CARIBBEAN
Here & Now

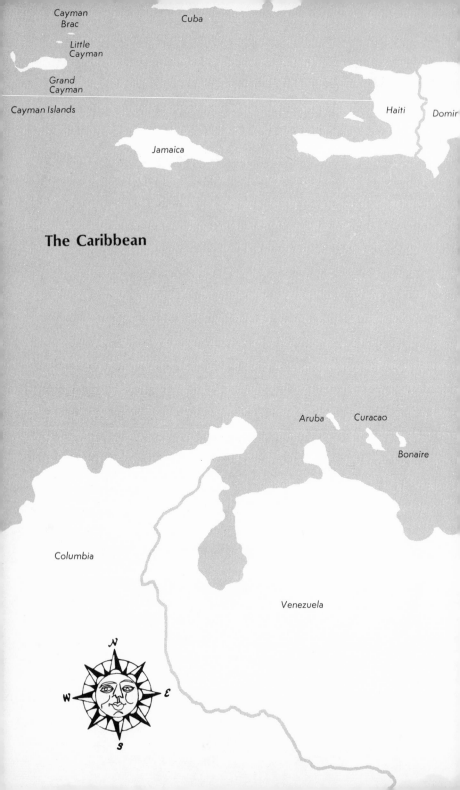

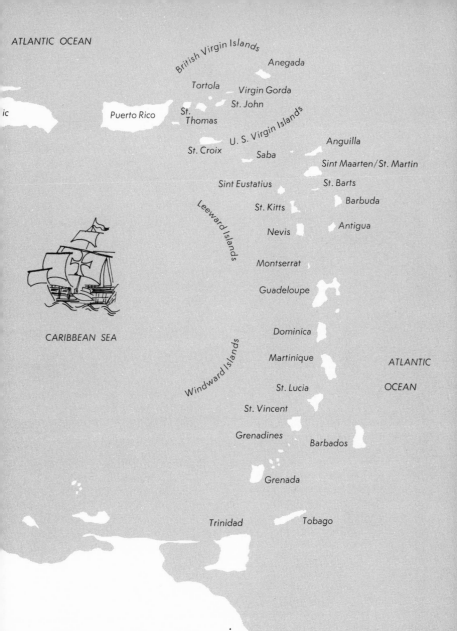

ATLANTIC OCEAN

British Virgin Islands

Anegada

Tortola

Virgin Gorda

St. John

Puerto Rico

St.
Thomas

U. S. Virgin Islands

Anguilla

St. Croix

Saba

Sint Maarten/St. Martin

Sint Eustatius

St. Barts

Leeward Islands

St. Kitts

Barbuda

Nevis

Antigua

Montserrat

Guadeloupe

CARIBBEAN SEA

Dominica

Windward Islands

Martinique

ATLANTIC

OCEAN

St. Lucia

St. Vincent

Grenadines

Barbados

Grenada

Trinidad

Tobago

SOUTH AMERICA

Guyana

Surinam

CARIBBEAN Here & Now

The complete vacation guide to 52 sunny islands in the Caribbean Sea by **JAMES RAMSEY ULLMAN** and **AL DINHOFER**, the editors of *CARIBBEAN BEACHCOMBER* magazine

THE MACMILLAN COMPANY · NEW YORK

COLLIER-MACMILLAN LIMITED · LONDON

Photo Credits

P.T. Huggins for Antigua Tourist Board, p. 3; Jack Waugh for Aruba Tourist Board, p. 15; Al Dinhofer, p. 22; W.E. Alleyne for Barbados Tourist Board, p. 31; Dutch Windward Islands Tourist Board, p. 43; British Virgin Islands Tourist Board, p. 50; Al Dinhofer, p. 63; Virgin Islands Government Information Office, p. 71; Fischer for Curacao Tourist Board, p. 73; P.T. Huggins for British West Indian Airways, p. 83; Virgin Islands Government Tourist Office, p. 94; Blonda for Dominican Republic Tourist Board, p. 96; Grenada Tourist Board, p. 107; Commonwealth of Puerto Rico, p. 116; Jocelyn Pierret for Guadeloupe Tourist Office, p. 125; Al Dinhofer, p. 137; Haiti Government Tourist Bureau, p. 144; Al Dinhofer, p. 147; Jamaica Tourist Board, p. 158; British West Indian Airways, p. 182; British West Indian Airways, p. 193; Commonwealth of Puerto Rico, p. 195; Commonwealth of Puerto Rico, p. 203; Commonwealth of Puerto Rico, p. 233; Dutch Windward Islands Tourist Board, p. 234; Jamaica Tourist Board, p. 239; Dutch Windward Islands Tourist Board, p. 247; Al Dinhofer, p. 248; P.T. Huggins for British West Indian Airways, p. 251; Haiti Government Tourist Office, p. 256; Commonwealth of Puerto Rico, p. 259; Charles Mauricette for St. Lucia Tourist Board, p. 265; Al Dinhofer, p. 273; Dutch Windward Islands Tourist Board, p. 275; P.T. Huggins for British West Indian Airways, p. 284; Harry W. Graff, Inc., p. 294; Noel P. Norton for Trinidad & Tobago Tourist Board, p. 307; Commonwealth of Puerto Rico, p. 317; Miles Raymond for U.S. Virgin Islands Information Office, p. 334.

CONTENTS

ABOUT THIS BOOK

It is unique in a number of ways.

• It has been produced entirely in the Caribbean by people who were born there or settled there long ago, or who otherwise know the islands intimately.

• It combines travel articles (personal impressions) with up-to-the-minute guidebook facts and concise information on tours, sports, resorts, restaurants and special events taking place on all the islands.

• It assumes the reader has a mind of his own—and is mature enough to evaluate first-person views and combine them with facts concerning specific prices and rates. The correlation adds up to the kind of Caribbean holiday an individual is seeking.

• Useful maps to help you get orientated, so you can do your free-port shopping and sightseeing without constant back-tracking, or zigzagging.

• Instant facts, so you're "with it" (historically, geographically), the moment you arrive.

• Where to stay—and what you pay, in winter or summer, at just about every hotel and guest house in the Caribbean. Also: Is it on the beach? Does it have a pool . . . golf course . . . tennis courts?

• Meet the people—names and phone numbers of officials of local civic-service organizations. You can seek out Caribbeanites with similar interests, professions, hobbies. (Instant friends.)

* * *

Essentially, we know better than most where to guide the Caribbean tourist.

CARIBBEAN HERE & NOW represents the first effort to create—from within the Caribbean—a fully rounded, fun-and-fact-packed travel guide. This volume, to be updated annually, is a literary spin-off of one of the largest regional travel magazines in the world, *Caribbean Beachcomber* magazine, published every other month in San Juan, Puerto Rico. The magazine constantly gleans facts and information related to all phases of Caribbean travel. The flow of tourism "news"—from dozens of our island-born correspondents —is distilled, here and now, while it's fresh and effervescent.

There are, generally speaking, two avenues for communicating travel information. There's the first-person travel book and the impersonally compiled guidebook. The travel book, or the travel article, is one man's response to new persons, places and things to see and enjoy. Such efforts (they used to be known as travelogues) offer an author's particular views, reflections, tastes. The reader assumes the travel writer, being something of a working-press tourist, calls 'em as he sees 'em. His suggestions are based on professional know-how, or—equally important—professional know-how-much.

We believe we have produced a new kind of guidebook, for the tourist with a mind of his own. We provide specific prices, rates, charges, etc. But we make no vague evaluations. We assume everyone has his own built-in evaluator for determining a dollar's worth. We do not, for example, say a hotel is expensive. What, after all, is expensive? And which reader's standards might we use as a gauge?

We list winter and summer minimum and maximum rates for hundreds of hotels and guest houses. We can tell you how many rooms in a hotel (to provide an idea of its size), whether it is on the beach, has a pool, tennis courts and golf course. We do not attempt to tell you if a hotel has "large rooms" simply because we have no comparative dimensions.

The same applies to our restaurant listings. We have avoided assiduously the spectrum of adjectives from tasty to yummy. To use the word delicious, to describe the fare in a restaurant, is an automatic jinx. It is a signal (via extra culinary perception) for the chef to disappear in a dinghy with the innkeeper's wife the day before you arrive. We confine our description to the location, decor, and mood of a restaurant. In some instances, where our local correspondent is on sure footing, we have noted a restaurant's long-standing "reputation" for superior food or service.

Note, too, that prices, generally speaking, are in flux. If you discover a hotel rate is slightly above the figures stated in our Where to Stay listing—well, we warned you. If your check in a restaurant is a dollar or so below what we reported, we hereby notify you that you owe our correspondent on that particular island a well-concocted rum drink.

Our introduction and eleven of the chapters in this volume lead off with first-person articles by James Ramsey Ullman. As *Caribbean Beachcomber* magazine's editor-at-large, Jim Ullman spends a good part of each year island hopping. His phenomenal career as globe-girding writer of fiction and journey journalist spans more than three decades. The success of his eighteen published works verifies a simple fact: he is a tireless investigator. When it comes to mining travel literature information, this man really digs. He seeks no short cuts, he cuts no corners. The result: that certain intimacy of reporting that makes a reader feel he is sharing the journey, traveling along on an inside track.

As travel writer-novelist, Jim Ullman is something of a maverick. After his first best-seller *The White Tower* (1945), his publishers attempted to cram him into the card-catalog category of mountain-climbing-type-travel-writer-novelist. He escaped several times, though, and returned clutching new manuscripts. One was set along the South American Amazon River region, *River of the Sun* (1951), and another, *Where the Bong Tree Grows* (1963), is an evocatively offbeat travel guide to the South Pacific. Jim Ullman's *Americans on Everest* (1964) is still among the Book-of-the-Month Club catalog selections. And his biography of the late renowned mountaineer, John Harlin, *Straight Up*, was released by Doubleday early in 1968.

The guidebook section of this volume is the domain of co-author Al Dinhofer. His forte appears to be chopping icicles off cold facts, so the reader can find information without getting lost in a tundra of gray-white pages.

Brooklyn-born Dinhofer, editor-*jefe* of *Caribbean Beachcomber* magazine, has about the best working-press job in the Western Hemisphere—certainly under the sun. In his reportorial travels, he tests beaches, reviews native shows, judges beauty contests, samples exotic foods and new rum concoctions and is ever on the lookout for potential tourist attractions. Dinhofer penned a daily column for the *San Juan Star* for five years before launching *Caribbean Beachcomber* in January 1965. He has been covering Caribbean show biz for *Variety* for almost a decade.

Three of the first-person articles in this volume (Cayman Islands, St. Martin, St. Barthelemy) are by Dinhofer, and one (Antigua) is by Jane Alderdice, *Caribbean Beachcomber's* special features editor.

The Research and Compilation Department for this guide is headed up by Lynn Feigenbaum, along with Jane Alderdice. The correspondents who help gather tourist information are far too many (and the turnover is much too fast) to be listed here. You need merely keep in mind that somebody out there on every island—representing this organization—likes you enough to see to it you always get your money's worth. That the travel information we publish is accurate. That whether you go Dutch, French, Spanish or English, there is a wide windward world of the Caribbean to be explored—before or after you've done the Leewards.

WHERE PARADISE IS FOUND

My title would seem to show some pretty positive thinking on the subject of paradise. Does it mean that I claim, actually, literally, to have found it? For both my own sake and our readers' (not to mention that of tourist boards and hotel associations), I wish I could say simply, "Yes." I would dearly love to share the belief of Voltaire's Candide, as he mused on the fabled land of El Dorado. "It is probably the country where all is well," he said, "for there absolutely must be one such place."

But Candide—if not Voltaire—was an optimist. Whether El Dorado or paradise, he didn't find it. Nor did I. In our 20th century, I'm afraid, one has to search for it farther afield than a few hundred miles from the coast of Florida (or Cuba). Farther, indeed, than the orbits of rockets and satellites. But short of it—short of the genuine, certified article—I'm happy to report that I've not done too badly. Until the real thing comes along, the Isles of the Caribbees are a pretty good substitute.

To get the non-paradisiacal side of things over with first: the Caribbean is poor. The great majority of its people are poor, and it can be disquieting for the visitor to live in beach-girt, air-conditioned, gourmet luxury, surrounded by tin-roofed shacks and squalid shantytowns. The islands have come a long way since the old days of slave-sugar-banana economy; but most still have a long way to go before they reach what Americans and Europeans consider a decent standard of living. Meanwhile, on the plus side, there is little of the grinding urban brand of poverty. With few big cities, there are few big-city slums. In the villages and countrysides, wants are simple and nature is kind.

Increasingly, industry is coming to the islands. And while this is, of course, basically good, it is not always so good for the Eden-seeker, who may find himself cheek-by-jowl with a bauxite mill or an oil refinery. In general, however, it's the heavier the industry, the bigger the island. And on the big ones there is room enough to live and let live. There are as yet few places where you have to worry about blast furnaces on your beach front or a film of smog on your frozen daiquiri.

One of the reasons is that *you*, in person, are the Number One Industry; and every tourist board, hotel and shop in the archipelago is dedicated to the proposition that you multiply and increase. Too dedicated at times, one would say: to the point where that *in person* seems forgotten and you become simply a statistic in the balance of trade. As the tourist tide swells, so, too, do the pressures of promotion and salesmanship. In season, planes, cruise ships and the more advertised resorts are jammed to overflowing. Far from getting away from it all, "it all" may follow you so relentlessly that you'll end up needing a holiday in the privacy of your own home.

To conclude the list of debits: even nature has occasional troubles living up to its publicized perfection. For one thing, by no means are all the islands emerald green. The low-lying ones, which get little rain, are more apt to be tan, or grayish, with sparse and scrubby vegetation. At the other extreme, the truly lush ones can get rain by the reservoir-full—though far more often on their island heights than along the shores. Even the trade wind is not *always* an unmitigated blessing. On some eastern and northern coasts it has a way of blowing, and blowing, and blowing, until you think it has gotten inside your skull and is swooping around in your brain.

Enough of such heresies. We are speaking of paradise. Well, almost-Paradise. And there are times and places, I can promise you, where the "almost" can be shelved. Having briefly maligned the trade wind, we will now concede that it is usually a delight. So, too, of course, is the famous Carib sun; and even the rains can be welcome, turning brown to green, and coming often at dusk, when you're tired of the sun and not quite ready for moon and stars. As for beaches (and I've been a longtime beach collector in many seas and oceans), it can be said simply that there are none better in the world. And if anywhere there are offshore waters of a lovelier blue or green or turquoise or azure or aqua, I have yet to find them.

The beauty of the Caribbean is known to everyone. What is less realized is its vast variety. It most definitely cannot be said, as of Gertrude Stein's famous rose, that "an island is an island is an island" for the differences between the islands are enormous. There are big ones and small ones, high ones and low ones, green ones and brown ones. Some are easy to get to, some are hard. Some are highly Americanized. Others are very British, very Spanish, very French, very Dutch. There are what can be called the "jumping" islands, full of jets, cruise ships, hotels, shops, night life. There are others where the only jumpers are frogs in the forest and fish in the sea.

In my own two years' wanderings, I have gotten to perhaps half the islands, or island groups. And each trip has been a new adventure, with little sameness or monotony. Here, in the sampler that follows, are some of the highlights as I individually encountered them:

JAMAICA: Big, high, green, and very beautiful—except for its capital city of Kingston, which runs to squalid slums. Jamaica, more than most, is the island that has everything (including poverty and political ferment); but for the vacationing visitor most of the "everything" is a delight. Along its north shore, it hops. Montego Bay and Ocho Rios are as lively and luxurious resorts as you will find anywhere. But a few miles inland you are off in another world of blue hills and emerald forests. (Don't miss the jungle rafting trip on the Rio Grande, near Port Antonio.) And the seven-mile beach at Negril, at the island's western end, is a marvel of untouched solitude and loveliness. For a first-time, one-island trip to the Caribbean, Jamaica, with its infinite variety, would be my number one choice.

HAITI: Also, big, high, green, beautiful. But there the resemblance stops; for while Jamaica is a tourist magnet, Haiti today is the forgotten island. Under "Papa Doc" Duvalier and his Tontons Macoutes, it has become a political and economic shambles. And a double pity it is. For in its mood, its color, its rich Afro-French-Caribbean texture, it is excitingly unique among the islands. Its native art is justly famous. Its few remaining hotels, though half-deserted, are excellent. Its Citadelle, the great fortress built by Henri Christophe during the wars of Haitian independence, is truly one of the wonders of the world. For the straight vacationer, no. For the adventure-minded, a treasure house of experience.

PUERTO RICO: Except in its physical features, the direct absolute opposite. Background and basic language are, of course, Spanish, but in all else it is thoroughly Americanized—for better or worse. Industry thrives, traffic rumbles, roulette wheels spin; and every time you turn around you see a new hotel, nightclub, or condominium highrise. In the interior and on the south coast things are quieter, but few visitors get there. In San Juan, and especially along its glittering shoreline, you are in a slightly Latinized extension of Miami Beach.

BARBADOS: A long jump from Puerto Rico, geographically and otherwise, it is very small and, though now independent, very British. Touristically, however, it is a "big" little island, for it has recently made huge strides in development and is now one of the prime resorts of the Indies. Apart from some small gems of beaches, nature has not been lavish. The terrain runs to low hills, scrub and sugar cane. But man has done well here; the island is more progressive and prosperous than most, and the so-called Platinum Coast on its western shore earns high marks for tasteful, and expensive, luxury. For adventure, no. For *la dolce vita*, yes indeed.

ANTIGUA: Also small, ex-British and very resort-minded. Low-lying and dry, most of its interior—plus its capital, St. John's—is downright ugly. But its ring of beaches, dotted with hotels, is unsurpassed in the Caribbean; and landlocked English Harbour is one of the foremost yachting centers in the islands. Whether for bathing, sailing or simply sunning and trade-winding, the prospect here is out to sea.

GUADELOUPE and MARTINIQUE: As French as Barbados is British: indeed more so, for they are politically part and parcel of France. Both are spectacularly mountainous and beautiful, and though the beaches are not the best in the world, they are far from the worst. From luxury hotel to wayside inn, the food is marvelous, the best in the Caribbean; and in the past few years there has been much development of tourist facilities. As noted, however, the islands are *very* French, and they are of no mind to turn somersaults to woo American tastes. If you meet them on their terms, not your own brought-from-home ones, you will find them richly rewarding. And it helps to have at least a working knowledge of *parlez vous*.

BRITISH WINDWARDS: From north to south, Dominica, St. Lucia, St. Vincent and Grenada. These, too, are beauteous islands, topped by mountains, bursting with greenery, and all are still well off the mainline of the tourist trail. St. Lucia, for obscure reasons, I have not yet visited. But the other three I commend to anyone seeking the *out* rather than the *in* in island living. Grenada is the farthest along as a resort: to my mind an almost perfect blend of the developed and undeveloped, the new and the old. Among its special attractions are a fine yacht harbor and, along a bay called Grand Anse, a dream beach if there ever was one. St. Vincent is also following the path toward resorthood, but a bit more slowly. And Dominica, a rough uncut emerald, is the slowest of all. Here, in outlying villages, there are still small commmunities of Carib Indians; and everywhere you will have the feel of what the islands were like before Columbus came—and then the rest of us.

U. S. VIRGIN ISLANDS: We were speaking of variety; and if you want it full in the face, make a quick hop from Dominica to St. Thomas. It is tiny, a mere dot on the map. But tourism is its only industry, and it has made more of it than many an island many times its size. Here, most emphatically, is a "jumping" island: in its hotels and night spots, on its roads and beaches; above all, on Charlotte Amalie's main stem with its jam-packed blocks of free port shopping. Even within so small a domain as the Virgins, however, there is change and contrast. Serene and slow-paced St. Croix, off to the south, is as different from St. Thomas as a dowager from a teeny-bopper. And on St. John, a rustic blend of Rockefeller and National Park, you are even more screened from the tumult and shouting. Here, notably, is a place where jumping is strictly for frogs and fish.

BRITISH VIRGIN ISLANDS: As may have been noted, I have not been listing my islands either by map or alphabet. They have simply been getting smaller. And by the time we reach the BVI's we are at very small ones indeed. Geographically, they are not remote: a mere puddle jump from St. Thomas and two of same from San Juan. But for beauty, they are unsurpassed. The Sir Francis Drake Channel, cutting its swath through the heart of them, is one of the great seascapes of the world; the islands themselves tiny gems of peace and beauty. Go if you can by small boat, for here sea and shores blend into one of the best yachting areas of the Caribbean.

GRENADINES: Here, finally, are the truly far-out islands, as tiny as the Virgins but much more remote. Stretching in a bright chain between St. Vincent and Grenada, they are divided administratively between them, but for the rare and lucky visitor they are a realm to themselves. Theirs too, are yachting seas, yachting shorelines; indeed, there is no way to get to most of them except by small boat. The comparatively larger islands are sparsely inhabited,

and a few small hotels have now begun to appear. But on the lesser ones
the population will be sea birds, sand crabs, iguanas, and yourself. Farthest
out of the Grenadines are the Tobago Cays; and farthest out of the Tobagos
is World's End Reef . . . which it really is.

That's been about it, thus far, for this two-year wanderer. From San
Juan's skyscrapers to World's End Reef; from Dominica's rain forests to the
Jamaica Hilton. And it has been a pageant, a feast of islands, never mo-
notonous, never dull. As is obvious from what I have written, I, like all of us,
have personal preferences. I tend to be a small-island man, an out-island man.
Your own tastes may be different. But what I have been trying to demon-
strate most of all in this guide is that, whatever they are, the Caribbean—
somewhere, somehow—can fulfill your tastes (unless, of course, you just
don't like tropical islands, and in that case you are hopeless).

For myself, the feast has been all I had hoped for, and happily it is far
from over. There will be second helpings. (On every island I have visited
there is more I want to see and experience.) And many new and fresh ones
as well. Ahead still lie Trinidad and Tobago, the somehow-skipped St. Lucia,
all the Dutch islands, St. Martin (half Dutch, half French), St. Barts, Saba,
Nevis, Montserrat, the Caymans . . . and the list goes on. The Dominican
Republic, after its strife-torn years, is again gradually opening up to vacationing travelers. And, who knows? One of these days, or years, it may again be
possible to visit long-lost Cuba.

That, presumably, will be rather less than paradise. Even my other ports
of call—other than World's End Reef—have had their flaws. But on balance
with the rest of the earth I have found no great cause for complaint. Big and
small, high and low, in and out, the Caribbees weave their magic. And the
feast will continue.

—*J. R. Ullman*

He who would bring home the wealth
of the Indies must carry the wealth
of the Indies with him.

> —*Samuel Johnson*

ANTIGUA

Despite its small size (nothing is more than 18 miles from anything else) Antigua is one of the Caribbean's big holiday resorts. It abounds in comfortable hotels, and has some of the most beautiful beaches in the Caribbean.

Down to the sea

If you are planning to spend a year on Antigua, it may be a comfort to know that you won't get bored with the same old beach. There are 365, which is certainly a very neat arrangement.

A large sign at the debarking passengers' entrance of Coolidge Airport advises the visitor that he is in "Antigua—Where Land And Sea Make Beauty." For once the phrasemakers have minted true, for it is in her beaches that Antigua's beauty lies.

The beaches of this small island are something to marvel at. One after another they ring the coast in powdery white sand, sometimes shading to a rosy white and all encircling little coves and harbors where the blue green water sparkles just like it does in the travelogues.

When we arrived in Antigua, we were immediately taken in hand by a taxi driver named Peewee. Peewee, like all taxi drivers from New York to Istanbul, drove half turned around facing the back seat and delivered himself of a running commentary on the life and times of Antigua (pronounced An-*tee*-ga).

Before we were off the airport road we knew that the tamarind is the native tree and the people of the island call the flamboyant tree the "June tree" and the local winery puts out a very gutsy rum called Cavalier. On the right we passed the cinema (Elizabeth Taylor in *Elephant Walk*) and then we were in St. John's, the capital, where Peewee was hailed by three or four friends with messages to be imparted later along the route.

Thinking that we might want to call someone sometime, we asked him about the telephone system.

"It's not too wonderful," he said. "When it rains you can't get it very clear, and when it doesn't rain it's not very clear too."

Many of the beaches of Antigua come equipped with modern, comfortable hotels which pamper their guests with chaise longues (no extra charge), umbrellas to lounge under and boats, large and small, for running up and down the coastline. The weather, from the tourist point of view, is perfect. Not much rain and one of the lowest humidity readings in the Caribbean.

Antigua is slow and quiet and the pace is unhurried. There really isn't much to do when compared with the fleshpots of the Indies. But the visitor should stir himself from the hammock and see what is to be seen. The best method is to rent a drive-yourself car or, if you're lazy beyond redemption, hire a car and driver.

The first step in renting a car is to present yourself at the police station in St. John's where, after a scrutiny of your driver's license and the transfer of 60 cents, you will be issued a visitor's driving permit. According to a blackboard in police headquarters, the number of registered vehicles in Antigua includes 2,079 automobiles, 254 trucks, four hearses, four ambulances, five cranes, 107 omnibuses, three fire trucks, 275 tractors, 608 motorcycles and 4,902 bicycles.

At the car dealer's (next to and part of the toy shop) we rented an English Hillman, $11 a day, right-hand drive, and inched our way out of town by asking directions every few feet. Antigua apparently has some local ordinance prohibiting street signs and road markers. The driver unfamiliar with the trails is quite likely to end up on the south coast when he wanted to go north.

But everybody is very friendly and informative and eventually we got out of town on a southeast heading. Our destination was Nelson's Dockyard on Antigua's south coast—Antigua's prime point of interest for visitors.

English Harbour, the site of the dockyard, is a beautiful landlocked anchorage which English ships used as early as 1671 as a refuge from hurricanes. The present dockyard was begun in 1746. The era of privateers, pirates and great sea battles in the Caribbean during the 18th century revolved around the dockyard at English Harbour. During the Napoleonic Wars it served Nelson, Rodney and Hood as a stronghold against the Spanish, Portuguese, French and Dutch.

The dockyard, with its stately buildings and elaborate ship-fitting facilities, was abandoned in 1889 and over the years allowed to fall into virtual ruin. Visitors and residents with a sense of history complained long enough and loud enough, and in 1951 the Society of the Friends of English Harbour was established with the object of preserving and restoring the dockyard both as an historic monument and as a yacht center. By 1956, an appeal sponsored by Lady Churchill had raised 50,000 pounds and Nelson's Dockyard was saved from oblivion.

The decision to combine the restoration with promotion of a yachting complex was inspired. Instead of the dusty do-not-touch atmosphere of a museum to the dead past, English Harbour today bustles with the everyday activity of a working dockyard.

The past is there in beautifully restored buildings, and the present is unmistakably with us. Bikinis are everywhere, on land and on sea. Private and charter yachts put in and out, and small boys in residence play with kites against a blue blue sky.

Restored to their original concept are the engineer's workshop (now locker space for yachtsmen); the master shipwright's house (police station

A quiet anchorage on the island of Antigua

with immigration facilities); the cooper and lumber store; the officers quarters (now rented to yacht skippers), and the paymaster's house (a yacht charterer's office). The canvas and clothing store is without a roof and is used for washing clothes and drying sail.

Tradition has it that Nelson stayed at the former house of the master shipwright in 1786 when he was captain of *H.M.S. Boreas* and acting as commander-in-chief of the Leeward Islands Station. The site is now occupied by the Admiral's House (built in 1855) and maintained as the dockyard museum, complete with ship models, figureheads, maps, prints and Nelson's bed (probably), a four-poster of gilded ivory-colored wood with a floral canopy. Behind Admiral's House is an old kitchen whose brick ovens are used by nearby villagers to bake cakes for festive occasions.

Perhaps the gem of the restoration is the building next to the great boathouse which housed the engineer's office and the lead and pitch stores. This has been turned into the 10-room Admiral's Inn and is a sight to delight the eye of anyone sick unto death with chrome and op and pop.

The Inn nestles behind a high stone wall and is entered past the porter's lodge. Inside, the lounge and bar are warm with hand hewn beams and mellow old brick. A shaded patio off the lounge looks out over the harbor, and it is not difficult to imagine that a candlelight dinner here would be graced by the ghost of Lord Nelson.

High above the harbor, on a hill commanding the approaches, are what at first, long-range glimpse appear to be Roman ruins. These are the remains of the garrison buildings of Shirley Heights, easily reached by car and worth the short drive. The fortifications and barracks on the hills above the dockyard were built between 1781 and 1791 under the direction of General Sir Thomas Shirley, commander and captain general of the Leeward Islands. The military garrison was stationed in Antigua to protect the island, and particularly the Naval Base, from attack. Far below, yachts bob at anchor in the now peaceful harbor, and Guadeloupe and Montserrat brood off in the misty distance.

Below Shirley Heights, on a hill overlooking the harbor, is Clarence House built in 1786 for the Duke of Clarence who later became King William IV.

On a hill near Clarence House, with a sweeping view of the dockyard and harbor, is The Inn, one of Antigua's most charming hotels. The Inn has cottage bedrooms, a bar that would spell sheer heaven to anyone fond of English pubs, and possibly the best food on the island. Down below on Freeman's Bay there are cottage bedrooms, a beach house and bar, and the up-above Inners are deployed to the beach via hotel-owned jeep.

On the trip back to St. John's we took the longer route along Fig Tree Drive, which is, as everyone will tell you, a must. But fig-lovers should be warned that in Antigua bananas are called figs, and the road follows along a very picturesque, winding course liberally lined with banana trees.

While on the subject of roads, it might be well to suggest that someone start a Society of the Friends of the Roads of Antigua. It is true that there are long stretches of road, sometimes extending for three or four miles, that are smoothly concreted and without major flaw. Then abruptly the concrete ends and great chunks of coral rear up to attack tires and nerve ends. Then the concrete resumes to lose itself shortly in pits and pots, and then it's back to the coral strand.

On one stretch of the worst road in Antigua the bone-crushing stone gives way to 50 feet of smooth macadam which begins and ends in mystery. We were told the reason for this 50-foot boon was that a truck loaded with tar broke down at this juncture and it was simpler to unload the tar right there before hauling away the truck. Whatever the reason, we were grateful.

Our favorite adventure in Antigua was breakfast at the airport on the morning of our departure. We ordered simply, we thought. Bacon, one fried egg, a glass of milk, toast and coffee. After a peaceful wait, the waitress put in front of us one plate holding two bacon, lettuce and tomato sandwiches. Now we are famous in our intimate circle for a certain unorthodoxy in breakfast fare, but it wasn't our morning for a double BLT. We asked her to take the plate back and bring us bacon, one fried egg, a glass of milk, toast and coffee.

After we ate the ham, scrambled eggs and the roll we went outside to wait for the plane. Just heading out the passenger gate to board a short-hop inter-island airplane was a family of four: mother, father and two teenage sons, who had been sitting at the table next to us in the restaurant.

At the very moment of departure our waitress came running up to them holding an order book in one hand and a plate in the other. We will carry with us forever the look on a young man's face as he walked to board his plane carrying two bacon, lettuce and tomato sandwiches on white bread.

—*Jane Alderdice*

Instant facts

Location: 300 miles southeast of Puerto Rico, 1,692 miles from New York.

Population: 64,000.

Capital: St. John's.

Nationality: Independent state in association with Great Britain.

Language: English.

Currency: East Caribbean (same as West Indian) dollar, worth 60¢ U.S., 64¢ Canadian, 4s 2d sterling.

Documentation: Proof of nationality for visitors from the U.S., United Kingdom or Canada who hold return tickets. No visa required. Vaccination certificate required for re-entry to U.S.

Climate & Clothes: Daytime temperatures average 80°. A perfect climate from a tourist's point of view since rainfall is slight and sunshine guaranteed practically every day of the year. Bring light clothes, summer suits, sportswear. Short shorts are worn only on the beach. Jacket and tie usually worn by men for dinner at hotels, though formal attire is not necessary.

Food: While continental cuisine is served in hotel restaurants, there are many tasty and exotic West Indian dishes prepared here. These include **souse**

(boiled pighead and trotters, seasoned and served with lime juice and cucumbers), **fungi** and **coo-coo** (cornmeal balls and okra). Native-grown vegetables are featured on many menus and fresh Barbuda-caught lobster is a treat.

Geography: Antigua has an area of 108 sq. miles and is about 16 miles across at its widest point. Most of the land area is flat. A hilly region in the southwest reaches its highest point at Boggy Peak (over 1,300 feet). The northern part of the island consists of the eroded remnants of long extinct volcanos.

History: From the visitor's point of view, Antigua today is a peaceful, tranquil island that echos to nothing more alarming than the sweep of the surf on countless beautiful beaches. But at one time in its history, it was a bastion of English military might, the chief British base in the eastern Caribbean. It was from Antigua that Admiral Nelson set off on his long pursuit of the French fleet, culminating in the Battle of Trafalgar which destroyed Napoleon's sea power.

Ruins of extensive fortifications on the headlands of the south coast testify to the days when Antigua was the "rock" that protected the British outposts of empire in the Caribbean.

Antigua was first discovered by Christopher Columbus on his second voyage in 1493. He named the island after the Church of Santa Maria la Antigua in Seville, and the pronunciation of the name has emerged as half Spanish, half English—An-tee-ga.

The island was visited by the Spanish in 1520, and in 1629 the French made an unsuccessful attempt to establish a colony. It remained uninhabited until 1632, when English planters from St. Kitts settled the land. The Carib Indians harassed the Englishmen, even to the point of kidnaping the governor's wife and children, but they were ultimately killed or driven off the island.

Antigua was raided by French, Irish and Caribs, but was finally ceded to England officially by the Treaty of Breda in 1667. In the 18th and 19th centuries, Antigua was the headquarters of the Commander-in-

Chief of the Leeward Islands Station, and was the principal British naval base in the eastern Caribbean during the Napoleonic Wars. Nelson was stationed in Antigua from 1786 to 1788.

Who flies here

The island has a full-jet airfield, Coolidge Airport, served by direct flights from the following major cities:

New York: BWIA, Pan Am. Round trip: $232–$323; 17-day excursion $161–$227.

Miami: BWIA, Pan Am. Round Trip: $181–$249; 17-day excursion $133–$185.

Montreal and Toronto: Air Canada. Round trip: $240–$344 (Canadian $259–$371); 21-day excursion $184–$274 (Canadian $198–$295).

London: BOAC. Round trip: $617–$931 (£220–£331 sterling).

San Juan: Air France, BWIA, Pan Am, Caribair. Round trip: $73–101; 17-day excursion $47–$90.

LIAT, ALM, Air France and other air charters provide service to many nearby islands.

Island transportation

Taxi service is readily available but prices are steep. If you don't mind an occasional wrong turn on Antigua's poorly marked roads, **car rentals** are the best bet. A Hillman Minx, for example, rents for $11 a day, $66 a week. Visitors may, upon presentation of a valid license from home, secure a temporary permit for 60¢ from the Traffic Department at the Police Station. Driving here is on the left.

Among the car rental agencies in St. John's are:

Alexander Parrish (Antigua) Ltd.
St. Mary's St., Tel: 187, 188

Lapps Car Rental, Ltd.
Cross St.

The Toy Shop
Long St., Tel: 132

Alexander Parrish and Lapp's also offer **tours** around the island. A 3-hour tour, without lunch, costs about $8.50.

Sights worth seeing

Antigua bows to no other island in the matter of beaches, but it has a number of other attractions, too. Anyone with a sense of history (even those without a sense of history will develop one) should not miss a visit to **English Harbour** on the south coast.

The dockyard at English Harbour was headquarters for the young Captain Nelson when he was Commander-in-Chief of the Leeward Islands Station from 1786 to 1788. It was used by Nelson and Admirals Rodney and Hood as the home of the British Fleet in the Caribbean in the time of the Napoleonic Wars.

In its heyday, Nelson's Dockyard was alive with the sights and sounds of men-of-war putting in to the harbor, of ships being careened and provisioned and fitted to put to sea again to engage the French and the Spanish, the Portuguese and the Dutch.

The dockyard was abandoned in 1889, and left to the attrition of time. But in the 1950's the Society of the Friends of English Harbour was formed with the object of preserving and restoring the dockyard both as a historic monument and as a yacht center.

Visitors assailed by thirst or hunger will be pleased by one flowering of the restoration, the 10-room Admiral's Inn that sits behind a high stone wall and is entered past the porter's lodge.

Three times a week, during most months, as night falls in Antigua, Lord Nelson and his dockyard come to life again. This is the striking *Son et Lumiere* production—the French innovation of combining floodlights, music, voices and a dramatic script to invoke the past for visitors of the present. Some of the world's most famous sites have inspired the *Son et Lumiere* dramas—the Acropolis in Athens, the Forum in Rome, the Pyramids of Egypt, the Tower of London and Hampton Court. Now English Harbour has joined the list.

High above the harbor, on a hill commanding the approaches, are the ruins of the garrison buildings of **Shirley Heights** (built between 1781 and 1791), easily reached by car.

Below the Heights, on a hill overlooking the harbor, is **Clarence House,** built in 1786 for the Duke of Clarence who later became King William IV.

If your expedition to the dockyard is starting off from St. John's, the most charming route to take is by way of **Fig Tree Drive.** The road passes by rolling sugar fields with old windmill towers and stone chimneys, through tropical fruit country, down Fig Tree Hill, and past west coast fishing villages. It is a beautiful trip, but don't expect to pick a fig. In Antigua, bananas are known as figs.

The sporting life

There are three nine-hole **golf** courses on the island—at the Antigua Beach Hotel and Halfmoon Bay Hotel. The Mill Reef Club also has golfing facilities but they are private and only members are welcome. Green fees start at $1.25 and clubs can be rented.

Tennis and **horseback riding** can be arranged through some hotels or you may call Dennis Armsby (Tel: 221) for information on riding.

Water sports: The first thing the average visitor wants to do is to get out on the beach as quickly as possible.

This is very easy, since oval-shaped Antigua is ringed by one beautiful cove and white sandy beach after another. Antigua's protected beaches guarantee superb **swimming,** and most hotels provide snorkeling and **water skiing** equipment—or else call Tony Johnson, c/o Antigua Water Sports, Tel: 258.

Arrangements for **fishing** can be made through Tony Johnson or Lee Westcott, Tel: 739. Top catches include bonefish tuna, barracuda, wahoo, kingfish and sailfish. Most hotels have fishing gear available or will make arrangements with local fishermen for reef fishing or expeditions to some of the islands around Antigua.

Boats for fishing, sailing or cruising can be chartered from the following services:

Lee Westcott
Crosbies, Tel: 739

Antigua Water Sports
P.O. Box 222, St. John's
Tel: 258

Tony Garton
P.O. Box 251, St. John's

Nicholson's Yacht Chartering Service
English Harbour

Whether your choice is a yacht trip or a sailfish, it is a good idea to make reservations in advance. Prices range from $2 an hour to $50 per person for a full day's outing.

A relaxing day cruise can be arranged through your hotel or Tony Garton aboard the 112-foot motor yacht *Warrior Geraint* at $13 a person. There are deck mattresses, easy chairs, sun and shade, changing cabins, fresh-water showers and a bar. The *Warrior Geraint* cruises close inshore for easy viewing, and puts in at Nelson's Dockyard for 2½ hours, allowing passengers time for exploring and for lunch at either the Admiral's Inn in the dockyard or at The Inn, a lovely hotel overlooking the harbor.

The *Warrior Geraint* also makes a trip to Maid Island, an uninhabited island off Antigua's north coast. There is snorkeling gear on board, the swimming is grand, and seashells can be collected by the bucketful. An Indian curry lunch, with 20 native side dishes, is served to the beachcombers. The "pickup" schedules for both trips are posted in most hotels.

Boats can be chartered for a day's sail to Barbuda and Redonda, Antigua's tiny island "possessions," for a picnic and swim on deserted beaches. For an even more nautical touch to a vacation, Antigua's Hawksbill Beach Hotel is offering a unique package plan, a combination of fun on shore (five days at Hawksbill) and two days afloat aboard the 50-foot motor sailer *Polonaise II*. On shore, the hotel offers dancing, steel bands, beach parties, arrangements for reef fishing.

Shopping buys

A casual few hours (at the most) can be spent visiting the craft shops in St. John's.

Clothing and fabrics are among the best buys (sea island cotton, Madras beach wear, Liberty of London and Thai silks). Other imports include French perfumes, liquor and Swiss watches.

There are also attractive local handicrafts. In addition to articles made from fiber, straw and tortoise shell, the ceramic figurines of steel bandsmen and limbo dancers are particularly recommended for souvenir hunters.

Dining, dancing and night life

In addition to dining and shows at the various hotels, visitors can find native dishes, as well as more familiar cooking, at these restaurants:

Al & Larry's: Market St., St. John's.

Chinese Garden: Newgate St., St. John's. Tel: S 698.

Fine Foods Snackette: Redcliffe St., St. John's. Tel: S 384.

The Kensington: St. Mary's St., St. John's.

Mac's Restaurant: The airport. Tel: S 292.

Mills Restaurant: Comacho's Ave., St. John's. Tel: S 594.

Spanish Main: Newgate St., St. John's. Tel: S 692.

The Towne House: Nevis St., St. John's. Tel: S 765.

Night life is not riotous but it is active. There are combos for dancing, and calypso shows do "one nighters" around the hotel beat. Hotels also schedule beach parties and barbecues, and the government-regulated **casino** at Marmora Beach Hotel is open till 4 A.M. if you like to stay up late with your money.

Night clubs and cocktail lounges around the island are:

Bill's Rum Soup: Popeshead St.

The Bucket of Blood: Coolidge. Tel: C 949.

The Catamarans' Club: Falmouth Harbour.

The Country Club: Donavans. Tel: S. 686.

El Tigre Supperclub: Old Parnham Rd.

The Jabberwock: Hodges Bay. Tel: C 48.
Joey's Flambouyant Club: Federation Dr.
Tel: S 680.
 Joyland: Fort Rd. Tel: S 87.
 The Pelican Club: Hodges Bay. Tel: C
66.
 Percy's Lounge: Federation Dr.
 The Strip: Cedar Grove.
 The Towne House: Nevis St., St. John's.
Tel: S 765.

Special events

 Carnival: Parades, floats, election of a
beauty queen, traditional "jump up" and
other festive celebrations. While Carnival
may begin at the end of July, it reaches
its peak on the first Monday in August to
celebrate emancipation in 1834.
 State Day: November 1.
 Boxing Day: December 26.

Meet the Antiguans

Organization	Official	Phone
Amateur Athletics & Cycling Assn.	J. O. Davis, Jr.	648
Olympics & Sports Assn.	Sydney Christian	136
Lawn Tennis	Lee Westcott	739
Netball Assn.	Miss Janice Dover	449
Basketball	Brother C. Seifert	127
Football Assn.	Henson Barnes	292
Fishing	Lee Westcott	739
Water Skiing, Diving	Tony Johnson	c/o 258
Rifle Club	Dennis Lambert	237 or 101
Boxing	Ivor Bird	33
Volley Ball	G. Flax	40
Yacht Services	Desmond Nicholson	106
Community Players (drama)	Mrs. G. Newby	411
Extra Mural Dept., U.W.I.	Mrs. E. Bird	781
Anglican Young People's Assn.		151
St. John's Masonic Lodge	V. E. Maynard	469
St. John's Ambulance Brigade	Nurse Olive Richardson	218
Chamber of Commerce	G. Maynard	743
Junior Chamber of Commerce	Vincent Derrick	524
British Red Cross Society	Eric Challenger	15 or 800
Y.W.C.A.	Miss Irene Roberts	775
Y.M.C.A.	Ercille Looby	834
Mental Health Assn.	Dr. Z. Wisenger	162
Girl Guides	Mrs. A. McDonald	167
Boy Scouts	H. Murdoch	620
British Medical Assn.	Dr. M. A. Lambert	693
Nurses Assn.	Miss D. Matthews	789 or 218
Civil Service Assn.	Dr. H. Tomlinson	398
Christian Council	Dean G. Baker	82
Teachers Assn.	Chas. Sampson	Michael's Village
Legal Assn.	Sydney Christian	136
Antigua Music Assn.	Dr. H. A. Rock	
Employers Federation	C. Cumberbatch	449
Society of Friends of English Harbour	J. Anjo	182
Son et Lumiere	E. Gibbons	291
Antigua Hotel Assn.	C. Cumberbatch or	449
	R. Davis	
Antigua Star (newspaper)	G. Joseph	80
Workers Voice (newspaper)	N. Richards	90
Antigua Tourist Board	Y. Maginley	29

Real estate and retirement

Antigua's stores carry a wide range of consumer products. Food, mostly imported, is more expensive than on the U.S. mainland.

Information on building sites and home rentals or purchases can be obtained from any of the following agents:

Gambles Estates Ltd.
P.O. Box 216, St. John's

Mr. Maurice Michael
Redcliffe St., St. John's

Mr. Ian Mair
High St., St. John's

Mr. Kenneth Gomez
High St., St. John's

Mr. Lee Westcott
Crosbies

Mrs. Allan Peters
Antigua Beach Hotel, Hodges Bay

Mr. John D. Miller
High St., St. John's

Mr. Rowan Henry
Church St., St. John's

A new residential estate is being built around the Antigua Golf and Country Club. There are, at present, three hotels, two clubs and more than 30 homes in the project. Information on this development is available from Canadian Marigot Ltd., Suite 429, 4999 St. Catherine St. West., Montreal, Canada.

Commerce and industry

Antigua's main industries are sugar and sea island cotton, but both have suffered a severe decline in the past decade. Fortunately, the decade has also seen a tremendous growth in tourism and the emergence of this centrally located leeward island as a veritable jet center. Antigua connects to over 30 cities around the world and, in turn, has direct flights to many of the Caribbean islands. In 1966 more than 54,000 tourists arrived in Antigua by air, plus another 1,500 by sea (cruise ship passengers not included).

There are now dozens of hotels and guest houses around the island.

The future of agriculture on the island is shadowed by the constant problem of drought. Even underground water sources are not useable since the limestone in which the water is trapped makes the water salty. Some parts of the island are entirely dependent on rain water and pipeborne supplies. Plans are being formulated for a desalinization plant.

A major new industry on the island is the West Indies Oil Refinery. The government offers incentives such as tax holidays and relief from certain duties to industries eligible for "pioneer" status, and to hotels. Detailed information is available from the Ministry of Trade, Production and Labour, Administration Bldg., St. John's.

Barbuda

A casual description of Barbuda doesn't make it sound like much. Small, flat, dry, scrubbily wooded—and hardly anyone has ever heard of it. It has, however, certain attractions that make it one of the more interesting vacation spots in the Caribbean.

Barbuda lies 40 miles north of Antigua and is a small paradise for hunters or fishermen or for beachcombers who like miles and miles of perfect beaches all to themselves. There is no lush tropical vegetation. The island is coral and flat, but the coral gives it its spectacular beaches of pure white powder sand that stretch unbroken and lonely for miles on both the windward and leeward coasts.

When beachcombing palls, there is hunting—for fallow deer, wild pig, guineafowl, dove and pigeon. Plover, curlew and snipe visit the island in August and September. Deer may be shot from January 1 to March 31 (a license may be obtained for a few dollars).

Fishing is excellent off Barbuda and small boats can be hired locally. Bone and tarpon are the most frequent catch—best between September and May—but barracuda, snapper, parrot fish and grouper are abundant.

Small though it is (68 square miles) Barbuda has a nicely tainted history. In 1691 the Crown gave the island outright to Christopher Codrington, then governor of the Leeward Islands, and it is said that Sir Christopher was not above making 7,000 pounds sterling a year on the "many lamentable wrecks" on the reefs which circle the island. He also used his domain as a breeding farm for slaves, choosing the sturdiest and tallest specimens he could find. The men of Barbuda are noted for their fine physiques and carriage and are superb fishermen and boatmen.

The island's only settlement is named, appropriately, Codrington. It fronts on a large, shallow, lobster-filled lagoon and tends to the dusty and dismal. But off the southern shore is Coco Point Lodge, a ten-room inn that envelops its guests in simple elegance. It is not for the indigent (rates are $120-a-day-a-couple, $70 single) but the tariff includes everything—tackle, boats, guides, water skis, sailfish, catamarans, horses and general cosseting.

The Lodge has aqualungs for divers who want to explore the 73 known shipwrecks on the reefs.

The guest book may yield some familiar names, among them H.R.H. Princess Margaret and Lord Snowden who spent part of their honeymoon at Coco Point.

If the pilot is in, the Coco Point plane will pick up passengers in Antigua. If not, Seagreen Air Transport has charters from Antigua for $54 round trip. LIAT flies from Antigua for $16.70, round trip.

Redonda

Redonda rises round and sheer from the sea 30 miles to the west of Antigua and has nothing much to recommend it except a bit of whimsical history.

In 1865 an Irishman named Matthew Shiel, who considered himself a descendant of Irish kings, sailed past the island and was moved to lay claim to it as a kingdom for his newborn son. In due time he brought his son, and a member of the clergy, to Redonda and officially

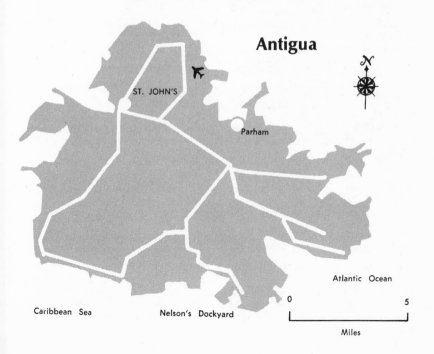

Antigua

ST. JOHN'S

Parham

Atlantic Ocean

Caribbean Sea

Nelson's Dockyard

0   5

Miles

proclaimed the young Shiel King Felipe I. The little group departed the next day.

A bemused Colonial Office in London actually did acknowledge the claim, and King Felipe subsequently appointed several of his friends as dukes. The King died in 1947, but before his death he named the poet John Gawsworth as his successor. Gawsworth became King Juan I and appointed his own friends, many of them well-known writers, as dukes of the kingdom.

Aside from its royal connections, Redonda is really a very simple island.

Even its name is simple. Spanish explorers saw it as a round island and put it down that way on their first charts—Redonda, Spanish for round.

The island, a mile long and half a mile wide, rises to a height of 1,000 feet and is a conspicuous landmark halfway across the channel between Montserrat and Nevis. In the early part of this century, it was worked by a labor force of some 100 men who dug phosphate from limited deposits. Today it is uninhabited except for a small herd of goats.

WHERE TO STAY — In Antigua

| | | Dec. 15-April 14 | | April 15-Dec. 14 | |
| | | **U. S. Currency** | | | |
	Plan	Double	Single	Double	Single
ADMIRAL'S INN	(MAP)	$28–44	$22–38	$23–30	$16–25
English Harbour	(EP)	$16–28	$16–28	$ 9–16	$ 9–16
(10 Rms.) (b)					
ANCHORAGE	(MAP)	$46–60	$32–46	$30–42	$18–30
Dickenson Bay (73 Rms.) (b, t)					
ANTIGUA BEACH	(EP)	$16–20	$12–14	$12–16	$ 8–10
Hodges Bay (40 Rms.) (b, p, t g)					
ANTIGUA HORIZONS	(MAP)	$54	$38	$28	$15
Long Bay (44 Rms.) (b, t)					
BARRYMORE	(AP)	$30	$18	$20	$12
Fort Road (20 Rms.)	(MAP)	$27	$17	$18	$11
	(CP)	$25	$14	$16	$10
BEACHCOMBER	(MAP)	$35	$25	$20	$14
Winthrop's Bay (16 Rms.) (b)					
BLUE WATERS	(AP)	$51–55	$40–42	$33–37	$20–24
BEACH	(MAP)	$46–50	$38–40	$28–32	$18–22
Soldier Bay	(EP)			$16–20	$12–16
(35 Rms.) (b)		(Dec. 15-April 21)		(April 22-Dec. 14)	
CARIBBEAN BEACH	(AP)	$31–36	$24–42	$21–28	$19–24
CLUB					
Dickenson Bay	(MAP)	$29–34	$22–40	$19–26	$-17–22
(57 Rms.) (b, p)	(EP)	$23–28	$16–34	$13–20	$11–16
CURTAIN BLUFF	(MAP)	$62–66	$44–48	$42–46	$32–36
South Coast (40 Rms.) (b, t)					
FALMOUTH HARBOUR	(EP)	$30	$25	$20	$18
BEACH APTS.					
Falmouth Harbour (9 Apts.) (b)					
GALLEY BAY SURF	(AP)	$55–63	$43	$33–41	$21
CLUB					
Five Islands	(MAP)	$50–58	$40	$28–36	$18
(16 Rms.) (b, t)					
HALF MOON BAY	(MAP)	$55–60	$50	$32–36	$22–26
(58 Rms.) (b, p, g)	(AP)	$60–65	$52	$37–41	$25–29
HAWKSBILL BEACH	(MAP)	$52–65	$42–55	$34–44	$21–34
Five Islands (36 Rms.) (b, t)					

JABBERWOCK BEACH (MAP) **CLUB**		$48	$35	$30	$18
Hodges Bay (16 Rms.) (b, p, t, g)					
JOLLY BEACH	(AP)	$66	$49	$40	$22
St. Mary's	(MAP)	$58	$45	$32	$18
(78 Rms.) (b, t)					
LONG BAY HOTEL		$40	$32.50	$30	$15
(20 Rms.) (b)					
MARMORA BEACH	(MAP)	$52–56	$38–42		
St. Paul's (100 Rms.) (b, p)					
SUGAR MILL	(CP)	$18	$12	$14	$ 9
Coolidge Airport (22 Rms.)					
THE INN	(MAP)	$52–57	$44–46	$32–37	$18–20
English Harbour (26 Rms.) (b, t)					
WHITE SANDS	(AP)	$44–50	$26–30	$29–32	$17–20
Hodges Bay	(MAP)	$36–42	$22–26	$21–24	$13–16
(30 Rms.) (b, p)					

LEGEND FOR HOTEL LISTINGS: (AP) American Plan (room and 3 meals); **MAP)** Modified American Plan (room, breakfast and dinner); **(CP)** Continental Plan (room and breakfast); **(EP)** European Plan (room only). All rates quoted on a per-day basis and subject to change. Confirmed reservations at specific rates desired are always recommended.
HOTEL FACILITIES: (b) beach; **(p)** pool; **(t)** tennis; **(g)** golf.

ARUBA

*There is one spot in Aruba where the susceptible will find themselves
listening for the thunder of hoofbeats and the crack of a rifle. The
terrain is so similar to what has become standard scenery in countless
Hollywood Westerns that it is difficult to believe you're only 15 miles
from South America and not in the American Southwest. One of the
finest beaches of the Caribbean stretches along the west coast. The island
is now firmly on the tourism map, with good accommodations and an
unusually hospitable people.*

Arriba, Aruba

Aruba is a small island way down in the southern Caribbean and is that
rarity in the age of air pollution—an excellent place to take a good deep
breath. The climate is almost desert-like, and the air is clean and exhilarating.

Aruba also offers hundreds of grazing goats and sheep, brightly painted
houses surrounded by cactus fences, a colorful outdoor market on the waterfront, abandoned gold-mining ruins, miles of sandy shoreline with perpetu-
ally calm, clear waters, sand dunes, Indian caves with clear hieroglyphics,
scores of weird divi-divi trees, and enormous free-form boulders scattered
over the countryside.

It is possible to see most of the island in eight hours of leisurely touring
—including time lost misinterpreting the generally unmarked roadways.
Car rentals are low and, with relatively few vehicles on the road, it is a
pleasure cruising around and about. Of course, one could take a guided tour
and do the island in less time. But Aruba is a delightful place for browsing
around and too small for even the most befuddled driver to remain lost
indefinitely.

This tiny Dutch island measures only 19.6 miles long by 6 miles wide.
Despite its petite dimensions, Aruba is—linguistically—quite cosmopolitan.
Most Arubans speak Papiamento, Dutch, Spanish and English, so there are
virtually no language barriers. Papiamento is a mélange of Spanish, Portuguese, Dutch and some Indian words.

At first glance, Aruba resembles a colorful sand dune bobbing in the
Caribbean Sea. Twelve degrees, 24 minutes from the equator (with most of
the land at sea level), one expects it to be sizzling. It can get pretty hot, but
the constant trade winds keep things from being too uncomfortable.

Due to the scarcity of rain, drinking water is distilled from the sea. Drinking water is so pure, as a matter of fact, that minerals must be added to give

*The strikingly contemporary Aruba Caribbean Hotel
on the island of Aruba*

it a taste. And being out of the path of hurricanes, Arubans live without fear of devastation from treacherous winds.

The island shows two faces: the western coast, on the leeward side, has a smooth, serene, sandy coastline; the eastern coast, facing the windward side, has a rugged, wild atmosphere.

A walk on the wild side takes in the dramatic natural bridge, high cliffs eroding from the pounding surf, swirling sand dunes. Caves covered with hieroglyphics may be seen at Fontein and Guadirikiri. Daily at 3 P.M. near the natural bridge, "the feeding of the sharks" takes place (Aruba's unique garbage disposal). It is said this also tends to keep the large fish on the wild side of the island.

On the serene side there are miles of calm, transparent waters rimmed with ideal beaches. A scenic tour includes the old Grist Mill, a stop at a small fishing village to watch the daily catch unloaded, then a drive to the most northern point near the lighthouse where pelicans dive pursuit-plane fashion into the sea.

The city of Oranjestad has a remarkably clean, scrubbed appearance. You might see some of the pastel houses receiving a fresh coat of paint. Dutch orderliness is omnipresent, even in the everyday business of delivering produce.

The Aruba Caribbean Hotel, the island's largest luxury resort, has a gambling casino, good entertainment in the Klompen Club, bright studio guest rooms (each with private terrace and a separate dressing room) and its own beach. Tourist facilities have been appreciably expanded with the opening of the Aruba Sheraton hotel, featuring a casino, fresh-water olympic-size swimming pool and dining facilities from the casual to the chic.

Glass-bottom boat passengers may view a partially submerged freighter which was wrecked on the coral reefs some 20 years ago. The submerged section of the freighter is now "home" for thousands of beautifully colored tropical fish and the twin masts above the water's surface are hunting perches for pelicans and seagulls.

Instant facts

Location: Most western of the Netherlands Antilles, 15 miles north of Venezuela, 42 miles west of Curacao, approximately 500 miles southwest of Puerto Rico.

Population: 60,000.

Capital: Oranjestad (Or-an-jes-tahd).

Nationality: One of the Netherlands Antilles, an autonomous part of the Kingdom of the Netherlands.

Language: Dutch, English, Papiamento, Spanish widely spoken.

Currency: The Netherlands Antilles guilder or florin, negotiated at 1.85 florin to U.S. dollar. (Most merchants offer a flat 2-1 exchange.)

Documentation: U.S. citizens do not need passports, but must have proof of citizenship, i.e. birth certificate. Naturalization certificate from naturalized citizens, re-entry permit or nonquota immigration visa from foreigners permanently residing in U.S. All visitors need smallpox vaccination certificates not more than three years old.

Climate and Clothes: One of driest islands in Caribbean. Temperature averages 83° in summer, 80° in winter. Light casual summer clothing is fine all year, although several hotels and restaurants require jacket and tie in the evening. Ladies are advised to wear dresses or slacks by daytime. Anyone in shorts in a downtown district can expect to draw stares. Arubans are not prudish, but they feel such attire should be left for sports and lounging.

Food: For Caribbean cooking, try iguana soup, roast pig or fresh seafood. Snipe, venison, pheasant, duck are other specialties. A gourmet treat is Indonesian **rijsttafel** (rice table), its elaborate preparation and exotic ingredients being a mixture of Dutch-Indonesian and Caribbean cookery. Rijsttafel ideally consists of seven groups of dishes, besides rice. However, it may include as many as 20 dishes and take three days to prepare. One set of dishes, **lalabs,** are vegetables cooked Chinese style, served cold. **Gareng** (crisp things) includes puffed shrimp mash and shredded chicken meat. Heavier offerings are **sajur,** something between soup and stew, and **sambelan,** mostly stew rich in coconut and tamarind milk, beef, pork, fish and hot peppers.

Geography: 19.6 miles long, 6 miles at widest point. Rocky island with cliffs on windward coast, flat beaches on leeward shores. Interior, with its many cacti and boulders, has been likened to U.S. Southwest.

History: Arawak Indians first settled in island caves. In 1499 Alonso de Ojeda claimed Aruba for Spain, but in 1634 the Netherlands won it in the Holy Wars. One early governor was Peter Stuyvesant, later governor of New Amsterdam, now New York. From 1634 to 1816 the island passed from the Dutch to the English and briefly to a Venezuelan "liberator." In 1816 the Dutch returned and remained.

Who flies here

Direct flights are available from the following cities:

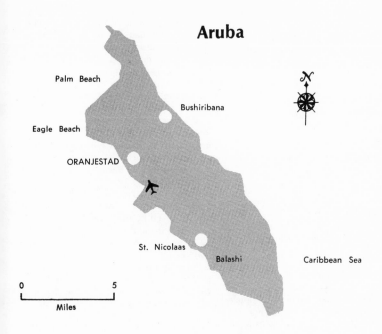

Aruba

Palm Beach

Bushiribana

Eagle Beach

ORANJESTAD

St. Nicolaas

Balashi

Caribbean Sea

0　　　　　5

Miles

New York: KLM Royal Dutch Airlines, Pan Am, Trans Caribbean. Round trip: $170-$403; 17-day excursion $150-$265; 30-day excursion $150–$190.

Miami: KLM, Viasa, Pan Am. Round trip: $205–$322; 17-day excursion $135–$195.

San Juan: Pan Am, Trans Caribbean. Round trip: $50–$179; 17-day excursion $35.

Island transportation

Taxis with English-speaking drivers are available, though cars may be rented by the day or week. To drive in Aruba, you need only a valid driver's license from your own country; no special permit is necessary. The following is a list of car rental agencies:

Avis Rent-A-Car
P.O. Box 254
Oranjestad, Tel: 1306, 2227

Bruno's U-Drive-It
Stadionweg 7
Oranjestad, Tel: 2423

Caribbean Express Co.
Wilhelminastraat 13
Oranjestad, Tel: 1992, 1993

Leer's Car Rental
P.O. Box 626
San Nicholas, Tel: 6046

Caribbean Car Rental
P.O. Box 252
Oranjestad, Tel: 2325

Enrique's Car Rental
Tanki Leendert 170
Tel: 1967

Hertz Rent-A-Car
P.O. Box 358
Oranjestad, Tel: 2714, 2250

Jansen Car Rental
Nassaustraat 167
Oranjestad, Tel: 2783

For those who prefer guided tours, the following agencies can arrange excursions and island-wide transportation:

Bruno's U-Drive-It & Sightseeing Tours
Stadionweg 7, Oranjestad
Tel: 2423

De Palm's Sightseeing Tours/
  Aruba Tours
c/o Aruba Caribbean Hotel, Palm Beach
Tel: 1813, 2250

Caribbean Express Co.
Wilhelminastraat 13, Oranjestad
Tel: 1992, 1993

Places to see

Interesting sights are easily reached by
car or on foot.
A walk on Eagle Beach will bring you
to the **Nurticulture Farm.** Here cucumbers,
tomatoes and other vegetables are grown
completely in chemicals rather than in
soil.
Oranjestad, the capital, is Caribbean in
its colors, and Dutch in its cleanliness.
Note houses painted pink, blue, yellow
and red. Tradition demands that neighboring houses never be the same color.
Even more colorful, **Wilhelmina Park,** on
the city's seaside, features flowers and a
statue of the Queen Mother. Nearby is
Schooner Harbour, one of the deepest
in the world and most modern in the
Caribbean. Stout-beamed sailing ships
dock alongside modern cruisers and, adjacent to the dock, open stalls display
wares from other islands. Fruits piled
high make good eating, and fish come in
all varieties.
The **Cunucu,** which in Papiamento
means countryside, is a desert-like area.
Here native homes wear "hex" signs to
ward off evil spirits. Cacti are used as
fences and clotheslines. Gnarled **divi-divi
trees** and **boulder formations** dot the
landscape. **Ayo** and **Casibari** have the most
impressive boulders. Ayo's rocks are
stacked one on top of another and are
full of Indian carvings. Casibari has "The
Doughnut" and "The Dragon's Mouth"
formations, favorite spots for photographers. The **Hooiberg** (haystack) is another
famous landmark, and for those who wish
to walk, there are steps carved to the top
of this hill.
Close to the south coast is **Canashito,**

site of Indian caves with wall drawings,
and home of Aruba's parakeet sanctuary.
Nearby is the **Balashi Gold Mill,** ruins exciting to visitors who have found gold
nuggets in the sand. Peaceful **Spanish
Lagoon,** once a pirate's den for repairing
galleons, is below the mill. Close by, the
Salt Water Distillation Plant, one of the
world's largest, is open for tours. Of historic interest is **Frenchman's Pass,** a breeding ground for birds and once a battle-
ground where Indians fought the French.
Fascinating rocks on the north coast
can be found at **Boca Druif,** a seaside
grotto near **Prins.** There are wall drawings
in the **Quadirikiri** and **Huliba Caves.**
Further northwest stands the **Natural
Bridge** carved by the sea in the coral cliffs
near the **Shark Feeding Grounds.** In the
same area are **Andicouri** and **Dos Playa,**
two coves for picnics and splashing.
Swimming for those who like it rough.
Near the north end of the island is **Pirate's
Castle** at Bushiribana. This old castle, now
in ruins, was once a gold mill and affords
a spectacular view of rough seas from its
site on a cliff. Tour groups are easily arranged from most hotels in Oranjestad.
Costs are reasonable and most of the island can be covered leisurely in one day.

The sporting life

The island is fast becoming a center for
deep-sea fishing. Chief sport fish are wahoo, blue and white marlin, kingfish, dolphin, tuna. Fully equipped boats may be
chartered for half or full day. **Skindiving,
snorkeling** and **water skiing** are popular
at **Palm** and **Eagle Beaches** where visibility
is excellent and water is calm. Even **sunk-
en ships** can be seen off coast. **Sailboats**
available are *Sailfish, Sunfish,* native
sloops. **"Watercycles,"** 11-foot catamarans
pedalled like bicycles, are popular with
the young set. **Glass bottom sightseeing
boats** and **moonlight cruises** are reasonably priced. Rates for water sports range
from $3–$6 hourly, depending on equipment, instruction needed. Hotels or Aruba Water Sports, Inc. on Palm Beach provide information and reservations.
Land sports include **tennis, golf, minia-**

ture golf and trapshooting. Aruba Caribbean Hotel-Casino has tennis courts, as do Tivoli, Caribe Club and Lago Sport Park—all with night illumination. There is one golf course, Aruba Golf Club, in Seroe Colorado. Miniature golf is offered at Arawak Inn in front of the Aruba Caribbean Hotel-Casino. Trapshooting is available at Aruba Shooting Range, Palm Beach. The tourist bureau and hotels make arrangements for land sports.

Spectator games, soccer, baseball, basketball and volleyball, are held at Queen Wilhelmina Stadium in Oranjestad, Lago Sport Park in San Nicolas, and at several clubs in villages.

Shopping buys

Though not a free port, savings of 50% are commonplace. There is no sales or luxury tax, no duty on some articles and low duty on other items. U.S. visitors are allowed $100 worth of goods duty-free. There are well-stocked shops in Oranjestad and San Nicolas and a shopping arcade at the Aruba Caribbean Hotel, Palm Beach. Look for these buys: diamonds, Delft blue pottery, Hummel figurines, Madeira embroidery, British woolens, Indonesian specialties, Italian wood carvings, typewriters and silk knits. Also, the standard Caribbean bargains in liquor, china, cameras.

Dining and night life

Entertainment after dark usually includes good dinner and drink but not necessarily a nightclub show. Arubans are not night owls. There are casinos at the Aruba Caribbean Hotel-Casino and the new Aruba Sheraton. The deluxe hotels feature big name entertainment. Combos and/or native-style drums are offered at Olde Molen Restaurant, Coral Strand Hotel, Cactus Inn and Bali Restaurant.

Aruba Caribbean Hotel-Casino: Palm Beach. Divi-Divi Coffeeshop, Papiamento Room dining salon, Klompen Club nightclub, and casino. American/international food, especially charcoal cooking. Recom-

mended: prime ribs of beef, lobster dividivi, pastries, coffee, pastrami. Famous for Zombies and Alexanders. Tel: 2250.

Astoria Hotel: Crijnssenstraat 6, San Nicolas. Chinese food: subgum wonton, moo goo gai pan, chow steak kow. Patio dining and bar. Tel: 5132.

Bali: Yacht pier opposite tourist bureau, Oranjestad. Floating restaurant and bar in converted houseboat. Home of famous rijsttafel and other Indonesian foods like nassi goreng, bam goreng. Allow two hours for 20-dish rijsttafel. Chosen "Best Restaurant in the Caribbean" by Caribbean Tourist Association, Bali attracted NBC newsmen to make film on decor and cuisine. Daily 10 A.M.–2 P.M., 4 P.M.–midnight. Tel: 2131.

Basi Ruti Hotel: Near Aruba Caribbean Hotel-Casino, Palm Beach. Oldest hotel on Aruba's beach. Italian specialties: canelloni, lasagna, scampi, veal scallopini. Also barbecues. Terrace or indoor dining; bars both places. Tel: 2222.

Cactus Inn Hotel: Oranjestad. Spanish, Aruban, international dishes in the Salon Madrid dining room. Entertainment occasionally. Most things happening weekends in the Cave Room cocktail lounge. Tel: 3100.

Coral Strand Hotel: Oranjestad, near airport. Talk of the Town dining room features beef fondue, red snapper, Aruban dishes, French food and dancing during dinner. Evenings, local entertainment. Tel: 3380 or 3381.

De Olde Molen (Old Windmill): Across from Aruba Caribbean Hotel-Casino. Restaurant, nightclub. Dutch windmill built in 1815, dismantled in Holland and reassembled on Palm Beach. Dining specialties: duck, wild boar, snipes, game food. 11 A.M.–2 P.M., 5–11 P.M. Upstairs, Miller's Wife offers nightly entertainment till 3 A.M. Tel: 2060.

Hong Kong Restaurant: 19 Adrian Laclé Blvd., Oranjestad. Bar-restaurant. Excellent shark-fin soup, chicken, lobster, sweet and sour dishes. Reasonably priced. Informal lunch and dinner. Tel: 2966.

Scala: Business section, Oranjestad. American cooking with U.S. meats. Tel: 1047.

Trocadero Restaurant-Bar: Near the harbor, Oranjestad. Seafood. Tel: 1756.

Special events, festivals, celebrations

New Year's Day: Pre-Carnival dances and nominations of Carnival Queen begin. Open house at Lieutenant Governor's home, Oranjestad.

Carnival Weekend: Four-day celebration. Children's parades—in San Nicolas, February 17 and in Oranjestad, February 18. Election of Carnival Queen in Wilhelmina Stadium, local talent show on February 22. Parade in San Nicolas, February 24. Grand Carnival parade, Oranjestad, February 25.

Queen Juliana's Birthday: Legal holiday, including fireworks, parades, sports events, dances. Highlight is "Aubade" (homage) to Lieutenant Governor by school children. April 30.

Labor Day: Island holiday marked by Maypole dancing to "Tumba" music at Aruba Caribbean Hotel-Casino and other places. May 1.

St. John's Day: Country people perform "Derramento di Gai," folk dance of Arawak Indians. June 24.

Aruba Sport Union Olympiad: Tournaments in soccer, basketball, tennis, baseball, volleyball, gymnastics, fencing. Last week in June.

Sint Nicolaas Arrives: Sint Nicolaas and helper, Black Peter, arrive by boat or plane and are met by an official delegation. They visit homes and clubs, giving gifts to good children and "punishing" the bad. December 5.

Kingdom Day: Island holiday observing Netherlands Antilles' achievement of semi-autonomy in 1954. December 15.

Boxing Day: Legal holiday during which friends and families exchange visits and greetings. December 26.

Meet the Arubans

Organization	Official	Telephone
Aruba Tivoli Club	Carlos F. Groes	1082
Caribe Club	Ruben D. Mansur	2493
Eagle Club	J. Downey	1940
Esso Club	M. E. Soderston	9-3307
Rotary Club	P. G. van Dam	1473
Lions Club	J. J. R. Beaujon	1835
Kiwanis	N. Schindeler	9-3516
Junior Chamber of Commerce	E. Villanueva	9-2661
Toastmasters Club	Kees de Jongh	2480
Cultural Centre of Aruba	J. H. Beaujon	1236
Free Masonry	Guenther E. Bosse	1686
Y.M.C.A.	Jorge Cuastavino	3072
Trade & Industry Assn.	G. G. A. Nouel	1563
Dental Society	Dr. Elroy Arends	1683
Medical Society	Dr. Hage	2796
Aruba Hotel Assn.	I. Cohen	3380

Real estate and retirement

Though living standards are high, costs of settling run about ½ to ¾ the costs of living in the U.S. in comparable style.

Land: Beach front lots on Palm Beach are government controlled, available for lease only. $79-$119 per year for ¼–⅜ acre, exclusive of taxes.

Construction Costs: Homes cost $95–$160 per sq. yard. A modest home can be built for about $13,000.

Taxes: No sales or luxury tax. Income taxes are on a graduated scale similar to the U.S., but rates are lower. (For example, a single person with an income of $10,000 pays 10.5% taxes.) Real estate taxes are divided into two categories—property (6%) and usage (5%).

Vacation and Retirement Homes: The

government encourages investments, providing information about construction and labor costs and current real estate buys.

Entry Requirements: Prospective residents must show a source of permanent income or permanent employment on island, have a home rented or bought and deposit $132.50 with the government for each adult member of the entering family. There are also health and vaccination requirements.

Complete information about settling is available from the tourist bureau.

There are four real estate firms:

Bouwmaatschappij Aruba N.V.
Druivenstraat 10

N. V. Arcu—Realtors
Anasastraat 4, Dakota

Notary C. W. J. J. Heufke
L. G. Smith Boulevard 25, Oranjestad

Notary F. E. J. Thijssen
L. G. Smith Boulevard 59, Oranjestad

Commerce and industry

After gold was discovered in 1826, several companies sought to exploit it. The last operation was at Balashi where the Anglo-Aruban Gold Mining Co. operated from 1910–1913, when World War I cut off the import of smelting chemicals.

Responding to government stimulation, the hotel and tourism industries are fast developing into important economic factors.

Tax advantages and monopoly privileges are favorable. The "Travel and Information Guide" available from the tourist bureau offers a brief discussion of investment opportunities.

WHERE TO STAY — In Aruba

| | | Dec. 15-April 14 | | April 15-Dec. 14 | |
| | | U. S. Currency | | | |
	Plan	Double	Single	Double	Single
ARUBA CARIBBEAN HOTEL-CASINO Palm Beach (212 Rms.) **(b, p, t)**	(EP)	$32–55	$27–55	$17–35	$13–35
ARUBA SHERATON HOTEL-CASINO Palm Beach (200 Rms.) **(b, p)**		Opening Dec. 1967 Rates on request			
ASTORIA San Nicholas (10 Rms.)	(EP)	$11–12	$ 8–9	$11–12	$ 8–9
BASI RUTI Palm Beach (15 Rms.) **(b)**	(EP)	$20–30	$14–22	$13–20	$ 8–14
CACTUS INN Oranjestad (21 Rms.)	(EP)	$17	$13	$13	$10
CENTRAL Oranjestad (25 Rms.)	(EP)	$10–13	$ 6–8	$10–13	$ 6–8
CORAL STRAND Oranjestad (28 Rms.) **(b, p)**	(EP)	$32	$26–32	$18	$12–18
MANCHEBO BEACH Manchebo Beach (48 Rms.) **(b, p)**	(EP)	$22–27	$17–22	$15–20	$10–15
NASSAU Oranjestad (11 Rms.)	(EP)	$13–50	$ 8	$13–50	$ 8
SCALA Oranjestad (18 Rms.)		Rates on request			

LEGEND FOR HOTEL LISTINGS: (AP) American Plan (room and 3 meals); **MAP** Modified American Plan (room, breakfast and dinner); **(CP)** Continental Plan (room and breakfast); **(EP)** European Plan (room only). All rates quoted on a per-day basis and subject to change. Confirmed reservations at specific rates desired are always recommended.
HOTEL FACILITIES: (b) beach; **(p)** pool; **(t)** tennis; **(g)** golf.

Typical get-away-from-it-all beach on the windward shore on the island of Barbados

BARBADOS

It may or may not have received its name from a fig tree. Legend holds that the name derived from the Portuguese "barbudos," after the bearded fig tree which sends down aerial roots from its branches. On the other hand, they marked it Bernardo on their maps, after St. Bernard. And then again there is the report that later Indian inhabitants were bearded and there is "barbudos" again. But fig tree, Indians or St. Bernard, it became . . .

Barbados, say its travel ads, is a singular island. But to me, at first sight, it looked as plural as you can get.

Seawell Airport was jammed. The road to Bridgetown was more so. As the schools let out, the armies of children all but hid the landscape. "The population of Barbados," my host Peter Morgan told me, "is a quarter of a million." Then he corrected himself. "But that was yesterday."

On an island only 21 miles long by 14 wide, this makes for considerable density per square mile and square inch. Indeed, in lack of elbow room Barbados ranks first in the Caribbean and close to first in the world. One of its major exports, for years, has been people. If it were not for this, one surmises, it would by now have settled like an overloaded ship into the sea. Yes, it's plural all right. But the ads don't lie: it is also singular.

Though without great natural beauty, it has pervasive charm. Though its resources, like its size, are small, it is far more prosperous than most of its sister islands in the Lesser Antilles. And in spite of its problems, it seems predominantly a happy place. The tourist brochures of every island in the sea proclaim that the inhabitants are "cheerful, friendly and courteous." When Barbados says so you can believe it.

Historically, Barbados is "singular" too, for it is one of the few of the West Indies that (a) was not discovered by Columbus and (b) has never changed hands between one European power and another. It was Portuguese explorers who in the early 1500's first put it on the map, coining its name, it is thought, from the "bearded" fig trees that then grew on the island. But this and a few pigs were all they bequeathed to it, and when the British appeared about a century later it was theirs for the taking—and for over three centuries until independence was granted in 1966.

If Columbus didn't sleep here however, another famous sleeper did. In 1751, aged nineteen, George Washington came to Barbados for two months with his half-brother Lawrence, on the only trip he ever made out of what was soon to be the United States. During his stay he caught smallpox, but not badly enough to keep him from writing that he was "enraptured with the beautiful prospects" of the island. Then he took off for home—and history—leaving Barbados to a very different history of its own.

For there was no revolution here. No fleets and armies and changes of government. As the years passed, Barbados became known as the "most British" of the British Indies. To the visitor, the manifestations are everywhere. It is the home of many English expatriates. Its landscape, though featuring cane rather than hedgerows, is as neat as that of Kent or Surrey. Cricket rivals the Anglican Church as the island religion. The center of its capital city of Bridgetown is called Trafalgar Square, and its harbor police still wear the historic uniform of Nelson's navy.

Yet in all this there is irony and contradiction, for however British the island may seem, it is simultaneously in the process of discarding the last vestiges of the old colonialism. For a time, a few years back, it was a member of the short-lived West Indian Federation. When that collapsed, it reverted to its status as a self-governing colony. And now it has total autonomy within the loose framework of the British Commonwealth.

You can feel new forces at work in the surge and bustle of Bridgetown. With a population of 40,000 plus, this is no sleepy insular Podunk but a true city, caught in transition between past and future. Most of the buildings are old and ramshackle, but new ones are coming. Around the rim of the harbor, called the Careenage, are rows of antique fishing and cargo sloops (with the Nelsonian floating police moving among them); but the thoroughfares roundabout present an all-day traffic jam that would do credit to a stateside Main Street. If the inhabitants don't precisely run, they walk briskly, as if they were going somewhere. The local businessmen favor dark suits and citified hats, more apropos to Madison Avenue than a tropic isle.

A fine place from which to view the lively scene is the balcony of a small pub-restaurant called the Flying Fish Club. (The "f.f.," you will soon discover, is not only the prime delicacy but virtually the national emblem of Barbados.) Yet surprisingly, on such a "touristic" island, there is not much else in the capital town to attract the visitor. It is hot, crowded and shabby, with few oases. Its stores run to the large, miscellaneous and routine. For handicrafts gifts and the general run of tourist purchases, it's best to go to Pelican Village, a new and attractive shopping center on Bridgetown's western outskirts.

Obviously, however, things are perking at the center. Bridgetown now has its first major resort hotel—the new Barbados Hilton, which, with 200 rooms, is by far the largest on the island.

Most of the island's pre-Hilton establishments are along the shore some miles north or southeast of the capital. And of these the *crème de la crème* tend to be on the northern stretch, known to travel-ad fame as the Platinum Coast. Here are such gems of the inn world as Sandy Lane, Coral Reef Club, Colony Club, Miramar and Eastry House: all luxurious, all expensive, and all designed, in spread-out cottage format, to give breathing room and pri-

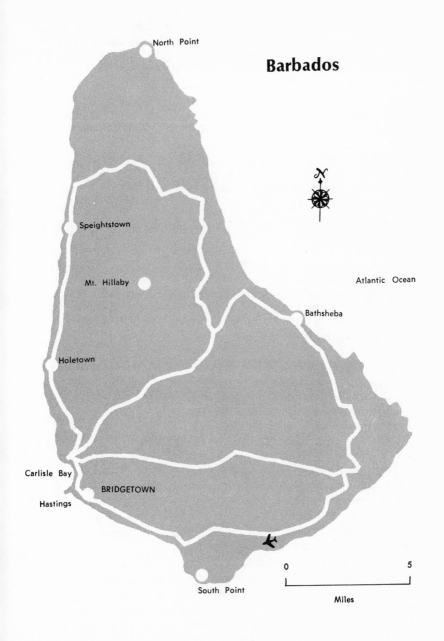

Barbados

North Point

Atlantic Ocean

Speightstown

Mt. Hillaby

Bathsheba

Holetown

Carlisle Bay

BRIDGETOWN

Hastings

South Point

0   5

Miles

vacy. Each, too, has its gleaming well-manicured beach. And Coral Reef, true to its name, has in addition a spectacular offshore submarine garden, with "aquanauts" Les and Muriel Wotton to take you snorkeling, diving or boating.

On the southern coast there are so many hotels and guest houses that it would take the rest of this report to list them. Overall, they are less luxurious and expensive than the platinum galaxy, and their beaches, if any, are apt to be much inferior. Oldest and largest (pre-Hilton) on the island is the Marine Hotel, which is not on the sea at all, but boasts a gargantuan swimming pool. And among the best known to old Caribbean hands is the St. Lawrence, run in a relaxed and genial fashion by Peter Morgan. Here, at Morgan's seaside caravanserai, is the type of place on the island for losing that touristy feeling and imagining yourself a veteran Bajan of years' standing. There are numerous like it.

It is both convenient and at times claustrophobic that most of Barbados' hotels are located cheek-by-jowl along their two coastal strips. There are, however, a few loners "out yonder," and notable among them is the renowned Sam Lord's Castle. Sam Lord was an 19th-century rogue, but the estate that bears his name is today a lovely and tranquil place of sweeping lawn, stately mansion, and rare period furnishings to gladden an antiquary's heart.

Among the many categories into which islands can be grouped are the "quiet" and the "lively" ones, and Barbados is definitely of the lively persuasion. By day you can find almost any warm-weather sport you can think of (except, God save the Queen, baseball); and at night, along the two "hotel rows," there is a pervading sound of clinking glasses and steel-drum bands.

There is, however, no gambling, and none of the neon-lit, gals-and-glitter type of nightclub. A few small spots near town, drawing a mixed crowd, sometimes swing into the small hours. And if you must have the *complete* roster, there was at last report still Harry's.

Harry's is a most un-Bajan place. It is a joint. In fact it is a men-only joint, except for the entertainers, and what the entertainers do, and wear, has long been a subject of bemused comment on the Caribbean grapevine. The Barbados Government and its Tourist Board want no part of Harry's. Though apparently unable to close it, they denounce it in the finest Victorian prose. In reply to a recent query as to what was going on with the place, came the statement that "the proprietor has been deemed a rogue and vagabond by Her Majesty's Court."

Barbados, like all Gaul, is divided in three parts. First and pre-eminent is the western and southern coastal section, based on Bridgetown, and already briefly visited. The second is the eastern coast, and the third is the island's interior, both very different.

Inland, one is almost instantly in another world—a world of sugar. Barbados is not a mountainous but a gently rolling piece of land, and valley and hillside are covered with yellow-green cane as far as the eye can see.

Almost as close, too, for often the cane grows so near and high that it seems about to engulf the roads and the houses beside them. Beyond Bridgetown's landward suburbs the traffic quickly thins out. Instead of cars and trucks there are goats and donkeys. At intervals one passes the ruins of old plantation houses and the ample buildings of modern ones.

The roads, on the whole, are narrow but good; far better than those on more rugged islands. And the villages, if not quite booming with prosperity, are less abysmally poor than on many of the Indies. The children, especially, are neat, spruce—and ubiquitous. A smile or wave from a passerby is the accustomed, not the unusual, thing. Barbados has little of the dramatic beauty of the neighboring British Windwards, with their bold peaks and rioting foliage, but it is a gentle and pleasant place under the caressing sun.

Then at last there *is* drama and beauty. You come—if you take the most rewarding cross-island route—to the top of Cherrytree Hill, and there spread before you is the east coast of the island. It is in total contrast to the soft domesticated shore on the west, a realm of crag and headland, wind and surf. For this is also the windward, the Atlantic coast, and on its shores, easternmost in all the Indies, beats a sea that has rolled unimpeded from distant Africa. It is a heady change of venue for the softened-up traveler. So heady that you may find yourself clutching the wheel of your small rented British car so that it, and you, won't blow away.

Midway along the east coast is its only town, Bathsheba, home port of the Barbadian flying fish fleet. Here the country runs to large scrubby dunes à la Cape Cod, with a few swimmable beaches—if you're partial to breakers. Not a few local residents have built small get-away-from-it-all cottages in this area, and the number increases as you work southward. Then comes the first outpost of the tourist world, Sam Lord's Castle. And beyond that you are back on the main stem.

Like its topography, Barbados' human content is divisible into three parts: the old-liners, white, Negro and mixed; the newer, largely part-time residents; and strictly short-term tourists.

Of the old-liners, the Negro and mixed form an overwhelming majority of about 95%. As noted, there has been much emigration over the years—particularly of young men, leaving a superabundance of adult females. But the birth rate has had no trouble keeping pace, and the outlook is for less and less elbow room as those armies of school children grow up.

This is probably not as ominous as it sounds, for Barbados has proven itself far ahead of most small West Indian islands in making a go of things economically. It has its sugar, its flourishing tourist trade, and a variety of other small diversified industries. Most important of all, it has—for obscure reasons—a harder-working and more ambitious population than most islands, with a tolerable standard of living already attained, and an even better one firmly in view.

As in all the predominantly black islands, except long-independent Haiti, the emergence of a one-time slave population into positions of power and prestige has been a recent development. And in Barbados, as in others, it has not happened without resistance from long-entrenched whites. No one —to add a twist to Noel Coward—can be more beastly to the British than the British; and in a recent issue of *Holiday*, Londoner Wolf Mankowitz joined the club with an acid portrayal of certain old-line white Bajans, insular and prejudiced, who cling to the illusion that they are still holding the thin red line of Victorian colonialism.

There is bound to be some of this in the remnants of a once overprivileged "plantocracy." I too heard racist talk in Barbados of the dire fate that would befall the island when the black majority gained total power. But it is my impression that by now this is the attitude of only a diehard few. Of the 12,000-odd white resident Bajans, most, if not born progressives, are at least realistic enough to know that history has turned a few pages, and that Barbados, as an independent country, is, will be, and should be essentially a black one.

Supplementing the old-line families, there has in recent years been a formidable influx of what might be called semiresidents. These include British, Canadians, Americans, and a scattering of others. Many are retired. Most range from well-to-do to big rich. And not a few (Lord Laseilles, Claudette Colbert, Ingrid Bergman, Sir Edward Cunard, Sir Ronald Tree come to mind) have a glamour-quotient of international celebrity. This has tended, inevitably, to make Barbados an "in" island, bestowing a social cachet of sorts for simply having been there. And it has—not at all incidentally— pushed up real estate values to the point where a choice piece of beach-front land on the Platinum Coast now sells for as much as $60,000 an acre. (Shelter extra.)

Let it be added, however, that—though it helps—you do not have to own a bank or be a film star to manage a week, a season, or even a home in Barbados. On the upper end of the island a new and ambitious cottage-plus-facilities development, called North Point, is beamed at middle-income families. More are sure to follow. Southeast of Bridgetown, among the non-platinum hotels, are guest houses and bungalows with modest rates. And if you'll settle for inland, with sugar instead of sand in your front yard, you may even find an old-fashioned bargain.

Like all resort islands, Barbados carries on an intramural debate on what sort of visitor it wants. "Is it the millionaires or the millions?" was the way one local hotelier put it. In point of fact the matter will be settled less by the Bajans themselves than by the combination of jet plane and widespread prosperity, which is bringing more and more visitors, of all breeds, to their shores. For the long run they will probably compromise happily on millionaires plus thousands—with the new Hilton adding more thousands than before.

In any case—as Caribbean islands go—Barbados flourishes. And Bajans will quickly "have you to know" that they intend to keep it flourishing. Though a little island, it is a *big* little island. It has its sugar. It has its long-term residents and short-term tourists. It has sun and beach, charm and gaiety. And along with these, in its people, drive and industry and ambition. One cannot be in Barbados long without searching for the word to describe the quality that sets Bajans apart from other islanders in the West Indies.

I think the word is pride.

—J. R. Ullman

Instant facts

Location: Most easterly of the Caribbean Islands, some 100 miles from St. Vincent.

Population: 250,000.

Capital: Bridgetown.

Nationality: Independent. Member of the British Commonwealth.

Language: English.

Currency: East Caribbean (same as West Indian) dollar—60¢ U.S., 64¢ Canadian and 4s 2d sterling.

Documentation: Persons entering the island must have some document (birth certificate not acceptable) satisfactorily establishing their nationality and identity. Passports are not required of citizens of the U.S., United Kingdom or Canada who hold a round-trip ticket or some other proof that they are on a bona fide visit to the island.

Climate and Clothes: Temperatures range between 75°–80°, rarely rising above 88°. A 10-knot breeze blows almost constantly, keeping humidity low. Rainfall averages 59 inches annually, slightly higher in the hills. January-June is the dry season. Lightweight summer clothes. Jacket and tie after 6 P.M. and for business appointments. Ladies are expected to wear dresses in Bridgetown rather than shorts. Cocktail frocks or late afternoon dresses after 6 P.M. Formal attire not usually necessary. Light wrap advisable for winter evenings.

Food: Chinese, Indian and English "pub style" cooking is excellent. Gourmet specialties are mostly seafood: green turtle steak or soup, flying fish—fried, broiled, boiled and in pies. Sea urchin eggs are a delicacy.

Several dishes worth trying: **black pudding** (a highly seasoned sausage stuffed with local sweet potatoes), **souse** (spiced pork made from pig's head and tongue), **coo-coo** (cornmeal and ochra puree), **cassava pone** (baked cassava, coconut and spices), **jug-jug** (traditional Christmas dish with beef, salted pork, corn flour and crushed green peas). Curries and stews are made with sheep, pig and goat meat.

There are more than 30 kinds of fruits and many vegetables, and of course Barbados rum mixed in drinks of all varieties. Be sure to try "sangaree," a cocktail specialty of the island.

Geography: Pear-shaped, 166 sq. miles (21 miles long by 14 miles wide). The southern half is very flat with land rising to a ridge near the center, the highest point of which is Mt. Hillaby at 1,104 feet. The northeastern half, called Scotland District, is rugged with cliffs and hills running to the sea.

History: Arawak Indians were the early inhabitants of Barbados. When the first settlers, an English expedition, arrived in 1625, they found a richly forested island which later was referred to as "the sanitarium of the West Indies" because the air was so healthful.

George Washington brought his half-brother Lawrence to Barbados in 1751 to recuperate from tuberculosis. Barbados therefore claims the distinction of being the only piece of foreign soil ever visited by George Washington.

The first English settlers were gentlemen farmers and their workers, and for some 20 years they cleared the forests and established tobacco plantations. Tobacco then commanded a high price in England.

In the 1640's, sugar cane was introduced into Barbados and from then until today sugar has been the most important economic activity in the island. Slaves were imported from Africa to work the cane fields, and Barbados flourished. The heyday of great wealth for the landowners was in the 18th century, and a lively trade sprang up with New England and Virginia.

Barbados is unique in West Indies annals in that it never passed from hand to hand during the colonial wars of the European powers. The island always remained English. The Dutch made an unsuccessful attack on Bridgetown in 1665, and there were many threats of attack by the French, but the Frenchmen never came. Barbados, however, was a heavily defended fortress island.

The abolition of slavery in 1833, and collapsing sugar prices, was followed by large-scale emigration, especially among the landowners, many of whom returned to England. The days of the sugar dynasties were over. But Barbados, more than any other West Indian island, was able to more or less hold its own in this transition period partly because of its policy of appointing an agent in London and partly because of the influence that some of its landowning families exerted in the British capital.

Throughout its history, Barbados has retained close links with the United Kingdom. Apart from assisting in military operations in the Caribbean, Barbados sent volunteers to fight in the Ashanti campaign, the Boer War and both World Wars.

Who flies here

Barbados has a modern jet airport at Seawell serviced by Boeing 707's, 727's, DC-8's, Viscounts and other aircraft. Airlines serving the island directly are as follows:

New York: Air France, BWIA, Pan Am. Round trip: $285–$436; 17-day excursion $189–$264.

Miami: BWIA, Pan Am. Round trip: $257–$354; 17-day excursion $161–$225.

Montreal and Toronto: Air Canada. Round trip: $316–$459 (Canadian $341–$495); 21-day excursion $213–$320 (Canadian $230–$345).

London: BOAC. Round Trip. $660–$1093 (£236–£390 sterling).

San Juan: BWIA, Pan Am, Caribair. Round Trip: $145–$219; 17-day excursion $85–$115.

Air France, Air Canada, BWIA, Pan Am, LIAT and other air charters provide service to other nearby islands.

Island transportation

The Tourist Board of this traditionally English island publishes a map for motorists, cyclists, walkers and tourists, that says a great deal about Barbadian verities. In an age when all of life seems centered around the internal combustion engine, Barbados has spared a thought for the vanishing eccentrics of the world who prefer a walk in contemplation or a leisurely tour by bicycle (rented for $1.20 a day, $6 a week or $16.80 a month).

Of course, for more advanced sightseeing a car is indicated. Taxis can be found almost anywhere, particularly around hotels, and buses (standard and open air) run regularly to and from Bridgetown. Car rental rates range between $30 and $45 a week, with an extra charge of 6¢ a mile over 250 or 300 miles, and daily rates are $7–$9, 6¢ a mile for over 50 miles.

Cars and motorscooters can be rented from the following:

Mobylette Autocycle
Fairchild St., Tel: 6871

Rent-A-Scooter
Opposite St. Lawrence Hotel
St. Lawrence Gap, Tel: 87767

Robert Thom
Bay St., Bridgetown, Tel: 6687

Dear's Garage
127 Roebuck St., Bridgetown, Tel: 3200

Gill's Garage
Fitts Village, St. James, Tel: 01222

Smith's Garage Ltd.
1st Ave., Belleville, Tel: 93233
St. Michael, Tel: 93747

Johnson's Stables & Garage Ltd.
Coleridge St., Bridgetown, Tel: 5186

Mending sail in the Careenage at Bridgetown on Barbados

If you are the holder of an international driver's license, it is advisable to register it at the airport upon arrival. Certain driver's licenses are valid but some drivers must take the test for a Barbados license, which costs about $3. Driving is on the left side of the road.

Chauffeur-driven cars can be hired by the hour or at flat rates. Tours can be arranged through hotels or directly from agencies such as Thom's Creative Tours, Bay St., Bridgetown (Tel: 4466).

Touring Barbados

The place to start is **Bridgetown,** in the parish of St. Michael. Bridgetown's old colonial harbor, called the **Careenage,** is a long inlet of sea, spanned by two bridges, that runs into the center of the town. The Careenage (the name derives from the old practice of beaching a ship, pulling it over on its side, and scraping the barnacles off the bottom) is faced with old warehouses and crowded at every hour with schooners and motor vessels loading and unloading every kind of cargo. It is patrolled day and night by the Harbour Police, who still wear the bell-bottomed trousers, middy blouses and beribboned straw hats of Lord Nelson's sailors.

The heart of the downtown section is **Trafalgar Square,** dominated by Sir Richard Westmacott's statue of Lord Nelson. Other points of interest are the **Legislature,** with its stained glass windows portraying British monarchs; **St. Michael's Cathedral** (Anglican); **Queen's Park;** Pilgrim House, now the **Governor's Residence** and the **Washington House,** a colonial home where George Washington is believed to have resided during the winter of 1751–52.

One lovely trip by car is along the **south coast** with its shell-strewn beaches, its fishing boats and coves. A good destination is **Sam Lord's Castle** where legend compounds legend. Sam Lord was a 19th-century rogue who pretty much ran the gamut of unpleasant things to do. Left as the executor of his brother's estate, he is said to have contrived the deaths of all but one of his nieces and nephews, to have cheated the surviving niece out of her inheritance, and to have kept his wife penned in a dungeon of the castle. When family skulduggery paled, he is supposed to have trained his slaves to act as wreckers along the coast at Long Bay, hanging lanterns in his coconut trees to lure ships onto the shoals. The looted cargoes were piled in his cellar. The evil Sam built the castle in 1830, but unlike him it is a thing of beauty. Set in 71 acres of gardens, with its own private beach, the plantation house is now a luxury hotel and retains the spaciousness and elegance of the Regency period.

East Coast: In Barbados, the eastern shore is known as the Windward Side. The trade winds, blowing uninterrupted from Africa, pile the waters of the Atlantic against the land in spectacular surf. Looking north up the coast, you can see the peaks of Barbados, including Pico Teneriffe, a pinnacled rock that thrusts up more than 1,000 feet.

About midway up the coast is **Bathsheba,** the island's most popular windward resort. Nearby is the village of **Tent Bay,** home of the flying fish fleet.

Every weekday morning these brightly painted boats, manned by native fishermen, head for the nearby fishing grounds where they net flying fish. The flying fish is Barbados' most famous taste treat, and is served at almost every hotel and restaurant. It is considered by many to be the most tasty tropical seafood.

Platinum Coast: On the leeward side of Barbados, leading north out of Bridgetown, is the St. James Coast Road which winds its way over what is known as the Platinum Coast. It is a narrow but well-kept highway which passes by clubs, luxury homes and hotel after hotel. The road keeps close to the sea and affords beautiful views of palm-lined sand beaches.

Ten miles along the road is **Holetown,** where the first English landing took place in 1625. Just beyond stands old St. James Church, its 17th-century façade still intact.

Near the northernmost tip of the island is Colleton House, a fine old plantation mansion.

The sporting life

No visit to Barbados would be complete without taking in a **cricket** match. Barbadians excel at this sport, and some of their players enjoy world-wide fame. Don't worry if the only thing you know about cricket is that there's a wicket. Everyone will be very happy to explain it all to you—in detail.

Polo is played between July and December, and very elegant **horse racing** meets are held annually in early March, early August and late November at Garrison Savannah. People enjoy **riding** in the countryside year round and horses may be hired from Chandler's Stables, Black Rock; Mangrove Riding School, St. Philip; Barbados Show Jumping Federation, Holder's Plantation, St. James.

There are two nine-hole **golf** courses, one at the Rockley Golf and Country Club (greens fees $3 a day, Tel: 7974), the other at Sandy Lane, St. James ($3.60 a day, Tel: 01493). Equipment may be rented.

There are **tennis** courts at the Royal Barbados Yacht Club, and at several other clubs and hotels. Arrangements can be made through your hotel.

Other popular sports include **football, some shooting, basketball** and **netball.**

Water sports: Barbados means **beaches,** both beautiful and accessible.

The west, or leeward, coast presents the placid face of the sea, perfect for swimming, snorkeling, floating or just dunking. One of the most beautiful beaches is at Freshwater Bay, now known as Paradise Beach. All along the west coast of Barbados fresh sheet water from underground reservoirs presses against the sea water and "springs" appear in the sand. A large number of these beach springs occur here.

The windward coast, on the east side of the island, is a place of pounding surf and spectacular scenery. Coral reefs around the west and south coasts protect the warm waters from dangerous fish, and are perfect exploring grounds for the skin diver and snorkeler.

Skindiving equipment, or aqualungs, with either a qualified instructor or a companion diver may be hired from Les Wotton (Tel: 01372 or 91352), West Coast Aquatic Sports. Aqualung instruction for more advanced expeditions are $15 a person. Mask and snorkel can be rented by the day and skindiving expeditions are made to a reef ($3.60) or to a sunken wreck ($6). A half-hour of **water skiing** instruction costs $7.

Fishing (trolling) here is usually done by line from a yacht or launch so that rod and reel are in rather limited supply. Best catches are bonito, Spanish mackerel, kingfish, dolphin, flying fish, black jack, crevalle and mackerel, with February–May the best months.

Fishing facilities are in limited supply. Fishing equipment can be rented from Les Wotton: a speargun for $1.30 a day, fishing rod for 90¢ an hour. For trolling or bottom fishing, a 25-foot launch can accommodate four people ($5 an hour, minimum 2 hours). Deep sea fishing, also for four, is $45 a half day, $81 a full day. **Small boats** for rent by the hour are canoes or kayaks ($1.30 per person) and rowboats ($1.30 up to 4 persons).

Yachts are available for charter from the following services:

Robert O'Neale
Tel: 91168

Carlo Mendoj, Colony Club, St. James
Tel: 01366 or 01248

Pat Fletcher, Barbados Aquatic Club
Tel: 5081

K. Murphy
Tel: 3763

L. V. Stoute
Tel: 4104

V. Burke
Tel: 3026

Les Wotton, West Coast Aquatic Sports
Coral Reef Club, St. James
Tel: 01372

For $2.10 an hour, one or two people can rent a sailfish through some hotels or from Les Wotton. This enterprising seaman also has hour-long **glass-bottom boat cruises** at $1.80 and **scenic coastline** cruises at $3.60.

For transportation to nearby Caribbean islands, you may contact the following agents:

R. M. Jones & Co.
Plantations Bldg., Bridgetown

DaCosta & Co., Ltd.
P.O. Box 103
Broad St., Bridgetown

Wm. Grannum
Plantations Bldg., Bridgetown

Shopping buys

Along the Princess Alice Highway that leads from Bridgetown to Deep Water Harbour there is a cluster of buildings with pyramided roofs set in three beautifully landscaped acres. There is Pelican Village, established by the Barbados Development Board as a center for the island's handicraft industry.

A modern craft center, Pelican Village includes 30 separate shops in which Bajan arts and crafts are exhibited and where some locally manufactured gifts and souvenirs are wrought, displayed and sold.

The Village itself is lovely, designed to be an integral part of its tropical environment. The shape and grouping of the wooden huts with their pyramided roofs of Wallaba shingles give the center the appearance of an African village, with modern overtones. Charming gardens and small orchards of flowering trees, shrubs and plants enhance the mood.

In addition to Pelican Village, Barbados offers other great shopping values. Bridgetown is a duty-free port with numerous shops for bargain buying.

Good bargains include duty-free cameras, china, cashmeres, gloves, silks and tweeds, perfumes, watches, liquor and many locally crafted baskets and pottery. Incidentally, gold, silver, platinum and diamonds are imported into Barbados duty free. Since the finished products are manufactured locally, all such jewelry is automatically considered duty free and not placed in bond.

Dining, dancing and night life

Barbados is not a place that jumps in frenetic neon after dark. But entertainment abounds. Evening is for making the rounds of hotels, or for attending a nightclub.

Hotels often stage beach barbecues and moonlight dancing. Some two dozen inns, nightclubs and restaurants listed have shows and dancing regularly announced in the press. There are many attractive restaurants along the St. James coast.

When you go out for an evening, you will find the music provided by a steel band, a small orchestra or a pianist. Floor shows usually include the diverting Calypso, modeled after the original Trinidad variety with impromptu verse-making and serenading, and the exciting limbo where agile dancers go under a bar sometimes only inches off the floor. The finest floor shows are provided by the hotels, and on "big nights" it is advisable to book tables in advance.

The island also has its share of late-late spots, mostly in Bridgetown. The moviegoer need not feel that he is removed from the world. There are several movie houses (cinemas, please) in Bridgetown and suburbs, and two drive-in theaters.

Accra Beach Hotel: On Rockley Beach, near Bridgetown. Popular family dining spot for snacks, light luncheons, hamburgers. Beautiful beach front.

Abbeville Hotel: Rockley Beach. Good English style cooking, with ocean view.

Bagshot House: St. Lawrence. Simple cuisine, occasional barbecues, informal atmosphere.

Bamboo: St. James Parish. Restaurant, cocktail lounge. Features steak. Music. 7 P.M.–wee hours. Tel: 01392.

Barbados Hilton: Needham's Point. New luxury hotel set in 21 acres on promontory over Carlisle Bay. Classic Hilton menu with local specialties. Entertainment, bars, coffee shops, dining room.

The Barrel of Rum: Broad Street, Bridgetown. Rendezvous of the local crowd. Lunch, cocktail hour and dinner. Has art gallery, good native dishes and potent drinks. No more than three of the following punches served to a customer: Henry Morgan, Cannon Ball, Parrot's Blood, Daisy Jones, Broad Side. Regular jam sessions and, during winter, dancing and entertainment till wee hours. Tel: 5715.

Beau Brummel: Balmoral Gap, Hastings. Cocktail lounge and nightclub with local entertainment, dancing. Floor show Wednesday.

Blue Water Hotel: Across from Rockley Beach. A lively dining room with regular entertainment. Steel bands and shows announced in the press.

Caribbee Hotel: Hastings on lagoon facing sea. Cocktail lounge, dining facilities and nightclub on roof. Dining roof features French and English cuisine, seafood at reasonable prices. Steel bands, limbo and calypso dancers on evenings when cruise ships dock.

Cloud Nine Nightclub: Bats Rock, on the sea. Favorite stomping ground for the late night set. Cocktails, chicken and chips, orchestra and floor shows. Open till late.

Colony Club: St. James, on beach. West Indian dishes expertly presented in relaxing but elegant surroundings. Buffets are a feature with dancing, shows regularly announced.

Coral Reef Club: St. James, on beach. Famous for Barbados barbecue, a deluxe buffet with six hot dishes, hot and cold soups, vegetables, salads. Very reasonable. Regular announcements of dancing, calypso shows.

Crane Hotel: St. Philip, on beach. Set on cliff with excellent ocean view from dining room. Seafood specialties, especially chubbs.

Driftwood Inn: St. Lawrence. Restaurant, cocktail lounge with late entertainment. Tel: 87152.

Eastry House Hotel: St. Peter, in gardens 200 feet above the sea. Cordon Bleu cuisine. Barbecues, steel bands, films and dancing.

Edgewater Hotel: Bathsheba on east coast. Dining room specializes in lobster, shrimp, puppy sharks and chicken.

Fiesta: Prospect, St. James. Cocktails and dining by candlelight to Spanish music. Features steak, lobster, lamb,

Devon sole, game hen with wild rice. Tel: 02286.

Flying Fish Club: Independence Square, Bridgetown. View of Careenage from cocktail lounge, dining room. Luncheons, buffets. Specialties: flying fish, homemade soups, curries, roti, souse, unusual sandwiches. Tel: 4724.

Half Moon Hotel: Dover Beach, south coast. Small, intimate dining room.

Harry's Nitery: Bay St., Bridgetown. An "infamous" late night place with steel bands and entertainment. Recommended for men only.

Hong Kong: Broad St., Bridgetown. Chinese luncheons and dinners. Recommended: chow kai cu, chow kai tier, shrimp chow mein, sweet and sour chicken, sweet and sour pork, chicken special. Tel: 6764.

Hotel Royal-On-Sea: Hastings, ocean front. Cocktails and good Bajan food served on terrace at end of hotel pier. Occasional dancing parties.

Island Inn: Garrison. Popular inexpensive menu. Steak is specialty. Meals served from grill or in tropical garden.

Le Bistro: St. James, adjoining Miramar Hotel. Nightclub. Music, dancing, shows, snacks. Tel: 01326.

Luigi's: Dover. Restaurant featuring Italian dishes with excellent wines. Music. Tel: 8318.

Lu-Mar Inn: Pollards on Highway B, St. Phillip. 18th-century manor transformed into hotel with English countryside manner. Popular place for lunch. Tel: 97256.

Marine Hotel: Hastings, set in tropical gardens. Cocktail lounge, dining room and ballroom setting for many gatherings among local crowd. Continental kitchen.

Miramar Hotel: St. James on the beach. Quiet, elegant setting in country garden with ocean views. A fashionable place for lunch, buffets. Steel bands, jazz, dancing and shows.

Number One Club: 1 Bay St., Bridgetown. Late night spot for jam sessions, occasional shows.

Oasis Restaurant & Cocktail Lounge: 31 Broad St., Bridgetown. Local and English dishes at reasonable prices, also snacks. Flying fish creole style is specialty. Near East atmosphere with "piano ramblings," limbo, fire-eating and belly dancing shows when cruise ships dock. Open for lunch, dinner till 2 A.M. Tel: 6625.

Ocean View Hotel: 2 miles from Bridgetown, on beach. English decor and cuisine. Good kitchens.

Paradise Beach Club: Black Rock, on beach, three miles north of Bridgetown. Informal hotel known for barbecues, picnics, West Indian kitchen. Dances and calypso entertainment regularly.

The Pelican: Princess Alice Highway, Bridgetown. (Pelican Village.) The place to eat when browsing through the village. Sidewalk tables for lunch, dinner and drinks. Specialties: flying fish platter, shrimp, porterhouse steak, Irish ginger beer. Tel: 6966.

Pepperpot: Nelson St., Bridgewater. Nightclub with steel band, dancing. Chicken and chips all night. Shows regularly featured. Tel: 5754.

Royal Caribbean Hotel: Hastings, across from beach. Poolside dining and Sunday buffet. Dancing regularly announced.

Sandy Lane Hotel: St. James. Luxury beach-front resort in 18th-century decor. Continental cuisine. Outdoor movies, dancing regularly scheduled.

St. Lawrence Hotel: St. Lawrence, on the ocean, four miles from Bridgetown. Informal atmosphere wtih buffet lunch regularly. Popular dish here is fish and chips. Occasionally, steel band and jazz trio for dancing, listening.

Sam Lord's Castle: St. Philip, on beach. Showpiece of Regency architecture, built in 1830 as private estate. Fine food, fine wine cellar. Films, calypso shows and dancing scheduled regularly.

South Winds Hotel: St. Lawrence beach, four miles from Bridgetown. Continental, American and local cooking. Good bar, weekly dances.

Sunset Lodge: St. Peter, across from beach. Georgian interior with two-acre garden. Informal atmosphere in dining room. Dancing, steel bands scheduled regularly.

Welsh Harp: St. James. Restaurant and cocktail lounge with entertainment some evenings. Tel: 01336.

Ying Yang Restaurant: Hastings. Chinese food. Tel: 70996.

Special events, celebrations

Carnival: Dances and celebrations. End of February.

Royal Barbados Police Display and Tattoo: February.

Beefsteak & Tripe Club Dinner: In honor of George Washington. On or near February 22.

Royal Barbados Yacht Club Regattas: February.

Horse Racing: Barbados Turf Club's spring meeting at Garrison Savannah. Late February or early March.

Easter Festivities: Easter bonnet parade, kite flying, picnics and dances. April 14.

The Queen's Birthday: April 23.

Labour Day: May Day Celebrations. May 1.

Polo Seasons: Beginning in July, polo and water polo played through December.

Emancipation Day: Usually celebrated the first Monday in August.

Horse Racing: Barbados Turf Club's summer meeting at Garrison Savannah. Early August.

Clerks Holiday: Usually celebrated the first Monday in October.

Horse Racing: Barbados Turf Club's autumn meeting at Garrison Savannah. November.

Annual Poppy Dance: November.

Remembrance Day: Services. November 13.

Independence Day: November 30. Festivities continue from November 27–December 3.

Agricultural and Industrial Exhibition: At Queen's Park. November or December.

Christmas Festivities: Celebrated by having open house for relatives, friends and acquaintances. Also, picnics and dances. Barbadians decorate their homes with such native vegetation as wild cherry, casurina and chrysanthemum rather than fir and holly. Bank holiday December 25–27.

Old Year's Night: Dances and other celebrations; also, "watch-night" service, after mass, to "watch" the old year out and the new year in. Banks celebrate, by closing, on January 2.

Meet the Bajans

Organization	Official	Phone
Amateur Athletic Assn.	Hamish McClurg	3596 or 87040
Olympic Assn.	Michael Simmons	2075 (at work)
Cricket Assn.	Ben Hoyos	7219 or 5770
Water Ski Assn.	Ralph Johnson	87101 or 01260
Game Fishing Assn.	Keith Murphy	3763 or 93698
Rally Club and Go-Kart Racing	Stanley Tryhane	6706 or 7846
Darts League	Maria Herbert	4255 or 70445
Rifle Assn.	Frank Edwards	92191 or 7222
Small Bore Rifle Club	Thomas E. Field	3636
Table Tennis Assn.	Keith Morris	02900
Lawn Tennis Assn.	Noel Symmonds	2564 or 3134
Light Aeroplane Club	Bruce Gibbons	3833 or 93104
Swimming & Water Polo Assn.	Dr. Peter Ward	7679 or 70639
Amateur Football Assn.	Christie Smith	3451 or 03530
Netball Assn.	Miss Pat Best	4427 or 92310
Cycling Union	S. Stoute	4720 or 2677
Rockley Golf Club	N. G. Pogson	7974 or 71165
Sandy Lane Golf Club	J. Thorne	01493 or 01148
Royal Barbados Yacht Club	William "Bill" Mason	7318 or 71125
Sailing & Cruising Club	C. Pilgrim	4434
Show Jumping Federation	Mrs. K. Frost	4750 or 03968
Rugby Union	Neil Thomson	3512
Amateur Weightlifting & Body Building Assn.	Carl Moore	3521

Organization	Official	Phone
Turf Club	G. A. Lewis	3980 or 92351
Polo Club	K. D. G. Frost	03968
Junior Chamber of Commerce	Noel Smith	4895 or 87533
Jaycettes	Miss Marvo Bonnett	2111
British Red Cross Society	Mrs. D. Kirchner	2052 or 7209
Rotary	Denis Bell	87161 or 70313
Dental Assn.	Dr. Randolph Greaves	6560 or 02253
Lions Club	E. Fitzpatrick	4260 or 8573
Y.M.C.A.	L. A. Hall	3910 or 6228
Y.W.C.A.	Mrs. Rita Parris	4953 or 7795
R.S.P.C.A.	Mrs. G. Barker	3077 or 70936
Youth Town	Frank Holder	3297 or 87533
Council of Women	Mrs. Thelma Ince	8554
Royal & Merchant Navy Welfare League	Mrs. S. B. Warren	4010
Children's Trust Fund	Mrs. Peter Branch	02800
Social Welfare Netball	A. St. Hill	4429 or 2926
Amateur Basketball Assn.	Allan Longe	03635
Interim Boxing Board of Control	George Spencer	4434 or 6958
Hockey Assn.	Tony Moore	0821 or 70340
T. B. Assn.	Mrs. E. R. L. Ward	7760
Road Safety Assn.	H. A. Black	2121 or 8620
Family Planning Assn.	Mrs. Elsie Gilkes	2027 or 92737
Medical Assn.	Dr. Edward Hutson	3893 or 0851
Nurses Assn.	Mrs. P. Sargeant	3618
Barbados National Trust	Donald Wiles	0821 or 93623
Mental Health	C. Bennet	02287
Teacher's Assn. (Elementary)	I. A. Norville	93223
Pharmaceutical Society	Hugh Mapp	3006 or 6407
Law Society	Edmond Bayley	3596 or 7379
Bar Assn.	A. K. Walcott	4147 or 03683
Automobile Assn.	Bill Mallalieu	4640 or 93783
Alliance Francaise	Mrs. J. Mitchell	70115
Press Club	Mitchie Hewitt	4718, 6191 or 92482
Green Room Players	Mrs. F. A. Collymore	7149
Soroptomists	Mrs. E. H. Walmsley	7418
Victoria League	Mrs. Thelma Ince	8554
The Jazz Club	Mrs. Everton Weeks	8687 or 3441
Arts Council	J. B. "Bob" Taylor	3615
U. S. Naval Facility	Mrs. A. Fryer	91294
The American Women's Club	Miss J. Lynn	7438
Horticultural Society	Mrs. G. Gooding	7442
Bridge Assn.	P. Griffith	4444
Canadian Women's Club	Miss Lucille Rousseau	7933 or 70176
Teacher's Assn. (Secondary)	David Pope	71217 or 95340

Musicians, museums and pretty gardens

Barbadian culture has a broad base of British historical tradition topped with Caribbean and African customs. In the Victorian Gothic Anglican Cathedral one hears, as well as Bach chorals, Negro spirituals sung with gusto. An unusual musical treat is a concert by the **Barbados Police Band.** Perhaps the most elegantly dressed orchestra in the Caribbean, the group performs mostly in its own Victorian band-box in Bridgetown. Its military stance and red, white and blue uniforms would do credit to any land, and its music is first-rate. (It has performed on the Ed Sullivan Show and in Macy's Thanksgiving Parade.)

The **Barbados Museum** in Bridgetown, once a prison, contains Carib and Arawak Indian relics, examples of birds, fish and marine life, and nostalgic reminders of life on the old sugar estates (furniture, glassware, china). The museum also houses an art gallery and a gallery for children.

Local bibliophiles are proud of the **Barbados Public Library,** with Bridgetown headquarters and seven other branches around the island. There is even a mobile service which visits 25 remote areas every two weeks, and facilities for some post-graduate students. The **Archives** in Bridge-town complement the library by keeping copies of all books locally published. Also in the Archives, wills and private records of the planters and pirates of early days have interested scholarly after-noon browsers.

Of interest to both scholars and holi-day sightseers is palm-fringed **Codrington College,** near St. John, its buildings on the shore of an artificial lake. The col-lege's namesake was a 17th-century gov-ernor of the Leeward Islands who be-queathed the estate, on his death, to a religious organization for the study of medicine and religion.

There are a number of beautiful gar-dens throughout Barbados. In the parish of St. Joseph are the **Andromeda Gar-dens,** complete with wild orchids, a small waterfall and species of the "bearded" fig tree that occupy such an important place in Barbados legend. **Welchman Hall Gully,** in the parish of St. Thomas, has 10 acres of lush tropical gardens in or-ganized abandonment. Purchased by the Barbados National Trust, it is being devel-oped as a natural tropical garden. In St. Andrew, **Turner's Hall Woods** stretches out over 45 acres of forest and features a "boiling" spring (actually activated by natural gas), rare birds and tall stately trees.

Real estate and retirement

Partly and fully furnished houses are in limited supply. When available, partly furnished homes rent for $90–$180 a month and, if you don't mind a some-what isolated beach cottage, $60–$90. Fully furnished places, including even linen and silver, are chiefly on the coast and rents range from $180–$300 a month (out of season), $300–$600 a month (in season). Tenants must pay extra for electricity or gas and for laundry services.

Also limited are unfurnished houses, averaging $90–$150 a month in rentals. Once in a great while, smaller houses are available for less. Buyers are a bit more fortunate. There are a good number of properties on the market. A 2–3 bedroom bungalow averages $12,480–$18,480. Prop-erties on the beach start at about $29,000. At the present time, the cost of buying land and erecting a building is more ex-pensive than purchasing an existing prop-erty the same size. Building costs average $9.60–$13.80 per sq. foot for a single floor, 10 foot ceiling structure.

Domestic help is obtainable for ap-proximately $9 a week. Taxes here are in-famously steep. Do not try to settle in Barbados unless you have an outside source of income as the government does not admit aliens who are seeking employ-ment.

The following is a list of real estate agents:

James M. Bladon Ltd.
Plantations Bldg., Broad St.
Bridgetown

Branker Trotman & Co.
Spry St., Bridgetown

L. B. Brathwaite
Pinfold St., Bridgetown

Realtore Ltd.
Colridge St., Bridgetown

D'Arcy A. Scott
Middle St., Bridgetown

Gerald Wood & Co.
McGregor St., Bridgetown

Holidan & General Services
Hastings House, Christ Church

Cecil Jemmot & Co.
Broad St., Bridgetown

R. Archer McKenzie
Spry St., Bridgetown

H. B. Niblock Co.
Bay St., St. Michael

Gonzalo Carillo
Seclusion Gardens, Black Rock
St. Michael

Ann Zimmerman Associates
Marhill St., Bridgetown

Commerce and industry

Throughout its history, Barbados' nummer one industry has been sugar. Even today, sugar and its by-products, rum and molasses, comprise 85% of its domestic exports and are a major source of revenue. However, tourism is now running a close second and is expected to overtake the sugar industry, which is faced with the problems of a shrinking world market and lower prices.

At the root of the island's industrial dilemma is the density of population. While the Family Planning Association is hard at work to lower future statistics, it cannot reduce the present ones. With food imports rising and much of the island's land area devoted to the cultivation of sugar, the government has had to insist that at least 12% of all estates over 10 acres plant other food crops. This scarcity of land also affects future hotel interests on the island, since the moderate amount of good coastal land is needed for residential, industrial and recreational uses also.

While there are still some problems affecting future tourism, such as the need for more sporting facilities (i.e., a championship golf course), tourism—in the form of short-term visitors, cruise-ship stopovers and "island-hoppers"—is expanding at a supersonic rate. The Hotel Aids Act of 1955 has encouraged hotel builders, and the newly opened Barbados Hilton, the first large hotel on the island, is certain to put Barbados firmly on the tourist track.

The government also has made an effort to attract industry to the island through the Industrial Incentives and Development Acts of 1963. An informative booklet, "Investing in Barbados," gives detailed information on what services the Barbados Development Board in Bridgetown is willing to render new industries. This little island has a number of advantages to offer interested investors, including a new jet airport and deep-water harbor, 800 miles of well-paved roads, good water supply, efficient electric and telephone systems and a stable government. Unemployment is uncomfortably high on the island and, up to now, many skilled laborers have been attracted to other islands.

WHERE TO STAY — In Barbados

	Plan	Dec. 16-April 15 U. S. Currency Double	Single	April 16-Dec. 15 Double	Single
ABBEVILLE Rockley (50 Rms.) (b)	(MAP)	$22–24	$11–13	$17–18	$ 8.50 $ 9
ACCRA BEACH Rockley (50 Rms.) (b) (CP)	(MAP)	$33–50	$26–28	$24–26 $20–22	$15–17 $13–15
ANDREA ON SEA (21 Rms.) (b)	(MAP)	$18	$10	$16	$ 8
BAGSHOT HOUSE St. Lawrence (16 Rms.) (b)	(MAP)	$36–42	$16–18	$22	$10–11
BARBADOS HILTON Needham's Point (158 Rms.) (b, p, t)	(MAP)	$60–64	$44–48	$32–36	$20–24
BENSTON BEACH Maxwell Road (15 Rms.) (b)	(AP)	$30	$15	$22	$12
BLUE CARIBBEAN St. Lawrence (10 Rms.) (b)	(AP)	$20–28	$14	$17–18	$ 9
BLUE WATER BEACH Rockley (30 Rms.) (b)	(MAP)	$38–40	$28	$24–26	$15
BONNIE DUNDEE St. Lawrence (24 Rms.) (b)	(MAP)	$36–42	$24–28	$22–24	$14–17
BUCCANEER BAY St. James (22 Units) (b)	(CP)	$30	$20	$22	$14
CARIBBEE Hastings (54 Rms.) (b)	(MAP)	$34–36	$25	$23–25	$16
COLONY CLUB St. James (55 Rms.) (b, p)	(MAP) (AP)	$54–66	$36–64	$30–40 $34–44	$20–30 $22–32
CORAL REEF St. James (50 Rms.) (b)	(AP) (MAP)	$58–68	$36	$34–44 $30–40	$22–28 $20–26
DRIFTWOOD INN (11) Rms.) (b, p)	(CP)	$10–12	$12	$ 7.50	$ 8
EASTRY HOUSE St. Peter (34 Rms.) (b, p)	(MAP)	$46–85	$42	$38–60	$24
EDGEWATER Bathsheba (21 Rms.) (b, p)	(AP)	$38–45	$20–25	$20–25	$12–15
FOSTER HOUSE INN St. Philip (4 Rms.) (b)	(AP)	$12	$12	$10	$10
GREENSLEEVES APARTEL (18 Rms.) (b)	(EP)	On Request		$21–30	
HALF MOON Dover Beach (9 Rms.) (b)	(MAP)	$40	$25	$20	$15
ISLAND INN Garrison (21 Rms.) (b) (MAP) (CP)	(AP)	$32–38 $28–36	$22–24 $18–22	$22–24 $18–20 $14–16	$12–14 $10–12 $ 6– 8
LU-MAR INN St. Philip (12 Rms.) (p)	(MAP)	$32–36	$22–23	$20–23	$14–15
MARINE Hastings (112 Rms.) (p)	(MAP)	$34–38	$17–19	$28–32	$18–22
MIRAMAR St. James (52 Rms.) (b, p)	(MAP)	$58–68	$40–58	$35–40	$21–25

NORTH POINT SURF **RESORT** (MAP) St. Lucy (11 Rms.) (b, p)	$40–48	$16–32	$25–30	$16–20
OCEAN VIEW (AP) Hastings (40 Rms.) (b) (MAP)	$36–42	$16–20	$24–26 $20–22	$13 $11
PARADISE BEACH (MAP) Bridgetown Area (100 Rms.) (b)	$40–50	$26–36	$26–32	$16–22
	(Dec. 16-April 15)		(April 16-Dec. 15)	
PENRITH RESIDENTIAL (EP) **CLUB** Worthing (6 Suites) (b, p)	$60 $87.50		$30–60	
ROCKLEY BEACH (MAP) Rockley (20 Rms.) (b)	$30–32	$22	$20–22	$13
ROYAL CARIBBEAN (MAP) Hastings (37 Rms.) (b, p)	$32–36	$18–24	$20–24	$12–14
ROYAL ON SEA (MAP) Hastings (33 Rms.) (b)	$32–36	$18–24	$20–24	$12–14
ST. LAWRENCE (MAP) St. Lawrence (22 Rms.) (b)	$30–36	$16–20	$11–12	$12–13
SAM LORD'S CASTLE St. Philip (40 Rms.) (b, p)	$50–60	$28	$36–50	$20
SANDY BEACH (Apts.) (EP) (26 Units) (Apts.) (AP) (Rms.) (b) (AP)	$24 $30 $24	$18 $20 $14	$16 $22 $10	$ 9 $12 —
SANDY LANE (MAP) St. James (70 Rms.) (b, g)	$66	$48–60	$38	$26
SILVER BEACH (AP) Rockley (12 Rms.) (b)	$22	$12	$18	$10
SOUTHERN PALMS (CP) **BEACH** St. Lawrence Gap (29 Rms.) (b)	$20–40	$18–38	$12–24	$10–22
SOUTH WINDS (AP) St. Lawrence Beach (MAP) (28 Rms.) (b) (EP)	$34–50 $30–46 $26–42	$21–24 $19–22 $17–20	$28 $25 $20	$16 $12.50 $10
STONEHAVEN INN (AP) St. Philip (12 Rms.) (b) (MAP)	$29–34 $25–30	$16–19 $14–17	$24–28 $20–25	$14–16 $12–14
SUNSET LODGE (MAP) St. Peter (16 Rms.) (b)	$40–60	$36	CLOSED DURING SUMMER	
WINDSOR (MAP) Hastings (42 Rms.) (b)	$30–35	$18–20	$22–24	$12–14

LEGEND FOR HOTEL LISTINGS: (AP) American Plan (room and 3 meals); MAP) Modified American Plan (room, breakfast and dinner); (CP) Continental Plan (room and breakfast); (EP) European Plan (room only). All rates quoted on a per-day basis and subject to change. Confirmed reservations at specific rates desired are always recommended.
HOTEL FACILITIES: (b) beach; (p) pool; (t) tennis; (g) golf.

BONAIRE

In ornithological circles Bonaire is considered for the birds. Thousands of flamingos make this small island their home, and dedicated bird watchers arrive from all over to observe the flamingos in their favorite nesting ground. Besides the birds, there are fish of all descriptions in lagoons and coral reefs, good beaches and gin clear water, and a constant supply of peace and tranquillity. There are good accommodations and good food, and for wilder moments a gambling casino decorated all in blue.

Where the flamingos go

A comfortable way to visit the salt mines is to travel to the small island of Bonaire, one of the Netherlands Antilles. Where slaves once mined salt under a tropical sun, waves of visitors are happily paying $32 a day (double room) to bask on Bonaire's beaches and look at Bonaire's birds.

The island offers splendid sailing, swimming, snorkeling and fishing, or just lazy beachcombing if that is your inclination. Travel connoisseurs who enjoy meeting new people will find Bonaire the "getaway" isle for those who live in larger neighboring islands. A weekend is likely to find the place full of Dutch, English, Americans, French, Venezuelans and Curacaoans.

The permanent population of Bonaire includes thousands of pink flamingos that nest and feed in shallow lagoons at both ends of the island. (The island is one of their few breeding places in the western hemisphere.) The flamingos can be observed at fairly close range all year 'round.

Great Salt Lake in the southern part is the flamingos' most important feeding and breeding site in the island. The road to the lake passes the salt pans and the old slave huts, built on such a scale that an adult could not stand upright. Nearby are the three brightly colored obelisks—one orange, one white, one blue—that marked the moorings for the old salt ships.

In and around the square salt ponds can be found a variety of other water birds—blue and white herons, snipes, sandpipers, several species of seagulls, ducks, pintails and pelicans, among others. Bonaire is by way of being a little bit of heaven for bird watchers. (Note: Bird watchers are advised to check far in advance with the Tourist Bureau for the best dates for bird watching.)

The island's scenery can be startling. In some areas millions of pieces of jagged coral intercept rolling combers and fling bright sea spray against the sky. The interior is dry and, in the north, hilly, and supports vast acres of cactus plants with here and there the weird divi-divi tree that bends always away from the wind.

Driftwood, conch shells and coral are there for the beachcombing on the windward side of Bonaire

There is an excellent system of roads that connects all parts of the island. Thoughtful planners have provided handy little walkways that lead down the sides of small coral cliffs to the edge of the sea.

Birds aside, most activity on Bonaire centers around the sea. The beaches are fine and white, and the sheltered Bay of Kralendijk is perfect for sailing and water skiing. Uninhabited—except for goats—Little Bonaire, just offshore, with its endless variety of plants, coral formations and colorful fish, is a favorite spot for skindivers. On "big" Bonaire, Lac, a large land-locked bay with sparkling clear water, is unsurpassed for spearfishing and underwater exploration. High piles of empty conch shells on the shore testify that conch meat is considered a delicacy on Bonaire. You are invited to help yourself to the shells.

At present, Bonaire has only two hotels: the relaxed Flamingo Beach Club, where dinner *without* coat and tie is *de rigueur*, and the larger, modern Hotel Bonaire (with gambling casino). Both hotels are situated on wide white stretches of beach and both have fine water sports facilities.

A $4 million, 250-room beachfront hotel—the Hotel Sorobon—is under construction at Lac Bay. Several other resort projects—a 120-room hotel, a retirement and vacation home development and a bungalow park—also are being built.

Instant facts

Location: 20 miles east of Curacao, 50 miles north of Venezuela.

Population: 7,400.

Capital: Kralendijk (Krah-len-dike).

Nationality: One of the Netherlands Antilles, an autonomous part of the Kingdom of the Netherlands.

Language: Dutch, Papiamento. English and Spanish are widely spoken.

Currency: The Netherlands Antilles guilder or florin, 1.87 florin per U.S. dollar (U.S. currency usually accepted everywhere).

Documentation: Presentation of vaccination certificate not more than three years old; return ticket to destination outside Netherlands Antilles. U.S. travelers: passport or birth certificate, if citizen; naturalization certificate if naturalized; re-entry permit or "non-quota" immigration visa, if permanent foreign resident of U.S.

Climate & Clothes: Completely outside the hurricane range, average annual temperature is 82° (January–February, 79°; August–September, 84°). Rainfall is 22 inches annually, coming in light showers in November and December. Casual summer dress is always appropriate. Sweaters and jackets are advised for cool evening trade winds.

Food: Seafood. Pickled conch shell meat is specialty. Chinese and Dutch cuisine available.

Geography: "L"-shaped and approximately 24 miles long, 5 miles wide. Northern half is hilly (highest peak: Mt. Brandaris, 784 feet); southern part, flat. Coast has many well-protected coves and beaches.

History: Original settlers were the Caiquetios, an Arawak tribe that raised sheep and goats in the hills. In 1499 Alonso de Ojeda discovered the island. For the next century the Indians were exploited by Spanish, Dutch and English pirates who visited regularly to plunder foodstuffs. In the 17th century Bonaire became a vast plantation and salt mining industry for the Dutch West India Company. Salt is still mined, but in much smaller quantities. The industry is now being reactivated.

Who flies here

Flights from New York, Miami and other major cities must make connections in Curacao. ALM (Dutch Antillean Airlines) has regular service from both Curacao (round trip: $18; 3-day excursion $13.50) and Caracas (round trip: $48; 17-day excursion $34.50).

Island transportation

Taxis and U-Drive-It cars are available at moderate rates. A U.S. license is valid. All taxis have fixed tariffs according to destination, route—if it is a tour—and time of day. (Night rates are higher.) There are three long tours offered by Bonaire Sightseeing: north, south and throughout the island.

The Flamingo Beach Club and the Hotel Bonaire provide free transportation between airport or dock and hotel. Tours, car rentals and taxis may be arranged through your hotel or directly from: Bonaire Flamingo Tours and U-Drive, Tel: 8310; Bonaire U-Drive, Tel: 8218.

Sightseeing

The capital, Kralendijk (Coral Dike), is small, neat and pretty. It is Dutch-clean, with buildings painted in orange, pink and green, and with small well-tended gardens. Its fort stands as a reminder of Bonaire's turbulent past, with cannon dating back to the time of Napoleon.

Locally, people don't bother too much with the word "Kralendijk." The capital is called simply "Playa," the Spanish word for beach. The island can be seen in one leisurely day. The northern hills are the most scenic. Visit **Goto-Meer**, the landlocked bay that is the abode of birds, including flamingos, and **Para Mira** (Stop and Look), a hill overlooking the tiny plazas and bright roofs of the village of **Rincon.** The road to the Indian cave at **Boca Onima** is lined with tropical fruit trees. At **Spelonk**, there is a Caiquetios Indian cave with inscriptions dating back 500 years. A side trip on the east coast to **Bolivia** or **Washikemba** is recommend-

ed. Here ocean waves break into high fountains against the rocky shore.

No southern tour is complete without a trip to the **salt pans.** After years of neglect they are being re-opened for industry. Three 30-foot **obelisks** in Dutch colors—blue, orange, white—were erected in 1838 to guide early salt ships to their moorings. The **primitive stone huts** were built for slaves working the pans, but on such a scale that no adult could stand upright. Also in the pans is the 765-foot antenna of **Trans World Radio,** the most powerful station in the western hemisphere. **Birds** are everywhere. Herons, snipes, sandpipers, ducks, pintails, pelicans are a few of the species that breed here. **Great Salt Lake** is the main nesting ground of the flamingos. Further down the coast is the island's oldest lighthouse, **Willemstoren,** built in 1837. Popular picnic spots are **Sorobon Beach** and **Boca Cai** at Lac Bay.

This sporting life

Life revolves peacefully around the sea. Off the coasts are practically virgin waters, excellent for **skin and scuba diving,** and suitably clear for underwater photography. It is wise to bring your own snorkel, regulator, fins and special gear because supplies are limited. Hotels will arrange for guides to help you explore the north coast and Lac Bay, where there are unsurpassed views of coral and sea life. Lac Bay has the best **fishing.** Breeding place of the huge conch, it is popular for spearfishing and hunting game fish. Sea crayfish and spine lobster thrive in shallows along all coasts and bottom fishing for red snapper is popular in slightly deeper depths. September–February is the best season for game fish, and trolling may net bonito, tuna, wahoo, barracuda, sailfish or an occasional kingfish. Dolphin season is March–August. Year round there are small tropical varieties and grouper.

Bring your own rod and reel, as standard local equipment usually includes only a handline. Hotel Bonaire and the Flamingo Beach Club offer free (row) **boats** to guests for bottom fishing. Both

Bonaire

hotels and local fishermen have other fishing boats available at reasonable rates. Sailing boats rent at $50 daily. Small charter boats rent at $4.50 per hour and $14–$22 for 5–10 hours. Large boats may be chartered at $5.50 per hour and $22–$32 for 5–10 hours. All rentals include boatman, tackle and bait.

Waterskiing is available at hotels at $5.50 per half hour, including boat and skis. Hour-long **glass-bottom boat** tours accommodate five passengers for $5.50.

Shopping buys

Though not a free port, low duty and low prices are advertised. However, a wider selection of luxury items and even lower prices can be found in neighboring Curacao. Best bargains are local artifacts: driftwood, gifts made of coral and conch shells, and tortoise shell jewelry—often inlaid with gold filigree. There are more than a dozen shops in Kralendijk, open daily except Sunday.

Dining, dancing and night life

Hotel Bonaire: Located on Playa Lechi, just outside Kralendijk. Modern coffee shop, cocktail lounge, dining room overlooking sea. International cuisine in informal atmosphere. **Gambling casino.** Music, dancing and shows. Jacket and tie in dining room and casino after 7 P.M. Tel: 8448.

Carib Theatre: Kralendijk. Music, shows. Tel: 8360.

Copa Cabana Restaurant: Nikiboko. Local specialties. Tel: 8365.

Flamingo Beach Club: Kralendijk Bay, on beach. Cabana resort with dining hall, cocktail lounge and terrace over the bay. Bar features ounce-and-a-half standard. Music, dancing, shows. Jacket and tie unnecessary. Tel: 8285.

Mona Lisa Restaurant: Kralendijk. Chinese and local dishes. Tel: 8308.

Orange Restaurant & Theatre: Antriol. Caribbean cooking with music and shows. Tel: 4279.

Palermo Restaurant: Antriol. Local specialties. Tel: 8271.

Zeezicht Restaurant: Chinese kitchen. Tel: 8434.

Special events, festivals, celebrations

New Year's Day: Masquerade, dancing in streets of villages and Kralendijk. Open house at Lieutenant Governor's mansion.

Children's Flower Parade: Religious procession. January 31.

"Simadan": Harvest month celebrated by folk dancing whenever crops are reaped. February.

Carnival: Dances, parades, fireworks. February.

Queen Juliana's Birthday: Sports events, music, festive atmosphere. April 30.

Labor Day: Island holiday with celebrations. May 1.

Ascension Day: Public Holiday. May 24.

Whitmonday: Public holiday. June 3.

St. John's Day: Folk songs and dances. June 24.

St. Peter's and St. Paul's Day: Local parties and dancing. June 29.

Sint Nicolaas Arrives: Sint Nicolaas parades through streets of Kralendijk to open Christmas season. December 5.

Kingdom Day: Celebration of autonomy gained in Netherlands Antilles Constitution. December 15.

Boxing Day: Families and friends exchange greetings. December 26.

Meet the people

Organization	Official	Phone
Baseball Assn.	Thomas Hernández	8395
Bonaire Cultural Center	Rev. J. Jonkman	8284
Bureau of Sports and Health	Edward Confesor	8329
Football Assn.	R. P. Saleh	8209
Lions Club	Rev. J. Jonkman	8329
Roman Catholic Boy Scouts	C. A. Nicolas	8241
Softball Assn.	P. N. Tromp	8444
Volleyball Assn.	Charles L. R. Ellis	8322

Real estate and retirement

The only real estate firm is the BEL-NEM Caribbean Development Corp., partly owned by Harry Belafonte, with a goal of building 150 permanent vacation homes and two hotels. Land is not available for sale, but the government offers 60-year leases at 3¢–30¢ per sq. meter. Construction costs range from $60–$80 per sq. meter. All ocean front property has been leased. Additional information is available at the Bureau of Economic Development and Tourism. Tel: 8322.

Commerce and industry

Until recently, Bonaire had practically no commercial development such as exists in her sister islands of Aruba and Curacao.

The most lucrative industry was salt, established in the 17th century, later declining in importance, now revived and modernized. The International Salt Company of Clark Summit, Pa., is now reactivating Bonaire's salt industry. The company has made a multimillion dollar investment in the project and is now constructing dikes and installing equipment. The first salt is expected to be harvested this year. International Salt has been very careful not to disturb the pink flamingos which nest in the salt flats, agreeing to detour its dikes around the birds at an additional construction cost of $100,000.

In the past few years the government has promoted expansion in tourism and other industries. The Trans World Radio, with the most powerful transmitter in the western hemisphere, and the Dutch World Radio are in Bonaire. Other harbingers of growth include a new textile factory, two

new banks, hotel expansions, and construction of the $4 million Hotel Sorobon
at Lac Bay. The water and power plant
has also been enlarged, and a pier is
planned at the site of the salt processing
center.

Low taxes, government monopoly privileges, and rights in the European Common Market are some incentives for
investment. The government welcomes
business—anticipating the time when
plans for the jet airstrip, marina and additional luxury hotels can be realized.

Detailed information is available at the
Bureau of Economic Development and
Tourism in Kralendijk.

WHERE TO STAY — In Bonaire

| | | Dec. 15-April 14 | | April 15-Dec. 14 | |
| | | U. S. Currency | | | |
	Plan	Double	Single	Double	Single
HOTEL BONAIRE (60 Rms.) **(b, p)**	(MAP)	$42–46	$28–32	$32–36	$21–25
FLAMINGO BEACH CLUB (21 Rms.) **(b)**	(MAP)	$32	$20	$23	$15

LEGEND FOR HOTEL LISTINGS: **(AP)** American Plan (room
and 3 meals); **MAP)** Modified American Plan (room, breakfast
and dinner); **(CP)** Continental Plan (room and breakfast); **(EP)**
European Plan (room only). All rates quoted on a per-day
basis and subject to change. Confirmed reservations at specific rates desired are always recommended.
   HOTEL FACILITIES: **(b)** beach; **(p)** pool; **(t)** tennis; **(g)** golf.

BRITISH VIRGIN ISLANDS

*The islands, islets, cays and rocks of the British Virgin Islands are strewn
like a broken necklace over the northeast corner of the Caribbean Sea.
The shores sparkle with small bays and hidden coves, and yachtsmen
consider these waters one of the world's loveliest cruising grounds.*

Uncut gems

A hop, step and jump—and there you are.

The hop is from San Juan to St. Thomas, the step from one plane (big)
to another (small), the jump from St. Thomas to Beef Island at the hub
of the British Virgins. In a few miles and a few minutes you have come from
the swarming center of everything to as far-out a realm as exists in the
Caribbean.

Call it a puddle jump. But what a puddle! Ranged in great arcs along
the central highway of Sir Francis Drake Channel, the galaxy of the Virgins
is a sight to transfix the eye and set the mind to dreaming. Progressively, as
one moves from the American to the British sector, the works of man drop
away behind. The world ahead seems to have risen newborn from the sea.

The British Virgins are not lush islands. Their climate is dry, and they
are short on bosky forests and purling streams. Their beauty is in their outlines: a sweep of cones and domes and castled crags against the shining sky.
In their bright scarfs of beach. In their connecting waters, deep and shallow,
carved into bays and inlets, a sea of prisms glinting in the sun.

There are about forty of them in all—the exact count depending on
where you draw the line between bona fide island and rock or reef. Biggest
and most important is Tortola—the Turtle-dove—some 12 miles long by
two-to-three wide. Next is Virgin Gorda, the Fat One. Others run a rich
gamut of nomenclature from plain Peter and Norman through Jost Van
Dyke, Dead Chest and Fallen Jerusalem, to Prickly Pear, Great Dog, George
Dog and Cockroach. If you get close in, and have a weakness for kooky
names, the going is even better. For instance, how about a morning sail from
Throw Way Wife Bay past Kitto Gut and Dicky Ground to Pull and Be
Damn Point?

In this labyrinth of land and sea there are less than ten thousand inhabitants, all but a handful of them Negro. Only a dozen of the islands
are inhabited, and only Road Town on Tortola, the British Virgins' capital-
cum-metropolis, could possibly, and barely, be called more than a village.
Elsewhere, man's hand has touched the islands lightly. The pervading sound
is the hum of the trade wind. The brightest lights at night are from moon
and stars.

Boating is a way of life in the British Virgin Islands

Tonight, at least. Perhaps tomorrow night. But not for much longer, for, as to all the Caribbean, change is coming to the BVI's. The wave of the future is coming. The wave of tourists. And preparations are underway to bid them welcome.

"The British Virgins," says my friend Ian Taylor, a three-year resident and devoted lover of the islands, "are in my opinion the crown gems of the West Indies. The gems are still uncut, but the polishing process is now taking place." Simultaneously, and more ominously, a recent news item announced: "The British Virgin Islands will soon employ a public relations expert to help them change their image."

For better or worse, as gem cutter or press agent, progress is obviously about to move in. But it will still be a while before anyone mistakes Road Town for San Juan or Cockroach Island for Montego Bay.

The chief reason why the BVI's, through the centuries, have been a Caribbean boondock is that they are so small and commercially unexploitable. The early tides of conquerors and colonists passed by and through them in quest of bigger game. Almost their only role in history was as a hideout for pirates and raiders, whose legacy remains today in a host of sunken wrecks and rumors of lost treasure.

In slave days, when sugar was king of the Indies, there were small plantations on the bits and pieces of arable land. But with slavery's end they collapsed. The old-line whites made a total withdrawal, and the freed Negroes reverted to a primitive life of fishing and subsistence farming. When, early in this century, the former Danish Virgins became American, there came a gradual development of a new export—manpower—with hundreds of islanders going to St. Thomas and St. Croix as labor for all manner of projects. (They still do.) But in the BVI's themselves there were no projects. An occasional British official came and went; an occasional adventurous yachtsman. The rest was sun, sea and stagnation.

It is only in the past few years, the years of the tourist, that the British Virgins have at last felt the true winds of change. The first to strike was quite a breeze indeed—a veritable manna-laden breeze—when Laurance Rockefeller and associates, who had already been active in Puerto Rico and the U.S. Virgins, moved into Virgin Gorda and created the resort of Little Dix Bay. Little Dix is still far and away the major contributor to the BVI's "new image." But with a Rockefeller leading the way, other bankrolls have inevitably followed. The polishing of the "uncut gems" is proceeding not only with enthusiasm but with increasingly visible results.

As of the present writing, there are, besides Little Dix, eight establishments in the islands ready and able to receive visiting (i.e., touring) firemen. Two are in Road Town, two in rural Tortola. Three are on small islands of their own, clustered close to Tortola's East End, and one is a neighbor of Little Dix on Virgin Gorda. None is big or deluxe by stateside or large-island standards. But this, it seems to me, is exactly as it should be, for bigness and deluxeness are precisely what a rational BVI visitor is trying to escape.

The people responsible for these and other recent developments are what might be called the New Breed in the British Virgins. Seniority among them goes to Louis and Beth Bigelow, semitransplanted New Englanders, who for some thirty years have been proprietors of the Guana Island Club on one of the satellites off Tortola's East End. The others are almost all of post-World War II vintage and include Englishmen, Canadians, Americans and hybrids (among the last being the aforementioned Ian Taylor, who is original English by way of Canada). Their personalities, of course, differ. Their projects differ. But I have never, anywhere, seen adopted islanders more united in enthusiasm and affection for their bumps of land in the sea.

This, to be sure, is not Eden, and there are problems aplenty—among them lack of money, lack of materials, lack of transport, lack of almost anything you can think of. A few short years ago the islands' economy was so miniscule it almost didn't exist, and even today it is a frail maverick thing perched precariously between British and American spheres of dominion. Politically, of course, the tiny realm is British. But the thin flow of worldly goods that has come its way has been so predominantly American that the U.S. dollar has become its official currency. Indeed—to the delight of philatelists—the BVI's are the only unit in the British Commonwealth on whose postage stamps the Queen shares billing with stateside dollars and cents.

Still, the Union Jack flaps proudly on shore and hilltop. And in business and finance a citizen of the Commonwealth receives preferential treatment. In the case of land, for instance, he may buy and sell at will, with no strings attached. But an American or other outsider must build and improve within a fixed period of time, or forfeit his title. The laudable purpose here is to fend off dollar speculation and get-rich-quick schemes which would be of no benefit to the islands themselves. But with dollars so much more available than sterling, the effect has also been a slowing of investment and development.

One of the pleasant things about small islands is the ease with which a newcomer can get acquainted. And in the BVI's the place par excellence for just that is Road Town's premier pub, The Poop Deck. By "premier" we imply no resemblance to "21" or the Waldorf's Peacock Alley. Floor, walls and ceiling barely manage to hold together. But under the aegis of expatriate American Hank Milstrey, The Poop Deck is a lively and genial place; and if you stay around you'll get the "poop" all right, about everyone and everything in the islands. No stagnant backwater here. For this is the New Breed's favorite forum, and the air is thick with talk of new plans, projects, dreams. Off in a corner, perhaps, you'll find a loner brooding over his beer: a hard core escapist in T shirt and tattered shorts who wants no part of any of them—just the good old days of classic beachcombing. But, alas poor fellow, he is brooding in a lost cause.

Roundabout sprawls the rest of Road Town in a confused state of flux between old and new. Most of the buildings are small and ramshackle. Beside the main dock a public privy overhangs the water. Dominating the view from the harbor is what looks like the abandoned palace of an Arab potentate: a nameless never-opened hotel that someday is going to be turned into something, but no one knows what.

At the two ends of town, however, two hotels, the Treasure Isle and Fort Burt, are functioning actively and attractively. A shop called Little Denmark, bulging with free-port bargains, could fit respectably into St. Thomas's Main Street. The new Barclay's Bank building boasts air conditioning no less, the first in the British Virgins. And along the waterfront an ambitious land reclamation project will provide acreage for a whole new "downtown business district."

In Ian Taylor's redoubtable Austin Champ (first cousin to a Jeep) I rode up, down and around the island of Tortola, and here too contrast was everywhere. Along the south shore, to either side of Road Town, the highway was new and excellent, with trucks and taxis breezing past in the best West Indian do-or-die fashion. But once we turned inland we were in an antique realm of ruts and bumps, donkeys and goats and chickens. On Tortola's heights we passed through the BVI's only rain forest, an almost untouched miniature jungle. But on a bare hilltop just beyond were rising the installations of a new Cable and Wireless station, a major link in Britain's international communications network.

Then came more wilderness. Close by, a maze of rocky hills and scrub. Far out, across sea and islands, a vast sweep of space and stillness . . . until the stillness was broken. Around a sudden corner a dinosaur of a yellow bulldozer was chomping the earth, and nearby a group of nonlaboring laborers was clustered around a portable radio listening to the World Series.

At intervals, on height and shore, we came to areas that had been staked out as realty developments and cottage colonies. One was called Spyglass Hill, a second Apple Bay, a third Arundel Estates. (Between them, I noted, were places called Shark Bay and Hell Hole, presumably *not* named by a realtor.) Most were still strictly in the surveying-and-hoping stage, with not a cinder block in sight. But at opposite ends of the island were Tortola's two "outback" establishments that are already functioning.

They are very different. One, Long Bay Estate, at the West End, is a combination hotel and housekeeping cottage colony that, after Little Dix Bay, is the largest resort in the BVI's. The other, Maya Cove, near the East End, is, in contrast, not a hotel at all but basically a private home which can accommodate only four paying guests. However, as run by a youngish American couple, Lee and Gale Johnston, it is probably—again excepting Little Dix—the most luxurious haven in the islands.

My own base in the British Virgins was not on Tortola but on a tiny fleck of land off its East End called Marina Cay. (Pronounced *key*, as are all such in the Caribbean.) I had work to do on a novel; for that I need solitude; and if the BVI's were the ideal hideout for pirates, I had reasoned, why not for a writer as well? Of all the refuges available, Marina Cay, with its six water-ringed acres, seemed best suited to my purpose. Indeed, its inhabited history had begun with a writer: a young American named Robb White, who in the 1930's had come to it with bride and typewriter and created a home and life, plus several books, out of almost literally nothing.

White had had a thousand-and-one problems to cope with, some of them pretty grim. I had only one, ironically pleasant, which was to keep myself in solitary confinement now that I had achieved it. The world beyond my cottage windows was so much more beguiling than my own company and sheets of blank white paper.

To begin with, there was Marina Cay itself, and its inhabitants. As run by Allan and Jean Batham, it was a far-out but totally civilized little community consisting of several scattered dwelling cottages, perched on bluffs above the sea, and a central hilltop "main house," mainly terrace, for dining, drinking and socializing. At the time I was there the premises were technically closed for off-season. But that by no means imposed Crusoesque alonesmanship, for the Bathams themselves were a numerous tribe.

On hand, besides Allan and Jean, were son Michael and wife and brother Richard with wife and daughter. There was a good-sized staff and a flow of visiting friends in all manner of boats. There were three dogs, one cat, one parrot, two turtles (huge), several hundred lizards (tiny), and squadrons of crabs, dove and pelicans. Topping it off, there was one sinister and strictly invisible inhabitant—suspected of being a coconut rat—who, in the absence of coconuts, dined exclusively on soap from the bathroom basins.

As headman of this formidable menage, Allan Batham was an outstanding specimen of the "new breed" of British Virgin Islander. Leaving his native England in 1958, with wife and son, he crossed the Atlantic in a 35-foot sailboat, theoretically en route to British Columbia. But one look at the BVI's and he was lost to them, becoming for nine years the proprietor and host of Marina Cay. Now, again bitten by wanderlust, he and Jean are off on a planned five-year world cruise. But the little Eden he created still flourishes under his brother's management..

And what an Eden it is!—the heart of a water-world of wonder and delight. I found I could not keep away from it. Thumbing my nose at typewriter and conscience, I donned mask and snorkel and floated over the coral castles and glinting fish-hordes of Marina's enclosing reef. In sailboat or Boston Whaler, I took off for the points of the compass. Marina is at the heart of a sweep of blue-green water called Privateers' Bay, and all around rose the carved and gleaming shapes of islands. On successive trips I went to Tortola, Virgin Gorda, Beef, Guana, the Camanoes, the Dogs—yes, even to Cockroach. And all were fascinating. And all were different.

Some are deserted; others in various stages of molding by the hand of man. On Beef Island today there are only the Batham's shipyard, the BVI's cow-pasture airstrip and, on an offshore cay, the small but attractive Trellis

Bay Hotel. But great plans are afoot: for a full-scale airport, a large real estate development, and a hotel-with-cottages complex. (If the crowded prospect fails to please, there will still be deserted Cockroach to escape to.)

When I put in at Guana Island, Louis and Beth Bigelow were away. Indeed, everyone was away; their establishment (basically a private club but with occasional nonmembers accepted) was not to re-open for another few weeks. But where man had withdrawn another species had moved in, and in Guana's beach-rimmed bay I encountered a sight that had to be seen to be believed. My first impression, on approaching the bay, was that the bottom had fallen out of it. Instead of the usual pale green of sand-paved shallows, its waters were dark cobalt blue, as above mid-ocean depths.

But the bottom was there all right. There were no depths, only shallows. What caused the darkness was a host of fry, minute baby fish by the million and billion, a mass so huge and dense that it seemed not an agglomeration of individual living creatures but a single vast organism wheeling and churning in the bay. Through the seemingly solid core of it thrashed a dozen or more big tarpon, having the meal of their lives. And competing from the air was a platoon of pelicans, almost hysterical with gluttony, diving with such wild abandon that it appeared sure that on each plunge they would break their necks. In all my travels, man's world had never seemed so remote to me. Here was the primeval sea as it had been through the eons, with myself an intruder from an age not yet born.

The scene changes. (That is one of the delights of the islands: the scene always changes.) The carnage of Guana Bay is gone, and in its place are a cool pavilion, the tinkle of glass and silver, and a headwaiter asking if you will have white wine or red. We have come to Little Dix Bay, five miles across the Sir Francis Drake Channel from Marina Cay, and if God's not in his heaven, man's at least back in his world.

As noted, Little Dix is the biggest and most elaborate of British Virgin resorts. A tremendous job was done in hacking its amenities out of the harsh terrain of Virgin Gorda. But its creators knew when to stop. It is no Fountainbleu or Hilton they have created on this remote island, but a happy compromise between simplicity and luxury, rusticity and sophistication. You won't experience as total a feeling of "far-outness" here as at other BVI retreats. But you also won't be so insulated from the world of nature that you can't even see it beyond the cabanas and casinos.

In the "new" category on Virgin Gorda, along with Little Dix are a small hotel called the Lord Nelson Inn, a marine research station run by the University of Pittsburgh, and a scattering of private homes built by pioneering types who don't like crowds and have the means to get away from them. Otherwise, things have changed little, and even regressed a bit, since the old days. Spanish Town, for instance, the island's only indigenous settlement, was once the site of active copper mining. But now the copper is gone, and all that is left is a sleepy village.

As you sail along Virgin Gorda's western coast, however, it is neither

British Virgin Islands

metallurgy nor demography that is apt to be on your mind, but only the wild beauty of the shoreline. Here, toward the island's southern tip, is a beach as perfect as any I have ever seen: an angled ramp of shining whiteness rising to a geometrically precise backdrop of green coconut palms. Then white and green alike are gone, and there is only grayness: the gray of rocks and boulders, huge and tumbled, rising like ruined castles from the sea.

Among them are caves and grottoes, called The Baths, in which one can swim through crystalline waters from light to shadow, from day to night. Beyond the castle walls, on the ocean floor, are sunken gardens, in ridges and valleys, swarming with the myriad life of the sea. Presently Virgin Gorda ends; there is only sea. But then the ruins rise again, still higher, wilder, in another island, Fallen Jerusalem. Sitting among its ancient stones, I can promise you, you will think long thoughts about earth and sea, and the little thing called man who likes to think himself their master.

Where now? We have not yet been to Anegada, outermost of the Virgins, lying low under the horizon to the northeast. But it is too late for that now. The sun is hanging low, like a blood orange, over the ridges of Tortola. So we head toward it—toward Marina Cay—across the Drake Channel and Privateers' Bay. When we are halfway there the sun is gone and the lights come up on the Cay, tiny but warm in the watery wilderness. Roundabout, the larger islands have lost their sharpness of outline. They are mere ghosts now, shapes of fantasy: fading, withdrawing, merging quickly into dusk.

Tomorrow we will go again to Road Town. We will sit in Hank Milstrey's Poop Deck and hear the talk of the New Breed. The talk will be lively, interesting, progressive. It will be about islands that should long ago have entered the 20th century, but are only now about to do so. It will be about money, tourists, hotels, homes, transportation, sanitation, education—and indeed everything that will serve to put the BVI's and their people more firmly "on the map."

So be it: the crown gems are being polished, and rightly so. But all that is for tomorrow. Tonight, on Privateers' Bay, there is no Road Town. No tourism. No politics or economics. There is only the sea, the stars, and the dark—islands ranged between them. The map that guides us is of Keats' ... "perilous seas in faery lands forlorn."

—*J. R. Ullman*

Instant facts

Location: A few miles east and north of the American Virgin Islands and 60 miles east of Puerto Rico. Some 1,450 miles from New York. Virgin Gorda and Tortola are 12 miles apart.

Population: About 8,000.

Capital: Road Town, Tortola.

Nationality: British.

Language: English.

Currency: U.S.

Documentation: International Certificate of Vaccination required. Passport required by all except U.S., Canadian and U.K. citizens with alternate proof of identity.

Climate & Clothes: Pleasantly breezy, thanks to the ever-present trade winds.

Subtropical temperature, varying no more than 6° from one "season" to another. Very casual clothing, ranging up to "cocktail" dress for larger resorts.

Food: Restaurants serve local seafood such as conch, whelks and lobsters, as well as continental dishes.

Geography: There are 41 islands—totaling 59 sq. miles—plus uncounted islets, cays and rocks. Of the dozen or so inhabited islands, all but Anegada (a hunk of coral) are of volcanic origin—an upthrust of rocky mountain ridges from a suboceanic plateau. The hilly areas of the islands have been cleared for use as pasture. Scrub growth covers much of the rest of the land. Most developed of the islands are Virgin Gorda, a humble 8.3 sq. miles of land area, rising to 1,359 ft. at Virgin Gorda Peak in the center; and Tortola, 21 sq. miles, with its 1,780 ft. high Mount Sage and many white sandy beaches.

History: A bit vague. Some believe that Columbus discovered the British and neighboring U.S. Virgin Islands and, impressed by their number, named them after St. Ursula and her 11,000 virgins. Other historians suggest that Sir Francis Drake dubbed them in honor of Queen Elizabeth I. Some natives claim that the group derived its name from early sailors' impressions of the isle of Virgin Gorda ("fat virgin"), which roughly resembles a woman of matronly proportions lying on her back. The islands later became a haven for pirates and buccaneers and, it will be noticed, their individual names are of less saintly derivation than those of other Caribbean islands. Dutchman's Cap, Rum Island, Dead Man's Chest, Prickly Pear and Fallen Jerusalem are typical.

The Spanish settled on Virgin Gorda in the 16th century to mine ore but the English later took over and both Virgin Gorda and Tortola were developed as agricultural estates. Principal crop was cotton, plus some sugar and indigo, and the economy was largely dependent on slave labor. Following the abolition of slavery, landowners abandoned their estates and laborers and their descendants took them over. Today agriculture is still the predominant activity though the major product is beef cattle.

Who flies here

Airlines based in San Juan, St. Thomas and St. Croix link the British Virgin Islands with major U.S. cities. The Little Dix airstrip receives daily flights from Puerto Rico and the U.S. Virgin Islands via Dorado Wings, V.I. Airways and St. Thomas Air Taxis. Antilles Air Boats also fly to the island. From San Juan, rates are $20–$25 one way depending on the season, $100 for a maximum of four people to charter a plane. The fare from St. Thomas, one-way, is $10 and from St. Croix $13.

There are scheduled flights to the Beef Island airstrip. LIAT has flights to Beef Island from both Antigua and St. Kitts. One-way fare is $29.

Island transportation

A few years ago Tortola didn't have any roads—not to mention cars—but it is now possible to **rent a jeep** from Tortola Car Rentals. The agency is located in Road Town (Tel: 2324 or stop at the Marine Store by Fort Burt Hotel). For those who arrive by ferry, air boat or yacht, see Paul Gouin at West End Yacht Services. Arrangements can also be made through hotels.

Tour operators on the island are Tortola Yacht Services (Tel: 2124/5), Tortola Travel Service (Tel: 2215) and Tour Tortola. If you're lucky, you may even chance upon an air-conditioned **taxi!**

Water sports

Wonderful **beaches** are a dime a dozen around these islands. **The Baths** on Virgin Gorda offer some offbeat swimming fun. This natural wonder is composed of gigantic boulders heaped upon each other, forming caverns and pools of water. The pools, quite logically, are called Male Bath and Female Bath and each has its own natural skylight.

There is no end to the boating, sailing and beach exploring offered by these small islands. In addition to facilities offered by some hotels, Paul West at Tortola Yacht Services, Road Harbour (Tel: 2124/5, offers just about every water sport and instruction (free with charter boats) in all but surfing. Boats and guides for **scuba diving** and **snorkeling** are available and, though they do not have their own rental equipment, they can obtain it on a day's notice. Masks, flippers and snorkel tubes are for rent or sale. Some of the best diving is around the island of Anegada, a treacherous bit of coral whose far-offshore reef has grounded many an unsuspicious vessel. Tortola Yacht Services has "exploited" these old shipwrecks and offers guided tours for divers in these virtually unexplored waters.

For **water skiing,** there are several ski boats and regular and slalom skis. **Surfing** is only fair in the Caribbean but during the winter months some beaches along the north coast of Tortola—especially Josiah Bay—can be surfed. No equipment available so bring your own.

Tortola Yacht Services also has two boats fully equipped for inshore and off-shore **fishing** which charter for $100 and $140 a day. All equipment, crew, bait and ice are furnished. They also have **boats** for exploring, beachcombing and island hopping: power boats from $12–$25 an hour, $35–$80 half day and $60–$140 full day. Sailboats for charter include a 23-foot locally built sloop with an auxiliary outboard, $30 half day and $50 full day. A 28-foot Parkwood sloop, Dutch design and diesel engine, charters for $65 half day and $80 full day, crew included. Cruises include stops at famous Deadman's Bay on Peter Island and the Treasure Coves at Norman Island.

Bareboat (no crew) rentals are available in Road Town on two brand-new sloops—the *Simoun* and *Corvette.* Weekly rates are $340 and $250 respectively.

Special events, festivals

Easter Monday: Picnics, dances, boat racing, horse races. April 15.

Whit Monday: Similar celebrations to those at Easter. June 3.

Festival Time: Traditional celebration to commemorate the abolition of slavery in 1838. Steel-band music, street dancing, parades, torchlight procession, fireworks, picnics, horse races, aquatic sports. First week in August.

Christmas Festivities: Street masquerades, torchlight procession, steel band tramp, carol singing, horse racing. December 24–26.

Meet the people

Organization	Official
Cricket Assn.	A. O. Shirley
Soft Ball Assn.	Gaston Penn
Young People's Assn.	Mrs. Riisa Rhymer
St. George's Fellowship	Rev. F. L. Norman
Red Cross	Ralph O'Neal
Girl Guides	Mrs. J. Poole
Boys Brigade	Rev. D. G. Mason
Life Girls Brigade	Rev. D. G. Mason
Methodist Women's League	Rev. D. G. Mason
Methodist Men's Fellowship	Rev. D. G. Mason
B.V.I. Society	J. R. O'Neal
The Players	Henry Milstrey
Jr. Chamber of Commerce	C. Dawson
St. John's Ambulance Brigade	J. Bailey, Chief of Police
Sea Scouts	Julian Carty
Civil Service Assn.	M. Winter
Teachers Assn.	E. Rhymer

Real estate and retirement

The government encourages land investment. However, it tries to discourage "get-rich-quick" speculators by insisting that something—house, hotel or highrise—be built on the land "within a reasonable period" after purchase. For example, the owner of up to three acres of land must invest slightly more than $2,000 an acre within a three-year period.

Land is available both from private investors and from the government. Choices range from a small chunk of a large island to a large chunk of a small one. Real estate agents are:

Smith, Gore and Co.
Road Town, Tortola

Mr. Richard Batham
Marina Cay

Mr. Frederick Clark
West End, Tortola

Mr. H. L. Stoutt
Long Bay, Tortola

Mr. I. Dawson
Ballast Bay, Tortola

Mr. Robert Dick-Read
Hannah Estate, Tortola

Col. John M. Begg
Island Investment Corp.
1714 Connecticut Ave.
Washington 9, D.C.

Commerce and industry

The British Virgin Islands, among the last remaining British dependencies, are just beginning to realize a need for greater self-sufficiency. The need, of course, stems from that age-old dilemma: lack of funds. This means shedding the not unfriendly but rather sleepy attitude towards tourism (though the ground was broken a few years back when Laurance Rockefeller built Little Dix Bay Resort on Virgin Gorda). Main regret among islanders is the loss of peace and quiet that ensues when visitors come looking for just those items.

In the past few years a number of steps forward have been made. More roads have been built, communication facilities (i.e., telephone) expanded and, most important for tourism, great improvement has been made in air transport to the islands. However, to attract more tourists many more improvements are called for in the future. Among these are better hotel and restaurant service in the capital, Road Town; more courteous and less costly taxi service; much better shops; and better sea transport to the neighboring U.S. Virgin Islands. Pending are plans to expand the airstrip at Beef Island and build a major one on the somewhat neglected island of Anegada. An agreement has already been reached for the development of most of Anegada.

The British Virgin Islands still have a primarily agricultural economy, based on livestock which is sold to Martinique and St. Thomas. They also export fish, fruit, vegetable and charcoal. The government has ordinances granting tax exemption and other incentives to industries, hotels and guest houses but there is still not enough employment for the male population. As a result, the islands' chief export is manpower.

WHERE TO STAY — In the British Virgin Islands

	Plan	Dec. 15-April 14 U. S. Currency		April 15-Dec. 14	
		Double	Single	Double	Single
BLOCH'S GUEST CENTRE (6 Rms.) **Road Town, Tortola**	(EP)	$ 7	$ 5	$ 7	$ 5
DRAKE'S ANCHORAGE **Mosquito Island** (8 Ctgs.) **(b)**	(AP)	$35	$25	$25	$20

HARBOUR VIEW (EP)	$16	$ 8	$16	$ 8
Cane Garden Bay, Torto a (12 Rms.) **(b)**				
LAGOON PLAZA (EP)	$14	$ 9	$14	$ 9
Road Town, Tortola (6 Rms.)				
LITTLE DIX BAY (AP)	$75–80	$65–70	$45–50	$35–40
	(Dec. 20-April 20)		(April 20-Nov. 1)	
Virgin Gorda (50 Rms.) **(b, t)**			$55–60	$45–50
			(Nov. 1-Dec. 20)	
LITTLE THATCH (AP)	$40	$20	$40	$20
RESORT Thatch Island (Ctgs.) **(b)**				
LORD NELSON INN (AP)	$35	$25	$26	$16
Virgin Gorda (10 Rms) (EP)	$20	$15	$10	$ 8
LONG BAY ESTATE (EP)	$20	$15	$17	$12
HOTEL				
Long Bay, Tortola **(Ctg)** (EP)	$30	$25	$26	$22
(8 Rms, 8 Ctgs) **(b)**				
MARINA CAY (AP)	$38–42	$25	$25	$18
Tortola Marina Cay (10 Rms.) **(b)**				
OCEAN VIEW	On Request			
Virgin Gorda (12 Rms.)				
SEA VIEW (EP)	$12	$ 6	$12	$ 6
Road Town, (AP)	$20	$10	$20	$10
Tortola (12 Rms.)				
SEBASTIAN'S ON (MAP)	$40	$30	$25	$15
TORTOLA Little Apple Bay, Tortola (6 Rms.) **(b)**				
SMUGGLERS COVE (AP)	$25	$19	$25	$19
Belmont Bay, Tortola (4 Rms.) **(b)**				
SOCIAL INN (EP)	$14	$ 7	$14	$ 7
Road Town, Tortola (4 Rms.)				
TREASURE ISLE HOTEL (AP)	$32–38	$18–22	$28–32	$16–20
Road Town, Tortola (16 Rms.) **(b)**				
TRELLIS BAY (AP)	$38	$25	$30	$20
Bellamy Cay (8 Rms.)				
WAYSIDE INN (EP)	$12	$ 6	$12	$ 6
Road Town, Tortola (14 Rms.)				

LEGEND FOR HOTEL LISTINGS: (AP) American Plan (room and 3 meals); **MAP)** Modified American Plan (room, breakfast and dinner); **(CP)** Continental Plan (room and breakfast); **(EP)** European Plan (room only). All rates quoted on a per-day basis and subject to change. Confirmed reservations at specific rates desired are always recommended.

HOTEL FACILITIES: (b) beach; **(p)** pool; **(t)** tennis; **(g)** golf.

CAYMAN ISLANDS

Three oases of peace and tranquillity are the Cayman Islands, lying
on the western edge of the Caribbean. Here is a small world that centers
around the sea, uncrowded stretches of powdery sand, superb fishing,
a snorkeler's paradise.

The good people of the Cayman Islands

Contrary to what some guidebooks will tell you, the Cayman Islands are not
"the islands that time forgot."

They are, rather, islands that have forgotten to get serious about the
fads and frustrations that time brings to the more progressive or dynamic or
so-called sophisticated areas of the world.

Time, as a result, has preserved the tiny Cayman Islands from the
onslaught of much man-made nonsense. One blessing, at least to over-
assaulted ears, is that the radio stations do not pour forth undisciplined
streams of rock 'n roll.

Caymanians have a deep love of their three islands and among the almost
10,000 inhabitants "everyone knows almost everyone else," according to one
senior citizen.

The Cayman Islands' most significant export for the past several centuries has been able-bodied seamen. One historian (writing in the Chronicle
of the West India Committee) has noted: "The land in Grand Cayman is
not as easy to cultivate as it is in Jamaica. There were never any large plantations there, and agriculture never became the mainstay of the population.
Instead, the inhabitants turned to the sea for their livelihood and became a
race of sailors and boat builders, possessing a skill and a hardiness unequalled
in the Caribbean. . ."

One American immigrant to these lovely shores (who has long since
become a Caymanian by adoption) points out:

"They're good sailors—the best—because they have grown up in the
family tradition of seamen. Their discipline is excellent. They have not been
spoiled by the rich-living ways of the world, and they do not ask more than
the going wage. They are a deeply religious people, so they are dependable
workers and they send their wages home to their families or wives. Add the
fact that they are fundamentally as honest as all get-out, and you can't find
a better shipmate anywhere."

The classic kidding the women take (even in local song lyrics) begins
with the question: "And what do the women do while the men are away?"

Replies another local observer: "Most pray—a few, though, play. . ."

"Our women are good women—in most ways the same as good women

Pedro's Castle, built by slaves in 1631, on Grand Cayman

everywhere," offers a retired Caymanian seaman who (after eight years at sea) lives comfortably with his wife and four children. "You can actually see what the women do with the money the men send them. Pretty soon you see a new sink or bathtub being delivered to the house . . . a new roof . . . better clothes for the children . . . and nowadays sometimes even a washing machine or those electric mixing machines. When that seaman comes home, he's got something to show for his years away—thanks to his wife." (Often, the women even supervise construction of the entire house.)

The Cayman Islands are peaks of a submarine mountain range. Geologists offer ample proof that these islands have been completely submerged at least three times. Ash-colored rock formations, high above water level, also indicate that waters surged over and around them for a long period of time, leaving them pitted and sponge-like in their appearance.

The Caymans' history, for the most part, has gone unrecorded. Brief and fleeting mentions of these islands appear in a few scholarly histories. A few facts have been combed from the sea logs and journals of captains and colonists. But far too many links are missing to provide an unbroken chain of historical occurrence.

Cayman Brac and Little Cayman—the lesser Caymans—were sighted by Columbus in May, 1503, while his caravels were moving hastily from Panama to Hispaniola. Chronicles liberally edited and annotated by Diego Columbus indicate that heavy storms (May is still among the wet months) made any attempt to land too risky. But noting the great number of turtles, Columbus named the islands "Las Tortugas," and sailed on. Early Spanish settlers in the New World renamed them the "Caiman" islands. Since caiman is the Spanish word for alligator, it is believed that when buccaneers and seagoing drifters spotted large iguanas and lizards on the shores they mistook them for baby alligators. It is also possible that Cayman Brac, long and narrow in geographical shape, may have inspired the name Caiman.

A map of the New World drawn by Benjamin Wright in 1616 identifies the main island as "Caiman-grande." Later in the same century we find these islands labeled "Kiemanus," "Caimanes" and "Caymanos." Finally, in the 19th century, we find the "Caiman Isles."

"At some time prior to 1734," writes Jamaican historian S. A. G. Taylor, "many, if not all, the inhabitants on Cayman Brac moved to Grand Cayman, and the first patents for land were granted. On November 9, 1735, Isaac Bawden, mariner of Caymanos, came to Montego Bay to marry Sarah Lamer, widow. In 1741, several other patents were granted, one of which was given to Mary Bodden and another to William Foster. Many of their descendants are still to be found in the islands."

The islands became a dependency of Jamaica in 1863 and held that status until an act was passed in 1958 giving statutory power to a new government, for the formal separation from Jamaica and the establishment of the Cayman Islands as a separate British territory.

Today the islands are "completely self sufficient" in the words of Administrator J. A. Cumber. Its police force (when we last visited) was made up of some two dozen men. Cayman Brac has exactly one law enforcement officer, a Constable McGlaughlin, who is said to be a "fine Sunday painter, a competent guitarist, and a fellow who pays a call every now and then to see that everything is in order, and stays awhile for a cool drink."

Grand Cayman now boasts more than a dozen first-rate hotels and cottage-colonies, with most tourism activities on West Bay, also called Seven Mile Beach. The fine-grain beach sand is so white "it hurts your eyes when you first get there," local residents like to boast. And true it is.

The aroma from the tall pine trees along these beaches blends with the sea breezes and anyone can become an addicted beachcomber after a week's visit. A reef that surrounds Grand Cayman is like a ribbon that delineates the beautiful bottle-blue ocean from the brilliant emerald of the shallow waters.

Grand Cayman's single impediment to active year-round tourism is a swampy plain in the interior that breeds mosquitoes which are a nuisance during the summer months. In addition to efforts by individual hotel owners to control this condition, a major government project is in full swing to rid the island of mosquitoes by draining the swampy areas and creeks around Little Sound in central Grand Cayman.

For the additional revenue necessary to accomplish its aims, the government has also put into effect a 10 shillings ($1.40) travel tax, collected from anyone leaving the island, local resident or foreigner.

Still another government project in the works is a plan to increase the sales of its postage stamps—a lively source of revenue. A small post office has been constructed in a section called Hell so that tourists (who see the humor in it) can mail their postal cards from there. Those convinced that the Cayman Islands must have some instant publicity agree the new post office is "one hell of a good idea."   *—Al Dinhofer*

Instant facts

Location: Grand Cayman is located about 180 miles west-northwest of Jamaica. Cayman Brac is 89 miles northeast of Grand Cayman and 5 miles east of Little Cayman. The island group lies about 475 miles south of Miami.

Population: Nearing 10,000.

Capital: George Town.

Nationality: British territory.

Language: English.

Currency: The Jamaican pound sterling, valued at $2.80 U.S. American and Canadian money is accepted everywhere but it is simpler to use the local currency when dealing with small amounts.

Documentation: Passports not necessary for visits of less than six months. Vaccination certificate required.

Climate & Clothes: Average temperature is 79.6°, with summers about 10° higher than "winters." Steady breezes are provided by the trade winds. Highest recorded temperature was 90°, lowest 58°. Slacks and beach wear almost always appropriate. If you are going at the height of the summer, it is wise to pack mosquito repellent in your bags.

Food: Turtles were once abundant in the islands, but Caymanians must now catch them off Central America. They are still a vital part of Caymanian diets and are prepared as soups, stews and steaks. Other seafood favorites are such delicacies as conch stew and raw conch cocktail (conch is similar to oyster meat) and crayfish, prepared in salt water and garnished with seaweed. Native crops include plantains, similar in appearance to bananas but larger and usually fried; the cassava root and yams. Rice is often prepared with coconut milk and curry.

Geography: Grand Cayman, the largest of the three islands, is about 20 miles long and 6 miles wide. Cayman Brac measures 12 miles long, slightly over a mile wide; and Little Cayman is 10 miles long and 2 miles across at its widest point. The total land area is about 100 sq. miles.

History: Christopher Columbus discovered the Caymans during his fourth voyage in 1503 and dubbed them Las Tortugas, or the Turtle Islands, after the turtles that once were prevalent in these waters. Its present name is thought to originate from early sailors mislabeling the islands' iguana "caiman," a type of tropical alligator. The islands weren't settled until the 18th century, but passing ships stopped in Cayman waters for turtles to add to their food coffers and pirates found the area a convenient haven between voyages. In 1670, the Caymans were turned over to the British along with Jamaica and not until the middle of the 19th century were all three islands permanently settled.

Who flies here

There are regular flights from:

Miami: BWIA, LACSA (national flag carrier of Costa Rica). Round trip: $95–$124; 17-day excursion $59–$79.

San Juan: BWIA. Round trip: $162–$182.

Kingston, Jamaica: BWIA, Cayman Brac Airways. Round trip: $51–$81; 17-day excursion $33.

The above airlines also provide service to other neighboring Caribbean islands.

Transportation / in and between the islands

Cayman Brac Airways, with headquarters on Grand Cayman, operates flights between the sister islands. Round trip fare between Grand Cayman and Little Cayman or Cayman Brac is $31.50, between Cayman Brac and Little Cayman $11.20. Certain excursion fares are less expensive.

Cars can be rented for about $10 a day or $60 a week from the following (don't forget—driving is on the left side of the road):

Bob Soto's Sports Fishing Hdqrtrs.
N. Church St., George Town, Tel: 2483

Captain Ertis' Jeep Rentals
West Bay, Tel: 230

Cayman U-Drive Ltd.
Fort St., George Town, Tel: 2448

Jim Bodden
P.O. Box 499
Grand Cayman, Tel: 2580

Cayman Transport Service Co.
Tel: 2671, 2428

Cico Rent-A-Car System
P.O. Box 400
Grand Cayman, Tel: 2468

Mango Tree Car Rental
George Town, Tel: 2532

Taxis are available for those who prefer not to rent a car, and Jim Bodden offers a **water taxi service** from the hotels to town. English **bicycles** can be rented at Caymandicraft in George Town.

Sights to see

On Grand Cayman, drive out the south shore to the popular **Tortuga Club** on the east coast. Wild orchids and wild parrots guaranteed enroute. Also fantastic seascapes. The Tortuga Club serves an excellent seafood lunch. Bring camera.

If the closest you've ever been to a **turtle** is turtle soup, don't miss ˙the opportunity of seeing the green giants in the turtle crawls of North Sound. When Columbus first sighted the islands he called them "Las Tortugas" because of the preponderance of sea turtles. The islands at one time had one of the largest nesting colonies of green turtles in the Caribbean and for a hundred years Caymanians were the world's most famous green turtle fishermen. Today, a section of North Sound known as Governor's Creek has been sealed off for a project to raise the giants in captivity.

Built by slaves in 1631 on the south shore, **Pedro's Castle** has been restored and is now the home of Tom Hubbel, the island's leading skindiver, marine photographer and collector of artifacts. Ancient coins and salvage from the age-old wrecks off the island are displayed.

Interesting historical artifacts and wildlife displays can be seen at the **Kiemanus Museum** in George Town and at **the Nook** in West Bay. The Kiemanus Museum features mementoes of bygone days, as well as live iguanas.

Water sports

Beaches: None better in the Caribbean. On Grand Cayman, West Bay Beach, now known as Seven Mile Beach, stretches for

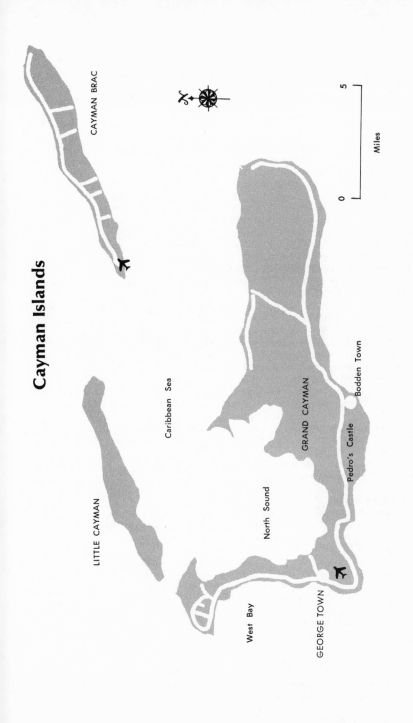

Cayman Islands

seven dazzling miles of white, white sand lined with tall Australian pines. Small coral reefs just offshore provide superb snorkeling ground for both the novice and the veteran. Beaches on the east and north coasts are equally good, and all are protected by an offshore barrier reef. Numerous beaches on both Little Cayman and Cayman Brac are so isolated you needn't worry about not going for a swim just because you forgot your suit.

Fishing: The waters off the Caymans are a practically untouched treasure trove of blue marlin, wahoo (best catches November–March), dolphin (plentiful in the spring) as well as amberjack, albacore, bonito and barracuda. Those who know their bonefish say the only place to go is Little Cayman or Cayman Brac. An official weighing station is located at the Sport Fishing Headquarters, where fishing equipment can also be rented.

In addition to angling, you can round up enough tropical fish to stock an aquarium. Royal grammas, jackknifes, jewelfish and the rare long nose butterfly are just a few of the species that abound in shallow water. Added attractions: airlines that serve the islands will assist you in getting your catch home.

Skin Diving: Some 325 wrecked vessels lie off the Caymans, some centuries old and others more recent, providing excellent sightseeing for underwater prowlers. Shallow-water coral gardens will intrigue underwater photographers, and spearfishermen will find groupers, snappers and other food fish in good supply. All equipment, from masks and fins to regulators and aqualungs are available for rent from the Sport Fishing Headquarters, owned and operated by Bob Soto, as well as from hotels throughout the islands.

Boating: The Sport Fishing Headquarters offers deep sea fishing expeditions, full day $85–$90, half day $50, for up to 10 people. They also charter boats for tours, water skiing and cruising and can be reached at P.O. Box 499, Grand Cayman (Tel: 2483). Charter fishing and sailing boats also are available from Jim Bodden, P.O. Box 499, Grand Cayman (Tel: 2580) and through Joe's Servicecenter, Box 55, N. Church St. (Tel: 2576). Several hotels maintain small boats and equipment for the use of guests at extra cost. Vallee Bodden, in Grand Cayman, offers the cruiser *Snoo* for fishing, water skiing or trips around the islands and also has a 16-foot outboard motor boat.

A boat trip across North Sound, including fishing and snorkeling on a barrier reef, can be arranged through your hotel. The trip includes a lunch of fresh-caught fish and lobster wrapped in foil and roasted over coals. While lunch is cooking, enjoy a cool drink at the Rum Point Club.

Glass-bottom boats are operated by both Bob Soto ($3 per person, minimum $6 a trip) and Jim Bodden.

Duck hunting is good here in the fall months.

Best shopping buys

The Caymans are a free port and many fine goods are sold at almost 50% of U.S. prices. Fine brand names can be found in fashions, jewelry, cameras and perfumes, and local seamstresses will be glad to whip up an exotic creation for you from Liberty of London and Irish linen fabrics. Duty-free liquor is also available though limited to one quart per person (over 21). Souvenirs from the islands are made from driftwood, sisal, shell, straw and, of course, tortoise shell.

Dine and dance

Blue Horizon: West Bay. Music and dancing.

Bothwell's: Lunch, dinner. Menu includes barbecued chicken, beef steaks, roast beef, turkey, ham and ice cream. George Town. Tel: 2479.

Buttonwood Club: George Town. Short-order American and native food.

Caribbean Club: West Bay Beach. European cuisine in formal surroundings. Cocktail bar. Jacket and tie required. Tel: 2593.

Cayman Arms: George Town. International cuisine, specializing in curries. Excellent paella, chicken chanticleer. Tel: 2626.

Club Inferno: West Bay (in the town of Hell). Music, dancing and occasional shows Tuesday, Thursday, Friday, Saturday.

Coral Caymanian Hotel: West Bay Beach. Attractive bar, native cookery.

Coronation Inn: George Town. Short-order American and native food. Tel: 2630.

Daisy Dairy: George Town. Milk bar. Tel: 2469.

Delmac's Super Club: West Bay. Music, dancing, Chinese and native food (try their turtle patties). Tel: 244.

Galleon Beach Hotel: West Bay Beach. Air-conditioned cocktail bar, restaurant.

George's: George Town and West Bay. Short-order American food. Tel: 2479.

Lighthouse Club: Breakers. Music, dancing, native food.

Mango Tree Drive-In: Crewe Rd., George Town. Tel. 2432.

Rum Point Club: Rum Point. Excellent seafood in informal surroundings.

Sunset House: S. Church St., George Town. Native or American dishes. Tel: 2511.

Tortuga Club: Colliers (East End). Excellent seafood lunch.

The islands have three outdoor movies and there are additional showings by the Hotel Assn. for hotel guests.

Meet the Caymanians

Organization	Official	Phone
Hotel Assn.	Mrs. C. MacTaggart	2551
Taxi-Cab Assn.	Ira Walton	2561
Chamber of Commerce	Paul Harris	2600
Agricultural Society	W. L. Bodden	2640
Horticultural Society	Mrs. A. L. Thompson	2417
Sailing Club	Maurice Muse	233
George Town Young Wives' Club	Mrs. Monica Bryan	
George Town Youth Club	Richard Ward	2511
West Bay Youth Club	Miss Marguerita Ebanks	216
Scottish Country Dance Club	Mrs. Effie Johnson	
Tennis & Sports Club	J. Conolly	2538
Boy Scouts	V. Anderson	2536
Girls Brigade	Mrs. O. H. Miller	2429
Red Cross	Mrs. E. Cook-Bodden	2505
Rotary	C. A. Hunter	2660
Civil Servants Assn.	L. Pierson	
Tourist Board	Eric Bergstrom	

Real estate and industry

A married couple coming to live in the Cayman Islands could probably manage on about $340 a month, including rent, food, light and some entertaining. There is no public water supply—rain water is obtained by individuals through wells and roof catchments, stored in cisterns and pumped when needed. All available land is privately owned and most costly, of course, on the beach where it is as high as $350 per running foot. Other coast land is much cheaper and lots inland cheaper still. Building costs vary between $12–$28 per sq. foot and there are a number of contractors on the islands. Real estate agents on Grand Cayman who can help newcomers with apartment rentals or the purchase of homes, homesites and business lots are:

Bodden-Creighton Development Co.
P.O. Box 499 (Tel: 2580)

R. S. Watler
P.O. Box 395 (Tel: 2601)

Alcopan Realty Co.
P.O. Box 355 (Tel: 2656)

Information on the new Palm Heights development is available from Cayman Supply Ltd., P.O. Box 261, Grand Cayman.

There is no taxation of any kind. Part

of the government's revenue is derived from import duties, a factor the newcomer will feel, for example, when doing his grocery shopping.

There is no unemployment on the Caymans due to the fact that a major export is manpower. Most male Caymanians are employed as merchant seamen and return home only to visit or take care of family affairs. A small cottage industry exists for the manufacture of thatch rope and there is a turtle processing plant. However, it is tourism that is rapidly becoming the Caymans' leading industry. Ample opportunity exists for setting up new hotels and nightclubs and the government is working on road improvement projects, the addition of a new jet landing strip, increasing its free-port facilities and ridding the islands of their major pest, mosquitoes.

WHERE TO STAY — In the Cayman Islands

		Dec. 15-April 14		April 15-Dec. 14	
		U. S. Currency			
	Plan	Double	Single	Double	Single
BAY VIEW	(AP)	$31–37	$18–21	$25–31	$15–18
Georgetown	(MAP)	$27–31	$16–19	$21–27	$13–16
(16 Rms.) (p)	(CP)	$20–26	$12–15	$14–20	$ 9–12
BEACH CLUB COLONY	(MAP)	$35–40	$20–25	$24	$12.50
West Bay Beach (18 Rms.) (b)					
BUCCANEERS' INN	(AP)	$35–45	$25	$25–35	$15
Cayman Brac (15 Rms.) (p)		(Jan. 15-Apr. 30)		(May 1-Jan. 14)	
CARIBBEAN CLUB		On Request		On Request	
West Bay Beach (18 Villas) (b)		(Dec. 1-Apr. 30)		(May 1-Nov. 30)	
CAYMAN KAI	(EP)	$25		$20	
North Shore (10 Cottages) (b)		(Dec. 1-Apr. 30)		(May 1-Nov. 30)	
CORAL CAYMANIAN	(EP)	$18	$15	$ 9	$ 6
West Bay Beach (17 Rms.) (b)					
GALLEON BEACH	(AP)	$40	$27	$30–32	$16–18
West Bay Beach	(MAP)	$36	$25	$24–26	$14–16
(37 Rms.) (b)	(EP)	$22	$18	$12–14	$ 7–9
GLEN & SANDY COTTAGES	(EP)	$25	—	$15	—
West Bay Beach (3 Cottages) (b)		(Dec. 1-Apr. 30)		(May 1-Nov. 30)	
PAGEANT BEACH	(AP)	$30–35	$16	$18–25	$14–15
Georgetown (19 Rms.) (b, p)		(Dec. 1-Apr. 30)		(May 1-Nov. 30)	
SEABONAIR COTTAGES	(EP)	$25	—	$18	—
West Bay Beach (4 Units) (b)		(Dec. 1-Apr. 30)		(May 1-Nov. 30)	
RUM POINT CLUB	(AP)	$40	$30	$30	$20
Rum Point (10 Rms.) (b)		(Dec. 1-Apr. 30)		(May 1-Nov. 30)	
SEA VIEW	(AP)	$25	$15	$15	$ 8
Georgetown (30 Rms.) (p)					
SELKIRKS COTTAGES	(EP)	$24	—	$12	—
Boddens Bay (2)		(Dec. 1-Apr. 30)		(May 1-Nov. 30)	
SUNSET HOUSE	(MAP)	$24	$15	$18	$10
Georgetown (7 Rms.)		(Dec. 1-Apr. 30)		(May 1-Nov. 30)	
TORTUGA CLUB	(AP)	$40	$30	$24–26	$15
Colliers Point (14 Rms.) (b)		(Dec. 1-Apr. 30)		(May 1-Nov. 30)	

WEST INDIAN CLUB	(EP)	On Request	On Request
West Bay Beach (9 Apts.) (b)		(Dec. 1-Apr. 30)	(May 1-Nov. 30)
WHITESANDS	(EP)	$25–30 $25–30	$15 $15
COTTAGES			
West Bay Beach (3) (b)		(Dec. 1-Apr. 30)	(May 1-Nov. 30)

LEGEND FOR HOTEL LISTINGS: (AP) American Plan (room and 3 meals); **MAP)** Modified American Plan (room, breakfast and dinner); **(CP)** Continental Plan (room and breakfast); **(EP)** European Plan (room only). All rates quoted on a per-day basis and subject to change. Confirmed reservations at specific rates desired are always recommended.
HOTEL FACILITIES: (b) beach; **(p)** pool; **(t)** tennis; **(g)** golf.

An ancient Caribbean inhabitant is this majestic specimen

CURACAO

Amerigo Vespucci, the navigator of the expedition that discovered
Curacao, went ashore on the supposedly uninhabited island in search
of drinking water and almost immediately discovered large footprints
in the sand. He and his men followed the track until they met five
women of such impressive tallness that Vespucci named the island the
"Island of the Giants." The women were Caiquetios Indians, members
of a robust tribe that also lived in Aruba, in Bonaire and in nearby
Venezuela. The Caiquetios disappeared from Curacao centuries ago,
to be followed by the Spanish, the Dutch and the English.

New world wonder, old world charm

No fewer than 50 nationalities are represented in Curacao's population—
16% of the population was born outside the Netherlands Antilles. While
Curacao (pronounce it cure-a-sow) is predominantly Catholic, the marvel-
ously preserved Mikve Israel-Emanuel Temple, in Willemstad, is the oldest
synagogue in the New World, a testimonial to the fine art of live and let live.

Curacao youngsters begin school studying Dutch then English, followed
by Spanish and French. Many complete their education with German and
Greek. Then, of course, there's Papiamento, the local language of casual conversation. Papiamento, according to an oft-quoted saying, is a colloquial
cocktail composed of three ounces of Spanish, one ounce of Dutch, a half
ounce each of French, African and English, and a good dash of Portuguese.
Like its native land, it is cosmopolitan.

The medley of different cultures vibrates through the music of this
Netherlands Antilles nation. There's the Curacao waltz, the polka and
mazurka, not to mention the catchy and popular tumba the band might
alternate with a frantic frug.

The farther out in the country you explore the farther out the sounds of
homemade music. There's the tambu (drums), benta (bow), cachoe (cow's
horn), heroe (rasping iron), and an instrument called the matrimonial
which is best described as a primitive tambourine. The concoction is rhyth-
mically fierce, almost barbaric. It is to standard dance music what pop art
is to painting—"fun" music is the only word for it.

But the really big news is that Curacao has evolved from a free port at
which cruise ships dock for a few hours, to a resort area with new and interesting accommodations, facilities and entertainment activities. Tourists
now stay longer and find more unusual ways to get away from the routines
of everyday life back home.

Schooner market at Willemstad on the island of Curacao

Although many visitors to Curacao look upon it as one big shopping bazaar (and with good reason) it has other fascinations to unfold for the visitor. It has, for instance, the world's only hotel insured against ship collision, and a famous pontoon bridge that swings open to admit incoming ships that sail right up the center of town.

There are good restaurants where the cuisine ranges from West Indian to East Indian to continental, fine hotels, a sophisticated gambling casino, all the water sports, and a capital city that is an architectural delight.

Willemstad is an old world city of gabled houses in the Dutch style, painted in colors that range from pastel tints to vibrant blues, reds and purples. This palette evolved, so the story goes, from the affliction of an early Governor of Curacao. The Governor suffered from severe headaches believed to have been caused by the strong sunlight glaring on the then white houses. A law was passed forbidding the use of white paint on any house in Curacao, and everyone painted his house in his favorite color.

The excellent condition of these colonial structures is unique in the Caribbean. In the 18th century, Curacao, a bustling Dutch trading port, escaped direct involvement in the battles between England and France in the Caribbean. The island did slip into British hands on two occasions, but Willemstad remained unscathed and her buildings stand as the purest example of a European city transplanted across the Atlantic.

The countryside offers a striking contrast to the bright hues of town. Dotted with nearly 100 hamlets and fishing villages, it is tawny brown and flat with an occasional hill where cacti or a divi-divi tree drink the meager rainfall. Here and there the ruins of a plantation landhuis recall the days when the island aristocracy kept large country homes.

Besides enjoying the beaches and visual pleasures in town and country, visitors are delighted with the number of festive occasions that pepper the calendar. There is a Chinese holiday, Jewish holidays, Spanish celebrations, and even a holiday for animals! The highly literate people of Curacao (98% literate) occasionally make a carnival out of "Book Week." Puppet shows, band music, raffles go on all during the sale of books, and few people bother to read until after the festivities.

Carnival or not there is always food vended on the streets of Willemstad, and the snacks range from hot and sweet dishes to plain fruits. For washing down tidbits and recuperating from the carnivals, shopping, and sports, there are a myriad of unusual Curacao liquor punches that cap any day.

Instant facts

Location: In the southern Caribbean just 38 miles north of Venezuela.

Population: 136,000.

Capital: Willemstad.

Nationality: Largest and most populous of the Netherlands Antilles, an autonomous part of the Kingdom of The Netherlands.

Language: Dutch. Papiamento, English, Spanish widely used.

Currency: The Guilder or Florin, about 53¢ U.S. American dollars are accepted everywhere.

Documentation: Transit,   including

cruise visitors, need proof of identity for a 24-hour (or less) stay. U.S. tourists do not need a passport but do need proof of U.S. citizenship. All temporary visitors must have a smallpox vaccination certificate not older than three years and a through or return ticket to a destination outside the Netherlands Antilles.

Climate & Clothes: Sunny days practically guaranteed since the island is almost rain-free, cooled by northeast trade winds. Annual average temperature is 81°. Curacao is outside the hurricane range. Light, casual clothes, sportswear, cocktail dresses, a sweater or stole for evenings. It is customary for men to wear ties at business appointments and after 6 P.M.

Food: Cosmopolitan. Gourmet dishes: **Java honde portie** (Java dog's portion), filet mignon topped with two fried eggs, surrounded by a mountain of rice, onions, tomatoes, peppers—all garnished with shrimp, curry seasonings, and coconut. **Keshi yena,** a whole Edam cheese stuffed and baked with fish, chicken or meats and raisins. Served with onions, tomatoes, olives, capers, plaintains. **Nasi goreng,** an Indonesian rice dish with meat, seafood, vegetables topped with egg and served with shrimp flakes **(kroepoeck).**

Snacking is a national pastime, and street vendors sell an almost infinite variety of exotic sweet and spicy tidbits. Famous sweets: **tentalaria,** peanuts, sugar and vanilla cooked in a big pan, cooled on a cold stone. **Fruta di pan,** cooked breadfruit eaten with raw coconut. **Chupa bebbe,** a homemade lollypop shaped like a goat or man. Cookies are also delicious, made from rice, egg and sweet breads. Spicy tidbits, usually made with beans, are also served as quick meals. Unusual spiced goodies: Dutch **rapucyners,** small beans with bacon, onions, beef, pickles. **Cala,** fried mashed beans with plenty of hot pepper. **Ayaca,** South American dumplings made from meat, prunes, with floury crust.

Staple foods served in all homes include **funchi,** a corn meal mush, and meat pies made from funchi or flour with chicken, fish, meat and various spices. Soups are full of exotic ingredients and may take hours to prepare. Favorites:

iguana soup (thought to preserve youth), **soppito** (coconut soup), tripe soup and okra gumbo. Chinese, Italian and Dutch restaurants insure hearty eating of nearly every kind of food. There is even **Chinese rijsttafel,** a variation of the famous 20-dish Indonesian rice feast.

Geography: A narrow, 37-mile-long island, 7 miles across at its widest point and only 2½ miles at its narrowest. Tiny bays and sandy inlets indent the coastline.

History: Alonso de Ojeda, a lieutenant of Columbus, discovered Curacao in 1499. Spaniards settled in the 1500's, but the Dutch captured the island in 1634. Peter Stuyvesant, later governor of New York, became governor in 1643. In 1800 Curacao came under a British Protectorate. It returned to the Dutch in 1802, was captured by the British in 1807, and finally regained by the Dutch by the Treaty of Paris in 1815 and the Treaty of London in 1816.

Who flies here

Curacao's big airport, Huehthaven Dr. Albert Plesman, is served by direct flights from the following cities:

New York: KLM, Pan Am, Viasa. Round trip: $266–$403; 17-day excursion $150–$265.

Miami: KLM, Pan Am. Round trip: $205–$322; 17-day excursion $135–$195.

Paris: KLM, Viasa. Round trip: $744–$1093.

San Juan: Pan Am. Round trip: $120–$179; 17-day excursion $35.

ALM (Dutch Antillean Airways) has flights to Curacao's two closest neighbors, Aruba ($26 round trip) and Bonaire ($18 round trip), as well as to other Caribbean islands. A three-day round-trip excursion to Aruba is $16.

Island transportation

Car and scooter rentals are available in Willemstad. Car rates range from $9–$12, not including gas. Scooters rent for $6. Taxis will sightsee in Willemstad for approximately $3.50 per hour. Minibuses with trained guides are popular for exploring the city and the island and for night tours. Approximate cost per person is $3 for a 1½ hr. city tour, $7 for a 2½ hr. city tour and $15 for a 4½ hr. island tour.

Information about rentals, taxis and tours is available directly from:

Curacao Sightseeing. Tel: 47054.

Ric Car Rental. Tel: 13686.

Dutch National Rent-A-Car and Scooter. Tel: 47054.

Hertz Rent-A-Car. Tel: 13686.

Taber Tours, S. E. L. Maduro & Sons, Inc. Tel: 11358 or 12500.

Universal Trading Inc. Tel: 23375.

If you feel like wandering about on your own, traffic keeps to the right-hand side of the road, as in the U.S.

Touring Curacao

Willemstad, the capital, has been called a great walking city. A good starting point is the **Queen Emma pontoon bridge** which joins the two major sections of town, the **Punda** and the **Otrabanda** ("other side").

The Queen Emma is a mixed delight to residents and a sheer delight to visitors. It floats on 16 pontoons over the deep channel of St. Anna Bay which leads from the Caribbean Sea into the huge inner harbor called the Schottegat. Since Curacao is the world's fourth port in tonnage of ships using it, the Queen Emma is quite often swinging either open or closed, and if you are going from Punda to Otrabanda, or vice versa, there may be delays.

The bridge is the only way cars can cross from one section of town to another, and consequently there are frequent lines of cars and pedestrians waiting for a ship to nose in or out. There is, however, a ferryboat which takes passengers across when the bridge is open.

Both bridge and ferryboat are free now, but at one time there was an assessment of two cents for pedestrians wearing shoes and one cent for those without shoes. It is said that some frugal visitors removed their shoes before crossing the bridge.

It is a three-minute walk in the **Punda Section** to **Fort Amsterdam,** which encloses the Governor's Palace, government offices and a Protestant church built in 1769. The modern Curacao Inter-Continental Hotel is built into the seaside Waterfort erected by the Dutch in 1751. Visitors may stroll or lounge on the 33-foot thick walls of the fortress, and the hotel's cannon walk is a favored spot for watching ships navigate the entrance of St. Anna Bay. (The Inter-Continental lays claim to a unique first—it is insured by Lloyd's against ship collision.) On the waterfront is the **floating schooner market** where a long line of small vessels sell produce and fish from neighboring Venezuela. It is most colorful in the morning. Nearby is **Mikve Israel Emanuel Synagogue,** one of the oldest in the western hemisphere.

In the neighborhood called **Scharloo** are the famous Dutch colonial houses painted in pastel colors and roofed with red tiles. Photographers appreciate the **Otrabanda section** for its waterfront views of the skyline. On a clear day the gabled buildings are mirrored in the bay, and color photos capture a bright scene. By car you can reach more distant spots of interest in town. One stop is the **Jewish Cemetery,** begun in 1650, one of the oldest burial grounds in the Americas. **Roosevelt House,** the American Consulate General, sits on Ararat Hill. The building was given to the U.S. by the people of Curacao in gratitude for American military protection during World War II. The **Water Distilling Plant** where most of the island's water is processed from the sea is an interesting point, as is Chobolobo, site of the **Senior Liqueur Factory** where the original Curacao Liqueur is distilled from oranges indigenous only to Curacao.

Fort Nassau, built in 1796 atop a 200-foot hill, affords a beautiful view of the harbor, the town and the island. Nearby is the harbor signal tower, and a restaurant with cocktail terrace is built into the ramparts of the fort.

Exploring the countryside by car makes a pleasant day's jaunt. The highway leading northeast out of Willemstad passes **Brievengat,** one of the old **landhuiszens** (plantation houses) of the 18th century with open arcaded galleries and antique Dutch furniture. It is privately occupied,

Curacao

West Point · Boca Tabla · St. Martha · Atlantic Ocean · Hato Caverns · WILLEMSTAD · St. Anna Bay

0   15
Miles

so make an appointment before stopping.

Two other interesting land houses well repay a visit. Perhaps the most unusual is **Landhuis Jan Kock,** a 200-year old home without radio, TV or electricity. Enjoy a glass of wine, bread and cheese in the old wine cellar where the furnishings are made from the trunks and branches of mahogany trees grown on the old plantation. If you arrive after sunset, you will find the house agleam with torches and old lanterns. The other plantation, **Knip Estate,** is a perfect place for light refreshments and a sea breeze after passing through **West Point,** a colorful fishing village on the beach. Wild sights include **Boca Tabla,** a coral-walled grotto on the north coast where the sea rushes in a burst of spray, and the **Grotto of Hato** with its unusual coral and limestone caves.

Although most tourist brochures don't mention it, one of the world's largest oil refineries is located in Curacao. The Shell Oil Refinery, just west of Willemstad, is not on the usual list of things-to-see-while-vacationing. But at night with lights ablaze and towers silhouetted against the Caribbean sky, it is a dramatic sight.

The sporting life

A wealth of coves and inlets and clear, clear waters concentrate much of the sightseeing in and around the sea.

Cruising: Boats are almost always available and standard rates for one to four passengers are $50 per half day, $80 per full day, not including meals. A delightful day's trip is to Little Curacao, a small island 10 miles east of Willemstad, with a lovely beach and lighthouse. Another trip is to Bonaire. Both islands can be visited on an overnight trip for approximately $125, including meals. A bargain yachting cruise runs down the coast from Piscadera to Spanish Water, stops for swimming at Spanish Water, then returns to Piscadera by sunset. Rates are $7.50 per person, with refreshments.

Deep Sea Fishing: Due to the sharp drop-off a few hundred yards off shore, conditions are excellent for catching marlin, sea bass, kingfish, sailfish and bonito. Charters begin at $75–$85 per day, $45–$60 per half day including tackle, six passengers.

Sailing: 14-foot "Flying Tern" class boats are available at $3 per hour for one to two persons, and 20-foot boats with guides for approximately $40 per half day.

Skindiving, Scuba Diving and Underwater Photography: Because waters are clear even far offshore, diving and photographing sea life are often combined with sightseeing and game fishing. Fins, mask and snorkel are $1 per day. Aqualungs are about $8 per day, not including equipment. Camera equipment costs about $8 per day.

Swimming: Although there are numerous unspoiled beaches easily "discovered" on any car trip, the best are on the northwest tip at Knip Bay and West Point, the latter a public beach. Other good beaches are Santa Cruz, Jan Thiel, Plantage Blauw and Santa Barbara.

Water skiing: Rates are approximately $2.50 per quarter hour with a minimum charge of $5.

Detailed information and arrangements for all water activities, including instruction, can be made through the tourist bureau, Taber Tours or hotels. Land sports include spectator games and **tennis,** and also **horseback riding.** The Shell Oil Company has a **golf** green open to visitors. **Baseball, soccer** and occasional **tennis** matches featuring international pros are also scheduled.

Best shopping buys

Willemstad's selection of goods is among the best in the Caribbean. Top buys: precious and semiprecious stones —especially diamonds, fabrics, china and silver, perfume, cameras, watches, radios, tape recorders and liquor. There is a compact shopping plaza in the Punda Section and one can easily hop from store to store. Shopkeepers are well informed on current duties and will suggest best bargains. The first $100 worth of goods are duty free for U.S. travelers.

Dining, dancing and after-hours spots

Aerovista Cafe Restaurant: Dr. Plesman Airport. Glass-walled dining room and cocktail lounge. Specialties: Russian eggs, sole Picasso, red snapper. Open 8 A.M.–11 P.M. Tel: 47122.

Airport Hotel Bianca: Near Dr. Plesman Airport. Dutch atmosphere and food, with **Koppensneller** (headhunters) outdoor bar. Dancing nightly. Tel: 47084 or 47120.

Americano Hotel: Center of Willemstad, facing harbor. View of pontoon bridge and city from cocktail lounge and terrace. New menu each day, international cuisine.

Avila Beach Hotel: Penstraat, ³/₄ mile east of Willemstad's shopping center. Outdoor dining room, schooner bar set in garden overlooking Caribbean. Local specialties, seafood, steak and chicken. Dancing nightly. Occasional entertainment and folk dancing. Tel: 11180 or 11182.

Coral Cliff Hotel: St. Martha's Bay, atop high cliffs overlooking sea. Dining room features European cuisine and starlight barbecues on terrace.

Country Inn: Groot Davelaar, near Willemstad. Homey atmosphere, poolside bar, cafeteria-style restaurant. Specialty is self-service barbecue. Tie and jacket for dinner.

Curacao Hilton Hotel: Piscadera Bay, 1¹/₂ miles from Willemstad. New luxury hotel. Cocktail bar, restaurants, casino, ballroom, convention facilities. International Hilton cuisine and local dishes.

Curacao Inter-Continental Hotel: Plaza Piar in center of Willemstad. Built into 18th-century fort, with views of harbor and Caribbean. Coffee shop adjacent to swimming pool; cocktails in the **Kini-Kini Lounge,** home of original recipe drinks; formal dining in the new **Rotisserie,** with dinner music; **discotheque** among arches of fort; gambling **casino** with blackjack, roulette, dice and slot machines. All food international with excellent keshi yena, nasi goreng. Jacket and tie after 6 P.M.

Formosa: Dr. da Gomes Plein, Willemstad. One of most popular Chinese kitchens for roast Chinese chicken, sweet and sour rice, rice à la Formosa. Tel: 12121.

Fort Nassau Restaurant: Just outside Willemstad in 18th-century fortress. Overlooks harbor, Shell Refinery and town. Several dining rooms in former barracks, cocktail lounge also upstairs on battery terrace near old cannons. International cuisine, good wine list. Open for lunch, cocktails, dinner Tuesday–Sunday. Open Monday if cruise ships dock. Strolling guitars week nights, dancing combo weekends. Tel: 13450.

Flamboyant Beach Hotel: Marie Pompoen Cove, 10 minutes from Willemstad. Relaxed atmosphere with ocean view. Coffee shop, restaurant, bar.

Lam Yuen: Suburban Willemstad, near Amstel brewery. Bar, restaurant specializing in Chinese dishes.

Lido Restaurant: Dr. da Gomes Plein. Willemstad. Favorite local spot for lunches, drinks and inexpensive dinners. Varied menu: wor hip har, subgum wonton, Indonesian rijsttafel, nasi goreng, Spanish chicken. 10 A.M.–midnight. Tel: 11800.

Peach Garden: Schottegatweg Oost 177. Informal cocktails and dining. Specialties: podjarka of chicken, sweet and sour dishes, Chinese rijsttafel (for four to eight persons). Open till midnight. Tel: 36108.

San Marco Hotel: Columbusstraat, Willemstad. Favorite place for breathing between shopping sprees. Snack shop features pizza, creole snacks, Italian ice cream and espresso. Dining room specialties: spaghetti, canelloni, ravioli, lobster. Tel: 12880.

There are numerous small hotels in the Willemstad area with restaurants attached.

Holidays

New Year's Day: Dancing and fireworks.

Sehoe (Harvest Festival): Songs and dancing in the countryside during the harvest. March.

Queen's Birthday: Public holiday and water festival, marked by young people serenading the Governor in Fort Amsterdam. Games and parties all over the island. Military parades, fireworks and fancy balls in Willemstad. April 30.

Labor Day: Official holiday. Parade by workers and other festivities in Union Hall. May 1.

Opening of the Staten (Legislative Council of the Netherlands Antilles): Governor goes to Staten to deliver his annual address. Soldiers stand along the route from the Governor's Mansion to the Staten and cannons are fired. Gala reception in evening. May.

Yule Season: St. Nicholas and his helpers, Black Peter and Sjaak Sjoerd, go to schools and clubs, giving out toys and—in theory, anyway—putting naughty children and adults in a large bag. Gifts are exchanged December 6.

Kingdom Day and **Antillean Flag Day:** Official holiday commemorating the granting of autonomy to the Netherlands Antilles and the hoisting of the first Antillean flag in 1959. December 15.

Dos Dia di Pascu: Official holiday. December 26.

Galleries, gardens and the arts

The many national groups living in Curacao have a strong pride in their development of a unified island culture. The **Curacao Museum** preserves some relics of the original Indian civilizations on the island and Venezuela and also boasts a collection of locally made cabinets. Of particular interest to the visiting *huisvrouw* is the old-fashioned Curacao kitchen. Special exhibits are regularly scheduled.

For art lovers, the **Gallery RG** opened recently in Willemstad and features a highly sophisticated exhibition of graphics and ceramics, most by Dutch artists. The **Arch Gallery** also offers periodic exhibits of paintings from Holland and the Netherlands Antilles.

The **Openbare Bibliotheek** (public library) has books in Dutch, Spanish, English and other languages, and the **Wetenschappelijke Bibliotheek** (Scientific and Learned Library) has specialized literature. Both are free to visitors. For those who appreciate outdoor browsing, Casa Cora includes the **Botanical Gardens, a zoo** and an unusual **Youth Traffic Park.** Here children learn to drive cars and obey signs, and their alternate successes and traffic jams are wonderful to behold.

Lucky visitors may have an opportunity to see the **Grupo Folklórico Antillano** perform by the docks and in the hotels. The group is reviving traditional folk dances and songs of the Netherlands Antilles. Organized two years ago, the musicians specialize in the **tambu,** the traditional dance of the island, and the **Curacao Waltz,** a Caribbean interpretation of the dance popular with former Dutch plantation owners. A famous treat comes when the group makes up lyrics commenting on family troubles, love affairs, jealousies, and other personal subjects.

To house the growing activities in the arts, the Central Pro Arte is under construction near Willemstad. It will have a concert hall and facilities for ballet, symphony orchestras, opera, and plays.

Real estate and retirement

Living costs are roughly the same as in the U.S. except for water, which is expensive. There are no real estate agents and houses are scarce, however advertisements in the local newspapers may net a temporary home from people who are going to Europe on vacation. Monthly rent on a two–three bedroom home, unfurnished is approximately $75–$125, furnished $100–$150.

General information on the cost of land and construction of housing is available from the Curacao Information Center, Willemstad.

Commerce and industry

Modern industrialization in the Netherlands Antilles began with the establishment of oil refineries in Curacao and Aruba in 1915 and 1928.

In 1915 Shell Oil Company chose Curacao as the site for refining and distributing Venezuelan oil. Standard Oil soon fol-

lowed with similar operations in Aruba, and both refineries are now among the world's largest. The consequent boom in the Netherlands Antilles continues. In Curacao alone, oil exports are 40 times larger than those of any other industry, and 50% of the ships docking in Willemstad are tankers.

Other exports include the famous Curacao liqueur (a basic ingredient is a bitter orange indigenous only to the island), and phosphate. These, however, are by no means as important as refining.

After World War II the government sought to diversify the economy with a series of 10-year plans attractive to other industries, especially tourism. Three features encouraging foreign investment are the 10-year tax holiday, the free zone, and associate membership in the European Common Market. Advantages include access to prime shipping facilities (Willemstad is one of the largest bunkerports in the world), duty-free import and export rights in the Netherlands Antilles and Europe, a $2/3$ cut on profit taxes, and competition in the Common Market on an equal basis with other members. Loans are available and monopoly concessions favorable.

Up-to-the-minute information on business and investment opportunities in Curacao is contained in two booklets. "Guide for the Establishment of Enterprises in Curacao," a 63-page booklet produced by the Curacao Bureau of Economic Affairs, contains general data plus sections on the tax holiday, the free zone, labor, land prices and building costs, and facilities for shipping and air transportation companies.

The 45-page "Investment Factors," published by the Netherlands Antilles Department of Social and Economic Affairs, includes information on taxation and tax concessions, the economy and prospects for development, money and banking, the labor market and general information.

Additional information may be obtained from the Curacao Bureau of Economic Affairs, 160 Scharlooweg, Curacao, Netherlands Antilles.

WHERE TO STAY — In Curacao

| | Plan | Dec. 15-April 14 | | April 15-Dec. 14 | |
| | | U. S. Currency | | | |
		Double	Single	Double	Single
AVILA BEACH	(MAP)	$28–46	$17–34	$20–34	$ 7–13
Willemstad	(CP)	$20–38	$13–31	$16–30	$10–12
(45 Rms.) **(b)**	(EP)	$16–34	$11–29	$14–26	$ 5–11
AMERICANO	(AP)	$24–27	$12–14	$24–27	$12–14
Brionplein (37 Rms.)	(EP)	$10–13	$ 6–8	$10–13	$ 6–8
BIANCA HOTEL	(CP)	$14	$ 9.50	$14	$ 9.50
Nr. Plesman Airport (21 Rms.)					
CORAL CLIFF	(MAP)	$40	$25	$30	$18
Santa Martha Bay (35 Rms.) **(b, t)**					
COUNTRY INN	(EP)	$16	$11	$16	$11
(72 Rms.) **(p, t)**					
CURACAO HILTON	(EP)	$32–65	$26–65	$22–45	$18–45
(200 Rms.) **(b, p, t)**					
CURACAO INTER-CONTINENTAL	(EP)	$30–34	$23–27	$20–24	$15–9
Plaza Piar (125 Rms.) **(p)**					
FLAMBOYANT BEACH	(EP)	$23–27	$20–24	$16–20	$12–26
Marie Pompoen (72 Rms.) **(b, p)**					
PISCADERA BAY CLUB	(CP)	$18–24	$13–17	$16–22	$11–16
Piscadera Bay (45 Rms.) **(b)**					
SAN MARCO	(AP)	$21–23	$14–16	$21–23	$14–16
Willemstad (23 Rms.)	(EP)	$12–14	$10–11	$12–14	$10–11

LEGEND FOR HOTEL LISTINGS: (AP) American Plan (room and 3 meals); **MAP)** Modified American Plan (room, breakfast and dinner); **(CP)** Continental Plan (room and breakfast); **(EP)** European Plan (room only). All rates quoted on a per-day basis and subject to change. Confirmed reservations at specific rates desired are always recommended.
HOTEL FACILITIES: (b) beach; **(p)** pool; **(t)** tennis; **(g)** golf.

DOMINICA

Dominica rises from the sea in great ramparts and towers, the very dream of a tropical island. Its peaks are often swathed in rain clouds, and hundreds of rivers and streams, pure and crystalline, course down its flanks.

Carib isle

With a slightly different historic twist of tongue and ear it could have been the Cannibal Sea—and "Cannibal Here & Now." For in origin, *Caribbean* and *cannibal* are one and the same.

Like so much in this part of the world, it began with Columbus. When he first reached the big islands that became Hispaniola and Cuba they were inhabited by peaceful agricultural Indians called Arawaks. But the Arawaks told of other Indians who held the smaller islands to the southeast, savage and powerful tribesmen who considered all other men their enemies, and not only killed but ate them. Some of the Spaniards heard their name as *Cariba*, others as *Caniba*, and thus both, with their eventually different meanings, entered the world's vocabulary.

To the Caribs themselves, their name meant *strong, brave, daring*. And they were all of that, with their other less beguiling qualities added. Indeed, to the oncoming Europeans they presented a special and brand new source of fear and awe. For this was before the opening up of interior Africa and the South Pacific, and the reason there was no prior name for cannibal is that none had ever before been known to white men.

For years before Columbus, the Caribs were the scourge of the West Indies. Starting from the Venezuelan mainland of South America, they had moved north in their war canoes from island to island, driving the Arawaks before them. When they captured prisoners, they killed and ate the men and children—the latter as a favorite delicacy—and took the women as combined servants and wives.

In a better world the coming of the Europeans might have meant salvation for the hapless Arawaks. But it was not to be. Enslaved and put to forced labor by the early Spaniards, they totally lost the will to live and were extinct within a few generations. The tougher Caribs, however, lived and fought on for centuries. In the whole history of American colonization, probably no Indian tribe anywhere put up fiercer resistance to the invaders.

Helping them was the fact that their main establishments were in the best natural fortresses of the West Indies: the rugged forested islands of Grenada, St. Vincent, St. Lucia and Dominica, later known together as the British Windwards. The Spanish, in quest of bigger game, largely passed

A sparkling silver waterfall in the deep green interior
on the island of Dominica

them by. But by the time the British and French arrived the pickings were slimmer, and both set to work at moving in on the Caribs.

It was a long and bloody business. To begin with, the two powers fought each other, with islands changing hands like playing cards; and then whoever gained possession, temporary or permanent, had to deal with the Indians. These, for their part, responded with a will—plus clubs, knives, poisoned arrows and cooking pots. It is on record, incidentally, that, as menu, the Caribs preferred French to English: an indirect and unappreciated tribute to *la cuisine Française*.

At last, after the Napoleonic Wars, the powers made their peace. France took over Guadeloupe and Martinique, Britain the so-called Windwards, except for the largest of them, Dominica. Here was an island so steep and wild, with the Caribs so entrenched in possession, that for a long while, by British–French agreement, it was left as undisputed Indian territory.

For a long while, but not forever. The tide of empire was irresistible, and in the end the wildest of the Indies also became part of the white man's world. Year by year, almost inch by inch, the French and then the English, returning, pushed the Caribs back, off the cliffs, into the sea, until finally their strength was broken and the Union Jack flew unchallenged over Dominica.

Still, the island and its Caribs remained unique. Elsewhere the Indians presently ceased to exist, not only as a nation but as people. Though the survivors of the wars did not wholly die off, as had the luckless Arawaks, they interbred and merged with the tide of African Negroes arriving as slaves, and ultimately disappeared in the vast Caribbean melting pot. In Dominica, however, they did not disappear. Here alone they retained their identity. Granted an area of what had become Crown Land by Queen Charlotte, wife of Britain's George III, they withdrew to its hills and forests, and from history into obscurity.

Obscurity has also, through the years, been the lot of Dominica itself. Tell your stateside friends (as I did) that you've been there, and they'll ask about its revolution and occupation.

"Not the Dominican Republic," you say. "Domineeka."

"What's that?"

Even Columbus gave it short shrift, leaving it with its name—meaning Sunday—and moving on. During the great plantation days in the Indies it was found too mountainous for profitable cultivation. And its scarcity of good harbors and beaches has, in our later day, held it back in the parade of tourism. Though one of the largest of the Lesser Antilles, with an area of some 300 square miles and a current population of about 65,000, it has remained a neglected boondock of the Caribbean.

But what a lovely boondock!

Rising from the sea in great ramparts and towers, it is the very dream of a tropical island. Its greenery gleams. Its shores are usually bright in sunlight, but its peaks are often swathed in rain clouds, and down its flanks, pure and crystalline, pour what Dominicans say are precisely 365 rivers and streams. While other lower islands roundabout suffer from drought and brown wasted landscapes, Dominica stands like an Eden, lush and teeming.

Yet here, if anywhere, is an example of "the fatal gift of beauty." For the bringing of the works of man to this tangled wilderness has been an enormous task. The few-years-old airport is a mere strip hacked out of wooded hillside on the northeast coast, capable of handling only smaller planes. The road from it across the hump of the island to its capital, Roseau, twists and turns for miles like a demented serpent. Not only are Dominica's roads hard to build in the first place. Once built, they require constant work and funds to keep them passable. And funds are one of many things in short supply.

Roseau, when at last you reach it, is, to face the facts, not much of a town. Though boasting a population of 14,000, one first-class hotel and one supermarket, it is for the most part nondescript and ramshackle, with little to attract the visitor other than its lively Saturday market. For commerce, its worst liability is that it has no protected harbor; for tourism, that there are no attractive beaches within miles.

Dominicans explain that Roseau is rather an "accident." Originally, Portsmouth, far up the western coast, was the island's principal settlement; but it proved a hotbed of malaria, and the center of population moved south. Now, though malaria is long since gone, the status quo remains, and no one seems very happy about it. "We just got stuck with Roseau," said one inhabitant ruefully.

Portsmouth today is little more than a village, but almost everyone agrees that it will loom large again in the island's future. Here there *is* a sheltered harbor. There *are* beaches. (Most of Dominica's meager strands are volcanic black, but these, if not dazzling white, are at least gray or beige.) And it seems sure that hereabouts will be the island's main resort area in years to come.

For the present, however, Dominica's prime attractions lie inland, in the wondrous green mountains and valleys that furrow its length and breadth. On the lower levels, everywhere, grows the tropical produce that provides its export income, most notably bananas and limes. Indeed, Dominican limes are world-famous, and have even helped add a word to the English language. The biggest landowners on the island are the makers of Rose's Lime Juice; and it was through the old-time use of Rose's on British ships, to ward off scurvy, that the English became known as Limeys.

Above the plantations, upon the mountainsides, cultivation gives way to primeval growth. Here in the deep rain forest is the pristine, the untouched Dominica in which the Caribs once roamed: a realm of giant trees and gleaming blossoms, of parrots and boa constrictors, of waterfalls and sulphur springs and boiling lakes, and finally of the highest peaks, the home of mist and cloud. No roads lead here; only faint tracks through a wilderness. The island's fairest wonders are hidden, and he who would see them must get there on his own two feet.

With this in mind, a Dominican friend told me that in his experience the island appealed most strongly to two extremes in visitors: the young and active who can climb and bushwack, and the elderly and contemplative who are content with peaceful beauty. For the in-betweeners, at present, there is not much to "do"; almost none, indeed, of the classic tourist activities to be found on more developed islands.

Night life, for example, is on a strictly do-it-yourself basis. To be specific, you drink or you go to bed.

Until very recently there was not even a likely place to do that. But now there are several establishments that provide the creature comforts in first-class fashion. Largest and liveliest is the Fort Young Hotel, in Roseau, actually and attractively built into the remnants of an old fort, with pleasant rooms, good bar and restaurant, and a patio swimming pool. To date, the Young's clientele has consisted largely of businessmen on the Caribbean circuit, but an increasing effort is being made to appeal to tourists.

Of a different genre—smaller, more elegant and more expensive—are Castaways and Island House, several miles out of town in different directions. Castaways, managed by Canadian Bill Harris, is on its own beach, black but silky, whereas Island House, a tiny but luxurious establishment owned and run by Floridians Peter and Marjorie Brand, is, in contrast, well up in the hills. Custom built along semi-Polynesian lines, with an exquisite landscaped pool, it is a lonely but lovely gem in a sweep of greenery and stillness.

Completing the where-to-stay roster are several guest houses of the Archbold Plantations (owned by a longtime Rockefeller associate); and in these, surrrounded by groves and orchards, one will perhaps best get the feel of the old island way of life. From one of them, Springfield, there is a fine vista down a long valley to the sea. At another, Clarke Hall, there is superlative fresh-water bathing in Dominica's largest river.

Few visitors come to the island simply by chance or because a travel agent sent them. Most, whether of the active or contemplative breed, come because they think Dominica is "their sort" of place, still unfouled-up by the 20th century; and not a few want to stay and dig in. Part of the appeal is that land is still comparatively cheap, in fact the cheapest in the Caribbean. But there is a catch here, for land is hard to come by. The island has not a single professional realtor. Established owners are reluctant to sell in the belief that land values are sure to rise. Finding that dream retreat is not wholly impossible (witness the Brands and a few others), but it takes some doing.

As on all "unspoiled" islands, there is difference of opinion among the residents as to the pros and cons of progress. The conservatives—who are apt to have it good as is—are resistant to change. The more numerous progressives want controlled but emphatic development. Most numerous of all, the rank-and-file Dominicans have few opinions one way or the other, for they are as yet scarcely conscious of the growing pressures from the outside world. In their back country villages they live much as they have for centuries. They speak their indigenous *patois* of mixed English-French-African, saving their school-learned straight English for the occasional outsider. Often they stare at the outsider as we would at a passenger from a flying saucer.

Even on Dominica, however, this will not last much longer, for change is coming. New roads are coming. Trucks and buses are coming. It will have new freedoms, and new problems. It will have more commerce, more industry, more tourists, more jobs, more everything; and the everything will flow across the island, in from its shores, up its hills and valleys, through its forests and streams. To its farthest outposts.

Even to the Caribs.

Indeed, with the Caribs the process is already well along. Read a guidebook of a few years back and it will say walk or ride horseback to reach the Indian reserve. Read one of only yesterday and it will prescribe a Jeep or Land Rover. But today you can reach the very heart of their realm in an ordinary car.

When I went, they were still working on the road. Ahead, against the forest green, above the high wild crags of Dominica's east coast, loomed a yellow bulldozer. A bit beyond it, walking pertly along, was a girl in pink Capri pants. A strayed tourist, I thought. But she was no tourist. She was not a Negro. Her black hair was straight; her skin was olive-yellow; between high cheekbones her eyes were as slanted as a Mongol's.

What next? I wondered. Caribs in bikinis? A cabana club? A discotheque? No—the pink-bottomed vision was a breed of one. The countryside continued wild and shaggy, and the Indians who subsequently came along wore the usual nondescript clothing of the rural Caribbean. One thing, however, continued to be *non*-nondescript. The faces. The features. One could see in them not only the lineaments of prehistoric America, but far back beyond that to lost origins in ancient Asia.

There is much disagreement as to how many "pure" Caribs are left today. Father Proesmans, a Belgian Catholic priest who has lived many years on Dominica, thinks about eighty. Another longtime resident, Douglas Taylor—an English student of Carib history and linguistics, who married a Carib —puts the figure somewhat lower. Other estimates run from a few hundred to a flat zero. Pure or mixed, however, the racial strain is genetically strong. On the Dominica reserve one feels oneself among true Indians, not among Negroes with some Indian blood.

The Caribs themselves have scant knowledge of their heredity. Along with almost everything in their history, it has receded into the mists of the past. Along with cannibalism have gone their other customs, costumes, weapons, artifacts and language—or rather languages, for once they had three: one for the men, one for the women (who were largely Arawak by birth), and one for ceremonial occasions. Now all that is left is what is contained in the research of Douglas Taylor and other scholars. The Caribs, like the surrounding Negroes, learn English at school and in everyday life speak the island patois.

There are today about 1,500 of them on the reserve. Maps show what purports to be their principal village, called Salybia, but there really is no village, only a district with the inhabitants spread out across hills and valleys. Many of these are planted with banana trees, for bananas are the Caribs' chief source of income, and the new road has been built by the government largely to help them get their produce to market.

There are also a few secondary "industries," and two stem from the past. The men still build rugged dugout canoes, which they sell to fishermen on Dominica and nearby islands; and the women weave sturdy and attractive baskets, which they sell to tourists. Also tourist-oriented, though scarcely traditional, is the part-time occupation of posing for photographs—with a firm financial deal usually made in advance. Most camera-toting visitors find this an unsettling procedure, a far cry from their romantic notion of "the noble savage." But today's Carib is neither savage nor romantic. He is, unfortunately but inevitably, a realist who knows he is a rare and curious specimen, with a cash value.

On my own visit, the first encounter with inhabitants en masse was at the Salybia school, and here was Carib-land at its brightest and best. There were no frills, to be sure. All 200-odd pupils, divided into six classes, were in one big barnlike room. The only visible appurtenances were blackboards and copy books, and the teachers, all Negroes, were, one surmises, not Ph.D.'s. The classes, however, were orderly and well mannered. Faces were lively, eyes keen, and hands popped upward at the teachers' questions. Here was the first generation of Caribs who would be almost wholly literate; and if the march forward would not be much above the primary grades, it would at least be far beyond that of all generations past.

Not far from the school was another of the reserve's principal buildings, the Catholic church. Together with most Dominicans, almost all the Caribs are at least nominally Catholic, and according to the French priest in charge make "fairly good" parishioners. The most notable feature of the church was its altar, an inverted Carib canoe. "It is hardly traditional, but it seems appropriate," said the priest with a smile.

Next along the winding road came a change of pace, the reserve store. No supermarket this. It was no more than a shed, with shelves two-thirds bare—except for one shelf lined with bottles of rum. Like his mainland cousins, the Carib has had his historic troubles with firewater; but unlike the United States, the Dominican government has not banned the sale of liquor to reservation Indians. In a land where it is so easy to "make your

own" it is certain that no such ban could be effective. And through the centuries the Carib has gone on drinking—into a bash, a rage, a stupor.

The road twisted on. We passed men cutting banana stems, gouging out a canoe, sitting idly under shade trees; women carrying loads and beating laundry on the rocks of stream beds. At intervals we came to Carib homes: all small, some decrepit shacks, some newly built of pressed construction board or plywood. The few we entered were at the same time sparsely furnished and cluttered. On the walls were colored pictures of Queen Elizabeth, the Crucifixion and the Beatles.

Then we came to a roadside opening, left our car, and descended a steep path toward the sea. On a level place above a steep bluff was a house similar to the others, but on the open ground before it, sitting, squatting and standing, was a group of about a dozen Indians. Here was the chief's home, and this was the Carib Council.

The men talked for a while in patois which I could not understand. Then one of them detached himself and came over to me. This I knew—for I had seen pictures of him—was the chief: a young man of about thirty, of medium build, with small, smooth, very Asian features. I knew, too, that, in accordance with recent tribal custom, he was not an hereditary but an elected chief, serving a three-year term; and I wondered if he had been chosen, despite his youth, at least partly because he seemed so totally pure Indian. There was nothing "pure" however, about his clothing, which featured a flowered sports shirt and a cricket cap. Nor about his name, which was Jermandois Francis.

He was pleasant, casual, and obviously used to talking to visiting firemen. The council, he said, met regularly to discuss and make decisions on tribal affairs, and only the most important matters were referred further, to the Dominican government.

"What sort of matters are those?" I asked.

"Mostly about land," said the chief. "Our Carib land as a whole. Outsiders are always moving in on us, and we go to the government to protect our rights."

"You reject all outsiders?"

"No. From the days when we fought the Arawaks we have taken women into our tribe. But not men." (He didn't elaborate on what used to happen to the men.) "Even our good friend, Douglas Taylor, who has married a Carib, cannot come and live here on our reserve."

"You want to keep the reserve, then?"

"Yes."

"Do you think the children who are going to school will want to stay here when they're older?"

"Yes," Jermandois Francis said again. But this second *yes* was weaker, and soon he changed the subject.

A little later I asked him, "May I take your picture?"

"Of course," he said politely. "The charge is three dollars."

Removing his cricket cap, he posed with ceremonial scarf and crown-topped mace that are his very British-looking symbols of office. When I had paid him I said I would also like to photograph an old and very Indian-looking couple who were standing close by.

"Surely," said the chief. "They are my father and mother. The charge is two dollars for one or three dollars for both together."

I chose the wholesale rate. We said a friendly good-bye, shaking hands and smiling. But it had not been a smiling time. It had, for me at least, been a sad time. And nothing—not even my departed six dollars—had been sadder than that sash and mace of office, in their setting of a small yard full of mud and rubbish.

It is easy to become sentimental about a small and dying people; to say that death should not and must not happen. But in the case of the present-day Caribs it assuredly will happen, and this will probably be for the best. There is no future for them *as* Caribs, except as a museum exhibit for anthropologists and tourists. Their only hope for a better life is to come out of their reserve, as many already have, out of their apartness and impotence into the mainstream of the world. That of course will mean general inter-breeding, and presently the Dominican Caribs, like Caribs elsewhere, will be gone. But in the process they will further enrich the wondrous mixture of humanity that inhabits what were once their islands.

We drove out of the reserve in the heat of the day. There were now no banana pickers, no canoe builders, no load carriers, no washwomen, but only an occasional figure dozing in the shade. Outside the grocery-liquor store a few men lounged on the steps, passing a rum bottle. Farther on, from a squalid shack, an old woman stared with blank and lifeless eyes.

Then, suddenly, we rounded a curve, and there was change. We had come to the school, and school was out, and the road was thronged with children. A group of girls came first, laughing and waving at us; then a brigade of boys, running, shouting, banging one another on the head with their copy books. Their young eyes shone. Their shouts and laughter filled the air.

That is how I want to remember the Caribs.

—*J. R. Ullman*

Instant facts

Location: 30 miles south of Guadeloupe.
Population: 65,000.
Capital: Roseau
Nationality: Associated state within the British Commonwealth.
Language: French Patois and English.
Currency: East Caribbean (same as West Indian) dollar—60¢ U.S., 64¢ Canadian and 4s 2d sterling.
Documentation: International certificate of vaccination required. Passport is required by all except U.S., Canadian and British citizens providing they hold proof of identity or round-trip ticket.
Climate & Clothes: Temperature varies from an average of 70° December–April to 90° May–November. Rainfall is 70 inches on the coast and as much as 300 inches in the interior. It is usually dry, particularly on the western coast, between January and June. Casual summer clothing—women should not wear shorts or slacks in town. Cocktail parties are quite dressy. Bring hiking shoes if planning interior exploration.
Food: Specialties are **crapaud** alias "mountain chicken" alias land frog. For frogs one usually thinks of *la cuisine francais* but Dominica's take second place to none.
Geography: 29 miles long and 16 miles wide with a total area of 305 sq. miles. The island is mountainous, highest peak being Morne Diablotin (4,747 feet). Dominica's unique feature is her rivers—365 of them. The island is of volcanic origin and has a rugged terrain, dense tropical forest, deep valleys and gullies.
History: Dominica, or Sunday Island, was discovered by Columbus in 1493, on his second voyage. For many years the French and English fought each other and the native Carib Indians, a fierce and warlike tribe, for possession of the rugged island. The English were granted rights to Dominica by the Treaty of Paris in 1763 but the French continued to invade the territory. In 1805 the French burned the capital town of Roseau and were only induced to leave upon payment of a £12,000 ransom.

Who flies here

LIAT services the island on north and southbound flights between Antigua and Trinidad. There is air service from the following islands, all fares round-trip:

Antigua $27
Barbados $57
Guadeloupe $15
Martinique $22
St. Lucia $27
St. Vincent $51

Island transportation

Plenty of **taxis** for drivers to all points on the island. Raymond Younis and "Pressy" Benoit (who knows the Caribs well) are excellent driver-guides. Drive-yourself cars are available for the intrepid from Archbold Plantations Ltd. and Rent-a-Car & Garage Ltd.

Wandering through Dominica

Excellent **river bathing,** a refreshing change from sand and surf. There are some nice beaches with ash-colored volcanic sand but beaches are not Dominica's forte. **Hiking** is a challenge in the upland rain forests and a popular walk is from Fresh Water Lake over the winding road to Rosalie. If that's too strenuous, wander through the fine **botanical garden** in Roseau.

A sight to see is the view from **Morne Bruce** (*morne* means hill) behind Roseau. More spectacular views from the north end of the island, toward Guadeloupe and its satellites; from the south, toward Martinique and its famous—or infamous— Mont Pelée. Catch a glimpse of **Morne Diablotin,** one of the Caribbean's highest peaks, on those rare occasions when it emerges from cloud. Rewarding trips are to the **Carib Reserve,** the rugged **North Coast,** the **Boiling Lake** and the **Sulphur Springs** at Wotton Waven.

For the sportsman, there is cricket, football, netball and spearfishing. The Dominica Club and Union Club, both private, feature tennis, billiards and bridge.

Best shopping buys

Grass floor mats, attractive and durable: on sale at the Convent Industrial School and the Dominica Handcrafts Company in Roseau. Also the expertly made baskets of the Carib Indians.

Dining out

Aside from hotels or guest houses, there is only one restaurant—**The Green Parrot** at Bay Front. Call Mrs. Daphne Agar, Tel: 200 (allow three rings). For beer drinkers there is a pub, **The Scenic,** run by Mrs. L. Benoit.

Special events, celebrations

Carnival: Shrove Monday and Tuesday. Street dancing, and other festivities.
Easter Monday: April 15.
Whitmonday: June 3.
Dominica Day: November 3.

Real estate and retirement

There is no real estate agent in Dominica and advertisement of property for sale is only now becoming common. Land purchases are usually the result of personal negotiation and potential settlers should pay preliminary visits to the island in order to make their own arrangements. Aliens wishing to purchase land must first obtain an Alien Landholders License from the Government. No figures on cost of land can be quoted since these vary tremendously throughout the island.

Furnished seaside villas may be reserved through Mrs. Celia Fadelle, 18 Rose St., Goodwill.

There are several country houses which may be rented. Write to Archbold Plantations, Ltd., Roseau or Mrs. C. J. L. Dupigny, Roseau. Food, being imported, is naturally somewhat high but domestic help is only about $8 a week. Taxes are steep but visitors can spend six months in Dominica without being liable for income tax.

Commerce and industry

Dominica is essentially an agricultural country as the soil is very fertile. The island is still largely undeveloped, offering good opportunities to the would-be investor. Chief industries are the manufacture of rum from sugar cane, copra from coconuts, cigarettes and cigars, canned citrus segments and juice, handcrafts, the growing of bananas, limes, cocoa and other agricultural products.

Encouragement is given by the government to the opening of new industries through incentive legislation, and there is definitely room for industrial expansion. The hotel industry, oils and fats, canning, livestock and agriculture all require further development. The Aid to Pioneer Industries Ordinance provides exemption from import duty on machinery and raw material, for five years and on export duty and from income tax for a similar period. The Hotel Aids Ordinance provides exemption from import duty on new hotel equipment and building material, and from income tax for those entering the hotel industry for 10 years.

WHERE TO STAY — In Dominica

	Plan	Dec. 15-April 14 U. S. Currency Double	Single	April 15-Dec. 14 Double	Single
CASTAWAYS Mero (12 Rms.) (b)	(MAP)	$35	$20	$25	$15
CHERRY LODGE Roseau (12 Rms.)	(AP)	$16	$9	$16	$9
CLARKE HALL PLANTATION Nr. Roseau (6 Rms.)	(AP)	$24	$18	$24	$18
FORT YOUNG Roseau (26 Rms.) (p)	(MAP)	$22	$12	$22	$12
ISLAND HOUSE Watten Waven (p)	(AP)	$45–50	$27–36	$23–30	$14–18
PURPLE TURTLE Beach Club (4 Rms.)	(AP)	$20.40	$12	$20.40	$12
ROXY'S GUEST HOUSE Laudat (3 Rms.)	(AP)	$20	$10	$20	$10
SPRINGFIELD GUEST HOUSE Nr. Roseau (4 Rms.)	(AP)	$24	$18	$24	$18
TRAVELODGE (4 Rms.)		$16	$8	$16	$8

LEGEND FOR HOTEL LISTINGS: (AP) American Plan (room and 3 meals); **MAP)** Modified American Plan (room, breakfast and dinner); **(CP)** Continental Plan (room and breakfast); **(EP)** European Plan (room only). All rates quoted on a per-day basis and subject to change. Confirmed reservations at specific rates desired are always recommended.
HOTEL FACILITIES: (b) beach; **(p)** pool; **(t)** tennis; **(g)** golf.

*Skindiving with snorkel is an easy sport to learn
for thrilling explorations of the Caribbean undersea*

DOMINICAN REPUBLIC

The Dominican Republic is a poor but beautiful land that emerged from 30 years of iron dictatorship only to plunge into a bloody civil war. Few tourists visit the troubled land although, as of this writing, there were signs of peaceful transformation after more than a year of representative democracy.

Touring the Island

If the Dominican Republic can ever solve its political problems, it has a great deal to offer the tourist.

There are a number of interesting tours to take through the country. On the north coast, washed by the Atlantic surf, is the most important northern harbor—PUERTO PLATA; attractive LONG BEACH and its hotel of the same name; and SOUSA, another beautiful beach originally settled by 20th-century German-Jewish immigrants.

East of Santo Domingo is the city of HIGUEY, founded in 1494 and the Lourdes of the Dominican Republic. Dominican–Spanish troops prayed to the Virgin of Altagracia while in desperate battle with the French and, when they won, adopted the Virgin as patron saint of the island-nation. Today sick and crippled persons come to the Sanctuary of the Virgin of Altagracia hoping to be cured and January 21 has been set aside as a national day of thanksgiving. Visitors will find the Cathedral itself an impressive structure.

Near Higuey is BOCA DE YUMA BAY, once an important landing place and a favorite spot for bathers since the days of Juan Ponce de León who used to swim there often. Boca de Yuma may one day become a major tourist spot. The area is excellent for hunting and fishing. Another good beach is at MACAO, best reached by jeep. Continuing up along the east coast you will reach the beautiful beach of SABANA DE LA MAR and the caves of Caño Hondo. Lobster fishing is excellent in this area. From here you can sail to the peninsula of SAMANÁ—in fact, you must go by boat as the road ends quite abruptly on the shore line. Arrangements for the trip can be made through the Agencia Marítima y Comercial (Tel: 2-9192/4) or the Department of Tourism (Tel: 9-2178/9).

The Bay of Samaná was once considered a vital body of water due to its location, between the Atlantic and Caribbean Seas. The Peninsula of Samaná and the Barracote Channels are similar to the Miami Everglades. Hunting and fishing is tops and, though there are no hotels, overnight stays can be arranged at some small native inns.

Also on the south coast, near Santo Domingo, are the beaches of Boca, Chica, Juan Dolio and Guayacanes, popular sites for swimming and other water sports. Be sure to stop off at LOS TRES OJOS (The Three Eyes). The "eyes" in this case refer to the sources of a spring of water—three underground pools in caverns about five minutes outside of the city. Visitors can swim here and sample the warm sulphur water, icy cold fresh water and lukewarm salt water, all in the same area.

Just a short, but pleasant, drive west of the capital is SAN CRISTÓBAL, where the Republic's first constitution was signed. Here also is a succession of excellent strands—Navayo, Palenque and the sweet water bath of La Toma. On the way is the Engombe SUGAR MILL, first such mill in the New World. It was built on the Haína River so that molasses and sugar could be easily transported to Spanish vessels waiting at sea. Ruins of the mill, mansion and chapel are being restored by the University of Santo Domingo.

A longer trip along the south shore is to BARAHONA. Here in the middle of desert country, and close to the Haitian border, is LAKE ENRIQUILLO,

View of Boca Chica Beach, Santo Domingo, Dominican Republic

largest lake in the Antilles. Swimming for those who don't mind crocodiles for company. Also, hundreds of flamingos inhabit the area. There are a number of interesting cities nearby. PARAÍSO has spectacular cliffs and the city of ALCOA (Cabo Rojo) is an oasis in the desert, a center for bauxite mining.

An especially interesting trip into the interior is the five-day excursion to SANTIAGO. On the way you will pass the very untropical LA NEVERA, actually freezing in the winter and covered not with palms but with pine trees. There is a lovely hotel in CONSTANZA, the Nueva Suiza, but you may very well find yourself the lone guest, such is the state of tourist affairs in the Dominican Republic right now. Constanza is the site of the Rio del Medio waterfalls. Onward to JARABACOA, another city with roots in the past and the site of three more waterfalls, impressive to visitors both visually and audibly. On the third day you should come to LA VEGA, at the entrance to the fertile Cibao Valley. An earthquake destroyed the original city and it was moved to its present site. The city is located at the foot of SANTO CERRO (Holy Hill), where Columbus placed the Spanish cross laying claim to the land. Parts of this cross can be seen in the Sanctuary of Santo Cerro, in the city of La Vega and in the Cathedral at Santo Domingo. The entire valley of La Vega is visible from the summit of Santo Cerro. In the city of SANTIAGO you can see the Monument of Heroes. View from the top includes Dominican shore line and rice fields.

Instant facts

Location: Some 1600 miles from New York and 880 miles from Miami.

Population: 3.8 million.

Capital: Santo Domingo.

Nationality: Independent republic.

Language: Spanish.

Currency: The peso, equal to the U.S. dollar.

Documentation: International certificate of vaccination required. Passport and visa not required by U.S., Canadian and British citizens. A tourist card, which can be purchased at the local airport for $1, is good for 15 days and can be renewed for another 15.

Climate & Clothes: Temperatures range from 72° in the winter months to 79° during the summer months, with trade winds to cool off coastal areas and cooler temperatures in the mountains. There is no official rainy season as such but most precipitation occurs between June and September. Sports clothes are appropriate only around hotels and on the beaches.

Food: Sancocho (a stew of various meats and root vegetables) and rice and beans form the better part of the native Dominican diet. Native fruits and vegetables include the plantain (a large, usually green banana-like fruit), cassava (like a potato, formed into cakes or bread), pineapple and coconut.

Geography: The Dominican Republic shares with Haiti the island of Hispaniola occupying the eastern $^2/_3$ with its total land area of 19,332 sq. miles. Three mountain chains run through the island and Pico Duarte, over 10,000 ft. high, is the tallest mountain in the West Indies. Rivers empty into both the Caribbean Sea and the Atlantic Ocean and one of these, the Artibonito, forms part of the natural border between the Dominican Republic and Haiti. A large lake, Lago Enriquillo, lies on the Republic's western border.

History: The island of Hispaniola was discovered by Columbus on December 5, 1492, and eventually became the base from which he explored other Caribbean islands. Lured by rumors of gold, Columbus' brother, Bartolomé, established the settlement of Santo Domingo de Guzmán in 1496. (During the Era of Trujillo the name of the city was changed to Ciudad Trujillo, but following the dictator's assassination in 1961 the old name, Santo Domingo, was restored.) Santo Domingo, considered to be the oldest city in the New World, was ruled for a time by Columbus' son, Diego, and welcomed the great *conquistadores* of the day. The island prospered and slaves were imported from Africa. When Spanish interest was diverted to Mexico and Peru, the French began to trickle in from the tiny pirate-dominated island of Tortuga, off the north coast of what is now Haiti, and for a time France claimed not only the western portion of the island but all of Hispaniola as her own. In 1809 Spanish rule was re-established, but in 1821 the Dominicans revolted and declared the country independent from Spain. The Haitians invaded and occupied the country for 22 years until the Dominican Republic was established following another revolution in 1844. In 1904, the unstable government requested American statehood and a motion to this effect was narrowly defeated in the U.S. Senate. The U.S. eventually stepped in to restore order and shore up the economy, and the country was occupied by U.S. Marines from 1916 to 1924. Generalíssimo Rafael Leonidas Trujillo Molina took over control of the country in 1930 and ran it virtually as a private fief until his assassination in 1961. Free elections were held in 1963 and Juan Bosch was elected president, only to be swept out seven months later by the military. The attempt to stage a coup and restore Bosch to the presidency in 1965 led to civil war that was checked by American intervention. On July 1, 1966, free elections were held and Dr. Joaquín Balaguer was elected president.

Who flies here

There are direct flights from the following major cities:

New York: Pan Am, Viasa. Round trip: $198–$285; 17-day excursion $155–$215.

Miami: Pan Am, Dominican Airlines.

Round trip: $85–$192; 17-day excursion $91–$125.

San Juan: Pan Am, Dominican Airlines, Caribair. Round trip $40–$63.

Service to and from other Caribbean islands via Dominican Airlines, KLM and Air France.

Island transportation

Car rentals are offered by the following Santo Domingo agencies; rates begin at about $7.50 and there is an extra charge for mileage.

Méndez Capellán C x A
Ave. Duarte 46
Tel: 2-9254, 2-9306

National Rent A Car
El Conde 9, Ave. Central cor. España
Tel: 2-2525, 2-3838

Santo Domingo Motors Co.
30 de Marzo #18
Tel: 9-1161

Nelly Rent-A-Car
Ave. Independencia 134
Tel: 9-1002

Quisqueya Rent-A-Car
Ave. Independencia
Tel: 2-8502

Renta Movil
El Conde 33
Tel: 2-2166

Hertz Rent a Car
Hotel Embajador
Tel: 3-2131

Santo Domingo Rent-A-Car
30 de Marzo #41
Tel: 2-8530

Taxis in Santo Domingo are unmetered and it is advisable to check on their rates before you take off. Fare within the city limits should be 75¢–$1. Another mode of transportation is the **carro público**—readily identified by its color scheme (blue and white, or blue and red-orange) and, upon closer perusal, the "P" on its license plate. These unmetered cars go just about anywhere, charging 15¢ in the city (more after midnight). **Buses** are less dependable than the ever-present públicos. They do, however, have scheduled routes in Santo Domingo and between towns. Fare is 10¢ in the city.

Interesting sights in Santo Domingo

As of late 1967 some of the following places were still closed down or neglected. It is hoped that they have been re-opened in the meantime.

The Cathedral of Santo Domingo: Built in the early 16th century, this impressive example of Spanish Renaissance architecture houses in its vaults jewelry and other artifacts by renowned artisans such as Benvenuto Cellini.

Tomb of Christopher Columbus: An ornate marble shrine in the Cathedral. Columbus died in Spain but his remains were brought to Santo Domingo.

Ruins of San Nicholas de Bari: On Mercedes Ave. The first hospital in America, built in wood in 1503 and replaced by the stone building 25 years later. Only the walls of the two-story high building remain.

El Conde Gate: At Parque Independencia. Built as a fortification in colonial times by the Spanish to protect the city against invaders. The three Dominicans who founded the republic in 1844 are buried here, the very site where they raised the first Dominican flag to declare the Republic's independence. Today it is a national shrine.

University of Santo Domingo: Now a modern group of buildings, the original university is the oldest in the Americas. It was established in 1538 by the Dominican Friars and today houses the Convent of the Dominics on Father Billini St. First student was, appropriately, Columbus' grandson Luis.

Columbus Castle: Built in the early 16th century by Columbus' son, Diego, then Viceroy of all Spain's conquests in the New World. The Alcazar, as it was officially called, is now restored and furnished with valuable antiques from this early era.

The Dancing Waters: On George Washington Ave. Though not dancing at the present time, the Teatro Agua Luz (Water and Light Theater) is well worth visiting

when it re-opens. The giant cascades fall in rhythm to music by known composers.

Chapel of the Rosary: First chapel built in the Americas. Dates from 1496, when Bartolomé Colombus originally founded Santo Domingo.

House of the Cord: Named after the cord of the St. Francis Order, in relief over the entranceway. Built in 1502, it was here that Francis Drake received the ransoms he demanded in exchange for not leveling the city of Santo Domingo. Columbus' son and granddaughters were born here.

Tower of Homage: First stone building in the New World (1502). It has flown seven different flags representing seven different countries that alternately ruled the young nation.

Columbus' Ceiba: Believed to be the tree where Columbus tied his ships on his third voyage to the island, 1498.

The sporting life

Baseball is the Dominican Republic's great sporting passion and the game is played throughout the year. Championships begin in October at the 16,000-seat Quisqueya Stadium in Santo Domingo and there are four teams—Licey, Escogido, Aguilas Cibaeñas and Estrellas Orientales. The first two are the favorites. Local enthusiasm is especially high due to the import of championship players from American major leagues. Other good stadiums at Santiago and San Pedro de Macorís.

Santo Domingo's one golf course, an 18-holer, is at the Santo Domingo Country Club (Tel: 3-1332). **Softball** stadiums are located at the Fairgrounds, Carretera Mella Km. 6 in Villa Duarte and near the Santo Domingo Country Club. Games are usually played on Saturday afternoons and on Sunday. **Horse races** are held at the Perla Antillana race track, near the airport, on Thursday and Sunday. Pari-mutuel betting. Betting also on **cockfights** every Sunday afternoon throughout the country. Largest cockfighting stadium in the Antilles is at Santiago. **Basketball** is most popular with the scholastic set but there are also night games in Villa Duarte on Tuesday and

Saturday. **Soccer** is played throughout the year and polo from January–April.

Hunters must go through a bit of red tape before leaving for the Dominican Republic. In order to get a hunting license upon arrival, they must first go to the Dominican consulate nearest their home and show them a license enabling them to hunt in their own country. Guns must be registered at the Customs House; cartridges can be purchased here. Certain fowl—heron, quail, partridge, wild turkey, native pigeons, little turtledoves—can be hunted year round while others are seasonal (limited to the fall months). Cayman (alligators) can be hunted throughout the year at Enriquillo Lake.

Contact the Hunting and Fishing Club, Centro de los Héroes (Tel: 3-1972), or the Dept. of Tourism (Tel: 9-2178/9).

Water Sports: There are many good beaches around the island. The best in the Santo Domingo vicinity is, of course, Boca Chica, some 20 miles away. Others throughout the island are at La Caleta, Long Beach, Guayacanes, Palenque, Macao and Villas del Mar. In the Hotel Hamaca at Boca Chica there are two Chris-Craft launches which can be chartered for fishing and water skiing. Spearfishing at Boca Chica is also good and the island, in general, is an angler's paradise.

Best shopping buys

Shopping here is not spectacular but there are some pretty good buys at the free-port shops—Japanese and German cameras, English fabrics, Italian accessories and French perfumes. Located in the Centro de los Héroes, the goods are in bond (duty-free to visitors only), which means that after you select the merchandise it is sent directly to the airport. Don't wait till the last minute or you'll be leaving *sans* goods.

Most sizeable stores are along Santo Domingo's Ave. Conde. In addition to local handicrafts, one unusual item that is both attractive and a conversation piece is amber jewelry. Although the settings leave something to be desired, the clear gold stone—a prehistorically petri-

fied sap—can be bought with (or without) bugs perfectly preserved within. Apparently, the more ostentatious or unusual the insect, the more valuable the gem. Prices are very reasonable and it's a fun purchase. Grasshoppers in your earrings, anyone?

Dining and night life

Bellas Artes: Ave. Independencia. Int'l cuisine, intimate atmosphere. Modern bar.

Chantilly: Ave. Máximo Gómez. French cuisine, modern bar.

El Dragon: Ave. Independencia #55. Chinese and Creole cooking. Tel: 2-3750 and 2-0086.

Europa: Calle Mercedes, corner 30 de Marzo. Modern *casino*, restaurant and bar. Tel: 2-4260.

Italia: Calle Juan Isidro Jiménez #1. Italian food. Tel: 9-2727.

Jasonied: Calle El Conde #73. Restaurant, very modern bar.

Lina: Ave. Independencia #4. Spanish and Creole food, modern bar. Tel: 2-0783.

Mandarin: Ave. George Washington #161. Tel: 2-2788 and 2-7687.

Mario: Calle Mercedes #4, in front of Independence Plaza. Chinese and Creole food. Tel: 2-3444.

Panamerican: Calle El Conde #75. International cuisine, modern bar. Tel: 9-5778.

El Pony: 30 de Mayo Highway, Km. 10½. International and Creole cooking. Tel: 3-1956.

Roxy: Calle El Conde #83. Modern bar, restaurant. Tel: 9-7370.

Toledo: Ave. George Washington. Modern bar-restaurant. International and Creole cooking. Shows with local and international figures.

Vesubio: Ave. George Washington #145. Italian food. Tel: 2-2766.

In addition to the Toledo Restaurant, there are **nightclubs and cocktail lounges** at the Night Club Radio Television Dominicana, Night Club Boringuén, the Moulin Rouge and in the El Embajador and Hispaniola Hotels. **Casinos** are at the Jaragua, Embajador and Paz Hotels, and at the Restaurant Europa.

Museums, gardens and the fine arts

Center of fine arts in Santo Domingo is the Palacio de Bellas Artes or Fine Arts Palace on Ave. Independencia #5 (Tel: 2-6384). In addition to an exhibition of paintings, concerts and recitals are held here regularly. At the Museo Nacional (National Museum), Centro de los Heroes (Tel: 3-1698) there are historic and pre-historic artifacts. Numerous public libraries, including one at the University, are open to visitors and the zoo and botanical garden—Bolívar (Tel: 2-6125)—is a family treat.

Special events, celebrations

Three Kings Day: Children celebrate the coming of the Three Kings, who leave presents in straw-packed shoes on the eve of January 6.

Virgin of Altagracia's Day: Official national holiday, celebrated with greatest devotion in Higuey, where a sanctuary dedicated to the Virgin is located. January 21.

National Independence Day: Carnival celebrations. February 27.

Holy Week: Marked by religious processions on Holy Wednesday and Good Friday (April 10 and 12).

Pan American Day: April 14.

Classical Music Festival: The National Symphony Orchestra and local and international artists are invited to play at the Fine Arts Palace. April.

Holy Cross Festivities: Religious celebrations, kettle-drum dances. Special festivities at El Seibo. May.

Merengue (national dance) Festival: July or August.

Our Lady of Mercy Day: Special celebrations at El Santo Cerro where legend says Lady of Mercy appeared to the conquistadores and Columbus. September 24.

St. Cecil's Day: Musicians, singers and dancers pay homage to the patron saint of music. Special programs sponsored by the National Music Conservatory. November 22.

Civic and social organizations—Santo Domingo

Organization	Address	Phone
Philatelic Society	Calle Isabel la Católica #54	
Academy of History	Calle Mercedes #50	9-4584
American Chamber of Commerce	Arzobispo Meriño corner Luperón, Box 850	2-1784
Hope Lodge	Calle Hostos #9	9-7263
Assn. of Architects and Engineers	Calle El Conde #79	2-5838
Ateneo Dominicano	Calle F. Mariano, Lluberes #18	2-3344
Junior Chamber of Commerce	Parque Eugenio María de Hostos	9-5355
Fine Arts Palace	Ave. Independencia #5	2-6384
Panamerican Union	Centro de los Heroes	3-1972
Bible Society	Calle El Conde #29	2-9528
Medical Society	Calle Arzobisbo, Nouel #106	2-3270
Club Libanes-Sirio Palestino Inc.	Calle M. Cestero #8	9-1075
Rotary Club	Calle Arzobispo Portes #70	2-2496
Lions Club	Ave. Venezuela, Ensanche Osama	5-1061
Sports Commission		
Professional Baseball League	Calle El Conde #83	2-7878
Dominican Scouts Assn.	Parque Eugenio María de Hostos	9-5355
Hunting and Fishing Club	Centro de los Heroes	3-1972

Real estate and industry

People aren't exactly looking to the Dominican Republic for retirement these days, but if you're interested in a home-site or property, there is a reliable agent at Calle Duarte #32, corner Luperón (Tel: 2-7005). Moving here is expensive,

Dominican Republic

housing is either prohibitively high in cost or low in quality and wages are lower still.

While property investment is risky because of political fluctuation it may bring in rich returns in the future. There is, at present, only one major real estate project geared to attract foreign investors. That is the Villas del Mar Development Company, which is offering beachside property some 15 minutes from the airport for cash or long-term payment. Information is available from the company on El Conde St. #33 (in the Hotel Commercial), Tel: 9-9484 and 9-2919.

The Dominican Republic's economy still is primarily based on agriculture and the country needs just about everything—low cost housing to stem slum growth, modern agricultural equipment, electric power projects and all sorts of industries. The Republic has more tourism potential than any other Caribbean country (with the possible exception of long-lost Cuba) and beautiful hotels built during the Trujillo regime. Yet little Puerto Rico is decades ahead of its unstable neighbor in both industry and tourism. Despite a law offering protection and industrial incentives to new industries, the Dominican government does not yet show any signs of long-range, full-scale cooperation with interested investors.

WHERE TO STAY —
In the Dominican Republic

	Plan	Dec.-April 14 U. S. Currency Double	Single	April 15-Dec. 14 Double	Single
EL EMBAJADOR INTER- CONTINENTAL Bella Vista (315 Rms.) (p, t, g)	(AP)	$22–26	$15–19	$16–20	$22–30
HISPANIOLA Santo Domingo (152 Rms.) (p)	(AP)	$28–32	$ 8– 9	$24–28	$ 7– 8

HOTEL COMERCIAL (EP) Santo Domingo (75 Rms.)	$20	$12	$20	$12
GUAROCUYA (EP) Barahona (22 Rms.) **(b)**	$ 8–25	$ 5–25	$ 8–25	$ 5–25
MAGUANA (EP) San Juan de la Maguana (19 Rms.) **(p)**	$ 7–20	$ 4–20	$ 7–20	$ 4–20
MARIEN (EP) Santiago Rodríguez (10 Rms.)	$ 5	$ 3	$ 5	$ 3
MATUM (EP) Santiago de los Caballeros (40 Rms.) **(p)**	$ 7–20	$ 4–20	$ 7–20	$ 4–20
MERCEDES (EP) Santiago de los Caballeros (40 Rms.)	$12–14	$ 4	$12–14	$ 4
MONTAÑA (EP) Jarabacoa (26 Rms.) **(p)**	$ 8–20	$ 5–20	$ 8–20	$ 5–20
EL NARANJO (EP) Higuey (40 Rms.)	$ 7–25	$ 4–25	$ 7–25	$ 4–25
NUEVA SUIZA (EP) Constanza (59 Rms.) **(p)**	$ 7–25	$ 4–25	$ 7–25	$ 4–25
SAN CRISTOBAL (EP) San Cristóbal (13 Rms.) **(p)**	$ 7	$ 5	$ 7	$ 5

LEGEND FOR HOTEL LISTINGS: (AP) American Plan (room and 3 meals); **MAP)** Modified American Plan (room, breakfast and dinner); **(CP)** Continental Plan (room and breakfast); **(EP)** European Plan (room only). All rates quoted on a per-day basis and subject to change. Confirmed reservations at specific rates desired are always recommended.
HOTEL FACILITIES: (b) beach; **(p)** pool; **(t)** tennis; **(g)** golf.

GRENADA

To much of the world, nutmeg is simply something one is required by law to sprinkle over the Christmas eggnog. There is much more to nutmeg than that. There is, for example, Grenada, where it all begins and where the air is filled with the scent of spices.

Still off the mainline

On the heights above St. George's, in Grenada, the soft air was filled with music. It wasn't Calypso; it was "Jingle Bells." And it came from the jail (with the best view on the island), where the prisoners' steel drum band was rehearsing for its Christmas concert.

In the harbor, a fleet of bright-sailed toy boats rode the waters. Commodore of the regatta, in a battered skiff, was a strapping local type in tattered shorts who looked as if he might hold his own with Cassius Clay. "He's going to try to sell them to us," one of our group said as we watched from a wharf. But he was wrong. The Commodore was just enjoying himself.

Out in the blue among the Grenadines there were the sea, the sky, the islands rising between them like wizards' castles. And then the dolphins. Picking us up off Cannouan, they escorted us on toward Bequia: leaping, plunging, grinning, all but winking at us, as they frolicked about our heeling cutter. They were enjoying themselves, too.

In harbor, at sea, perhaps even in jail, enjoyment comes easy in these islands called the British Windwards. Way down the line in the chain of the Lesser Antilles, they are far-out but friendly, rugged but gentle, and as lovely to the eye as islands can be. Still jetless (for their airport runways are small), they are out of the rush and bustle of the Caribbean mainline, oases to be cherished in the wastes of a mechanized world.

They comprise four main islands. Farthest north, least developed and visited, is the steep jungle land of Dominica. Then, after a jump past Martinique, which is French, comes St. Lucia, then St. Vincent, then Grenada. Between the last two, lost, tiny and alluring, are the strung-out beads of the Grenadines.

(Note to neophytes: In the Caribbean, many names, including its own, are pronounced eccentrically, e.g., St. Lucia is *St. Loosha* and Grenada is *Grenayda*. Bequia, gem of the Grenadines, is *Beckwee*.)

I came by way of Barbados—on the mainline—to Pearls Airport in Grenada, a thin seaside slot in a forested mountainside. And from there the journey continued, by car, over the mountains to the capital town of St. George's. Resident Grenadians, taxi drivers excepted, are less than enthusiastic about this obligatory 16-mile roller-coaster ride, which takes twice as long as the flight from Barbados. But for the first-timer it provides an ideal introduction to the island.

Grenada is steep, but not barren-steep. It is green and lush. Once a major sugar producer, it has long since almost eliminated cane and become, as it calls itself, "Spice Island of the West." Nutmeg is the prime crop. About a third of the world's total of nutmegs come from its tight 133 sq. miles. But it also grows cinnamon, ginger, cloves and tonka beans—plus cocoa, its largest export—in aromatic profusion. In my own travel experience, it is one of the few places on earth where the good smells outdo the bad.

Sweeping up over the island's hump is an emerald cloak of growth. ("Drop a few seeds anywhere," say the Windwardians, "and you have an instant jungle.") And like scattered rents in the cloak are the roadside villages. Some have English names, some French, for Grenada has had a speckled colonial history. At the topmost crest of the hills is one of the island's notable "sights," the Grand Etang, or Big Pond, a broad gleaming lake in the green crater of a long-dead volcano. A bit farther on is a lovely forest-hemmed cascade called Annandale Falls.

The sight of sights in Grenada, however, is less nature's handiwork than man's. This is its metropolis, St. George's, clinging to the steep slopes of its southwestern coast, which many travelers have compared to the Italian coastal towns south of Naples. As Caribbean communities go, it is a big one, with roughly a third of Grenada's 90,000-odd population living in and around it. And with its twin harbors, flanked by old forts and bold headlands, it is spectacularly beautiful. In 1955, along with the rest of Grenada, St. George's was hit and devastated by the only hurricane in its history. But today, to a visitor's eye, scarcely a scar remains.

The only hotel of any size in town, the St. James, caters mainly to a commercial trade. But there are two musts for visiting firemen of any breed: both handily in the same waterfront building and both run by Americans. One, upstairs, is The Nutmeg, a cheerful restaurant-cum-bistro presided over by ex-New Yorker Carl Schuster. The other, downstairs, is The Sea Change, a book-and-gift shop (featuring spices, what else?) operated by Mrs. Frances Brinkley, ex-several places including West Virginia.

Not only these establishments, but their proprietors, too, are well worthy of acquaintance, for both are prize specimens of contented escapees to a tropic island. Do not, however, expect to find them lounging under frangipani trees nibbling lotus—or nutmeg. Both will assure you that in the Isles of Sweet Languor you have to work twice as hard for the same result as in Manhattan's canyons or those West Virginia hills.

Virtually all Grenada's resort hotels are clustered on the island's southwest peninsula, beyond St. George's. First, out from town, is The Islander, high on a bluff above the harbor, which a few years back was the locale for many scenes in the film *Island in the Sun*. Next is Ross Point Inn: small, informal, and noted for its West Indian cuisine. Beyond this begins the proud two-mile sweep of Grand Anse, one of the great beaches of the Caribbean, and here, along its bright perimeter, are what could be called The Big Four of Grenada's hostelries.

They are, in order, Silver Sands, Grenada Beach, Grand Anse Riviera and Spice Island Inn. All are brand new, or the next thing to it. All are low-lying and well spread out. And all, though top bracket of their kind, are moderate in price compared to similar hotels on mainline islands such as Barbados or Jamaica. Of the four, Grenada Beach Hotel is the largest. Silver Sands, I would say, is the "homiest." The Riviera offers an all-season choice between hotel living and bungalow housekeeping. And Spice Island, as run by Alan Krassner, another happily displaced New Yorker—and undisplaced gourmet —is, in my opinion, a small gem of innsmanship.

Grand Anse isn't quite done yet. Beyond Spice Island Inn, at the far end of the beach, is the Flamboyant, an easygoing cottage colony plus beach front bar operated by Californians Jim and Knight Needham. Knight, to my surprise, proved to be a Mrs.; and Bebe, another member of the family, turned out, when introduced, to be a Grenadian monkey. A small place, the Flamboyant, but not a dull one.

Across the southwest peninsula, opposite Grand Anse, stands the newest of the new among Grenada's hotels, a trim and elegantly landscaped inn-with-cottages called the Calabash. And east of it, on a sub-peninsula of its own, is another and different development that is perhaps the most interesting on the island. Called Westerhall Point, this is a residential project—no hotel, only homes—launched by an English architect, Beresford Willcox, and his Scandinavian architect wife. Unlike many such projects in the islands, it is not merely on paper. It exists. Already on the Point there are some twenty-five homes, secluded and lovely, with a list of tenants so international that it reads like a U.N. General Assembly roll call. More are coming, too. And understandably. For Westerhall is one of the best of its kind I have seen in the Caribbean.

It is easy for the short-term visitor to spend all his time in this blossoming southwest sector that forms about a tenth of the island. But the other nine-tenths merit a visit, too, if only because they are so very different. If you feel rugged and thrifty, take one of the public buses: short on comfort but long on wondrous names like *Courage de Luxe* and *God Is Love*. More sedately, there are taxis and drive-yourselves. And best of all, if you are lucky, as I was, there is the car-plus-company of Mrs. Gertrude Protain, executive secretary of the Grenada Tourist Board. In her charm and helpfulness, knowledge and enthusiasm, Mrs. Protain is no less an asset of her island than St. George's Harbor or Grand Anse Beach.

Whatever your conveyance and company, north and east of St. George's you will soon be out of the tourist world. Hotels are gone. Tourists are gone. In their places are mountain and valleys, and the islanders living largely as they have for centuries past. There are groves of nutmeg and other spices, and the mills that process them. There are plantations of cocoa, mile upon mile.

Here and there are indications of the "New Grenada" that in time will move up from its southwestern foothold. Near the island's northeastern tip, at Levera Beach, a Canadian realty firm is engaged in an ambitious project of hotel and home development. In the adjacent town of Sauteurs is a fine new school that would do credit to any stateside community; but around it is the old, unchanged island world of goats and chickens and shacks and immemorial poverty.

The future seems distant here, the past very close. It is in the name of

Terrace dining overlooking the harbor of St. George's on the island of Grenada

the town itself, for Sauteurs means Leapers; and the Leapers were a band of Carib Indians who, back in 1652, chose to plunge to death from a nearby cliff, rather than submit to the French colonial forces that were besieging them.

All is quiet now at this cliff on the northern coast of the island. The last of the Caribs have long since vanished, and the realtors and hoteliers are yet to come. There is only gray rock, green growth, bright beach, blue water—and across the water, gleaming in sunlight, the serried islands of the Grenadines.

Make no mistake about it: the jets will come to Grenada. More ships, hotels and tourists will come, and presently it will become part of the mainline. What is all to the good economically may, of course, seem something quite else again to the escape-minded traveler. But let him not wholly despair, just yet. It will take more than a quick infusion of "progress" to banish the songs from the jail, the toy boats from the harbor, and the grinning dolphins from the sea.

—*J. R. Ullman*

Instant facts

Location: Southernmost of the Windward Islands, Grenada lies 90 miles due north of Trinidad.

Population: About 90,000.

Capital: St. George's.

Nationality: Independent state in association with Great Britain.

Language: English. A French-English patois, interlaced with a few African and Carib phrases, is still spoken in some parts of the island.

Currency: The East Caribbean (same as West Indian) dollar, worth 60¢ U.S., 4/2 in sterling, 64¢ Canadian.

Documentation: International certificate of vaccination required. Passport required by all except U.S., Canadian and U.K. citizens with alternate proof of identity.

Climate & Clothes: Average temperature 80°. Naturally air-conditioned by the trade winds. Cool summer clothing, but the ladies might find a light sweater welcome in the evenings from January to May. Sportswear is very popular, although feminine visitors are advised not to wear short shorts in town.

Food: Continental specialties and Creole dishes found almost everywhere. A great local delicacy is nutmeg jelly.

Geography: 21 miles long, 12 miles wide—120 sq. miles of lushly forested mountains and idyllic beaches.

History: Discovered in 1498 by Columbus. A company of London settlers arrived in 1609, but the Carib Indians were so inhospitable the settlement was abandoned within a year. The Caribs successfully discouraged further attempts at settlement until the French purchased the island from the Indians for knives, hatchets, beads and two bottles of brandy. During the Carib uprising of 1652, the remnants of the Indian band leaped from a cliff into the sea. During the dynastic wars of Britain and France, the island changed hands several times, and was finally ceded to England in 1783.

Who flies here

There are no direct flights from major international cities but the following islands connect with Grenada:

Barbados: BWIA, Caribair, LIAT. Round trip: $32; 17-day excursion $22.

Trinidad: BWIA, Caribair. Round trip: $29–$48; 17-day excursion $18.

Tobago: BWIA. Round trip: $29–$48.

San Juan: BWIA, Caribair. Round trip: $152–$222; 17-day excursion $97.

Island transportation

Self-drive cars are available for about $7 a day upon presentation of a driver's license. For those who prefer to let someone else cope with Grenada's hilly terrain and left-handed roads, local drivers offer tours at moderate rates, particularly when there are three or four persons in a car. These tours usually include a knowledgeable dissertation on Grenada's many fruit and spice trees.

Around Grenada

By far the most spectacular mode of arrival in Grenada is by boat. St. George's, a town of picture-postcard beauty, curves around the end of a winding bay and comes into view as your boat tacks in from the sea. At the harbor entrance you will sail under the guns of **Fort St. George,** built by the French in 1705 and now serving as the police barracks. The town has spread up and over its peninsula and from the sea there is a fine view of the Grenadian architecture, which seems to be about half French provincial and half country English.

As in many of the other islands, the bricks used in the older buildings came to the island as ballast and they have kept remarkably well their hues of rose, sienna and ochre.

High on a hill overlooking the downtown section is **Government House,** a stately colonial mansion with a broad veranda. The Botanical Gardens will be a treat for those interested in the many unusual and colorful trees and flowers of the Caribbean.

A tunnel, built almost 75 years ago, joins the part of St. George's known as **Carenage Town** with Bay Town, over the hill. Also on the hill are the photogenic Roman Catholic Church with its brightly colorful interior, the Scotch Presbyterian Church and its view of Bay Town through the branches of a brilliant flamboyant tree, and the Anglican Church whose walls tell the history of Grenada through a series of engraved memorial tablets.

A drive around the island makes a pleasant day's tour with a stop for a picnic lunch at the Tourist Board's Picnic House at Levera Beach. The road skirts the coast and the first small towns encountered are Concord and Gouyave where it becomes immediately obvious why Grenada is called The Spice Isle of the West.

Concord is a receiving depot for nutmeg and mace while **Gouyave** has a nutmeg factory which you can visit and where pretty Grenadian girls are busy cracking and sorting the seeds. Next comes **Sauteurs,** where Caribs' Leap offers a grim reminder of that warlike tribe of aboriginal Indians who chose death rather than surrender to the French in 1652.

Driving from Sauteurs to Grenville on the Atlantic side of the island you will pass **Levera Beach** which has a protected swimming area from which the wild breakers of the open sea can be seen but not experienced. Still farther on are **Lake Levera** and **Lake Antoine,** both nestling in craters of the now-extinct volcanos whose eruptions formed the island eons ago. Continuing around the island after a look at the colorful Grenville markets, the mountains recede and the land becomes flat grazing country. On the south coast, between Westerhall Bay and Chemin Bay, is **Westerhall Point,** an ambitious project for land development. On the southwest tip of Grenada is **Point Saline** with its unique view from the lighthouse of the point where the Atlantic joins the Caribbean: on one side is a dramatic, sparkling, slate-black beach of volcanic sand; on the other is the brilliantly bright white coral sand beach called **Grand Anse,** known to beach buffs as one of the world's greatest.

From Point Saline it is but a brief drive along this stretch of beautiful beach back to the town of St. George's. Another interesting tour can be enjoyed on the way to **Pearls Airport.** It is the road across the island from St. George's to Grenville which climbs 2,000 feet to the mountain ridge which forms the backbone of the island and winds through the cool highlands past **Grand Etang,** another crater lake.

If time permits, take the side road which leads to magnificent **Annandale Falls.** The area around Grand Etang is a forest reserve and bird sanctuary where you may see wild pigeons and mountain doves.

Sports

Quite naturally, sports in Grenada center around the magnificent waters which surround the island and which are world-famous for brilliant clarity and color. At beautiful Grand Anse Beach, changing facilities are available at the Flamboyant Beach Bar and Morne Rouge Beach Club for a dollar entrance fee.

Game fishing is excellent in Caribbean waters: marlin, wahoo, dolphin, tuna and kingfish abound. A fully equipped twin diesel Sportfisherman with an experienced skipper is available for charter for either full ($80) or half day ($45). Refreshments are served on board without charge.

Grenada is the home of one of the Caribbean's newest and largest fleet of **charter boats,** with a number of well-equipped, skillfully staffed sailing yachts of varying designs and capacities available.

These yachts can be chartered for daysailing in Grenadian waters or for longer cruises up through the lovely Grenadine Islands to the Windward and Leeward Islands and the Virgin Islands. Rates average about $15 per person for a day-long trip around Grenada's coastline. Longer cruises are available through the Grenada Yacht Services, P.O. Box 183, St. George's (Tel: 2508 or 2883); "Island Yachts," also of St. George's; or Windward Island Tours, 172 Park St., Montclair, N. J.

Sailfish, cozily suited for one or two persons, are also rented by the hour ($3), half day ($10) or full day ($15). A three-lesson sailing course is offered for $15.

Grand Anse Bay is a superb spot for **water skiing,** as more and more people are finding out. There is a special beginners' course with a well-qualified instructor and the available equipment includes standard, slalom, trick, shoe and children's skis as well as a disc. The beginners' course of six lessons costs $25 and skiing rates start at $3 for 7½ min.

Some of Grenada's most exciting sightseeing is from the water and a special **cruise** oriented toward photographers has been arranged which, for a rewarding 1½ hrs., goes past Grand Anse Beach and Fort George, then into Carenage and the Yacht Marina, past the old quarter of St. George's and finally back to Grand Anse Bay. The price is $3 per person.

The perfect way to end a day in Grenada is a 1½-hour cocktail cruise in romantic Caribbean waters. Drinks are included in the $8 price.

Skindiving and **spearfishing** are just beginning to come into their own and Grenada is right in the swing of things with rental masks, fins, snorkels and spearguns, as well as experienced guides, at $4 per person. If that isn't quite your line, you can see the same reefs from a slightly different angle via glass-bottom boats on a 1½-hour cruise, $3 per person. There are innumerable varieties of tropical fish and coral.

Other beach equipment, rented by the hour, includes two-seater Pedalos ($2), sets of masks and fins (50¢) and beach floats ($1). To arrange for fishing, sailing, water skiing, skindiving or cruising, Grenada Water Sports is located in the center of Grand Anse Beach (Tel: 4239, Ext. 191) or arrangements can be made with them through your hotel.

Shopping buys

Fashionable imports and colorful souvenirs are featured side-by-side in St. George's dozen or so stores. In Bond (duty free) goods are available only at Y. de Lima Ltd., though the Spice Island Talent Shop carries In Bond liquor. Good buys range from the more sophisticated merchandise—Liberty of London fabrics, Pringle of Scotland, French perfumes, Royal Holland pewter, Omega and Tissot watches and other international name brands—to island souvenirs, such as spice samples arranged in bamboo gift baskets, in fish-net bags or in baskets held by West Indian dolls. Spices, of course, are a must on visiting housewives' shopping lists.

At Dinah's Originals you will find a large assortment of batik and Calypso print dresses, shirts, blouses, skirts, bikinis and swimsuits. Dinah can also whip up an original creation in just a few hours, for delivery to your hotel or ship.

Dining—and thereafter

Nutmeg Bar & Restaurant: The Carenage, St. George's. Good dining, pleasant atmosphere. Tel: 2018.

Rocky's Terrace Bar: The Carenage, St. George's. Chinese food featured. Tel: 2352.

Franco's: The Shopping Center, St. George's. Delicious ice cream. Tel: 2194.

Nick's: The shopping center, St. George's. Air-conditioned haven for thirsty shoppers. Tel: 2368.

Dolphin Club: Grand Anse, near leading hotels. Grenada's only night spot! Terrace and dance floor overlook the sea. Informal dining from 8:30 P.M. on vine-covered patio. Small menu offers steaks, chicken, hamburgers or sandwiches. Italian night on Wednesday. Dancing till 1:30 A.M., closing time around 3 A.M.

During the season it is necessary to make reservations for dinner. There are restaurants in most hotels.

Holidays and festivals

New Year Fiesta: Yacht Club Dinghy Regatta and horse racing. January 1–2.

Carnival: A week or so of pageantry—Calypso, steel band processions, floats and parades, masked balls. Officially begins the Monday before Ash Wednesday with the opening celebration, "J'our Ouvert," at 6 A.M. February 26.

Statehood Day: March 3.

Easter Monday and Tuesday: Yacht Club Inter-Island Regatta, horse racing. April 15–16.

Labour Day: Street processions. May 1.

Whit Monday: Yacht Club festivities. June 4.

Corpus Christi: Religious processions. June 13.

Queen's Birthday: Military parades, honor awards. June 8.

Emancipation Day: Carriacou Yacht Regatta, horse racing. August 5–6.

Remembrance Day: Church parades. November 10.

Boxing Day: Continuation of Christmas Day festivities. December 26.

Meet the Grenadians

Organization	Official	Phone
Amateur Athletic & Cycling Assn.	C. Francis	2225
Cricket Assn.	R. Robinson	2371
Rifle Club	A. Fakoory	2680 or 2459
Table Tennis	J. A. C. Steele	2486
Lawn Tennis	D. A. Renwick	2049 or 2031
Grenada Yacht Services	R. Petersen	2508
Grenada Water Sports	M. Snare	4239
Netball Assn.	Mrs. M. David	2399 or 2406
Amateur Basketball Assn.	M. Scipio	2087
Football Assn.	G. Renwick	5-253 or 2479
Golf Club	C. E. Hughes	2455 or 2000
Physical Culture Club	T. M. Bedeau	2500
Grenada Racing Co.	A. Creft	7-531
Grenada Yacht Club	R. Smith	4-225 or 2022
Water Skiing	M. Matthias	4-219
Ambulance Brigade	J. Dumont	2244
Ambulance Assn.	Miss L. Commissiong	2789 or 2031
Chamber of Commerce	D. M. B. Cromwell	2020

Organization	Official	Phone
Junior Chamber of Commerce	E. Ross	2635
Lions Club	J. Dabreo	2393
Nat'l Youth Council	N. Barriteau	7-212
Red Cross Society	Mrs. I. Thompson	2330
Council of Women	Mrs. U. Sylvester	2450
Y.W.C.A.	Miss P. Osbourne	2122 or 2111
Anti-T.B. Assn.	E. Gittens	2340 or 2070
Mental Health Assn.	Mrs. U. Sylvester	2450
Boys Brigade	G. A. Southwell	2389 or 2225
Police Boys Club	Corp. C. Bartholomew	2244
Duke of Edinburgh's Award Scheme	E. M. A. Welch	2768 or 2225
British Medical Assn.	Dr. E. P. Friday	2263 or 2051
Nurses Assn.	Mrs. W. Robertson	2082 or 2051
Police Welfare Assn.	Sgt. J. Robinson	2244
Civil Service Assn.	R. Noel	5-213 or 2271
Grenada Teachers' Union	A. Abraham	2280
Family Planning Assn.	Mrs. M. Pressey	2560 or 2100
Assn. of Masters and Mistresses (Secondary Schools)	H. D. Baptiste	2642 or 2092
Grenada Law Society	H. E. L. Hosten	2437
Alliance Francaise	Mrs. M. Hughes	2455
Arts Council	Miss M. Blundell	5-258 or 2451
Inter-Church Council	Miss D. Hopkin	2275 or 2345
Veterans' Assn.	G. Solomon	2621
Blind Welfare Assn.	Mrs. S. Neckles	2014
R.S.P.C.A.	Mrs. S. Renwick	2323
Employers' Federation	D. M. B. Cromwell	2020

Real estate and retirement

While land costs have gone up in recent years, it is still possible to settle in Grenada on less than a royal pension. Married couples can probably manage on $360 a month, a single person on $240. Visitors eager to settle on Grenada are better off renting a house for several months to see how they acclimate to the peace and quiet. Real estate agents in St. George's who can be of help include:

Donovan & Associates
Grand Anse
Tel: 4-327

A. N. Hughes & Sons
Halifax St.
Tel: 2426

L. C. J. Thomas
Grenville St.
Tel: 2335

F. J. Archibald
Melville St.
Tel: 2028

M. A. Bullen & Sons
Halifax St.
Tel: 2114

J. Pitt
Old Fort Rd.
Tel: 2039

Lots may be purchased at prices ranging from 22¢–54¢ a sq. foot (about $3,000–$6,000 a half acre), depending on terrain and location. While it is no longer possible to snap up beachfront property for a few beads and trinkets, lovely hillside property can be bought for about $3,600 a half acre. Non-British citizens must obtain permission from the government before purchasing any land.

There are a number of new developments, the most well established being at Westerhall Point, a privately owned peninsula a little over a mile long and averaging 200 yards wide. Westerhall has five beaches, its own yacht club and promises future privacy (no hotels, not more than 80–100 houses). Lots range in size from 20,000 sq. feet to two acres and cost 25¢–60¢ a sq. foot, with water, electricity, phone service and an adequate road available. Inquiries may be addressed to the managing director, B. Willcox, at The Carenage, St. George's (Tel: 2746). Other developments are the Levera Beach Development, P. O. Box 230, St. George's and Mt. Alexander Estate, St. Patrick's (Tel: 3-240).

Moving to Grenada is a costly venture, though $2,100 worth of household goods can be brought in without duty (cars not included). Taxes, too, are pretty steep but full-time domestic help is only $15–$24 a month. Most food is imported and, as a result, more expensive and available in less variety and varying degrees of freshness.

Commerce and industry

Although tourism is becoming a major factor in Grenada's economy, agriculture is still of chief importance. Major export crops are cocoa, nutmeg (with its co-product, mace) and bananas, while sugar cane and coconut are consumed locally. There are more small landowners here than anywhere else in the West Indies, and a small fishing industry that could profit from expansion.

The government offers concessions to new industries and hotels interested in establishing in Grenada. Detailed outlines of these incentives and other information on business opportunities can be obtained from the Grenada Tourist Board and the Grenada Chamber of Commerce.

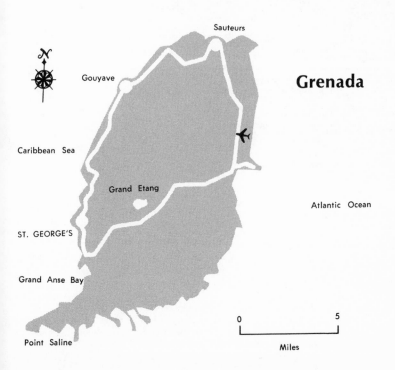

WHERE TO STAY — In Grenada

	Plan	Dec. 15-April 14 U. S. Currency		April 15-Dec. 14	
		Double	Single	Double	Single
BLUE HORIZONS Grand Anse (12 Apts.) **(b)**	(EP)	$18	$13	$12	-$ 8
THE CALABASH L'Anse Aux Epines (Ctgs.) **(b)**	(AP)	$60 (Dec. 1-Apr. 15)	$40	(Rental) $51–60 a week (Apr. 16-Nov. 30)	
CRESCENT INN Belmont-Grand Anse (12 Rms.)	(AP) (MAP)	$18–30 $16–26	$10–18 $10–16	$14–24 $12–22	$ 8–14 $ 8–12
GREEN GABLES GUEST HOUSE St. George's (14 Rms.)	(AP) (MAP)	$12–13 $11	$ 6 $ 6	$12–13 $11	$ 6 $ 6
GRENADA BEACH St. George's (60 Rms.) **(b)**	(MAP)	$55	$45	$30	$16
ISLANDER St. George's (28 Rms.)	(AP)	$40	$25	$30	$20
RIVIERA Grand Anse Beach (20 Rms.) **(b)**	(AP)	$52	$35(MAP) (EP)	$25 $13	$15 $ 8
ROSS POINT INN St. George's (12 Rms.) **(b)**		$35	$20	$21	$12
ST. JAMES St. George's (21 Rms.)	(AP) (MAP) (EP)	$18–20 $14–16 $8–10	$10–11 $8–9 $5–6	$18–20 $14–16 $8–10	$10–11 $8–9 $5–6
SILVER SANDS Grand Anse (20 Rms.) **(b)**	(MAP)	$25–42	$15–28	$21	$12
SPICE ISLAND INN Grand Anse (20 Rms.) **(b)**	(AP) (MAP)	$60	$45	$36 $32	$21 $19

LEGEND FOR HOTEL LISTINGS: (AP) American Plan (room and 3 meals); **MAP)** Modified American Plan (room, breakfast and dinner); **(CP)** Continental Plan (room and breakfast); **(EP)** European Plan (room only). All rates quoted on a per-day basis and subject to change. Confirmed reservations at specific rates desired are always recommended.

HOTEL FACILITIES: (b) beach; **(p)** pool; **(t)** tennis; **(g)** golf.

THE GRENADINES

Many old Caribbean hands consider the isles of the Grenadines the nearest thing to paradise the world has to offer. On countless isolated beaches the only sounds are the scuttling of a crab and the splash of a pelican diving into the blue-green reef waters.

A cruise through the "somewhere else" islands

Cooking, seaborne housekeeping and coddling her menfolk were Joan Georgeson's specialties. Not navigation. Her rule of thumb for that was "By the time you get there you're somewhere else."

It occurred to me that this could be said of not a few human activities. A somewhat depressing thought. But there was no depressant in Joan's "somewhere else," for we were cruising the Grenadines, where one "else" is as good as another. Indeed, the whole of them are the very essence of Elsewhere—a miniature world beyond the world, tiny, secret and lost.

I had come to Grenada, southernmost of the Windwards, and my following stop would be at St. Vincent, the next big island to the north. There is, peculiarly, no direct plane service between them. If you insist on flying, it has to be along two legs of a triangle by way of Barbados.

I didn't insist. As far as I was concerned, all planes could be given back to the Wright Brothers. What I wanted was to sail to St. Vincent; for sailing meant the in-between Grenadines, and I had had eye and heart on them for a long time.

Only a handful of cruise ships ply these far-out islands, and these pass through quickly, with few stops. Commercial motor-sailers out of St. George's (Grenada) and Kingstown (St. Vincent) rarely go the whole length of the chain; and besides, their accommodations are better designed for goats, chickens and bananas than for *homo sapiens*. This leaves charter yachts, and it was a yacht I was after. I had decided that on my second morning in Grenada I would start shopping around.

I didn't have to. At my first night's dinner at Spice Island Inn, I had no sooner told my host, Alan Krassner, of my plans than he went off across the terrace. A few minutes later he was back with Fred and Joan Georgeson. They were the proprietors of the 36-foot Bermuda cutter *Alano*. They were taking off two days later for a week's sail to St. Vincent. They already had one passenger signed on but could accommodate another. Was I interested? Foolish question.

The word yacht has an expensive sound, and I had been leery of that part of it. But the tariff seemed to me not too lethal. It was then $35 a day, covering everything except drinks and smokes, which would be at free-port

A fishing sloop in Caribbean waters

prices. This, I discovered, is the generally standard cost for one person on a yacht of any size in the Caribbean, provided all berths on the craft are filled.

The next day I met my fellow charter. (For obscure reasons, hirers of yachts are called charters, not charter*ers*.) His name, in full panoply, was Alexander Fitzmaurice MacLaren, which soon, welcomely, became Maurice, pronounced Morris; he was a Canadian from Barrie, Ontario, in flight from skies, skates and chilblains. Though a frequent visitor to the West Indies, he had never deep-sea sailed before, and was as pleased at the prospect ahead as—well, as I was.

St. George's small boat harbor is an up-to-date place, with all manner of maritime and marina facilities provided by Grenada Yacht Services. It is also a busy place, for Grenada is the southern terminus of the traditional Caribbean yacht run, of which St. Thomas, in the U. S. Virgins, is the northern end and Antigua's English Harbour the midpoint. Berthed and anchored around us, as we prepared to put off, were craft of many sizes and designs. And of many nationalities too: American, Canadian, English, French, German. There was even a Chinese junk, but its flag was the Union Jack.

Then came *the moment*. Lines were loosened and coiled, the engine hummed, and *Alano* moved out into the main harbor of St. George's. At any time it is one of the loveliest harbors of the West Indies: deep, steep-rimmed, with the town tiering high above it, and around the town green hills and headlands. But now, in the blue and gold of early morning it was more beautiful than ever . . . or perhaps it only seemed so in that magical time of setting sail.

The town receded, vanished, but not the land. We would be in sight of land of one sort or another through the whole trip; and now, during the first morning, it was the long western coast of Grenada. This is the leeward coast. The island's mountainous spine blocks and deflects the northeast trade winds, and in the resultant semicalm we had to use engine as well as sail.

"I hate the damn thing," said Fred Georgeson, a true sail-sailor. But he conceded that without it we'd be getting nowhere fast.

Fred, in his late fifties, was an expert yachtsman but, interestingly, not a long-time one. He and wife Joan, married for more than thirty years, had for most of them lived a strictly landlocked life in their native California. All along, however, they had dreamed of becoming seaborne, and eventually, when he was fifty, Fred found himself able to turn dream into fact. Going to England, he had *Alano* built to his long-planned specifications. He studied seamanship and navigation. For two years thereafter he and Joan cruised the Mediterranean; then alone together crossed the Atlantic to the West Indies.

Now, for five years past, the Caribbean had been home. More specifically, *Alano* had been home, for they had none ashore. When "charters" appeared, they chartered. When they didn't, they cruised on their own or lay over in island harbors. Was it the good life they had dreamt of? Mostly yes, they agreed. Now and then they felt a certain loneliness and rootlessness. Keeping *Alano* shipshape could be hard dirty work, and sometimes its tiny dimensions seemed confining. But beyond these were always the wide and wondrous dimensions of sea and islands. They were free to roam them . . . Yes, on balance, life was good.

Toward noon of that first day we passed the northern tip of Grenada. The trade wind, now unobstructed, hit us, and with engine off we moved on mainsail, staysail and jib. *Alano* heeled. The sea hissed and gurgled on our leeward gunnel. Ahead were the Grenadines.

Overall there are hundreds of them—if you count reefs, rocks and bumps —stretching for 75 miles between Grenada and St. Vincent. Only a quarter of them, however, are true islands; and of these a mere dozen-odd are inhabited, with a total population of about 14,000, mostly Negro. Politically their southern sector is controlled by Grenada, the northern by St. Vincent. But politics and such seem as remote as Mars (remoter, for here there are no spaceships) as you push out into their wild blue yonder.

First, with Grenada astern, came the islands called Ronde and Diamond, the latter better known to fame as Kick-em-Jenny. There are two theories as to how it got this name. One is that early British seamen performed linguistic mayhem on its original French name, *Cai-qui-Gene* (cay that give trouble); the other simply that the winds around it give it a kick like a mule. Either way, it is less an island than a towering rock, designed strictly for sea birds, or perhaps a maritime pillar saint.

North of Jenny came several miles of open water and then Carriacou, our first-day destination. This is the largest of the Grenadines, both in area (13 sq. miles) and population (7,000), and in its metropolis of Hillsborough boasts one of the few settlements in the islands that could be called a town. We did not go straight there, however, but anchored in a nearby cove, sheltered and deserted, called Tyrell Bay.

Then followed what was to become our standard evening routine: a swim over the side in limpid waters; drinks; dinner (served by Joan in the cockpit); moon and star watching; then sleep. Joan and Fred slept by choice in the roomy cockpit under an awning, Maurice MacLaren and I in the cabin below. In the morning, the sun and we rose simultaneously. Maurice took a pre-breakfast dip, while Fred and I made snide comments about hardy north-woodsmen. And soon we were off to Hillsborough.

I've called it a town, but let's change that to village. There was one scraggly street, two rows of houses, and one hotel, no less, The Mermaid Tavern. Lord of the Manor here is J. Linton Rigg, widely known yachtsman and yachting writer, whose career has spanned oceans and continents, but who now, in his bachelor sixties, has chosen remote Carriacou as his home. In 1965 he organized a midsummer sailing regatta which brought a whole fleet of visitors to its usually quiet waters. But the rest of the time he has The Mermaid largely to himself.

Inland from Hillsborough, Carriacou has two notable features: a modern well-equipped hospital and an astonishing network of roads. The roads were built long ago when the French owned the island, as an aid in moving guns around to ward off British intruders; and now they provide more than ample service to Carriacou's 32 (at last count) cars. Roundabout them, between the steep hills, grow the cotton, corn and limes that are the island's main crops.

In Hillsborough's bay is a small patch of land called Sand Cay, where we had fine snorkeling over coral sea gardens. And in this area, too, there are "tree-climbing" oysters, which cling to the roots of mangrove trees in shallow waters. Here, however, this oyster-lover met with his one major frustration of the trip. My companions were less bivalve-minded than I. Time was pressing. (Yes, even in the Grenadines.) My next oysters would be Cape Cods in Boston, two weeks later.

Boston! It was almost impossible to visualize it, in that warm, still, shining realm that cradled us. Or San Juan either, with its tall towers, its traffic, its crowds. The churning slam-bang world of cities and nations was lost beyond far horizons. What was real was sky and sea and castled islands, and sunlight glinting on the silver wings of flying fish.

Off to the east, past Carriacou, was Petit Martinique, known for boat building, fishing and—*sotto voce*—smuggling. But we sailed on, close-hauled into the wind, toward Union Island. Like Carriacou, it is a big one, as Grenadines go, with two towns called Clifton and Ashton and two small hotels. We didn't go ashore, however, preferring to savor the beauty around us from a marvelous anchorage in Chatham Bay. The most mountainous of the Grenadines, topped by sharp spires and soaring ridges, Union has often been likened to Moorea, in French Polynesia. I myself cannot go quite all the way. For me, nothing matches Moorea, except possibly nearby Bora Bora. Until these two are moved to the Caribbean, however, Union will do quite nicely.

During the whole of our cruise the only shapes in the sky were clouds and sea birds. Until we reached Bequia, practically on St. Vincent's doorstep, the only ships we saw, and these always at a distance, were small trading schooners and a few yachts like our own.

If we had been "far-out" all along, we were soon to be farther. From Union we cruised northward, past the large low-lying island of Mayero and then east to The Tobago Cays. These consist of four uninhabited islets, plus a great network of sub-islets, shoals and sandspits sweeping out to an ultimate rim called, appropriately, World's End Reef. And here we dropped our hook in the very heart of Elsewhere.

Fred, however, was a prudent sailor. Mooring *Alano* in a safe deep-water channel between two of the larger islets, we used its dinghy for the

Grenadines

ST. VINCENT

BEQUIA

CANNOUAN

MAYERO

UNION

MUSTIQUE

Caribbean Sea

PALM   TOBAGO CAYS

RONDE

CARRIACOU

Atlantic Ocean

GRENADA

exploration of the labyrinth. And what a labyrinth it was! There was blue water, green water, white water. There were dark rocks and shining beaches, and behind the beaches green ramparts against a sun-drenched sky. Amid the green gleamed the bright blossoms of frangipani; on the beaches were scuttling crabs, darting iguanas; in the air, flights of pelicans, now cruising placidly, now plunging vertically into the crystal sea.

We too plunged, though less professionally, and floated face-down in our masks above sunken seascapes. Begging crabs' and iguanas' pardon, we took over the beaches. And in the evening, from *Alano's* cockpit we watched a sunset to end all sunsets over the spires of distant Union. Then came night, but not darkness, for the stars blazed, the moon was full. Beneath them, the beaches around us gleamed like floodlit stages, and it seemed that in their stillness, at any moment, a ghostly ballet would begin. . . . Of crabs and iguanas, perhaps. Or of long-dead pirates. Or mermaids.

It was not easy to leave those Tobago Cays. Even the anchor seemed reluctant to come up. But come it did, and off we went toward Bequia, northernmost of the Grenadines. Again Mayero floated past; then two other large islands, Cannouan and Mustique. These, by repute, are the "depressed area" of the chain, whose inhabitants were long held in virtual serfdom by absentee owners, and who even now live in stark poverty. Much of the land, however, has recently changed hands. As on other islands, there is talk of hotels, resorts, airstrips; and when they come, presumably—and hopefully— the condition of the people will be bettered.

Like all paradises, the paradise of the Grenadines is flawed. But it was hard to credit it as *Alano* surged on through a flawless world of sea and space. We took our tricks at the wheel, lay sunning ourselves on the deck, or clung to the bowsprit in showers of spray. Quickly, seemingly from nowhere, came other showers, a torrent of rain; then as quickly vanished, and in their place was a rainbow. (I have never seen such rainbows as in these islands.) Presently a school of dolphins picked us up and frolicked with us almost to the entrance of Bequia's Admiralty Bay.

Bequia—pronounced Beckwee—lies only nine miles from St. Vincent. It is by far the most visited of the Grenadines; and whereas at our other anchorages we had been totally alone, here we were surrounded by a small fleet of other yachts. Soon, too, we had a bigger neighbor, as the Norwegian cruise ship *Meteor* appeared and put a hundred-odd passengers ashore for a few hours' visit.

Bequia's town-village, Port Elizabeth, is no bigger than Hillsborough; its roads are not up to Carriacou's. But otherwise it is several miles, or years, ahead of its sister islands. It has two small but first-rate hotels: the middle-aged Sunny Caribbee, also known as the Bequia Beach, close to town on Admiralty Bay, and the brand new Friendship Bay, two short but hilly miles across the island. It has several attractive resort homes. (One was the winter haven of Anthony Eden, Lord Avon, until he suffered a heart attack and moved to Barbados, with its better medical facilities.) And it has Princess Margaret Beach (yes, she too has been here), one of the prize strands of the Caribbean.

Based on *Alano*, we lived an amphibious life between shore and harbor, and in the latter we were very much in the world of yachtsmen. It is a very special world, both tight and broad, provincial and cosmopolitan. Everyone talked sailing shop. Everyone knew everyone else: from Newport, Cowes, Bermuda, Gibraltar, the Canaries. And everyone, including his grandparents and grandchildren, seemed to have crossed the Atlantic in a catboat.

Ashore it was cosmopolitan, too. There were British, Canadians, Americans, Europeans: some there for a day, some for a week, some hoping to stay for the rest of their lives. There were Thomas and Gladys Johnston, escapees from New York and Chicago, who have built a home in which one of the rooms is a ledge on a cliff. There was St. Vincentian Noel Agard, who after the rigors of building his Friendship Bay Hotel, was hoping to reverse the trend by vacationing in New York or Chicago. There were old-line Bequians who are among the few small-boat, hand-harpoon whalers left in the world. And there was the middle-aged lady, also Bequian and looking very "native," whom I met in a palm grove beside a beach.

"Would you like to buy this land?" she asked me.

"Well—" A few blinks. "Do you own it?" I asked.

"Yes."

I looked around. "And live here?"

"No, I'm just visiting. I live in Brooklyn now."

"Oh."

"Where do you live?" She asked.

"Boston."

She nodded. "My son lives in Boston," she said. "He's getting his M.D. next June at B. U."

"Somewhere Else" was fading, the rest of the world coming back.

—*J. R. Ullman*

Instant facts

Location: A chain of about 600 islets, stretching for 60 miles from northeast to southwest between St. Vincent and Grenada.

Population: About 14,000.

Capital: None.

Nationality: The northern half is administered by St. Vincent, the southern by Grenada.

Language: English.

Currency: East Caribbean (same as West Indian) dollar—60¢ U. S., 64¢ Canadian and 4s 2d sterling.

Climate & Clothes: Temperatures average 80°–85°. June to December is the unofficial rainy season but the sun usually makes an appearance every day of the year. The Grenadines are not in the normal hurricane belt. Wear what you will.

Geography: The islands are either a few sq. miles in area or, in some cases, a rocky bump in the sea. Largest of the islands is Carriacou—7 miles long, 2 miles wide and 13 sq. miles in total land area.

Palm Island

One of the gems of the Grenadines long rejoiced in the name of Prune Island until a kindly benefactor-developer changed the Prune to Palm, a change rather more in keeping with the whisper of the trade winds.

Prune or Palm, this small island (half a mile long by a quarter of a mile wide) midway in the chain of the Grenadines is as well endowed as any tropical isle can be. There are four white coral sand beaches, and its western strand, Casuarina Beach, is said to be the finest in the area. Palm is surrounded on its north, east and south sides by offshore coral reefs and the view of some 12 nearby islands and islets—all three to four miles distant— makes a splendid scenic panorama.

Until recently, Palm Island was admired and enjoyed mainly by passing yachtsmen, and a herd of wild goats which ate the young palm trees planted in a beautification program.

The planter of the trees, John Caldwell, is an author and owner-skipper of the 45-foot ketch *Outward Bound,* well known in the islands. Caldwell's hobby is planting trees on the treeless beaches of the Windward Islands, but the goats of Palm, formerly Prune, were eating the trees as fast as he planted them. Caldwell offered to rent the island for a year from the government of St. Vincent, which administers the island, get rid of the goats, plant it extensively in trees and turn it back to the government for development.

The government suggested Caldwell be the developer, with the government as a $12^1/_2\%$ shareholder. Caldwell obtained the island on a 99-year lease and set about readying it for paying guests.

The first ten rooms of the 20-room cottage-style Palm Island Beach Club opened early this year. The design is West Indian, with the duplex cottages grouped village-style around a central garden.

Palm also offers a 1,500-foot-long private airstrip, with members of local Aero Clubs welcome to fly in.

Plans are to have a private plane connecting with Sun Jet flights into St. Lucia to enable guests to reach Palm Island within five hours after leaving New York.

WHERE TO STAY — In the Grenadines

	Plan	Dec. 15-April 14		April 15-Dec. 14	
		U. S. Currency			
		Double	Single	Double	Single
ADAMS **Union Island (b)**		$14	$ 8	$14	$ 8
FRANGIPANI **Bequia (b)**	(AP)	$19–21	$11–12	$15–16	$ 9–10
FRIENDSHIP BAY **Bequia (b)**	(AP)	$25	$15	$18	$ 9
PALM ISLAND BEACH CLUB **Palm Island (20 Rms.) (b)**		Rates on request			
SUNNY CARIBEE **Bequia (9 Rms.) (b)**	(MAP)	$18–20	$14–15	$14–16	$11–12
SUNNY GRENADINES **Union Island (b)**		$16	$ 9	$16	$ 9

LEGEND FOR HOTEL LISTINGS: (AP) American Plan (room and 3 meals); **MAP)** Modified American Plan (room, breakfast and dinner); **(CP)** Continental Plan (room and breakfast); **(EP)** European Plan (room only). All rates quoted on a per-day basis and subject to change. Confirmed reservations at specific rates desired are always recommended.

HOTEL FACILITIES: (b) beach; **(p)** pool; **(t)** tennis; **(g)** golf.

GUADELOUPE

The butterfly-shaped island of Guadeloupe combines the Caribbean complement of beautiful beaches and soaring mountains with an ambience all its own. As a Department of France, it is very Gallic in its customs, its outlook and, like its sister island of Martinique, is an outpost of French gastronomy.

Vive la différence

President de Gaulle should be told about a subversive operator in the French island of Guadeloupe. His name will here be given as Monsieur X, and by profession he is a maître d'hôtel.

Monsier X is French, very French. But he is also international, for he has spent many years working in foreign lands. When I first met him, he was maître d' at one of the top American hotels in the Caribbean.

Now, on second meeting, he was on vacation in Guadeloupe. Ostensibly he was on vacation. Privately, and with dedication, he was on a mission that, if successful, could shake the very foundations of *la république.*

"Zese Guadeloupiens," he told me in his finest Franglish, "zey are good cooks, we French have taught zem zat. But ze serveece! *Mon dieu,* ze serveece! Zey know nozzing. And I tell zem zat. I have many friends in hotels here, and I tell zem, 'You want ze business, yes? You want ze American tourist business. But you will never get it if you do not learn ze serveece— *le service moderne et international.'* "

Opening his briefcase, Monsieur X produced a book. "I show zem zis," he said. "I read it to zem in French. I read it to zem all, so zey will understand how a meal should be served."

He handed me the book, and as I held it I could hear the bones of Escoffier and César Ritz rattling in their graves. It was a *Manual of Table Service* issued by the School of Hotel Administration of Cornell University.

No, I don't think it likely that there will be another Fall of France. Even less likely is a fall of Guadeloupe or its sister island of Martinique, for, if anything, they are more French than France itself.

For one thing, the old colonial families are still well entrenched, and highly conservative. The run of French officialdom, sent over from the homeland, is conservative, too. Further, the status of the island has in recent years been changed from that of colonies to *départments,* or integral states, of the Republic. While once-imperial Britain has allowed its West Indian domains to move ever farther, in some cases all the way, toward independence, France has assiduously tied hers more and more closely to *la patrie.*

Both Guadeloupe and Martinique, to be sure, feel to a degree the climate of the times. There are partisans of independence, sporadic rumblings from the left, and it is hard to prophesy what the long-range future will bring. Politically, that is. But not otherwise. In their culture, their ambience, the ways of thinking, doing, being, Guadeloupiens and Martiniquaises are totally French, and neither Monsieur X's subversive campaign nor anyone else's is going to effect a major revolution.

This extreme "Frenchness," I would say, is both good and not-so-good. For the islanders themselves it provides a strong sense of identity and security, but it also shuts them off to a large degree from the more open and cosmopolitan societies of the Caribbean community. For the visitor it presents a marvelous change of atmosphere from the British, Dutch and Spanish-American islands—a sample of France itself on our continental doorstep.

The number-one practical problem is language. For there is far less English spoken than in France itself, and unless your high school French is still usable you are going to have problems. Even in the hotels there is apt to be only one linguist on the staff, and if he or she is not on duty, it's either *parlez vous* or *sauve qui peut*.

Further, there is a problem beyond practicalities: the subtle, personal problem of a stranger in a strange land who feels cut off from all around him. And the situation becomes worse if he feels that those around him like things just that way. This is not to imply that French West Indians are surly or unfriendly people. Far from it. But they are provincial. They live in a tight and closed society. They are not used to spreading the welcome mat for outsiders, and are not quite sure that they want to.

In Tahiti, another chip of France in the tropic seas, there used to be a joke that the motto of the *Bureau du Tourisme* was "Don't bother coming. Just send your money." And there have been those with rather the same impression of the French Antilles. As a result, the flow of American tourists has thus far been largely limited to cruise boat passengers, who sightsee, shop and move on in a few hours, without really leaving their own shipboard world. Those who come for a week, a month, or more have been few and far between.

This is slowly changing. The jet has come, the ranging traveler has come: to Guadeloupe and Martinique as to elsewhere. And waiting to greet him is a new and growing breed of islander who knows that the old "closed corporation" is no longer either desirable or possible. On both islands, fine new hotels have opened, with more to come. More locals dealing with tourists are becoming bilingual. Who knows? One day (but don't count on it) a maître d' may even read his staff the riot act from the Service Manual of the Cornell Hotel School.

Thus far we have been considering both Guadeloupe and Martinique, for in general terms they are very much peas in a pod. Coming now to par-

Hotel La Caravelle on the island of Guadeloupe

ticulars, however, we shall focus only on the former, for each *has* its own particulars, its own special ingredients.

To begin at the beginning, then: Guadeloupe was discovered by Columbus. There followed the usual extermination of the Carib Indians; later the usual alarums and excursions between British and French. But the British, though they won their share of battles, never took a truly firm hold on the island, and France has now been in total possession for 150 years.

Lying between the British islands of Antigua and Dominica—with Martinique beyond Dominica—Guadeloupe is, next to Trinidad, the largest of the lesser Antilles. The vast majority of its almost 300,000 people are Negro. But, the French being easier-going about such things, there has been far more racial mixing than in the British domains, and the resultant crossbreed is one of the happier products of the Caribbean melting pot.

Also, the island itself is immensely attractive—beginning with its overall shape, which is that of a butterfly. Actually, the two wings are different islands, separated by a narrow strait called the Rivière Salée, or Salt River; and each has its own name, Grande-Terre and Basse-Terre. The French they are a funny race, however, and the names are exactly the reverse of what they should be. Grande-Terre, meaning Great Land, is the smaller of the two and comparatively low-lying, while Basse-Terre, meaning Low Land, is larger and steeply mountainous.

Guadeloupe's principal city, Pointe-à-Pitre, is at the heart of the butterfly, on the Grande-Terre side of the Rivière Salée. And it *is* a city, not merely a town, of about 60,000 inhabitants. Unlike almost all the rest of the island(s), it is not very attractive: a place of crowds and noise and slums and industrial suburbs. But it is active and vital. Its sea front and airports hum. Its markets teem. Among the jerry-built shacks and decaying 19th-century houses are rising modern office buildings, schools, housing developments, even a midget skyscraper or two.

Of recommendable activities in Pointe-à-Pitre, girl-watching is one of the best. Black, white or *café-au-lait*, its young women run to the pretty, the formful, the chic. They have likely bought their clothing for a few francs at the counters of the *Prisunic* (the supermarket); but like their overseas cousins on the Champs Elysées, they wear them as if they had emerged from Dior or Balmain.

Then of course there is eating. *Mon dieu*, such eating! Basically and classically French, the cuisine is richly supplemented by Creole island specialties, notably seafood. (A small, succulent clam, the *palourde*, is, to my taste, the last word in shellfish.)

And the menus, to my surprise, were as varied and tempting as along the boulevards of Paris. One major problem is the virtual impossibility of avoiding two full multicourse meals a day: a regimen that in the tropics leaves you barely able to move or breathe. Another, perhaps, is the nonobservance of the codes of the Cornell Hotel School. But there are compensations galore. (Among them, no tipping.)

Out of Pointe-à-Pitre and on into Grande-Terre, one is almost immediately in agricultural country. Here sugar is king, and the undulating miles are clothed with cane fields. Now and then, however, the land undergoes a change. Small hills close in. In place of cane are slopes of grass and forest, blossoming trees and bubbling streams, and one moves through a miniature Land of Oz sort of country, tiny, trim and emerald green.

Along the south shore of Grande-Terre are Guadeloupe's best beaches, white and gleaming, and at its far-eastern end, called Pointe des Chateaux, is one of the prime "sights" of the island. The "chateaus" here are not man-made. They are castles of nature, huge towers of rock carved by wind and sea; and against them, in an eternal boil of foam and breaker, beat the waters of the open Atlantic.

The other wing of the Guadeloupien butterfly, though called Basse-Terre, is the high island. Indeed, its interior is simply one long mountain range, culminating in the volcano Soufrière, 4,800 feet high.

Soufrière is quiescent but not dead. One of the most spectacular roads in the West Indies curls up through dense rain forest to within a short distance of its summit, and from there, if ambition dictates, you can climb up among the steaming vents of its rugged cone. Should the skies be clear, you will have a view of Guadeloupe and its surrounding seas that will knock your eye out. But no weather guarantee is issued, for a peak like Soufrière manufactures its own cloud and rain.

As Caribbean roads go, Guadeloupe's are among the best. To the north of Soufrière a brand-new one, cutting across the spine of Basse-Terre, is a gem of both engineering and scenery; and the older one that circles the island's rim provides a half-day (fast) or full-day (slow) drive of marvelous beauty and variety. Here on the steeper ground there are fewer cane fields than on Grande-Terre; in their place stand tall tiers of banana groves. Half-way down the eastern shore, one comes—inevitably, as on almost every island—to the site of Columbus' first landing. Farther on, from Basse-Terre's southern tip, there is a view across the sparkling (usually) sea to the Iles des Saintes.

These Isles of the Saints are Guadeloupe's most attractive satellites. Small, green and hilly, they are only a few miles from the "mainland" (which is what Guadeloupiens call their big butterfly), but also as "far-out" and primitive as any escapist could wish. They can be reached by ferry-launch, or more comfortably—and expensively—by chartered sailboat, and few Carib islands can match them for loveliness and peace.

Ironically, back in 1782 their offshore waters were the scene of one of the greatest naval engagements between French and British: the decisive battle of the Saints, in which Admiral Rodney defeated and captured Admiral de Grasse. But today, where cannon once roared, there is only the soft lapping of the wavelets and the occasional cry of a sea bird.

Augmenting natural beauties, the people of the Saints are also interesting. On one of the two main islands, Terre de Bas (Lowland), they are almost all Negro. But on the other, Terre de Haut (Highland), they are predominantly white—a tight, deeply inbred community, running to tall big-boned blondes, descended from migrant Breton and Norman fishermen of centuries back. Uniquely among the islanders, they weave, and wear, wide parasol-like straw hats that from a distance make them look like Oriental coolies.

Besides the Saints, Guadeloupe has other outliers, of which the largest are Marie-Galante and La Désirade. But these are strictly sugar islands, with few attractions for visitors. Much farther off, the French sector of St. Martin (shared with the Dutch) and the pinpoint of St. Barthélemy (St. Barts) are also politically administered by Guadeloupe, but geographically and touristically are no part of it at all.

Near Basse-Terre's southern point, on the west coast, is Guadeloupe's second city, also called Basse-Terre. Strangely, this, and not larger, centrally located Pointe-à-Pitre, is the island capital. And it is a quieter, cleaner and more provincial place than the metropolis on the Rivière Salée.

North of it, fronting the Caribbean for some 20 miles, Basse-Terre's

Guadeloupe

western shore offers some of the finest and wildest of West Indian scenery. It is a region of bluffs and headlands, deep bays and jungled valleys, and the road, now high, now low, curves through it like one of the *corniches* of the French Riviera. There are, however, no Cannes, Nice and Monte Carlo along the way, for this is primitive, sparsely settled country. The few settlements are largely fishing villages, and close by them one sees long swathes of brightly colored nets drying on the beaches. The beaches themselves are darker than those of Grande-Terre: beige to brown rather than creamy white. But they have a wild, almost forlorn beauty that holds the eye and stirs the heart.

Grand-Terre, Basse-Terre, all around the butterfly. And again and again the prospect changes. I would say that, of all the charms of Guadeloupe, the most pervasive and appealing is its almost limitless variety.

Until very recently, few outsiders experienced it. Except for cruise passengers, who rarely got farther than Pointe-à-Pitre, the island was not catering to the tourist trade, and even the basic matters of where to sleep and eat were major problems. Now at last, however, that situation has changed. There are as yet, *a la bonheur*, no "Gold Coasts" or "Hotel Rows," as in, say, San Juan or Montego Bay. But there are a few scattered establishments as good as any in the Caribbean.

Two are of the order of what the French called *de grand luxe*. These are the Fort Royal, in the northwest corner of Basse-Terre, and the Caravelle, on the south shore of Grande-Terre, both of which are big, elegant, and equipped with all the appurtenances of a top-flight resort. The food at both runs from excellent to superb. (But this would seem to be the case everywhere on the island, where I did not once have a substandard meal.)

The only possible drawback shared by Fort Royal and Caravelle is that they are a long way from town, each other, and almost anywhere else.

Straight *de luxe*, without the added *grand*, are the smaller Auberge de la Vielle Tour and La Pergola de Gosier both on Grande-Terre's south coast. On the other hand, the veteran Grand Hotel in town is, despite its name, not grand at all, a place for visiting businessmen rather than pleasure-bound tourists.

Even the tiny Iles des Saintes have their hotel. This is the Fort Joséphine, a mainhouse-with-bungalows affair on a tinier-than-tiny islet consisting only of a hilltop (with a glorious view) across a bay from Terre de Haut. In contrast, back on the "mainland" of eastern Grande-Terre, is what will be, when completed, the largest establishment in Guadeloupe. Called Les Alizés (The Trade Winds), it is the project of a French Canadian syndicate, and will include hotel, cottages, and an adjacent real estate development.

We are late in mentioning the French Canadians. For a long time they have been the backbone of the slim tourist trade of Guadeloupe and Martinique. For the French French, even in the jet age, the islands are far away. For English-speakers, as noted, there is the language problem.

But, as noted too, things are changing.

Hoteliers, businessmen and the Tourist Board are actively out after the American trade. To British West Indian Airways, Air France and Pan American, the airlines serving Guadeloupe, there has now been added Caribair, based in Puerto Rico, and it has ambitious plans for sales and promotion. The Manual of Table Service of the Cornell Hotel School may not yet be required reading in the island schools. But a new generation is at least learning that to be true citizens of *Les Antilles Francaises*, they do not necessarily have to live in padlocked isolation.

To end with a question: As of right now, in its present stage of development, would I recommend Guadeloupe to American vacationers?

My answer is that if you speak even a little French, absolutely yes. If you speak no French but like a bit of challenge, yes, too. If you speak no French, and prefer the easy, the familiar, the everything-as-usual in your resorts—then my answer is no, not yet, wait a bit. In a few years, for better or worse (and it will be both), the French islands will be totally girded for the North American tide.

Meanwhile, for my money, *vive la différence!*

—*J. R. Ullman*

Instant facts

Location: 310 miles southeast of Puerto Rico, 500 miles northeast of Venezuela.

Population: 310,000, including the dependencies.

Capital: Basse-Terre.

Nationality: Overseas department of France. Guadeloupe has several island dependencies, including Désirade, Marie Galante, Les Saintes, St. Barts and the French half of St. Martin.

Language: French.

Currency: New Franc, 20¢ U.S.

Documentation: International certificate of vaccination. Passport required by all except French nationals, U.S. and Canadian citizens who hold alternate proof of identity. U.S. and Canadian citizens staying longer than 10 days require a passport, plus a visa for stays of over three months.

Climate & Clothes: Temperatures average 77°–86° in coastal areas, 66°–81° inland, with year round trade winds. There are three "seasons": "Carême" (Lent)—mild and dry, from the end of February to April; "Hivernage" (rainy season)—warm and wet, from July to October; and a relatively cool season from November to February. Summer clothing is appropriate throughout the year.

Food: Excellent! Most restaurants serve French cuisine, modified over the years by the use of local fruits, vegetables and seasonings. Many of the smaller, more out-of-the-way restaurants serve creole cookery.

Geography: Guadeloupe, a total of 532 sq. miles, is really two islands, separated by a narrow sea water channel, Rivière Salée. Its shape resembles a butterfly. The highest of the two is, ironically, Basse-Terre (meaning "lowland") while Grand Terre (or "great land") is indeed, the smaller. Unlike Grande-Terre, with its rolling hills, Basse-Terre to the west is a rugged, mountainous island, dominated by the volcano of La Soufrière (4,812 ft.).

History: Columbus discovered Guadeloupe on his second voyage in 1493 and gave it the name it bears to this day. Two early attempts to colonize were unsuccessful and the island was abandoned to the Caribs in the beginning of the 17th Century after the Spanish had failed in their attempts to subdue the warlike

Indians. The French came along in 1635 and for the next 80 years, like so many other Caribbean islands, it went back and forth between the English and the French. It finally became French forever at the Treaty of Waterloo and received departmental status in 1946.

Who flies here

Direct flights to the International Airport of Le Raizet, five minutes from Pointe-à-Pitre, are available from the following cities:

New York: Air France, Pan Am. Round trip: $251–$344; 17-day excursion $161–$227.

Miami: Pan Am. Round trip: $200–$266; 17-day excursion $138–$195.

Paris: Air France. Round trip: $669–$931 (3305–4600 francs).

San Juan: Air France, BWIA, Pan Am, Caribair. Round trip: $86–$128; 17-day excursion $63–$80.

Island transportation

Thanks to the relatively new road, hacked out of the jungles of Basse-Terre's mountains, driving through Guadeloupe is no longer much of a strain. To further facilitate getting around on your own, all major intersections have signs and here, unlike in the neighboring British isles, driving is on the right. Visitors may use hometown licenses for a short time or, better yet, international permits. **Self-drive** cars rent for about $9–$12 a day ($8–$10 if rented by the week), 7¢ a kilometer extra, and are available in Pointe-à-Pitre through:

Hertz (Caribcars S.A.R.L.)
26 rue Vieux-Bourg (Abymes)
Tel: 351

Guadeloupe-Cars
rue Hincelin Assainissement
Tel: 1094

Garage Narcisse
41 fbg. Alexandre Isaac
Tel: 654

Marie-Gabrielle
21 rue Alexandre Isaac
Tel: 538

For those who don't object to less luxurious seating and tooth-rattling speed, there are numerous **buses** going from one end of the island to the other at moderate prices. Cars can be hired with a chauffeur, both for **tours** and transport around the island, from the following Pointe-à-Pitre agencies:

Maurice Bellon Tours
B.P. 331
Tel: 634

Entreprise Marie-Gabrielle
2 rue Alexandre Isaac
Tel: 538

Taxis can be hired at the entrance of the dock, Place de la Victoire, and Le Raizet Airport.

Places of interest

One of the prettiest drives on the island is from Point-à-Pitre to Basse-Terre, across the drawbridge connecting the two sectors. Some of the sites you will see are:

Square Sainte-Marie (Capesterre): Where Columbus is supposed to have disembarked in 1493 after discovering Désirade and Marie-Galante. A statue of the famous navigator marks the spot.

Trois Rivières: Site of a large rock covered with drawings by the pre-Columbian Carib Indians, and other Carib relics.

Fort Richepanse: A well-preserved castle in Basse-Terre, built in 1647 and resting place of early generals and governors.

Not to be missed is a trip to **La Soufrière.** Basse-Terre's new road leads, without too much interruption, to a parking area near the summit of this volcano, presently dormant but constantly emitting clouds of steam, sulphurous gases and boiling water. Ambitious hikers may walk to the very top and cross the moist crater floors, now overgrown with vegetation. Starting points for this trip are Basse-Terre and Saint-Claude and the ride takes one through the dense tropic growth of the Bains Jaunes forest. For those who shun cars altogether, arrangements to climb the volcano can be made through the Mountain Climbing Club in Basse-Terre.

In Gosier (Grande-Terre) the **Fleur d'Epée Castle**, an 18th-century fortification, is now open to the public as a museum with prints, documents, coins and other mementos of Guadeloupe history.

The sporting life

Guadeloupe **beaches** come in living color—white, orange or black—depending on the type of rock surrounding them. If you visit Moule Beach (that's Mussel Beach in French), on the east coast of Grande-Terre, you may come across some bleached bones lying on the sand: there was once a cemetery nearby and the changing face of the coastline has exposed it to the sea.

Other excellent beaches on Grande-Terre are St. Anne and Gosier on the south. On the west coast, at Grand Cul de Sac Marin, are the beautiful beaches of Anse-Bertrand and Port Louis—highly recommended for the underwater fisherman.

Boats can be chartered at the Yacht Club, in Pointe-à-Pitre; at Le Mouillage, Bas du Fort or, easier still, through your hotel. Besides volcano climbing, other Guadeloupe sports include tennis, fishing (arrangements can be made through your hotel) and bicycling.

Best shopping buys

French luxury items (perfumes, wines, brandies and the like) are what attract most tourists to the bustling narrow streets of Pointe-à-Pitre. Purchases are duty free if brought directly from store to airplane but, as in France itself, prices are high. Customs here is very casual—declaration is entirely oral. In addition to shops carrying French merchandise and a few selling jewelry, there are a number of boutiques catering exclusively either to madame or monsieur. Among local products, the native dolls top the list.

Dining, dancing and night life

As for the national sport of eating, this too is expensive. At one of the better hotels, a full dinner for two, with wine, will easily top $20. Advice: Forget the tab and enjoy it. Forget the calories, too.

The following restaurants are recommended:

Au Poisson D'or: Port-Louis. Tel: 22.

Au Tonneau D'or: Gosier. Orchestra, nightclub. Tel: 70.

Aux Raisins Clairs: Saint-Francois. Tel: 19.

Les Bambous Du Rivage: Sainte-Anne. Tel: 17.

Le Boukarou: Gosier. Orchestra, nightclub. Tel: 37.

La Bourgeoise: 13 rue A. René-Boisneuf, Pointe-à-Pitre. Tel: 400.

Caravelle: Sainte Anne. Orchestra, nightclub. Tel: 1400 (Pointe-à-Pitre).

Chez Mariepan (formerly La Tortue) Gosier. Orchestra, nightclub. Tel: 72.

Chez Paul: Saint-Claude (Matouba). Tel: 21.41.77.

La Creole: Gosier. Tel: 34.

El Dorado: 32 rue Sadi Carnot, Pointe-à-Pitre. Tel: 322.

Folies Plage: Anse-Bertand. Tel: 17.

Grand' Anse Hotel: Trois-Rivières. Tel: 47.

Grand Gousier: Gosier.

La Halte du Bas du Fort: Route du Gosier. Tel: 651- P-à-P.

Luna Roc: Gosier (Saint-Félix). Orchestra, nightclub. Tel: 47.

Le Mabouya: Baillif (Madeleine). Orchestra, nightclub. Tel: 21.17.25.

L'oasis (Chez Beauvais): Corner, rues Nozières and A. René-Boisneuf. Tel: 270.

L'oiseau Des Iles-Madras: Pointe-à-Pitre (Raizet). Tel: 11.67.

La Pergola: Gosier. Tel: 14.03.

Le Robinson: Basse-Terre. Tel: 21.11.52.

La Rocade: Sainte-Rose. Orchestra, nightclub. Tel: 40.

Vieille Tour: Gosier. Tel: 14.04.

Le Zombi: Basse-Terre (Rivière des Pères). Nightclub, orchestra. Tel: 21.17.50.

In addition to nightclubs in some of the above restaurants, **La Cocoteraie** in Gosier (Poucette) has shows, dance music.

Civic and social organizations

Organization	Address	Phone
BASSE-TERRE		
Chamber of Commerce and Industry	45 rue du Dr. Cabre	21.16.56
Consul General	Palais du Conseil Général	21.11.25
Syndicat d'Initiative	45 rue du Dr. Cabre	21.16.56
Banana Growers Assn.	16 rue Baudot	21.13.30
Notaries Assn.	rue Baudot	21.16.04
Préfecture		21.15.60
POINTE-A-PITRE		
Sous-Préfecture	Place de la Victoire	1100
Chamber of Commerce and Industry	5 Square de la Banque	115
Junior Chamber of Commerce	B. P. 505	
French Red Cross	2 rue Victor Hugues	1221
Tourist Office	Immeuble S/Préfecture	930
Syndicat d'Initiative	28 rue Sadi-Carnot	72
Producers & Exporters of Sugar and Rum	11 rue Schoelcher	762, 763
Medical Assn.	Place de la Victorie	166
Bar Assn.	37 bis r. A. Grégoire	1454
Druggists Assn.	48 rue Frebault	231
Architects Assn.	35 rue Boisneuf	1310
Family Planning Center	106 rue Schoelcher	1712
War Veterans' Assn.	11 rue Victor Hugues	
Free French Assn.	31 rue de Nozières	1204
P. O. W. Assn.	Recette Principale Douanes Quai Lefèvre	144

Industry and real estate

The economy of Guadeloupe remains to a large extent agricultural. Most vital segments are the production of sugar cane (with its popular by-product, rum) and bananas, though much of the island's banana crop was damaged by hurricane winds in 1966. Meanwhile, public authorities encourage investment in industry and hotels, and liberal laws have been instituted to attract promoters. A very thorough booklet, entitled (with customary Gallic verbosity) "Financial and Tax Benefits Available on Industrial and Hotel Investments," is available from the Industrial Development Board (Tel: 21.15.60).

Projects currently being considered include a cement works and mining facilities. Almost 600 hotel rooms have been built and many seaside cottages are in the last stages of construction. Other improvements on the island include modernization of the harbor and channel, a boon for Guadeloupe's important fishing fleet as well as for attracting cruise ship traffic; the new road cutting through Basse-Terre; and the restoration of Basse-Terre's historic old fort.

There are no restrictions on aliens settling here, though there is some French red tape. Islanders are somewhat phlegmatic about promoting real estate. We recommend inquiring at the French Government Tourist Office, 610 Fifth Ave., N.Y., N.Y. 10020. Prices are still fairly low as a big building boom has not yet hit the island.

Désirade

Guadeloupe's outpost to the east is the flat-topped island of Désirade. Cotton is the chief crop on its 10 square miles and the natives are fishermen who bring their catch in by sloop to Pointe-à-Pitre in Guadeloupe.

Désirade's chief distinction is that it was the first land sighted by Columbus as he sailed into the New World on his second voyage in 1493. There is a small French leper colony in the eastern end of the island.

Marie-Galante

Marie-Galante, the largest of Guadeloupe's island dependencies, is quite undeveloped and owned in large part by well-to-do Guadeloupiens. It lies 25 miles from the Basse-Terre wing of the Guadeloupian butterfly and has a population of about 30,000.

There is a fairly good shore road that makes an almost perfect circle around the island and a protected beach at Grand Bourg, the chief town. The people raise a high grade of cotton and also sugar, which they distill into rum.

The Hotel de la Concorde rises gracefully to all demands on its kitchen with good food served in the French manner.

Iles des Saintes

The Iles des Saintes are tiny French satellites of that very French island, Guadeloupe. They are usually visited on a day's excursion from the mother island, but such is their unusual charm that they will well repay a longer stay.

Les Saintes are lovely islands lying six miles south of the Basse-Terre coast of Guadeloupe. They are easily accessible by boat leaving daily from Trois-Rivières on the "mainland," although the crossing is apt to be choppy with a generous amount of spray. But if the sea is calm, the trip to **Terre de Haut** (Highland), one of the two larger Saintes, takes less than two hours.

The village on Terre de Haut very nicely lives up to that overworked word, charming. The houses are brightened by red or blue doorways and the single street follows the curve of the harbor. There are balconies and Victorian gingerbread embellishments and a little town square and small bistros. There is even the touch of the eccentric in a large house, built in the shape of a steamship, jutting out of a rock cliff.

The real surprise of Terre de Haut is the people. Largely descended from Norman and Breton stock, they are fair-skinned, blue-eyed and often blond. Many of them have preferred inbreeding to intermarriage.

Almost a trademark of Les Saintes are the curious, Oriental-styled straw hats worn by the men of the islands. The hats, called *salacos*, are made of split bamboo with fine white cloth stretched tightly over the frame. They offer protection from the sun and give the *Saintois* a look all their own.

The other chief *ile* of the Saintes is **Terre de Bas** (Lowland) where the people are almost all pure Negroes. Intermarriage has been rare, although Terre de Haut and Terre de Bas are so close together.

The men of Les Saintes are renowned as seamen. Fishing is the chief occupation, officially, and the unofficial occupation is smuggling. The islands abound in good swimming beaches and interesting places to stop for a picnic. For longer stays, there are a small hostelry in Terre de Haut and a small cottage resort on another Sainte, Ilet à Cabris. This is the Hotel du Fort Joséphine under the direction of Marie Petrelluzzi of the justly famed La Pergola in Guadeloupe.

WHERE TO STAY — In Guadeloupe

		Dec. 15-April 14		April 15-Dec. 14	
		U. S. Currency			
	Plan	Double	Single	Double	Single
AUBERGE DE LA VIEILLE TOUR (45 Rms.) **(b, p)**	(MAP)	$42–44	$30–32	$26–30	$18–20
CARAVELLE Sainte-Anne (112 Rms.) **(b, p)**	(MAP)	$52–56	$38	$36–40	$24

FORT ROYAL **Deshaies** (100 Rms.) **(b, p, t)**	(MAP)	$50–60	$36–42	$32–38	$21–24
GRAND **Pointe-a-Pitre** (65 Rms.)	(MAP)	$20–32	$13–24	$18–28	$12–22
LES ALIZES **Le Moule** (128 Rms.) **(b)**	(MAP)	$40	$34	$24	$19
FORT JOSEPHINE **Iles des Saintes** (8 Ctgs.)	(EP)	On Request		$10	$10

LEGEND FOR HOTEL LISTINGS: (AP) American Plan (room and 3 meals); **MAP)** Modified American Plan (room, breakfast and dinner); **(CP)** Continental Plan (room and breakfast); **(EP)** European Plan (room only). All rates quoted on a per-day basis and subject to change. Confirmed reservations at specific rates desired are always recommended.
HOTEL FACILITIES: (b) beach; **(p)** pool; **(t)** tennis; **(g)** golf.

GUYANA

In Georgetown, Guyana's capital city, the streets are wide and shaded and many of the buildings are in the comfortably opulent style of the 19th century. In the country's interior, dugout canoes are still the favored means of transportation on jungle rivers and jaguar is hunted in the forests.

Safari country

On the northeast coast of the South American continent, Guayana (formerly British Guiana) is a land of superlatives. It has the largest of this, the rarest of that and a culture and a way of life in sharp contrast to the American scene.

It is not, as of now, to be confused with the great tourist meccas of the Caribbean—luxury hotels do not rear up around every bend and the beaches are not dotted with striped umbrellas. But tourism is a coming thing. British Overseas Airways Corp. (BOAC) is building a 100-room resort hotel overlooking the Atlantic, the Demerara River and Georgetown, with the opening date scheduled for the latter part of 1968. Hotel Tower, on Main Street, is adding a modern wing and numerous other hotel projects are in the making. In the meantime, Guyana has much to offer those seeking a bit of the offbeat, the uncommon.

The people of Guyana are of varied origin: African, East Indian, British, Portuguese, Chinese and Amerindian, with a considerable degree of mixture between the races. The largest segment of the population is East Indian, descendants of indentured workers brought from India in the latter half of the 19th century. The second largest ethnic group is African in origin.

GEORGETOWN, the capital, is called the "Garden City" and also basks under the unofficial title of The Best Laid Out City in the Caribbean. The reasons for this pleasant state of affairs are both historical and geographical.

The city lies by the Atlantic Ocean on the right bank of the Demerara River estuary. Early Dutch settlers chose the site for a fort to guard settlements upriver, and in time it grew into a sizable trading port. The city is laid out in a rectangular pattern, with the streets meeting at right angles. This followed logically, since the land is flat and because the old sugar estates were built from the river or sea coast inward as long rectangles. The same pattern remained when they became part of the town.

Many of the old canals, built by the Dutch, have been filled in to form tree-lined avenues, pleasant for strolling. A nice bonus from the historical and the geographical.

Georgetown also boasts some of the finest Gothic architecture in the

A masterpiece of gingerbread architecture,
Georgetown's City Hall on the island of Guyana

Caribbean. There is St. George's Cathedral, dedicated in 1892 and the tallest wooden building in the world, with a 132-foot spire. Happily, it is beautifully maintained. City Hall, another wooden structure, is an exceptionally handsome piece of colonial architecture. Painted powder blue, it also enjoys a fine state of preservation.

Inland trips

Most visitors who come to Guyana will want to see something of the interior with its vast upland savannahs, rain forest jungles and endless variety of birds and animals. The open savannahs of the south stretch for miles— here is cattle country, rodeos, Indian tribes (friendly) and a feeling of limitless space.

The dense forests provide a natural haunt for tropical birds, the toucan and the macaw, and wild orchids grow everywhere. GAME HUNTERS (and camera enthusiasts) will find the interior ideally suited to safaris. The jaguar (largest tree climbing cat in the world), the capyhara (world's largest rodent), the fleet-footed deer and numerous wild ducks all make Guayana their home.

FISHERMEN can have a try for the Arapaima, the largest fresh-water fish in the world. The Tourist Officer will arrange for hunting and fishing guides, and prices are reasonable.

In addition, there is creek swimming, rowing, horseback riding, mountain climbing and visits to numerous Amerindian settlements where life is lived much as it was centuries ago.

The most famous and spectacular sight of the interior highlands is KAIETEUR FALLS, five times the height of Niagara Falls and with a sheer drop of 741 feet. On the Potaro River, amidst dense jungle, the grandeur of the Kaieteur bursts on the viewer with startling beauty. A curtain of mist sparkles in the sun and a permanent rainbow hovers over the falls like a protective arch. Enhancing the natural beauty of the falls is the cola-colored water, which glistens in topaz and amber hues.

The Kaieteur can be reached by charter plane which lands on the POTARO RIVER above the falls, or by overland (and overnight) trek by jeep and by foot. Plans are underway to build a landing strip and guest house near the falls to further open up the area to visitors.

Visitors who want to extend their exploration into the interior must be prepared for a bit of roughing it. Facilities, such as guest houses, are adequate but still on the primitive side. But if you are not irrevocably chairbound to the 20th century the natural beauty and splendor of the land will far outweigh the lack of luxury.

Instant facts

Location: On the northeastern shoulder of South America, bordered by Surinam to the east, Brazil to the south, Venezuela to the west and the Atlantic Ocean.
Population: 675,000.
Capital: Georgetown.

Nationality: Formerly British Guiana, Guyana is now an independent nation.

Language: English.

Currency: Guyana dollar—60¢ U.S., 64¢ Canadian and 4s 2d sterling.

Documentation: International certificate of vaccination required. Passport required by all except U.S. and Canadian citizens holding proof of identity or roundtrip ticket.

Climate & Clothes: The climate varies considerably from region to region. The low coast land, site of the capital city, Georgetown, is cooled by the North-East Trades from the Atlantic, with temperatures ranging about 80°. The rainy season is mid-April to mid-August. In the interior the dry season is from October to March when nights are clear, winds cool and conditions pleasant. The rainy season inland can be fraught with insects. Light, informal attire in town and casual safari clothes (khakis and sport shirts for men, slacks for women) for treks into the interior regions.

Food: The country's six races have each produced its traditional foods including Indian curries, Chinese noodles, English roast beef, Portuguese garlic pork, African metemgee and Amerindian pepper pot. These can be enjoyed in any of the many restaurants.

Geography: The coastal plain, where most of the population live, is intensely cultivated, with rice and sugar cane the main crops. Inland, vast savannahs stretch away to thickly forested mountains. Four great rivers flow through Guyana—the Demerara, the Essequibo and the Berbice, which gave their names to the country's three counties, and the Corantyne which forms the border with Surinam. Guyana, in fact, is an Amerindian word meaning "Land of Many Waters." Land area: 83,000 square miles.

History: The legend of El Dorado runs through the history of the Guianas like a counterpoint to reality. To the Spanish and English explorers and adventurers of the 16th and 17th centuries the legend was reality—somewhere in that great uncharted vastness on the northeast coast of South America there existed a fabulous city of gold.

The El Dorado of legend did not exist. It was a dream city built on the exaggerations of men who had seen fool's gold shining from the rude household utensils of the Indian inhabitants and who had heard of the custom of one of the tribes of sprinkling their chiefs with gold dust at religious ceremonies. But El Dorado was the lure that opened up the region to exploration and caused the British, Spanish, Dutch and Portuguese to fight over it for centuries.

The Guiana of those days is now three countries—Surinam (formerly Dutch Guiana), Cayenne or French Guiana and the newly independent nation of Guyana, formerly British Guiana.

Guyana was discovered by Spanish sailors in 1499, but the earliest European settlement was made by the Dutch. The Dutch settlement was destroyed by Spaniards and Amerindians and by 1596 the settlers had withdrawn to *Kyk-Over-Al* ("Look-over-all") on the Essequibo River where they established a new fort.

The Dutch held Guiana, though sometimes yielding to the English, French and Portuguese, until 1796 when it was captured by a British fleet. It was restored to the Dutch in 1802 and finally ceded to Great Britain in 1814. In 1831 the area was united under the name of British Guiana, and remained under British rule until it attained independence on May 26, 1966.

Who flies here

There are direct flights to Guyana's Atkinson International Airport, located about 30 miles outside of Georgetown, from the following places:

New York: Pan Am, BWIA, KLM. Round trip: $346–$479; 17-day excursion $247–$357.

Miami: Pan Am, BWIA. Round trip: $282–$396; 17-day excursion $210–$290.

London: BOAC. Round trip: $744–$1,093.

San Juan: Pan Am, BWIA. Round trip: $208–$263; 17-day excursion $151–$204.

Barbados: BWIA. Round trip: $98–$141; 17-day excursion $57–$85.

Trinidad: BWIA, BOAC, KLM, AF, Pan

Am. Round trip: $84–$114; 17-day excursion $52–$80.

Touring Guyana

Cars can be rented at reasonable cost but it's advisable to hire a car with driver since the roads leave much to be desired. The following tour operators are recommended for car and airline (see Guyana Airways) transportation:

Sandbach Parker & Co., Ltd.
(Travel Dept.) 45-47 Water St.
Tel: 61487

Kaitur Travel Service
Tel: N.A. 2166

Guyana Travel Tours
A102 Issano Place
Bel Air Park, Tel: 61063

Louis Chung & Sons Ltd.
51/53 B Lama Ave.
Bel Air Park, Tel: 5842

Miss M. Rockliffe
343 Middle and Cummings Sts.
Georgetown, Tel: 4847

Guyana Airways Corp.
32 Main St., Georgetown
Tel: 2455

The sporting life

Hunting and fishing: See "Inland Trips." There are virtually no beach facilities in Guyana; here, rivers are the scene of most water sports. The Demerara Rowing and Aquatic Club, Ruimveldt, East Bank, Demerara offers special membership to visitors. Water skiing is a bimonthly event on the Demerara River, exact dates depending on the tide. Speed or sail boats are not readily available but can be arranged for through the Club or by contacting the Tourist Officer, Guyana Development Corp., Bank of Guyana Bldg., High St., Georgetown.

Best shopping buys

One of the fascinating sites of Georgetown is Stabroek Market where almost everything under the sun can be bought.

There are good buys in gold jewelry (raw gold can be bought and made into custom designs in 48 hours) and several stalls in the market are literally a glow of gold. Tray after tray of homemade jewelry—earrings, bracelets, necklaces, pins, rings —spill over in dime-store profusion.

Two of the best goldsmiths and jewelers in Guyana are L. Seepersaud Maraj & Sons, in the Stabroek Market, and Parmeshwar Singh at 6 First St., Alexander Village. Mr. Singh, in fact, is known as "Goldfinger" and is famous throughout the country for his delicate work in gold in both the traditional and modern styles.

Dining, dancing and night life

Night life in the capital is not raucous but rather pleasantly unobtrusive. There are a number of good combos playing here and there, both steel bands and dance bands, and there is good food in good restaurants. A prime steak can be enjoyed for as little as $1 or $2, and here may be found what is probably the only five-cent glass of soda pop extant.

Belvedere Hotel: 234 Camp St., Georgetown. Pleasant indoor setting. Nightly dancing in Calypso Tent. American and English dishes in The Hut. Open for luncheon and dinner. Saturday nights the band plays. Tel: 2871.

Brown Betty Snack Bar: Hincks St., Georgetown. Tel: 4626.

Cactus Club: 74-75 Main St., Georgetown. Poolside bar and patio. Air-cooled restaurant, elegant dining room. Indoor bar and bar lounge, dance floor. Buffet supper every Saturday night. Jukebox. Open for luncheon and dinner. Tel: 62011

Carib: 2 Liliendaal, East Coast, Demerara. Light luncheons served in open-air terrace facing the sea. Dancing, floor shows on Saturdays nights every two weeks. English, Creole and American cooking. Tel: 4644.

Farm Fresh Inn: 43 Robb St., Georgetown. English, American, Indian and Chinese dishes. Famous for filet mignon, bhoonjal curry, barbecued chicken and "chicken-in-the-rough." Air-conditioned.

Golden Lotus Night Club: Dancing to band every Saturday night. Tel: 3445.

Half-Way Inn: Supply, East Bank, Demerara. English, American, Indian and Chinese dishes.

Kool Korner: 11 Strand, New Amsterdam, Berbice. Elegant dining in pleasant surroundings. English, Chinese and American dishes. Bar and lounge, dancing Saturday nights. Tel: N.A. 91.

Moonglow: 41 Newmarket St., Georgetown. Open-air luncheon and dinner, specialty: broiled steak. Air-conditioned bar and lounge. Dancing every Saturday night. Tel: 2696.

Oasis: 64 Robb St., Georgetown. Indian and American dishes. Tel: 3520.

Palm Court: 35 Main St., Georgetown. Pleasant open-air setting. Specializing in "chicken-in-the-rough," filet mignon and barbecued steaks and chickens. Bar, dancing every Saturday night. Tel: 3026.

Penthouse: Commerce St., Georgetown. Dining, live music every Saturday night and most Friday nights. Tel: 5355.

Rendezvous: 77 Robb St., Georgetown. Favorite place for "chicken-in-the-rough." Air-conditioned restaurant. Newly opened *Rendezvous Gardens* — open-air dance floor. Tel: 5575.

Russell's: Main St., Georgetown. Restaurant.

Special events, celebrations

Pagwah: Hindu feast. March.

Eid-Ul-Azal: Celebrated in March or April. Moslem holiday.

Easter: Celebrated from April 13–15.

Labour Day: May 1.

Independence Day: May 26.

Youman Naubi: Moslem feast celebrated in June.

Commonwealth Day: First Monday in August.

Dipavali: Hindu feast celebrated in October.

Boxing Day: Continuation of Christmas celebration. December 26.

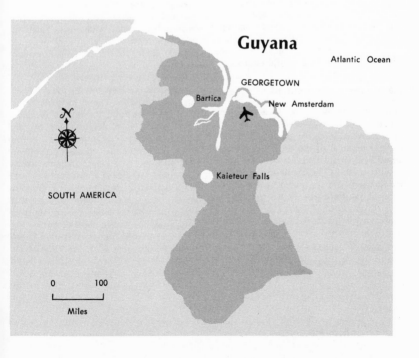

Guyana

Atlantic Ocean

GEORGETOWN

Bartica

New Amsterdam

Kaieteur Falls

SOUTH AMERICA

0   100

Miles

Flora, fauna and the dramatic arts

The **Guyana Museum of Natural History** contains some rare specimens of the fauna of the country, including the Giant Armadillo, largest and rarest of the armadillos, and the tapir, largest indigenous land mammal in Guyana. (If you don't really feel like going off into the jungle the Museum affords a tame close-up of some of the world's exotica, and museum director Mahamad Hanif is always pleased to answer questions and explain the exhibits further.)

Guyana's flora is in spectacular profusion at the **Botanic Gardens** in Georgetown where tropical flowers and trees grow over 180 acres. Among it all is the Guyanese Victoria Regina water lily, the world's largest leafed aquatic plant. The Guyana Zoo is housed in the Botanic Gardens.

The **Promenade Gardens** in Middle St., a small, park-like garden enclave, is another pleasant stop and an ideal spot to enjoy a sandwich lunch.

The **Theatre Guild of Guyana,** with its own 200-seat playhouse in Georgetown, is one of the most active dramatic groups in the area. The guild stages eight productions annually—including musicals, dance concerts and original dramatic efforts.

Real estate and retirement

Persons wishing to settle in Guyana will, on arrival, be granted permission to stay in the country for an initial period of three months. At the expiration of this period, an application for an extension, in writing, must be made to the Chief Immigration Officer, who will decide whether permission will be granted or not.

Information on real estate is available from:

Clarence H. Nelson
7 Croal St., Georgetown
Tel: 5805

Information on income tax rates can be obtained from the Inland Revenue Dept., Georgetown.

Commerce and industry

Guyana is a country rich in natural resources but poor in the capital needed to develop its vast potential. To attract the necessary capital, the government has put out the welcome mat for investors in the form of the Guyana Development Corp., charged with stimulating and facilitating economic development from mining and manufacturing to hotel building and tourism.

The country already has a healthy bauxite industry and its fertile coastal plains have made it the rice bowl of the Caribbean. But its great mineral wealth is still relatively untapped, vast stands of timber are untouched, and the door is wide open for the manufacture of consumer goods. (Guyana has been favored by nature in the matter of transportation. Four great rivers flow through the country, and its 83,000 sq. miles are crisscrossed by smaller waterways. Small air strips are dotted about the interior to further open up the land to development.)

To date, the Guyana Development Corp. has awarded concessions to over 120 enterprises, including chemical, metal, electrical, garment, food and related products, hotels, plastics, exploration for oil and other manufactures. Through the corporation, the potential investor is offered the following incentives: income tax exemption; duty-free importation of some raw materials, machinery and building materials; accelerated depreciation; tariff protection; loans; and special benefits for companies located in the interior.

Further information is contained in five booklets, available from the Guyana Development Corp., Bank of Guyana Building, High St., Georgetown, Guyana, S.A.

Meet the Guyanese

Organization	Official	Phone
Guyana Amateur & Athletic Assn.	J. A. Alexander	2375
Guyana Cricket Board	A. Abdool	3404
Guyana Cycle Union	B. Massay	5402
Guyana Basketball Assn.	H. Henry	
Guyana Football Assn.	C. Romallo	3061
Guyana Rowing and Aquatic Club	W. K. Potter	2078
Red Cross Society	Mrs. M. Douglas	5174
Tuberculosis Society	Dr. Thakre	3400
Children's Dorcas Club	Miss Ivy Franker	4761
United Sad'r Islamic Anjuman	Muhammad Zahur	5797
Sanatam Dharam Maha Sabba	Pandit Reepu Daman Persaud	3902
Girl Guides Assn.	Mrs. Muriel Wight	
Boy Scouts Assn.	L. B. Thompson	61573
Guyana Assembly of Youth	George de Peana	
Y.W.C.A.	Mrs. May Rodrigues	5160
Y.M.C.A.	Justice P. A. Cummings	61632
Friends of St. George's Cathedral	Miss W. Daniels	
Catholic Youth Organization	Miss P. Sylvester	
St. John's Ambulance Brigade	F. A. D. Cleare	61376
Theatre Guild	Pat Magalee	
Georgetown Dramatic Club	W. R. Robinson	2691
Georgetown Toastmasters' Club	G. Thompson	62011
Lions Club	John Fernandes Jr.	3211
Dental Assn.	Dr. M. I. Tallim	5435
Forest Products Assn.	P. Welshman	2520
Frontiers of America Service Club	Eric Shepherd	2696
R.S.P.C.A.	Mrs. S. Dalgleish	4237
St. Vincent de Paul Society	Albert Rodrigues	4631
Boy's Brigade	C. E. Martindale	61753
Bolivarian Society	J. A. Brown	3614
Guyana Legion	Ivelaw Miranda	4608
Society for the Blind	H. Whitley	4496
Georgetown Rotary Club	H. de Cambra	61489
National Assn. of Surinamers	C. Wright	3251
League of Coloured Peoples	Dr. C. H. Denbow	4014
Music Teachers' Assn.	Miss Lynette Dolphin	5406
Women's League of Services	Mrs. G. B. F. King	5633
Music Festival Assn.	Miss Lynette Dolphin	5406
Georgetown Jaycees	Ed. Gordon	62111
British Medical Assn.	Dr. V. Shury	5835
National History & Arts Council	Basil De Rushe	3081
Consultative Assn. of Guyanese Industries	Col. G. B. Thompson	5341
Chamber of Commerce	M. B. Gajraj	4844
Chinese Assn.	Chow-Kee	4859
Society of Medical Technologists	Ramjass Tiwari	3231
Guyana Museum	M. Hanif	4251
Tourist Committee	Insan Ali	3096
Georgetown Gardeners' Club	A. D. Thompson	2491

WHERE TO STAY — In Guyana

	Plan	Dec. 15-April 14		April 15-Dec. 14	
		U. S. Currency			
		Double	Single	Double	Single
BELVEDERE Georgetown (18 Rms.)	(EP)	$ 6–10	$ 5– 6	$ 6–10	$ 5– 6
PARK Georgetown (46 Rms.)	(AP)	$12–21	$ 7–13	$12–21	$ 7–13
PENGUIN New Amsterdam (11 Rms.)	(EP)	$9 –15	$ 5– 9	$ 9–15	$ 5– 9
TOWER Georgetown (60 Rms.) (p)	(EP)	$17–21	$12–14	$17–21	$12–14
WOODBINE Georgetown (21 Rms.)	(CP)	$11–18	$ 6–11	$11–18	$ 6–11

LEGEND FOR HOTEL LISTINGS: (AP) American Plan (room and 3 meals); **MAP)** Modified American Plan (room, breakfast and dinner); **(CP)** Continental Plan (room and breakfast); **(EP)** European Plan (room only). All rates quoted on a per-day basis and subject to change. Confirmed reservations at specific rates desired are always recommended.
HOTEL FACILITIES: (b) beach; **(p)** pool; **(t)** tennis; **(g)** golf.

Native boats at Ibo Beach, Gulf of Gonave, on the island of Haiti

HAITI

An oppressive dictatorship and pervading poverty are the everyday facts of life in Haiti. Despite these misfortunes Haiti somehow remains a vital country, rich in color and texture, rich in history, and rich in its blend of African, French and deep-down Caribbean.

Haiti: the forgotten land

Short of Cuba, the *out* place in the Caribbean these days is Haiti. In the thriving, thronging world of the West Indies, the historic Black Republic is ignored, forgotten, lost.

Apply for hotel accommodations and you will see. Elsewhere, in season, it is almost worth your life—and life savings—to get a room, but in Haiti, in or out, you can have your pick. With a cruise ship, on the other hand, you will have no pick at all, for scarcely any go there; and of the airlines, only Pan American flies in and out. As you swoop in toward landing you will see beauty and magic spread out beneath you, and perhaps wonder briefly why *everyone* doesn't come to enjoy it. But once you're down you won't be long in learning a few reasons.

The decrepit airport reeks of poverty. Smells and beggars press in on you. And from a poster on the walls the eyes of Big Brother—alias Papa Doc, alias Francois Duvalier, alias *President* à *Vie de la République*—look down on you enigmatically. Of the other eyes around, not a few are hidden by dark glasses, and you are aware that these are virtually the trademark of Papa Doc's personal police squad, the Tonton Macoutes. You think of the Haiti of Graham Greene's novel, *The Comedians.*

A casual visitor, to be sure, is in no danger. This is a dictatorship. Intrigue and violence lie close beneath the surface. But unless you yourself start intriguing (advice: don't), the violence will stay hidden. You will merely wonder about it. Just as you will wonder if your heap of a 1950 taxicab is going to make it in one piece from the airport to your hotel.

Interestingly, and rather pathetically, Haiti *wants* tourists. It wants them badly, for its economy needs every dollar—or shilling or franc or gourde (its own money)—that it can get. With this in mind, it played host in 1966 to the annual convention of the Caribbean Travel Association, and did an efficient and gracious job, with only a very few police state overtones. One of these was at a reception in the Presidential Palace. Every door and window was guarded by a soldier with rifle and bayonet. But there was a nice Caribbean touch unofficially added when, during the ceremonies, most of them dozed on their feet.

The average visitor won't be involved with such as this. But there is plenty that he can become involved in—with no hazard and much pleasure —for Haiti is many things besides a political and economic mess. To begin with, it is beautiful. Its western third of the island of Hispaniola (which it shares with the Dominican Republic) is a collage of blue mountains, green valleys, gleaming bays and sculptured headlands. It is rich in color and texture, rich in history, rich, above all, in its blend of African, French and deep-down Caribbean that make it unique in the West Indian world. In a way, its misfortunes have also been its blessing. While jet, cruise ship and Yankee dollar have imposed on most other islands a certain standardization, Haiti, the neglected stepchild, has remained fascinatingly itself.

What that self is depends partly on where you look. At first sight, as noted, there is its beauty. At second—and third and fourth—there is its poverty. Of the country's jam-packed population of almost five million (next to Cuba's the largest in the Caribbean), all but a very few live on the barest subsistence level; and the standard of education is the lowest in the islands. Home is a shack. Food is what can be scraped from the soil. But this has been going on for a long time now, and the Haitian is used to it. He finds his escape in indolence, in laughter, and in the world of spirits. More specifically, in voodoo. By official statistics, Catholicism is the dominant religion. And there are many churches and churchgoers. But beneath the facade are deep layers of ancient African superstition and ritual, which have persisted more strongly in Haiti than perhaps even in Africa itself.

Will you hear drums in the hills at night? Almost surely yes. Will you be able to see a genuine voodoo ceremony? Probably not, unless you stay around a while and make "connections." There is what might be called *pseudo-voodoo* on view everywhere, watered down for the commercial purposes of public entertainment. But the genuine article, the voodoo of barbaric fetishes, catatonic trances and animal sacrifices, is usually hidden away in rural boondock or city slum. The church, of course, takes a dim view of its practice. And so too, officially, does the government. But the latter, at least, tends to look the other way. It is Papa Doc's proud claim that he "understands" his people as does no one else, and part of that understanding is to allow them to exorcise their frustrations and miseries in the wild release of voodoo.

A long way from both voodoo and poverty are the small group of Haitian Creoles who for years have formed the country's aristocracy. Descended from long-ago French settlers, with varying admixtures of Negro blood, they identify themselves not with Africa but with France, where, over two centuries, many of them have been educated. Not a few are wealthy, the rest at least prosperous. Almost all are cultivated, multiligual, cosmopolitan, and their women have long been famous for their *café-au-lait* beauty.

In today's Haiti, however, their interlocked families have lost their former power. Duvalier's government is black-directed, black-oriented; and while it has not liquidated the Creoles, it has reduced many of them to roles of

School girls in Port-au-Prince on the island of Haiti

decorative impotence. With a Tonton Macoute behind many a bush, they don't air their true feelings. But the more enlightened among them will concede that their decline is, at least in part, their own fault. Like many aristocracies before them, they had, while in power, so little social conscience or responsibility that they virtually invited the dictatorship that shoved them aside.

Of a middle class in Haiti there is almost none. Its one-time small group of business and professional men have fled en masse to more liberal and prosperous climes, and if it's a doctor or lawyer you're in need of, you had better flee, too. The capital of Port-au-Prince, on its beauteous bay, is today a sprawling run-down city, relieved only by the ornate white Presidential Palace, a few other government buildings, and a posse of prideful statues to bygone heroes.

Yet it is part of Haiti's magic that it is not truly a depressing slum. It is too alive, too full of color, sound, smell and human juices. The Iron Market, spread over acres, selling everything under the Haitian sun, is surely one of the top sights and experiences of the Caribbean. The streets roundabout are no less full of seething life. There are beggars, yes. There are vendors and peddlers in maddening profusion and persistence. But here again is the magic. For what they are trying to sell you, as likely as not, isn't soda pop, postcards or gimcrack souvenirs—but genuine works of art.

Haiti's art explosion of recent years is now internationally known. At its top level it has produced artists of formidable talent and sophistication, known to museums and collectors throughout the world. But even the more primitive creations of grass-root and sidewalk painters brim with color and vitality. Perhaps the most impressive works on public view are the murals in, strangely, not the Catholic but the Episcopal Cathedral in Port-au-Prince. And fine collections are on exhibit, and for sale, at numerous galleries. Besides painting, much excellent wood carving is done and the prices of both are low by off-island standards.

For a long time the Haitian *ambiance* has attracted outside artists and writers, and two Americans in particular, writer Selden Rodman and the late DeWitt Peters, have helped immensely to encourage artistic talent. Since the political blight, however, artistic as well as run-of-the-mill visitors have tended to seek other pastures.

Nowhere, of course, is the decline more evident than in what has happened to the hotels. In the last several years many of the better ones have closed down, and how the rest keep going is as mysterious as voodoo. No less mysterious is that they function well. Most are attractively built, surrounded by terraces, gardens and pools, and their cuisine, a varying blend of French and Creole, ranks with the best in the Caribbean. The one thing they won't provide is much company—except on occasional party evenings when some of the more solvent local citizenry may show up.

In the Port-au-Prince area, the best-known establishment is probably

Grand Hotel Oloffson, a bizarre gingerbread museum piece that, in palmier days, was headquarters for many VIP's in the realms of art, writing and theater. Atmosphere it still has in abundance. And if your inclination is toward a beard, bare feet and beachcombing (though without a beach—just a bar), it's a likely place for you.

At the other extreme is the nearby Hotel Castelhaiti, the country's newest and largest. Built on a hillside, with a stunning view, it rises still higher on its own to a local skyscraper record of eight stories, and provides Haiti's nearest approach to a Sheraton or Hilton. Others in town are the Sans Souci and the Splendid (with no *e* on the end, despite its semi-French ancestry), both run, and run well, by Haitians, and catering largely to a local clientele.

For the rest, it's up the hill to Pétionville, Haiti's premier resort town, some seven miles inland and 1,500 feet high. Here, as in the capital, several of the old hotels have vanished. But several also remain, and they are good ones: notably El Rancho, the Villa Créole, the Choucoune and the Ibo Lélé. Of the four, El Rancho is the most luxurious and expensive. The Ibo Lélé, being the highest, is also the coolest, commanding a magnificent sweep down the hillside toward Port-au-Prince and its harbor.

This hotel was formerly operated by the late André Roosevelt, of the French branch of the Republican Roosevelts. Its present proprietors are Robert and Tamara Baussan. He is a member of one of the long-established Creole families, she an exiled White Russian (by way of Paris), and in their culture, manners and way of living, they represent the best of what is left of the old cosmopolitan Haiti. In their eyrie at Pétionville, one feels as if he is in a villa above the Côte d'Azur, rather than a few steaming miles from the clatter of Port-au-Prince.

Still higher in the hills, and almost temperate in its climate, is the smaller town of Kenscoff. Once, it too was the site of several hotels; but now they are gone, leaving only a restaurant, Le Perchoir (The Perch), boasting the definitive view-of-all-views. Beyond this, there is little for the tourists, short of distant Cap Haitien on the northern coast. Nothing, that is, except Haiti itself.

Blue mountain and green valley, rutted road and lost village, barking dogs, crowing cocks, braying donkeys, thumping drums. There are no Creoles (or Russians, or Americans) here. Black faces are everywhere. They are in the village shacks, by the dusty roadsides, on the roads themselves.

The procession may be in the direction of a market, laden with fruits, greens and squawking chickens. It may be homeward bound, carrying a few gourdes' worth of store goods. In either case, it is on the march for miles: uphill, downhill, through dust and rain and tropic sunbeat. When at ease, rural Haitians are apt to be totally at ease, and for good reason. When they work, it is in a grinding marathon of drudgery that no white man could long endure.

Even in a car, a trip through hinterland Haiti is a rugged experience.

Most visitors confine themselves to the gentler amenities of tourism. There are the good hotels, the good food, the exciting art world, and the no less exciting scenery, to be seen comfortably from a terrace with a cool drink in hand. Also, there are facilities for most warm-weather sports, including plenty of swimming pools. But the true beach-lover will find slim pickings. Though Haiti, like every tropical island, has its coastal strands, there are few of great attractiveness, and these are discouragingly far from the central resort area.

As compensation, though, there is Sand Cay. A few miles out in the bay from Port-au-Prince, this is a shallow sweep of crystal water and tiny islets, encompassing marine gardens of marvelous beauty. You go out to it by launch from the city's waterfront, and once there, have the choice of peering down through the craft's glass bottom or taking a snorkeling tour with one of the crew. Even if you have seen the other famous reefs of the Caribbean (such as Buccoo in Tobago and Buck Island off St. Croix), Sand Cay will not disappoint you; it is a miracle of life and light and shimmering color. For a while after, even the bright hues of Haitian painting will, in comparison, seem drab to your bedazzled eyes.

When the sun goes down and the moon comes up, some islands go to sleep. But not Haiti. Whether for the elusive tourist dollar or simply for its own pleasure, the nighttime island hums and hops. On any given night your own hotel may be deserted, but at least one of them (they take turns) will be swinging, with music and revelry. The most elaborate of the shows are at the Hotel Choucoune in Pétionville and the International Casino on Port-au-Prince shoreline. And the Casino—with an alleged assist from New York's Mafia—will also be happy to take care of your gambling requirements. In almost all the shows presented here and elsewhere there are over-and-undertones of voodoo, dramatically presented.

On a check list of Haiti and things Haitian, one item remains. A big item; perhaps, the biggest. Its history.

Not its recent history. Since long before Papa Doc its rulers have been a succession of petty dictators and strong men so dismally alike that it is hard to tell them apart. Not even the 20-year occupation by U.S. Marines, from 1915 to 1934, seems to have any notable effect on its cutthroat politics and depressed economy. For Haiti's days of fame and glory one has to go back to the beginning of the 19th century.

This was the time when, long before any other West Indian nation, it won its independence from Europe. It was the time of its national heroes: Toussaint L'Ouverture, Christophe, Dessalines, Pétion. Statues of them fill the squares of Port-au-Prince. Mementos of them fill the National Museum. But by far the greatest relics—among the greatest in the world—are a long way from the capital, in the mountains behind Cap Haitien. These are the two huge structures built by Christophe, alias King Henri I: the palace of Sans Souci and the fortress known both as La Ferrière and the Citadel.

Until recently they were reachable from Port-au-Prince only by a long and rough overland journey. Now, however, you can fly in less than an hour to Cap Haitien (where there is a lonely but very pleasant hotel called L'Hostellerie du Roi Christophe), and in another short hour, by taxi, you are at the gates of "Christophe country." Of Haiti's pantheon of early heroes, this illiterate giant who crowned himself king was, historically, probably the least important. But romantically he was the very model of a primitive conqueror, a real-life Emperor Jones of the tropic islands, and he built his castles to the scale of his dreams.

Approaching from the nearby town of Milot, you come first, at the head of a valley, to Sans Souci, a vast and stately mansion, now a ruin, built in the style of the great palaces of Europe. Here, once, were pomp and luxury, polished floors, fine furniture and works of art. But beyond and above it, then as now, was only the wildness of forest and mountain. Christophe, wanting his Citadel to be just that, an impregnable fortress, built only a rough trail to its heights, and that is all there is today. To reach it, you ride on scraggly rented horses, which look as if they will never make the next step, but eventually make thousands.

The ascent takes about two hours, and it is not until near the end that you first see your goal. When you do, however, you *see* it; and you will never forget it. The West Indies are full of ruins, especially hilltop ruins—the old

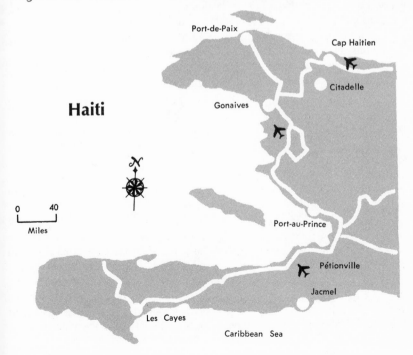

forts of British, French and Spaniards. But The Citadel is nothing like these. It stands out not on a hill but on a mountaintop. It is ten, twenty, fifty times the size of anything you have seen on another island, a thing on the scale of the Pyramids or the Coliseum.

Its battlements soar above you. A thrust of stone, like a ship's prow, cleaves the sky. Then at last you are at its base, you have entered it, and it is even vaster than you had thought. Christophe built it to house a garrison of ten thousand, and you can spend hours moving from level to level, through halls and courtyards, galleries and terraces, without once retracing your steps. At the top you emerge on a platform in space. You try to imagine the king on this platform, his ten thousand around him, surveying the miles of his realm. Now there are only a few tourists, a few guides. There are moss-grown stone and rusted cannon. As later, descending, you look back and upward, The Citadel seems no longer a solid fortress but a tower of dreams, alone and sleeping in the sunlit sky.

Still later, back in the 20th century, you try to rub the ache from your much-abused buttocks. You take your last swim in your hotel pool, eat your last fine meal, enjoy your final evening of music and dancing. In the morning you look for the last time at the gleaming hills and, down in Port-au-Prince, pick up the lovely paintings you have bought. Then you drive through the city, through the sea of poverty, to the airport. There, beggars pluck at your sleeve. From the wall Papa Doc looks down enigmatically. Roundabout stand the Tonton Macoutes, their eyes hidden by dark glasses.

On the plane you try to cast up accounts, to decide what you will say or write about Haiti. And it is not easy. Is it pleasant? No. Is it well run? No. Is it happy? No. Is it beautiful? Yes. Is it fascinating? Yes. Is it magical? Yes.

Should you go there? Make up your own mind.

—*J. R. Ullman*

Instant facts

Location: 1,300 miles from New York, 640 miles from Miami and 50 miles southwest of Cuba.

Population: About four million.

Capital: Port-au-Prince.

Nationality: An independent republic.

Language: French, a little English, Creole.

Currency: Gourde (20¢ U.S.) but U.S. currency accepted everywhere.

Documentation: International certificate of vaccination required. For a stay of up to 30 days, only proof of identity is needed.

Climate & Clothes: Temperatures average 70°–85°, with only slight variation between summer and winter. Light summer clothing appropriate year round. Most hotels require tie and jacket for evenings.

Food: Most of the food served at hotels and restaurants is local. Favorite dishes include **langouste** (rock lobster), **cabrit** (goat, usually barbecued and marinated a la Creole), **rice and beans** Haitian style, **griot** (a sort of pot roasted pork which often appears at banquets and voodoo festivals) and **tassot** (an old Indian recipe of dried meat or fowl soaked and served in marinades). For desserts, try something French and fattening or one of the many varieties of tropical fruits.

Geography: The Republic of Haiti, with a total area of 10,700 sq. miles, is in the western third of the island of Hispaniola.

Haiti, meaning "high land" in Indian dialect, has a mountainous terrain with peaks up to 9,000 feet.

History: Originally settled by the peaceful Arawak Indians, Haiti was discovered by Columbus in 1492. He named the island La Española, later corrupted to Hispaniola. The first settlers were primarily interested in gold but later arrivals started sugar plantations, importing Negro Africans for slaves. Haiti became a prosperous agricultural center under the French, originally buccaneers who moved in from the nearby island of Tortuga. The western part of Hispaniola was ceded to France under the Treaty of Ryswick (1697). After bitter struggles, Haiti achieved its independence in 1804. Among the island's heroes were Toussaint L'Ouverture, Jean Jacques Dessalines, Alexandre Pétion and Henri Christophe (King Henri I, first and only king of Haiti). For a short while, Haiti ruled the entire island of Hispaniola but a revolution quickly ended that arrangement. Since the founding of the Dominican Republic in 1844, the two nations have shared the island.

Who flies here

There are direct flights available from the following cities:

New York: Pan Am. Round Trip: $225–$320; 17-day excursion $165–$222.

Miami: Pan Am. Round Trip: $120–$179; 17-day excursion $91–$125.

San Juan: Pan Am. Round trip: $71–$99.

Santo Domingo: Dominican Airways, Pan Am. Round trip: $29–$44.

Island transportation

Cars can be rented, with or without chauffeur. Cost of car and driver is $3 an hour, $20 a day (10 hrs.) in the Port-au-Prince area, maximum four persons. To drive yourself, a permit will be issued if you have a valid hometown driver's license. Agencies include Avis Rent-A-Car, Heraux Tours, Agence Citadelle, Magic Island Tours and Southerland Tours. There aren't many gas stations so fill 'er up when you see one. Sightseeing facilities offered by these travel agencies in

Port-au-Prince: Agence Citadelle, Heraux Tours, Magic Island Tours, Southerland Tours, Haiti Holiday Tours and Carib Tours. In Cap Haitien: Royal Tours and Cap Haitien Travel Service VM2.

There are also plenty of **taxis,** identifiable by a red flag on the hood or radio aerial and a "P" on the license plates. An "L" on the plates means the driver is English-speaking and covered by passenger accident insurance. Rates are fixed and should be attached to the back of the driver's seat. If not, ask for a rate sheet.

The Haitian Airline COHATA provides **plane** transportation from Port-au-Prince to Cap Haitien and to Port de Paix, $16 and $18 round trip respectively. There are also frequent flights to Hinche, Gonaives, Jacmel and Les Cayes.

Places of interest

A tour of **Port-au-Prince** includes a look at imposing public buildings like the National Palace. Afterwards, visitors get a first-hand opportunity to push their way through the crowded Iron Market and, as a finale, tour the modern residential sections and factories where Haiti's gleaming mahogany ware and furniture are produced by hand.

Haiti's **Cul de Sac plain,** and its apricot, plum and apple-green mountains are displayed in two separate tours. The first takes travelers through sugar cane fields, sisal plantations and thatched-roof villages. The other winds up to **Pétionville,** mountain suburb of Port-au-Prince where homes and hotels, veiled in cascades of coral bougainvillea, perch 1,000 to 2,000 feet above sea level. The roller-coaster road spirals up to Kenscoff where the air becomes misty, pine trees replace palms, and children sell bouquets of daisies, geraniums and carnations for a few cents.

On the way back to the capital, a different route is taken to **Boutillier** to see the panorama of the Bay of Gonave, sparkling white Port-au-Prince, the plain's pea-green patchwork and a majestic range of mountains.

Inland is Haiti's great **Pine Forest,** 60 miles east of Port-au-Prince—15,000 acres of timber. This is the habitat of the rare musician bird—and Lake Saumatre, famous as a hunter's haven, is on the way to Pine Forest. Sixty miles south of Port-au-Prince is the former pirate stronghold of **Jacmel,** on the southern peninsula. More recently a coffee center, the town has handsome buildings, spacious parks and silvery-white beaches. **Les Cayes** is an important business center some 130 miles southwest of Port-au-Prince. Here Simón Bolívar took refuge and obtained military aid from President Pétion in 1815.

Cap Haitien is only a 40-minute flight or a scenic six-hour drive from Port-au-Prince. An inexpensive package tour covers three days and two nights. The tour operator arranges round-trip automobile transportation, hotel, meals, and sightseeing in Cap Haitien, plus a horse and guide for the trip to the Citadel fortress. Many prefer to drive to Le Cap and return by air.

The 198-mile drive to Cap Haitien never lacks interest. The road curves around the Bay of Gonave, winds through tropical plantations, cuts through mountains, dips down forest glens, skirts brooks, crosses rivers, and, during the last two hours spirals up 3,000 feet. En route, it passes through the drowsing seaside town of **St. Marc** and bustling **Gonaives,** where the independence of the French colony of Saint Domingue was proclaimed under the Indian name of Haiti in 1804.

French buccaneers founded Cap Francais —as Cap Haitien was called originally—in 1670. Less than two hundred years later Le Cap had become France's wealthiest colonial capital. Its surrounding sugar and cocoa plantations supplied half of Europe. Today Cap Haitien is a symphony of colors. Red tile roofs surmount houses that are a pastel rainbow of creme de menthe, yellow, pink and blue. Tall, massive colonial doors are red, green and blue. Despite fire and earthquake, it is still a true yesteryear town, with its wrought-iron balconies, high walls, hidden gardens and flowering patios.

The 17th-century cathedral dominates the huge Place d'Armes, where patriots were put to death in 1791. On one corner is the 137-year-old Union Club, housed in a gracious mansion almost as old. A block away, a residence built more than a hundred years ago houses a small museum. A chalk-white building dating back to French colonial times serves as part of a 225-bed government hospital.

Although the old Latin custom of promenading in the dark to the accompaniment of band music prevails in Le Cap, there are two nightclubs featuring dance music and native shows. Three miles from the city is excellent ocean bathing at Cormiers beach. Virtually unchanged since Columbus sailed past in 1492, it can be visited by car, with time for a two-hour swim.

Accommodations are modern and reasonable in Le Cap. Hotel du Roi Christophe is a 200-year-old mansion, gleaming with tiled floors and polished mahogany, boasting a tropical garden, outdoor swimming pool, and an open air nightclub. For mountainside living with broad terraces and views of harbor and town, there's the Mont Joli and Hotel Beck, the latter with a swimming pool.

To reach the massive **Citadelle,** tourists drive to the little town of Milot and from there go on horseback for the bumpy two-hour climb up the mountains, past the ruins of Sans Souci. The Citadelle towers 130 feet above a 3,000-foot summit called *Bonnet a l'Eveque* (Bishop's Hat) which plunges in an almost sheer drop to the plain below. The Citadelle was built by thousands of men, women and children, forced laborers of King Christophe. The huge blocks of masonry, the 365 cannon, some weighing five tons; the thousands of cannon balls, were dragged by these people from the plains over the narrow, rock trail that tourists ascend by horseback. Walls are from seven to 10 feet thick and over 100 feet high. It has vast galleries and deep, pitch-black dungeons. From the roof the whole valley and the bay at Cap Haitien can be seen.

Hopeful treasure hunters will be interested in the trip to **Tortuga** (Tortue), the small island off Haiti which was once a haven for pirates. Embarkation point is

Cap Haitien and a large sailboat with an auxiliary motor transports visitors to the island. While not much remains of the original pirate settlements, visitors have been known to probe the island for reputed buried loot.

The sporting life

There is a nine-hole mountain **golf** course at Pétionville Club and a golf course at the International Country Club. Arrangements for **horseback riding** can be made through hotels; facilities at the International Country Club.

Hunting in Haiti is year round although the best season is the October–April period, when ducks are migrating in great number from the U.S. and Canada. There are no "bag" limits and no license is required, just a permit to bring a gun into the country (write Chief of the Army, Quartier General, Port-au-Prince).

As many as 63 different species of water fowl can be found in and around Haitian waters. Haiti has numerous lakes, the largest situated in central, southern and western portions of the country. They are easily reached by car from Port-au-Prince. Alligator hunting is also a listed sport.

Water sports

Good swimming at Kyona Beach, outside Port-au-Prince, complete with restaurant and changing facilities. Other good **beaches:** near Jacmel and Cap Haitien. Sail and motor **boats** can be chartered at International Casino Pier. Glass-bottom boats make a morning-long trip to Sand Cay ($6), a colorful coral reef, leaving each A.M. from International Casino Pier. Excellent **spearfishing** here. La Gonave is headquarters for sport fishermen, with cruisers at Port-au-Prince.

Best shopping buys

While Haiti is not a free port, prices are definitely competitive with those of its Caribbean neighbors. In addition to primitive paintings (see "Art Centers"), there are many interesting items for sale in cool, dim shops tucked in massive colonial structures. These include: voodoo inspired copper and brass jewelry, wood sculptures, folklore recordings and handloomed candlewick fabrics whose counterparts now adorn the United Nations building in New York. Haitian rum is worthwhile sampling; it is made from sugar cane cuttings rather than from molasses, and is quite distinctive. Continental imports are also good buys. These include German cameras, Swiss watches, French perfumes, etc.

Dining and nights outs

Africana: Oppo. Dept. of Tourism. Lots of atmosphere.

Aux Cosaques: Chemin des Dalles. Creole cuisine. Highly recommended.

Au Reservoir: At Bourdon. Rotary dinner-meeting here Monday nights.

Nobbe et Bondel: Exposition Grounds. Dining with a Teutonic accent.

Picardie: Pétionville. French–Haitian menu.

Le Rond Point: Exposition grounds. French cuisine.

Sunset Lodge: Haitian dishes; American, too, for homesick tourists.

Saturday night means a rendezvous at the **Cabane Choucoune,** one of the most unique swinging nightclubs of the Caribbean. Built in the round, it resembles an oversized and well-kept African tribal hut (seating capacity 550). It is located in Pétionville, about 20 minutes by car from Port-au-Prince. The Cabane offers its guests one of the country's leading bands and floor shows by Haitian dancing troupes.

A far cry from the Cabane is the modern, air-conditioned **International Casino.** By no means limited to the gambling set as it also offers dancing and floor shows. Other shows can be seen at Haiti's leading hotels. Night life tours, at a small cost, take tourists to a voodoo temple where ceremonial dances are performed, to an exuberant rural social get-together, locally known as a "bambouche," and to the continental-type nightclubs patronized by the Haitian elite.

Voodoo—of sorts

Practically every traveler wants to see a voodoo ceremony, and an authentic one at that. It's difficult, for voodoo basically is a true folk religion with rituals often continuing for 12 hours or more. There are, however, excellent voodoo shows in and around Port-au-Prince, notably at **Habitation LeClerc,** where a *houngan* (priest) and a large group of worshippers perform the classic rituals in an open-air *hounfour* (gathering place) surrounded by seated spectators.

Even in sophisticated nightclubs, solo dancers, teams and groups usually pattern their routines on colorful, intricate and sensual rites adopted from the voodoo religion. Those visitors determined to view a genuine voodoo ceremony should listen to Haiti's omnipresent drums. These sacred drums, basic to voodoo, whose constant beat exerts a strange compulsive effect, serve as a beacon. Often, the throbbing of drums across the night signify a voodoo ceremony is taking place. So, follow the sound to its source, generally a neighborhood *hounfour*.

If the visitor respectfully asks to watch and is sincerely interested, frequently admission is granted. The hounfour probably will be a shack, half open to the warm night, where he may view an exhausting all-night ordeal. Occasionally, a participant will become—or appear to be —"possessed" or entranced by the accelerating rhythms of the drums. Other times, the worshipers become completely enveloped by ecstasy, the essence of a mystic experience similar to that of other world religions. Voodoo seen by tourists may not be this authentic but it always is a unique and exciting spectacle.

Special events, celebrations

Independence Day (New Year's Day): Official celebrations throughout Haiti and particularly in Port-au-Prince. January 1.

Ancestor's Day: January 2.

Carnival (Mardi Gras): All three days preceding Ash Wednesday. Parade of floats with colorful decorations, costume balls and other activities. February 25–27.

Good Friday: Rara. Peasant carnival which takes place just before the crop season. Holy week, April 7–14.

Anniversary of Toussaint L'Ouverture's Death: April 7.

Pan American Day: Official celebrations. April 14.

Agriculture and Labour Day: Parade of field workers and Agriculture Fair. May 1.

Flag and University Day: May 18.

Anniversary of Dessaline's Death: October 17.

United Nations Day: Official celebrations. October 24.

All Saints Day: November 1.

All Souls Day: November 2.

Armed Forces Day: November 18.

Columbus Day: Official ceremonies in honor of discovery of Haiti. December 5.

Art centers

Haiti is the only Caribbean country considered to have a distinctive art form and original works may be purchased at bargain prices. To duty-conscious travelers, mindful of the lowering on the amount of tariff-free goods that can now be brought back, U.S. Customs regulations place no limit on "bona fide" works of art.

While Haiti is noted principally for its primitive art, an unusually fine crop of talented artists has ranged into more modern forms such as abstract and realistic impressionism. Sculptors, too, have moved on from the "fertility goddess" and tribal mask stage to finely executed statues and busts, mainly in mahogany and other woods.

Two of Haiti's top galleries—**Centre d'Art** and **Gift Fair**—are located in the heart of Port-au-Prince. **The Artist's Fingers** on Bourbon St. is on the way to Pétionville, and the **Red Carpet** faces the entrance to the **El Rancho Hotel** in suburban Pétionville. The **Corner Store** also has an excellent section of Haitian art.

The Art Center, founded in 1944 by the late American painter DeWitt Peters, is the oldest gallery and pioneered the art movement in Haiti. Prices at the Art

Center range from $25 to $200 and a few of the finer works go as high as $1,000. Located at 17 rue de la Revolution, the Center represents such distinguished masters as Hector Hyppolite and Philome Obin as well as many brilliant young artists.

At **Issa's Gallery,** on a hill overlooking the city, as many as 10 painters put in an eight-hour day painting six days a week. Blanchard, Normil and Abelard are perhaps the best-known painters working on the premises. The Gift Fair, behind the Post Office in Port-au-Prince, shows some of the lesser Haitian works in a large salon fronted by a gift shop. Prices here range up to $100. The Artist's Fingers is owned and operated by twin brothers, Joseph and Jean-Baptiste Maurice, who also are fine wood carvers. The Maurice brothers feature sculptured pieces at their establishment but also represent a number of painters, notably the well-known Max Pinchinat. Watercolors can be obtained at the Artist's Fingers for as low as $10 while oils go for from $40 to $300.

At the Red Carpet, the top artist is Jean Nehemy, whose works hang alongside those of the veteran Pétion Savain, 62, and the 23-year-old Bernard Wah. Prices here range from $25 to $400 with most in the $25 to $200 class.

WHERE TO STAY — In Haiti

| | | Dec. 15-April 14 | | April 15-Dec. 14 | |
| | | U. S. Currency | | | |
	Plan	Double	Single	Double	Single
BEAU RIVAGE (AP)		$12–24	$ 8–10	$10–12	$ 6– 8
Port-au-Prince (40 Rms.) **(p)**					
CASTEL HAITI (AP)		$32–40	$18–22	$27–29	$15–17
Port-au-Prince (70 Rms.) **(p)**					
CHOUCOUNE (AP)		$35–40	$20–25	$26–28	$16–18
Petionville (30 Rms.) **(p)**					
EL RANCHO (AP)		$55–60	$35–45	$32–40	$20–25
Petionville (55 Rms.)**(p)**					
IBOLELE (AP)		$28–42	$16–24	$26–42	$14–24
Petionville (70 Rms.) **(p)**					
MARABOU (EP)		$14	$ 8	$10	$ 6
Petionville (15 Rms.) **(p)**					
MONTANA (AP)		$35–55	$20–29	$24–29	$14–19
Petionville (36 Rms.) **(p)**					
OLOFFSON (AP)		$39–42	$24–26	$24–26	$14
Port-au-Prince (20 Rms.) **(p)**					
PLAZA (AP)		$15	$ 8	$12	$ 6
Petionville (30 Rms.) **(p)**					
VILLA CREOLE (AP)		$35–40	$18–21	$26–28	$14–16
Petionville (40 Rms.) **(p)**					
VILLA QUISQUEYA (AP)		$18–28	$10–15	$15–25	$ 8–15
Petionville (13 Rms.) **(p)**					
SPLENDID (AP)		On Request		$18–22	$10–12
Port-au-Prince (37 Rms.) **(p)**					
ROI CHRISTOPHE (AP)		$25	$14	$18	$10
Cap-Haitien (20 Rms.) **(p)**					
SANS SOUCI (MAP)		$28	$15	$28	$15
Port-au-Prince (18 Rms.) **(p)**					

LEGEND FOR HOTEL LISTINGS: (AP) American Plan (room and 3 meals); **MAP)** Modified American Plan (room, breakfast and dinner); **(CP)** Continental Plan (room and breakfast); **(EP)** European Plan (room only). All rates quoted on a per-day basis and subject to change. Confirmed reservations at specific rates desired are always recommended.
HOTEL FACILITIES: (b) beach; **(p)** pool; **(t)** tennis; **(g)** golf.

Drifting down Jamaica's Rio Grande on a bamboo raft

JAMAICA

The Arawak Indians—the pre-Columbian inhabitants of Jamaica—named it Xaymaca, "Land of Wood and Water," and its beauty is legendary. A great ridge of blue-green mountains dominates the island. In the interior, tropical birds sing and exotic flowers grow and unexplored territory—the Cockpit Country—still exists. On the coastal plains the ruins of great plantation houses are silhouetted against the hills in moody evocation of the past. On the north coast, white sand beaches, a sapphire sea and luxury hotels have made Montego Bay and Ocho Rios the Riviera of the Americas. Jamaica has been a lure to pirates and explorers. Today its visitors come in search of the perfect vacation isle.

This gem Jamaica

The Union Jack of Imperial Britain has been gone now since 1962. The flag of free Jamaica is green, gold and black.

The colors are there wherever you look: the green in the hills and valleys, the gold in the sunlight, the black in the faces of its people. They shine and gleam. They intermingle. They blend with other colors: the blue of sky and sea, the white of beaches, the yellow of fruits, the red of earth.

Putting first things first, Jamaica is beautiful. It is also big (as Caribbean islands go), with an area exceeded only by Cuba's and Hispaniola's and a population pushing toward two million. No "pancake with a palm tree," Jamaica is a land of many moods and aspects, faces and voices. Of lagoons and mountain peaks, cane fields and bauxite, orchids and traffic jams, hotels and history.

"Yes, sir," a taximan said proudly, "our island's got about everything there is." Then he added, "Except money."

But even that seems to be coming.

I flew into Kingston, its capital, from San Juan and was immediately aware of a vivid contrast between the two cities. Culturally, San Juan is Spanish and American, Kingston British and Negro. In commerce and tourism, San Juan is a prime boomtown of the 1960's; Kingston, though one of the largest cities of the Caribbean, is emerging from the 19th century. It sprawls and swarms, but 99% with homegrown Jamaicans. Other than the short-stay passengers on winter cruise ships, the mainstream of visitors prefer the north shore resorts, where the beaches are. Except for the newish Sheraton-Kingston Hotel, which caters as much to local as to foreign trade, there are none of the gaudy pleasure palaces that line the Condado strip of San Juan.

Short of palaces, however, there is a scattering of pleasant havens. Best known from days of yore is the Myrtle Bank, smack on the waterfront, now venerable and a little dated but picturesque and fascinatingly "in and of" the city around it. The central section of the hotel was burnt out in 1966 and a new but smaller structure has been built to replace it. Farther out in the byways, small but inviting, are the Terra Nova, Courtleigh Manor, Liguanea Terrace and others.

Across the harbor at historic Port Royal is the only beach resort in the area, an attractive hotel called Morgan's Harbour. In the nearby hills is Blue Mountain Inn, where food and view alike are to be cherished.

Tired of sun and surf and cocktail bar? Kingston soon convinces you Jamaica is not exclusively a 4,411-square-mile country club. At its bustling center are the Victoria Crafts Market, with all manner of island products on exhibit and sale, and the Institute of Jamaica, a combined library-gallery-museum in which you can trace the island's history from Arawak Indians to Playboy Club.

In the city's northeastern outskirts are the Hope Botanical Gardens, a splendiferous array of tropical flora, with a few fauna added. Close by is the University of the West Indies (associated with the University of London), with a new and lovely campus and platoons of red-robed students. In the Institute you can see Jamaica's past. In the University you can see, or at least powerfully feel, its future.

We have mentioned Port Royal; and here, too, is past and future, all in one. At the tip of the long arm of land that forms the outer rim of Kingston's harbor, the old town was long the capital of Jamaica, the stronghold of Henry Morgan and his co-buccaneers, once known as the "richest and wickedest" city in the world. In 1692 (presumably as the wage of sin) Port Royal was stricken by an earthquake that tumbled most of it into the sea. Later, in a second incarnation as Fort Charles, it served as a British naval base in the days of Nelson and Rodney. Now, on its thin spit of land, there is little to be seen but rubble and ruin.

Great plans are afoot, however. In recent years undersea exploration has revealed much of the contour and layout of the sunken city. No less than $19 million in private capital has been raised for historical restoration. Soon, on this barren sandspit, there will rise a replica of old Port Royal, comparable to restored Williamsburg in Virginia. Far and away the most ambitious of Jamaica's tourist projects, it should one day be a true wonder of the Caribbean.

Swinging back to central Kingston, there is one further place that should be mentioned: if not a sight for seeing, at least a site for handy reference. This is the Jamaica Tourist Board, an organization that can serve as a model of its kind for any country small or large. The prime function of the JTB is to get you to Jamaica in the first place, and this it works on (via your favorite magazine and TV station) with might and main.

But once it has you, be assured, it will not drop you like a gutted coconut. If you're lost, strayed, or need anything from a historical date to a hotel room, the Board, located on Harbour Street, will cheerfully help out. (Indeed, the only thing they cannot supply is cigarettes at a reasonable price. The cost of a smoke in Jamaica is horrendous.)

After two days in Kingston (just right, I should say, in a two-week trip) I took to the road in a rented car. This is no project to be undertaken lightly. One's hired car is tiny, frail, and driven by clutch and gearstick on the left side of the road. Opposition cars, trucks and buses are often huge and ferocious. They roar around Jamaica's five-million blind curves at fifty-per, neatly straddling the central dividing line.

Even if your nerves are not quite those of an astronaut, the strain is worth it. For the island's interior is surpassingly lovely. On the flat coastal plains you are flanked by seas of sugar cane. As the road rises and twists you come to the realm of bananas, coffee, cocoa, bamboo, breadfruit and yams. When the land steepens into true mountains, the way lies through deep gorges and grottoes, their walls lined with almost vertical hanging jungles.

At the top of a rise, unexpectedly, there may be a bare plateau, with the raw red earth and looming sheds of a bauxite plant. But these are soon gone. There is again only the green of forest until you top a final rise and see, far ahead and below, the shining blue miles of the Caribbean.

On my island circuit I went first from Kingston to Spanish Town. This, as the name implies, was Jamaica's metropolis during its long-gone days under the rule of Spain, which ended in 1655. It is one of the few places where traces of the *Conquistadores* can still be found. Beyond it, the main road bears north straight across the island to the Gold Coast playgrounds of Ocho Rios and Montego Bay. But I swerved to the west. For the next few days my route would be through Jamaica's southwestern quadrant which is least visited by travelers.

Came first a day and a night in the town of Mandeville, 2,000 feet in the hills. For years Mandeville has been the holiday refuge of Kingston Britishers seeking the coolness of elevation. But the genus North-American Tourist, seeking not coolness but warmth, has avoided it.

Old English Mandeville moved closer as I came to the town green and its foursquare Anglican Church, looking as if it had been transported intact from Kent or Surrey. In its quiet graveyard I found a true memento of empire, a tablet fixed in the stone of a moss-green wall. The tablet read: *In sacred memory of Walter Henry Nightingale, First Battalion, West Indies Rifles, died in Sierra Leone, 1913.* In my antique hotel room, with its Morris chair and coil of punk to ward off insects, I half expected the door to open and Kipling or Chinese Gordon to come in and join me.

Westward from Mandeville are villages with wondrous names: among them Pepper, Gutter, Lilliput, Maggotty. Here are goats, donkeys, roosters. Here are naked, wide-eyed children and kerchiefed women beating their wash against the stones of stream beds.

It is not all pastoral idyll, for in the village one finds a gas pump, a Coke dispenser, and a sign saying F. WATSON, OFF-COURSE BETTING. And along the roadside are groups of men, young and old, loafing the day away. In spite of Jamaica's great strides in agriculture, industry and tourism, there is still noticeable unemployment on the island. In the southwestern area, most jobs for men are on sugar plantations. But sugar is a seasonal crop, and this was not the season.

Snaking down to the coast, the road goes from Black River to Savanna-la-Mar. Here are perhaps the best fishing grounds in Jamaica. But they have been barely probed. And along the whole shore there is only one small traveler's haven, Whitehouse Inn. Talking with Oliver Holroyd-Smyth, a genial Anglo-Irishman who owns the one charter fishing boat in the area, I found his frame of mind typical of outlanders everywhere, who have settled in remote and lovely places. Half of him yearns for a build-up of Jamaica's southwest; for hotels, tourists, charters, dollars. The other half no less fervently hopes the unspoiled, uncommercialized Eden he inhabits will never change.

In Savanna-la-Mar sugar is king, and I visited one of the large plantations. More vivid in my mind, however, is another very different sort of visit—to Miss Evangeline Davis of the U.S. Peace Corps. To most travelers, as to myself, it may come as a surprise that the Corps operates in Jamaica. For one sees nothing of its volunteers in the gilded realms of Touristia. But they are there all right (about 100 of them at this writing) tucked away in small towns and villages, living not as outsiders but as part of the communities in which they serve.

Most of them teach school and they are badly needed, for Jamaican illiteracy is still a problem. The educational system is so short of teachers (not to mention money) it has been, to date, impossible to make schooling compulsory.

Young, pretty and dedicated, Vangie Davis of Washington, D.C., was doing her share of bridging the gap by teaching in Savanna's junior high. She lived in the nearby home of middle-class Jamaicans. She was familiar with the local food, customs and dialect. Riding around town on her bike, she seemed to know everyone. She and her fellow Corpsmen, one feels, may be accomplishing more for Jamaica—and Jamaica's feeling for the U.S.—than all the traveler's checks in the coffers of resort hotels.

Soon Vangie and Savanna recede, and ahead is something new. What gleams now is a beach, one of the great beaches of the world. We have come to Negril, at the island's far-western end. Ahead, for long miles, are bows and arcs and crescents of virgin sand. Like Port Royal, Negril is to be one of Jamaica's major projects-of-the-future. The government has already put some $7 million into it, draining adjacent inland swamps and building (parallel to the beach), the finest highway in the island. It has been waiting for private capital to do the rest.

Until now, private capital has responded with one small hotel, the Sundowner, a small open-air restaurant specializing in seafood and some beach cottages that can be rented.

Here I stopped, changed into swim trunks. It was one of the memorable experiences of a lifetime, for on those seven sweeping miles of beach I was the only human being. Leaving sand for silken water, I was the only visible living creature in all the miles of the Caribbean.

Later, back on the shore, a few men and boys appeared to work on a small beached boat a few hundred yards from me. But they stayed only a short while. A small crab sidled up, seemed to eye me curiously and took his departure. All that was left were sun, sea, sand and self.

It was hard to believe that the languorous fleshpots of Montego Bay were just a few miles to the northeast.

"Mo" Bay was there all right, as lush and plush and lovely as I remembered it from my last visit: a resort that, to my mind, comes as near to having everything as any in the world. True, there is no single spectacular beach like Negril's. But the justly famous strand of Doctor's Cave (public) and those of many of the hotels (private or semiprivate) are, on a smaller scale, pure gems. Day or night in Montego there is always something to do, and better yet, perhaps it is the perfect place for doing nothing.

Dining is lavish and cosmopolitan. Almost every room in every hotel is air-conditioned. Outdoors, on most days, you find the even better conditioner of the trade winds.

Montego's establishments run the gamut from the top-bracket cottage colonies (Round Hill, Half Moon, Racquet Club, Miranda Hill), through the more conventional resort hotels (Casa Montego, Casa Blanca, Montego Beach, Royal Caribbean), to a host of small inns and guest houses with modest accommodations and rates. Some are close to town, some are out a way. Some are on the shore, others on the hillsides a short distance inland. A few, notably the prestigious Sunset Lodge, operate less as hotels than as private clubs.

Round Hill and one or two others are strictly winter resorts. In line with Jamaica's campaign to become an all-year playground, most are open around the calendar. Make no mistake about it, however. The "high season," in Montego as throughout the Caribbean, is still between Christmas and Easter. At other times accommodations are less expensive and easier to come by.

One of the first, and still one of the foremost, of West Indies resorts, Mo Bay has in the past few years, I would say, been suffering from a slight case of schizophrenia, or, in Madison Avenue parlance, "image trouble." Its original image, carefully nurtured, has been that of affluence, luxury, exclusivity. This it still preserves to a large degree. But recently as a result of boom times in the States and elsewhere, it has found itself playing host to many visitors whose tastes and pocketbooks require more mundane fare. Realistically, if sometimes painfully, it has tried to compromise, to keep its old-line colonies of long stayers and big spenders and at the same time attract the come-and-go budget vacationer. Thus far it has managed the balancing act rather well.

In the old days (meaning fifteen years ago) the north shore of Jamaica, for the tourist, meant Montego Bay, *period*. Now the whole 150-mile sweep is on its way to becoming a tropical Riviera. But there are still a few gaps in the Parade of Progress.

East of Montego the hotels dwindle off. Cane fields reappear, and among them stand several of the great houses of the old slave-day plantations. Farther back is what is known as Cockpit Country, once the historic refuge of rebellious slaves, called Maroons, and still a region of wild and savage inaccessibility. A special daily train from Mo Bay, named the Governor's Coach, offers thrice weekly round trips into the interior touching the fringes of this district. But a true trip *into* it would resemble an expedition to the mountains of the Moon.

At Discovery Bay, some 35 miles from Montego, Columbus, in 1494, made the first European landing on Jamaica. Runaway Bay, a bit beyond, is the place from which the last of the Spanish garrison made their escape when the British took the island. And St. Ann's Bay, still farther on, was the one-time site of Sevilla Nueva, the first town established in Jamaica after its discovery. East of St. Ann's, history fades again. The Gold Coast re-arises. We have come to Ocho Rios.

There is some confusion as to what Ocho Rios is. Basically, it's a town, a very small town with a big traffic circle. But for touristic purposes it has given its name to the whole strip of shore from St. Ann's Bay to Port Maria. A traveler who says he is going to Ocho Rios may be bound for a hotel ten miles or more on either side. Town or strip, it is beautiful, more so, I would say, than Montego Bay, though it still lags behind its older rival in tradition and cachet. And it offers much to see and do. Close by, on the main route to Kingston, is Fern Gully, a road built in an old river bed that for two miles bores an emerald tunnel through the heart of a lush overgrowth. To the west is Dunn's River Falls, a cascade of silver water flowing directly into the sea over rocks so smooth yet unslippery that one can climb right up them to the heights. Farther afield, near Port Maria, is Brimmer Hall, a working plantation which conducts tours through its groves of banana, coconut, citrus and pimento. If you think a plantation tour sounds dullish (as I did), you will be mistaken. With its fabulous flora and top-drawer guides, Brimmer Hall is a 90-minute delight, topped by a dip in a pool and a planter's punch.

Then, of course, there are hotels, hotels, hotels—seventeen major ones in all by the latest count. The two largest are farthest from Ocho Rios town, the Jamaica Hilton to the west and the Playboy Club to the east. In between, among others, are the Shaw Park, Sans Souci, Jamaica Inn, Plantation Inn, Island Inn, and, second to none, the veteran Tower Isle.

Well, second to *one* let us say. For my own brief visit, the Playboy Club must rank first. But there is a catch: the Playboy was temporarily closed. As I wandered through its vast halls and terraces (it is the largest hotel in Jamaica) I was alone as on the beach at Negril. Into the VIP Room I went. No VIP's. Into the Playmate Bar. No playmates. The Bunnies had taken to the woods, leaving not even a pair of ears behind. But all was not lost. Around the pool bar, across the broad central lawn, in nonchalant procession and pecking busily, there came marching a mother hen and six chicks!

Port Antonio, the third of the north coast's prime resort areas, and one with a bright future, is near the island's eastern end. Smaller than Montego Bay and Ocho Rios, it has a languorous far-out atmosphere that can drive some visitors away in a day and a night and make others feel they have at last found Eden.

Scenically it is gorgeous. As backdrop, there rise the highest peaks of the Blue Mountains, and front and center are deep bays and bold headlands. Also, it is the greenest and lushest section of the island, for which a price must be paid in more rain. But the rains are quick, heavy, and suddenly gone. Green and gold return, richer, brighter than ever.

There are three hotels in Port Antonio: the Bonnie View, high on a hill-top (which has a bonnie view, indeed); the Jamaica Reef, on the promontory of land that separates Port Antonio's two harbors; and the De Montevin. The Reef is the oldest hotel on the island, originally called the Titchfield and built by the United Fruit Company in 1892. Later it became the personally owned playground—and part-time boxing ring—of the late Errol Flynn. It has survived its vicissitudes handsomely and today is a happy hideaway.

In September, Port Antonio's twin harbors fill up with small craft, as the town stages an international fishing tournament. The rest of the year the main traffic is the coming and going of banana boats. With a little imagination one can conjure up still another fruit-bearing ship from times gone by, for this was the West Indian port to which Captain Bligh, after the *Bounty* mutiny, finally brought his cargo of breadfruit from the South Pacific.

Today, however, the star aquatic attraction of the area is not offshore but inland. This is rafting on the nearby Rio Grande, which has now been going on for a half century and has become one of the island's popular tourist attractions. Unique among island rivers, the Grande presents an eight-mile course of pools and channels, rapids and spillways. Long bamboo rafts, poled by expert "captains" and with a thronelike seat for two passengers, makes the kaleidoscopic run in two hours. As luck (bad) would have it, I made the trip alone. Even so, it was a delightful joyride. With a soft and perhaps slightly nervous female hand to hold, it would have been even better.

At Port Antonio we are almost at the end of Jamaica's fabled north shore.

But not quite. Beyond it are two phenomena that are—well, phenomenal.

The first is a hotel. Its name is Frenchman's Cove. Its claim to fame is that, in the high season, it makes a strong bid to be the most expensive hotel in the world. Its slogan: *two for two for two*, meaning $2,000 for two persons for two weeks. But this, I understand, was for the pinchpenny days of the previous season; for the coming one, rumor had it, the rate would move up to $190 a day. Through summer and fall, it must be added, the tab is considerably less stratospheric. But at no time of year is Frenchman's Cove to be confused with the YMCA.

For such prices, to be sure, you get something in return. Each resident couple occupies a large and luxurious cottage, complete with maid and butler, library, hi-fi and, if you want it, a piano. The grounds with a crystal stream running through them, are a landscaper's dream, and to-and-fro transportation is by private electrical golf cart. If you want to go by car or plane to other parts of the island, the trip is on the house. All drinks are on the house.

During the lower-rate season the bag of goodies is rather less lavish. But as I can testify from a brief visit, you don't live like a pauper.

The second of far-eastern Jamaica's wonders is Blue Hole. If Frenchman's Cove is largely man's handiwork, this is nature's alone. It is a salt-water inlet with a narrow opening to the sea. On all other sides tall green-sheathed cliffs shield it from the world beyond. Its water, deep and clear, is a dark blue, an ultramarine, so pure and gleaming the eye watching it becomes almost hypnotized. Mindful of its splendors, and of the semantics of salesmanship, the Tourist Board is currently changing its name on maps and folders from Blue Hole to Blue Lagoon. I concede the improvement. But hole or lagoon, it is as fair a sight as you will see on earth.

I was lucky there. Blue Hole—or Lagoon—is among the most photographed spots in Jamaica; but when I came down the steep road that leads to its shore, there was no one else to be seen. I was alone again, as at Negril. But everything else was different. At Negril there had been lapping of surf, the cawing of gulls. Here all was stillness. There the prospect had been out to the sea, to space, to miles beyond measuring. Here was closeness, intimacy, sanctuary.

For an hour I stayed in sanctuary. I sat on its shore. I swam in its waters. Then through the stillness I climbed up to the road and my car, and began the drive along the east coast to Kingston.

Soon the stillness gave way. Trucks and buses roared past. Horns honked. Overhead, a jet screamed up from Kingston's airport. The 20th century was back in business.

—*J. R. Ullman*

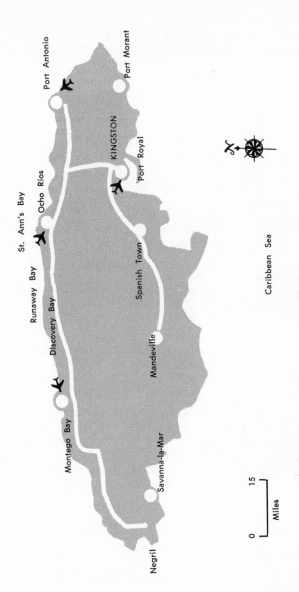

Jamaica

Atlantic Ocean

Port Antonio

Port Morant

St. Ann's Bay

Ocho Rios

KINGSTON

Runaway Bay

Port Royal

Discovery Bay

Spanish Town

Mandeville

Montego Bay

Caribbean Sea

Savanna-la-Mar

Negril

0   15

Miles

Instant facts

Location: About 700 miles south of Miami.

Population: Approaching two million.

Capital: Kingston.

Nationality: An independent nation, member of the British Commonwealth.

Language: English.

Currency: Jamaican pound sterling, 7 shillings to the dollar. Most places will accept American currency but Canadians are advised to change their dollars in a bank.

Documentation: Passport required by all except citizens of the U.S., U.K. and Canada who have proof (i.e., a round-trip ticket) that they are bona fide tourists. Smallpox vaccination not required by passengers from Aruba, Bahamas, Bermuda, B.W.I., Canada, Cuba, Curacao and U.S.

Climate & Clothes: Cooled by year-round trade winds, winter temperatures are in the mid-70's and summer in the mid-80's. Although there is no definite rainy season, it is dampest in May and October. A wrap or other light covering is recommended for evenings, particularly in the winter season.

Food: Jamaican cookery has a liberal application of spices and peppers, originally introduced to disguise the taste of preservatives in the days before refrigeration. Continental cuisine is everywhere but some local dishes worth sampling are **rice and peas, salt fish and ackee** (an exotic tree vegetable); **curried goat and rice, jerked pork, run down** (made from salted shad and coconut oil), **mackerel and bananas, pepperpot soup, fricasseed chicken** (actually a thick stew) and **roast suckling pig.** Jamaica also has a wide variety of the usual and unusual in fruits. An exotic fruit dessert is **Matrimony.**

Geography: Roughly 146 miles long by 51 miles at its broadest, Jamaica is a mountainous island with its tallest peaks (over 7,000 feet) in the Blue Mountain Range. It is the third largest island of the West Indies.

History: The island was first visited by Columbus in 1494 but was originally inhabited by the Arawaks, a peaceful and now extinct race of Indians. For 150 years the Spanish occupied Jamaica (although little trace of their occupation remains) until it was conquered by British forces in 1655. The island became the stronghold of Caribbean buccaneers, who transformed the old capital of Port Royal into the Sodom and Gomorrah of the Western Hemisphere. Its most famous buccaneer, Henry Morgan, was ultimately knighted and served as Jamaica's respected governor.

Who flies here

Jamaica's two jetports, one at the north shore city of Montego Bay and the other at Palisadoes near Kingston, are served by nine international airlines. Direct flights leaving regularly from major cities around the world are:

New York to Kingston or Montego Bay: BOAC, Air Jamaica, Lufthansa, Pan Am. Round trip: $225–$325; 17-day excursion $155–$215.

Miami to Kingston or Montego Bay: BWIA, Air Jamaica, KLM, Pan Am. Round trip: $117–$154; 17-day excursion $64–$90.

New Orleans to Montego Bay: Delta. Round trip: $180–$245; 17-day excursion $144–$195.

Toronto to Kingston or Montego Bay: Air Canada. Round trip: $236–$344 (Canadian $254–$371); 21-day excursion $172–$248 (Canadian $186–$268).

Montreal to Kingston or Montego Bay: Air Canada. Round trip: $250–$346 (Canadian $270–$373); 21-day excursion $184–$271 (Canadian $198–$292).

London to Kingston or Montego Bay: BOAC. Round trip: $608–$956 (£217–£341 sterling).

Frankfurt is served by Lufthansa via New York while Mexicana provides flights to Mexico and the West Coast.

Getting around Jamaica

By Car: Greatest mobility is afforded by renting a car, self- or chauffeur-driven. Martin's Tours, Hertz Rent-A-Car and Avis Rent-A-Car operate from offices in Kingston (including Palisadoes Airport), Ocho Rios and Montego Bay. Limousine service and car rentals are also available from more than 20 other agencies.

Rates vary widely, depending on the type of car, length of rental and time of year (the steeper winter season ranges from December 16 to April 15). Some agencies offer a flat weekly rate, with unlimited or partial mileage charges. Usual rates, however, range from $6–$11 a day or $35–$50 a week plus a mileage charge of 7¢–10¢. The Jamaica Automobile Association, for a modest $2 fee, assists visitors in much the same way that its stateside equivalent, the AAA, does (free service in case of a breakdown, map, handbook and a helping hand should you get a ticket).

Jamaica Tours has a sightseeing bus in operation, and other transfer and tour agencies, headed by Martin's Tours, offer varied itineraries throughout the island. If you choose to drive yourself, a network of good roads crisscrosses Jamaica and the distance and direction to towns and villages are clearly marked. Count on roughly 2½ hours for trips from Montego Bay or Kingston to Ocho Rios and about 3½ hours to get from Port Antonio to Ocho Rios or to Kingston.

Kingston and Montego Bay have metered taxicabs with government-controlled rates: 28¢ U.S. for the first mile for one passenger, each additional mile 18¢ and each additional passenger 11¢. Visitors are cautioned to ask the fare of any privately operated, nonmetered cab before starting their trip.

Buses are available in Kingston and its suburbs but are not reliable on an island-wide basis.

By Train: Diesel coach service has been introduced by the government-owned Jamaica Railway Corporation, offering a leisurely four-hour trip between Montego Bay and Kingston ($4 one way) and a three-hour trip to Port Antonio ($2 one way). A day-long "Governor's Coach" trip out of Montego Bay includes a visit to a typical village, sugar estate, rum distillery and some caves. Frequent stops for photographs and picnic lunch by the river ($11 per person).

By Air: For convenient resort-to-resort service, daily shuttle flights via Jamaica Air Service and BWIA link the island's major cities. The following round-trip rates are presently in effect:

Kingston-Montego Bay: $17–$21 ($12–$16 for a one-day excursion).
Kingston-Ocho Rios: $16.
Kingston-Port Antonio: $16.
Montego Bay-Ocho Rios: $16.
Montego Bay-Port Antonio: $24.

Jamaica Air Taxi also offers charter flights. Numerous landing strips are available for entry by private aircraft. Arrangements should be made with the Civil Aviation Dept. before departure though there are no restrictions at either Kingston or Montego Bay.

Things to do / the offbeat, the unusual

Rafting: A safe but thrilling experience for two, this trip down the rapids of Port Antonio's Rio Grande takes about two hours with a stop for lunch. Each raft is constructed of 12 to 14 bamboo poles securely lashed together and is guided by an experienced native helmsman.

"Alligator" Hunting: Need a new belt or pocketbook? The Jamaican alligator—rightfully referred to as a Crocodilus Acutus—provides a unique target for would-be safari hunters. Expeditions can be carried out in swamps near the Hellshire Hills and around Aguilar Pond, at Portland Point, Milk River and the Black River areas. For information, contact Bernard Cridland in Aguilar's sports shop, Harbour St., Kingston.

Plantation Tours: Visitors can tour Brimmer Hall, one of Jamaica's largest banana and coconut plantations, on a comfortable tractor-drawn "jitney." Another interesting tour is conducted at Runaway Spice Estate, an historic plantation still in operation today growing pimento or allspice.

Spelunking: An unusual treat for cave addicts is the Green Grotto in the Runaway Caves, located on the Northshore Highway near Runaway Bay. There is boating on an underground lake in the grotto, studded with stalagmites and stalactites. The Caves have a romantic history connected with the defeat of the Spanish in the 17th century.

Waterfall Climbing: At Dunn's River Falls, near Ocho Rios, the water bursts down deep ledges on its way to the sea. Here, experienced guides take visitors to the top, an exhilarating if somewhat dampening experience. Also near Ocho Rios are the Roaring River Falls and the eerily beautiful Fern Gully, once a river bed but now a road where ferns grow so high they blot out the sun.

Luminous Lagoon: The water in this unusual lagoon lights up like a lamp when agitated, sparkles in your hand and etches the fish in streaks of light as they swim. Located at Rock Bay, Falmouth, some 25 miles from Montego Bay. Visitors can stop for refreshments at its two hostelries (Glistening Water and Fisherman's Inn) from whose docks a boat can be taken on the lagoon.

Banana Loading—Banana boats load regularly at Montego Bay, Oracabessa and Port Antonio. Spectators can watch either from the wharf or from the boat itself as the huge stems of bananas are transported from the lighter to the hold. Speedboat trips to the banana ships go from some Montego Bay hotels.

The above tours can be arranged through most hotels or touring agencies.

The sporting life

Golf: Of the island's 10 golf courses, four are considered championship: the Caymanas Golf and Country Club near Kingston, Tryall Golf Club west of Montego Bay, the Half Moon-Rose Hall Club east of Montego Bay, and the Runaway Bay Golf Club on the north coast road to Ocho Rios.

A fifth 18-hole course is the Constant Spring Golf Club at St. Andrew. There are two nine-holers near the south coast, at the Liguanea Club in Kingston and the Manchester Club in Mandeville, and one at San San opposite Frenchman's Cove. Although Jamaica's golf clubs are for the most part private, guests of affiliated hotels are entitled to lower greens fees.

Tennis: Excellent tennis courts can be found at or near most hotels throughout the island. (See "Where to Stay" listing.)

Polo: Regular matches are held at Drax Hall near Ocho Rios on Saturday afternoons, and at Hanover Polo Club near Montego Bay every Sunday at 4:30 P.M.

Horseback Riding: For the horse fancier, the Good Hope Hotel in Montego Bay offers over 200 miles of plantation trails. Tryall Hotel and Circle Seven Ranch in the Montego Bay area also have good riding facilities.

Horse Racing: Racing enthusiasts can follow the horses at the large, modern track as Caymanas near Kingston. Meets featuring cup and stake races are held each Saturday throughout the year and on public holidays. Pari-mutuel bets may be made.

Cricket: In line with Jamaica's British heritage, cricket matches are played on the green all over the island much of the year. There is no baseball in Jamaica.

Water sports

Underwater: Skindiving, snorkeling and scuba diving are popular sports in Jamaica. A rocky reef extends eight miles east of Kingston and the Cays of Palisadoes are excellent hunting grounds. Along the island's north coast are a great many coral reefs whose protected waters are safe and harbor tiny fish, brilliantly hued anemones and undersea plant life. Most river mouths offer good sport and game fish such as snapper, grouper, barracuda and yellowtail, as well as lobster and shrimp, that can be stalked by spearfisherman and cameraman alike.

Water Skiing: Facilities for water skiing are offered by most hotels and there is an annual championship run-off in Kingston at Morgan's Harbour, at Ocho Rios and Montego Bay. Surfboards are also available at most sea-front hotels.

Swimming: There are fine beaches all along Jamaica's north shore. Most of the hotels in the Montego Bay area have access to a beach or have beaches of their own. In the Ocho Rios area all hotels have sea frontage. In Port Antonio, swimming is available at San San Beach; at Blue Lagoon, a mysterious deep hole in the sea bottom where the water is a deep ultramarine; and along the mile-long stretch of Long Bay.

There are beaches near Kingston, but none in the city itself. At Lime Cay, about a mile south of Port Royal, there is a white sand beach on a tiny island. There is also a public park and swimming is permitted at Gunboat Beach. Other beaches, of dark, volcanic sand, are located to the east of the city, and there is a new beach area at Port Henderson across the harbor to the west of the city.

Fishing: Located directly in the migratory path of many species of fighting trophy-fish, Jamaica is a mecca for deep-sea anglers. Marlin, sailfish, wahoo, dolphin, tuna, bonito and barracuda, to name a few, abound in its deep coastal waters. Whitehouse, on the southwest coast, offers a kind of "sure thing" fishing as its three banks are protected from Jamaica's southwesterly trade winds. Though not a resort, limited accommodations are available at Blue Water Club, 35 miles from Montego Bay.

In Kingston, charter boats fish from Morgan's Harbour Marina, located on the Palisadoes at Port Royal. A blue marlin tournament is held here annually around Christmas. The Jamaica International Fishing Tournament, held off Port Antonio, and the Montego Bay Blue Marlin Tournament both take place in October. A lack of sufficient, well-equipped charter boats has been a problem, though an increasing number of these craft are available in Ocho Rios and Port Antonio. The Montego Bay fleet consists of 11 sports fishermen, all equipped with tackle and bait.

For fresh-water enthusiasts, river fishing for mullet, calipoeva, snook, tarpon and snapper is excellent and there are over 40 rivers in which to fish. Proven streams are Martha Brae at Falmouth (contact Good Hope Plantation); Dunn's, White, Roaring and Rio Nueva rivers near Ocho Rios (contact Don Sutton-Brown, Silver Seas Hotel); the Rio Grande at Port Antonio (contact Mr. D. Smith-Bingham, Portland Fishing Club); and the Black and Cabarritta Rivers on the South Coast (contact Mrs. F. Bailey, Blue Water Fishing Club). In Kingston, advice can be had from Aguilar's sports shop, Harbour St.

Boating: Not many sailing ships are available for charter in Jamaica, although these can sometimes be arranged through the Montego Bay Yacht Club, Morgan's Harbour Yacht Marina in Port Royal, the Royal Jamaica Yacht Club in Kingston, and the Ocho Rios Sailing Club, which races catamarans and sailfish. Every two years in March the Biennial Miami–Montego Bay Yacht Race is held.

For the less adventurous, large glass-bottomed boats take visitors from hotels out over reefs, chasms and gorges of underwater mountains made of twisted limestone formations and giant growths of coral.

There is a day's cruise starting at Kingston's Victoria Pier, stopping at Morgan's Harbour Hotel for rum punch and lunch and on to Lime Cay, little islands close to Port Royal, for swimming and skin-diving. Contact Martin's Tours for information.

There is no restriction on the entry of private yachts at any of the island's ports. Arrangements for fuel, water and anchorage may be made with the Harbor Master, Kingston; or with the aforementioned yacht clubs in Kingston, Port Royal and Montego Bay.

Shopping buys / something interesting, something exotic

Jamaica offers some of the finest shopping items in the Caribbean, thanks to the free-port status of almost 50 stores in Kingston, Montego Bay and Ocho Rios. There is also the huge bazaar-like Victoria Crafts Market in Kingston where straw hats, baskets, placemats, needlework and other evidences of the island's handicraft are sold. And fresh and colorful concepts in jewelry, clothing and even footwear are featured by the owner-designers of shops both in and out of the resort belt.

Free-port shopping is a privilege extended only to nonresidents of the island. Visitors select merchandise from sample goods in the "In Bond" shop and are issued a receipt upon payment. These goods are delivered to the purchaser at the airport before his departure from the island. Free-port concessions are also located at both Kingston (Palisadoes) and Montego Bay airports.

Savings for U.S. and Canadian citizens are generally up to 60%. Excellent buys include liquor, English china (Minton, Spode, Wedgwood), Swiss watches (Ernest Borel, Omega, Rolex, Nivada), perfumes (Dior, Ralphael, Dana, Chanel, Carven) and cameras (Nikon, Leica, Bolex, Konica, Olympus, Minox, Hasselblad).

A complete listing of the free-port shops is usually available upon arrival. These stores carry a wide range of merchandise in addition to those mentioned—from hairbrushes and golf balls to silverware, cutlery and cashmere sweaters.

Designer goods in convenient American sizes can outfit visiting shoppers from head to toe. "Tie-heads" (Jamaican for scarves), African-style caftans in colorful prints, bush jackets for men, original ceramic jewelry, and a wide (and wild) variety of sandals are available along with elegant hand-embroidered cutwork and the more conventional wardrobe items.

Dining, dancing and night life

KINGSTON

Blue Mountain Inn: At elevation of 1,100 feet on banks of Mammee River. Once the Great House of a coffee plantation. Choice wines, blazing log fire impart elegance. Jacket and tie compulsory, ladies advised to take a wrap. Both a-la-carte and table d'hote menus available. Count on a tab-for-two of at least $25, with wine and tips. Reservations recommended. Tel: 77400.

Calabash And The Sombrero: For dancing. Features island's top bands with the new "pressure" beat.

Cathay Club: 88-92 Orange St. Old, established and highly regarded Chinese restaurant. Roof garden, cocktail bar. Wear what you like and expect good food and service. Tel: 22725.

Cloud 9: At Half Way Tree. Air-conditioned cocktail lounge. Operating in an atmosphere of intimate gloom. Excellent Italian pizzas and cold Lowenbrau beer

on tap. Dancing, no cover charge. Tel: 65444.

Club Havana: Near the harbor. A circular room with an under-the-stars dance floor. Drinks for two only $1.50. For the more adventurous. Tel: 81935.

Continental: At Half Way Tree. Noted for cuisine and management's practice of sending a goblet of wine to each diner. Air-conditioned. Dinner for two within $10. Tel: 67979.

Courtleigh Manor Hotel: Dancing, entertainment nightly in the **Grotto Bar** and **Celebrity Room.** Visitors are welcome to Tuesday night poolside barbecue, and a special Jamaican dinner Sunday.

Ferry Inn: On main road between Spanish Town and Kingston. 300-year old tavern with Cordon Bleu cuisine. Dinner for two well within $10. Dress and atmosphere strictly informal. Tel: 38573.

Flamingo Hotel: Dining, dancing, entertainment, floor shows. Tel: 65535-6.

Golden Dragon: 7 Constant Spring Rd. at Half Way Tree. Dining, dancing, entertainment. Orchestra and calypso band. Open-air garden club.

Hummingbird Restaurant & Cocktail Lounge: 34 Beechwood Ave. off Half Way Tree Rd. Mostly Jamaican cuisine. Dinner reservations advisable. Tel: 66821.

Jamaica Arms: 14 Port Royal St. Air-conditioned. Tel: 22103.

Liguanea Terrace Hotel: On Old Hope Rd. just Below Hope Gardens. Lunch and dinner in open-air dining room. Native and American cuisine. Tel: 77721-4.

Mayfair Hotel: 4 W. Kings House. Good English-style food, fish and chips on Friday. Tel: 69419.

Mee Mee Restaurant: Just above Liguanea Plaza on Hope Rd. Very elegant, very Chinese. Tel: 79361.

Oriental Restaurant: At Tropical Plaza, Half Way Tree. Light, crisp Chinese fare. Open for lunch and dinner. Tel: 68864.

Premium Juice Bar: At Victoria Crafts Market. Attractive bar serving fresh Jamaican fruit juice. Don't miss the chance of sampling some of Jamaica's more unusual fruit juices: mango, tamarind, soursop.

Queen of Hearts: Oxford Terrace. Candlelight dining-dancing, cocktail lounge.

Orchestra. Open till you leave. A gathering place for Kingston's jazz buffs. Tel: 67504.

Rodney Arms: In Port Henderson, across harbor from Kingston. Seafood served in 18th-century village atmosphere.

Sheraton-Kingston: Entertainment and dancing nightly in **Jonkanoo Lounge.** Have dinner first in attractive **Spanish Main Dining Room,** which offers an excellent menu. **Pepperpot Coffee Shop** open till midnight. Tel: 65432.

Shish Kebab: 7 Beckford St. A bistro with lamb kidneys on a spit and labban, in authentic Arabic style. Tel: 24382.

Swiss Chalet: Kingston's newest and fanciest. Gracious dining, vintage wines.

Terra Nova: Waterloo Rd. Food, service and wine list will please the discriminating. Specialties of the house: escargot and Chicken Kiev. Dinner for two easily runs to $25 with wine and tips. Tel: 66540.

Tip Top: 43 Half Way Tree Rd. From wienerschnitzel to apfelstrudel, this specialty German restaurant also features smoked blue marlin, many varieties of German sausage. Tel: 68805.

Treasure Chest: On King St. at Victoria Crafts Market. attractively primitive setting.

Wing Shinn: 31 Luke Lane. Chinese food. Tel: 23072.

The V.I.P.: 84 Half Way Tree Rd. Dining, dancing and entertainment under the stars. Good band.

For the young set who like to move: the **Copa, Blinking Beacon, Blue Mist** and **Johnson's Drive-Inn.**

MONTEGO BAY

Buddies Drive-In: At Reading. Waterfront restaurant complete with moonlight and oil lamps. Lobster, chicken. Tel: Reading 261.

Campbell's Airport Restaurant: Air-conditioned and popular even with nontravelers. Cocktail lounge and soda fountain. Open 8 A.M.–midnight. 24-hour service cafeteria (downstairs). Tel: 2145.

Cats Corner Club: Opened last winter. Posh, soundproof, private club for members and guests.

The Cellar Club: Union St. Popular downtown restaurant. Italian food and imported steaks, drinks in the cellar. Tel: 2667.

China Doll: 35 St. James St. Chinese cuisine. Tel: 2461.

Club 35: Smart club, elaborate lighting decor and floor show nightly.

Fisherman's Inn: At Luminous Lagoon, Falmouth. Fresh seafood such as mullet, snapper, lobster and crayfish.

Great House At Sign: 10 minutes ride from town. Six-course native luncheons with donkey ride and tour of the property thrown in. All food served is home-grown.

Harmony House: A small hotel featuring a garden restaurant. Attractive, reasonable prices.

Hilton's Restaurant: At City Centre shopping arcade, upstairs. Good, reasonably priced meals. Lunch and dinner.

The Little Inn: On Orange St. downtown. Excellent place for light lunch. Brick-built, old-world bar is one of the town's pleasantest drinking places. Tel: 3095.

Lotus Room: Church St. Chinese food.

Miranda Hill: Crystal, fancy chandeliers and hand-rubbed furniture contribute to gracious atmosphere. Fine food. Tel: 2161.

Montego Bay Racquet Club: Hilltop hotel and restaurant perched high above bay and town. Continental and American cuisine. Table d'hote and à la carte. Reservations necessary. Tel: 2165.

Montego Inn: On Fort St. close to town. Air-conditioned, à la carte. Popular with local business people.

The Old Mill: A steakhouse and restaurant at Coral Springs, between Falmouth and Duncans. A pleasant stopover.

Pelican Grill & Coffee Shop: Gloucester Ave. Air-conditioned and good halfway house for those walking into town. Lunch and dinner served.

The Playmate Club: Adjacent to Sunset Lodge on Kent Ave. Music is loud, continuous and the latest. Drinks only $1 apiece and a $5 minimum.

Poinciana Inn: On Gloucester Ave. Serves good seafood and steaks in a delightful garden setting.

Reef Club: About five miles out of town. An attractive nightclub specializing

in Italian food. Dancing, nightly entertainment. Tel: Rosehall 292.

The Rice Bowl: On Market St. second
floor. Somewhat off the tourist track.
Top-notch, low-cost native cuisine.

Ridgely's Plaza Steakhouse: At Ridgely
Plaza Hotel. Prime imported steaks, prime
prices. Open for dinner. Coffeeshop service on Bay Terrace for luncheon. Tel:
2541.

Rum Barrel Inn: On Market St. Small
lively restaurant and bar. Has a touch
of the English "pub" flavor but the cuisine is mainly French. Features seafood,
including baked crab and baked stuffed
lobster.

Verney House Hotel: Leader Ave. Buffet
every Saturday 7–11 P.M. Good Jamaican
food, dancing to Calypso band.

White Sands Inn: Kent Ave. Dining in
secluded tropical garden. Reservations
necessary. Tel: 2314.

Yellow Bird: On Church St. A lively
swinging nightclub. Dancing, down-to-
earth native show. Popular with locals.
Tel: 2929.

OCHO RIOS

Bird and Bottle: On Main St. Open air
dining, air-conditioned cocktail lounge.
Chicken in the basket and charcoal-
broiled steaks. Dishes of particular country feature Thursday nights. Most meals
around $2 and drinks in the dollar range.

Brown Jug Club: Lively downtown
night spot. Activity till the wee hours.

Club Maracas: Every night of the week.
Chinese cuisine by reservation only. Activity until the small hours, with dance
band, Calypso, limbo and show.

Golden Head Hotel: Barbecue steak dinner on the pier every Tuesday where
banana loading can be watched at nearby
Oracabessa Harbour.

Jamaica Hilton: Full entertainment program, varied cuisine. **Limbo Room** has
native floor shows with dancers who double as chambermaids, cashiers, or bell-
boys during the day. Coffeeshop offers
snacks or full meals, open daily 10 A.M.–
I A.M. Always informal. Tel: St. Ann Bay
382-6.

The Little Pub: At Celia Byass Centre.

Quality Jamaican food as well as banana
splits and other soda fountain delicacies.
Lunch and dinner.

Playboy Club: In Jamaica Playboy Club-
Hotel at Oracabessa. Air-conditioned.
Good music, top entertainment. Dress is
informal in **Bunny Bar** and **Patio,** jacket
and tie in dining room, nightclub and
penthouse.

The Ruin: Recently restored, 40-foot
high-and-wide waterfall and three acres
of tropical gardens. Luncheon and dinner
with dancing, entertainment nightly.
Open 11 A.M.–3 A.M. Tel: 333.

Tower Isle Hotel: Visitors are welcome
to dine at this old-established and famous
hotel whose international cuisine is well
known.

Special events, festivals, celebrations and all that calypso

Jamaica New Film Society Festival: An
outstanding film is shown at the Little
Theatre, Kingston, on the second Tuesday of each month. Throughout year.

Annual Jamboree Tournament: At Tryall, Half Moon-Rose Hall Golf Courses,
Montego Bay. January.

Annual National Exhibition of Painting:
At Institute of Jamaica, Kingston. Late
February–March.

Flower Show: Annual exhibition of St.
James Horticultural Society, Montego
Bay. March.

Yachting: Annual Regatta of Montego
Bay Yacht Club. March.

Flower Show: Annual exhibition of Jamaica Horticultural Society. April.

Queen's Birthday Celebration: Sailing
regattas at Kingston and Montego Bay.
Special Trooping of the Color at Up Park
Camp. June 10.

Independence Day Celebrations: Ceremonial parade at National Stadium; exhibitions, arts and crafts, culinary competitions. July–August.

International Fishing Tournament: At
Port Antonio. October.

International Bill Fish Tournament:
Morgan's Harbour Beach Club & Marina,
Port Royal. November.

Yachting: Annual Regatta. At Royal Jamaica Yacht Club, Kingston. November.

Christmas Day Celebrations: Junkanoo bands, holiday concerts and street celebrations. Similar events on Boxing Day, December 26.

The galleries / the gardens / the lively arts

Combining museum, art gallery and library, the Institute of Jamaica is a mélange of the topical and traditional. Exhibits range from relics of the island's early aboriginal inhabitants, the Arawaks, to contemporary works of art by Jamaican and visiting artists. Artifacts from the island's past also are on display at the White Marl Museum, 10 miles west of Kingston, at the recently excavated site of an early Arawak village.

Art galleries are abundant throughout Jamaica, though many works of art can be seen at sidewalk exhibitions. Viewings in private studios may be arranged by calling the Jamaica School of Arts and Crafts. Sculptress Edna Manley's large wood panel is in the Sheraton-Kingston Hotel and other examples of her work can be seen in the Kingston Parish Church and in the little town of Morant Bay.

Galleries in Kingston include Hills, on Harbour Street, and the Contemporary Artists Association of Jamaica, on Constant Spring Road. If you're on the north coast, the little town of Rio Bueno offers an enchanting small gallery run by artist Joe James, and Gloria Escoffrey's private studio, which you can visit in the evenings and on weekends. Eastward along the coast, between Ocho Rios and Oracabessa, is the Galina Point Studio of the two Parbosinghs where visitors are welcome. On the way to Montego Bay, stop in the old town of Falmouth and visit Herbert Palmer's Art Gallery. And once in Montego Bay you can visit Michael Lester's Gallery and the Neville Budhai Art Gallery.

For those interested in drama and dance, the Little Theatre in Kingston offers both in the Jamaican tradition and its *tour de force* is the annual Pantomime, a Jamaican stage entertainment. The National Dance Theatre Company specializes in modern dance influenced by the island's music and legends.

Largest of several public gardens is Hope Botanical Gardens in suburban Kingston. In addition to its exotic flora and artificial lake, it also contains an aquarium and the island zoo. Other outstanding gardens are: Castleton Gardens, over 100 years old, on the route linking Kingston with the north coast; Fern Gully near Ocho Rios; the 200-year-old Bath Gardens in St. Thomas with its rare trees; and Cinchona (the Hill Gardens), just under 5,000 feet high in the Blue Mountains.

Real estate and retirement

There is a wide variation in property values depending on situation and land use. Agricultural land is, naturally, much lower in cost than land in development or tourist areas.

In the resort area of Montego Bay, inland lots of 1/3 of an acre start at $2,900 and go as high as $19,600 an acre in top developments such as Rose Hall or Tryall where there is a championship golf course. Homes start at about $14,000 and it is possible to rent houses for $140 to $1,400 per month and apartments for as little as $84.

In Ocho Rios large parcels of land are available and, consequently, are considerably cheaper. Also, some lands not on the beach enjoy beach privileges. Homes start at about $16,000.

In and around Port Antonio, only the San San Estate has been developed as a resort area, and this includes a nine-hole golf course. Prices range from $2,240 to $5,600 per acre but, at present, there are no sea-front lots available. Homes in this area are all comparatively new and modern, with excellent facilities and landscaping. As a result, even very small homes with no appreciable land are quite expensive.

On the westerly tip of the island, the Negril area is being developed. Plans include a permanent community, hotels, a yacht club, golf course and large tracts for recreational activities. Further information can be obtained from Negril Land Authority, Box 67, Savanna-la-Mar.

While certain unavoidables (i.e., income tax) are pretty steep, such luxuries as maids, gardeners, chauffeurs and "bearers" (messengers) will not overly burden a budget. However, Jamaica is still primarily geared to a higher cost of living and social security will *not* cover living expenses.

For a complete guide on land and homes, information may be obtained from:

The C. D. Alexander Co. Ltd.
77 Harbour St., Kingston.

The Jamaica Company
1 King St., Montego Bay.

Graham Associates Ltd.
1 King St., Montego Bay.

Lord Ronald Graham & Co. Ltd.
1 Pineapple Pl., Ochos Rios.

Mr. Denis Smith-Bingham
San San Estate, Port Antonio.

Industry and commerce

Until postwar years, the most important factor in the economy of Jamaica was agriculture. Sugar was the island's mainstay, backed up by extensive cultivation of bananas, citrus fruits, coffee, coconuts and pimento (allspice). The discovery of bauxite added a new and important industry. Jamaica now provides approximately ⅔ of the world's supply of the ore that goes into aluminum.

A government-backed Industrial Development Corporation is sponsoring vigorous expansion of the island's manufacturing potential. Important concessions regarding investment, tax relief, duties on imported raw materials and machinery have been made. Major industries have been lured to Jamaica's shores but at a much slower rate than, say, to Puerto Rico, with its Operation Bootstrap. This may be partly due to the Jamaican's ambiguous attitude toward progress—he would like to "make good" but not at the expense of changing his leisurely, relatively unautomated way of life.

This same attitude held true for the tourist industry. But in the last few years, Jamaica has gone all out for its "guests." The island has opened its doors to the middle-income visitor rather than catering exclusively to the very (very) wealthy. Customs officials and taxi drivers have been encouraged to smile, hotel facilities are under constant scrutiny and free-port shops are a major attraction. Jamaica also produces a wide variety of handicrafts, made mostly in the country and sold in specialty shops throughout the resort areas. These hand-crafted items include straw goods, embroidered dresses and beads made from local plant seeds.

Meet the Jamaicans

Organization	Official	Phone
Jamaica Amateur Radio Assn.	Mr. E. M. Metcalf	78774 (Kingston)
	Mr. Leslie B. Fletcher	2602 (Montego Bay)
Antiques	Mr. Henry Vendryes	24644 (Kingston)
	Miss Susie Latreille	491 (Ocho Rios)
Astronomical Assn. of Jamaica	Mr. Charles Hanna	323 (Stony Hill)
	Mr. Leslie Powell	78499 (Kingston)
Biology	Dr. J. R. Parnell	70383 (Kingston)
Birdwatching	Mrs. Phoebe Hart	41216 (Kingston)
	Mr. Herman Douce	2909 (Montego Bay)
	Mr. Patrick Tenison	289 (Falmouth)
Botany	Dr. G. H. Sidrak	70309 (Kingston)
Jamaica Bridge Assn.	Mr. George Desnoes	23905-7 or
		26538-0 (Kingston)
Butterfly Collecting	Mr. Peter Gunter	RH 387 (Kingston)

Organization	Official	Phone
Jamaica Caving Club	Mr. A. E. Teulen	77258 (Kingston)
Coin Collecting	Mrs. Greta Barrow	77451 (Kingston)
Fencing Assn. of Jamaica	Mr. Raymond Jackson	25461 or
		25464 (Kingston)
Kingston Fencing Club	Mr. Ronnie Nasralla	22321 or
		22772 (Kingston)
Hiking	Mr. Derrick Dyer	79642 (Kingston)
Jamaica Horticultural Society	Mr. P. W. C. Burke	42658 (Kingston)
Jamaica Orchid Society	Sir John Carberry	76553 (Kingston)
Cornwall Horticultural Society	Dr. Ferdinand Levy	2024 (Montego Bay)
History	Mr. Clinton Black	79257 (Kingston)
	Mr. Paul White	2224 (Montego Bay)
Jazz	Mr. Jimmy Carnegie	83202 (Kingston)
	Mr. Seymour Mullings	208 (Claremont)
Shell Collecting	Mr. George A. Rutherford	2708 (Montego Bay)
	Mr. Patrick J. Tenison	289 (Falmouth)
Stamp Collecting	Dr. Don Gore	70727 (Kingston)
	Mr. Patrick J. Tenison	289 (Falmouth)

WHERE TO STAY — In Jamaica

Kingston Area		Dec. 15–April 14 U. S. Currency		April 15–Dec. 14	
	Plan	Double	Single	Double	Single
ABAHATI Kingston (26 Rms.) **(p)**	(CP)	$10–18	$ 5– 8	$10–16	$ 5– 8
CLIEVEDEN COURT Kingston (28 Rms.) **(p)**	(MAP)	$25	$15	$20	$12–50
	(EP)	$18–20	$12–13	$13	$ 9
	(CP)	$20–22	$13–14	$15	$10
COURTLEIGH MANOR Kingston (67 Rms.) **(p)**	(AP)			$40–44	$22–26
	(MAP)			$34–38	$19–23
	(CP)	$26–30	$16–20	$24–28	$14–18
FLAMINGO Kingston (60 Rms.) **(p)**	(MAP)	$30–32	$20–22	$24–26	$15–16
GREEN GABLES Kingston (12 Rms.)	(EP)	$10–12	$ 4– 6	$10–12	$ 4– 6
LIGUANEA TERRACE Kingston (37 Rms.) **(p)**	(MAP)	$22–25	$13–15	$20–25	$12–15
MAYFAIR Kingston (10 Rms.)	(MAP)	$16–18	$10–12	$16–18	$10–12
MELROSE Kingston (25 Rms.) **(p)**	(EP)	$10–20	$ 5–10	$ 8–14	$ 4– 7
MIMOSA LODGE Kingston (18 Rms.) **(p)**	(AP)	$20–22	$10–12	$16–18	$ 8–10
	(MAP)	$18–20	$ 9–11	$14–16	$ 7– 9
	(CP)	$14–16	$ 7– 9	$12–14	$ 6– 8
MONA Kingston (30 Rms.) **(p)**	(MAP)	$34	$15	$30	$13
MORGAN'S HARBOUR Port Royal (37 Rms.) **(b, p)**	(MAP)	$32–34	$18–20	$28–30	$15–16
	(EP)	$20–22	$12–14	$16–18	$ 9–10
MYRTLE BANK Kingston (52 Rms.) **(p)**	(MAP)	$32	$18	$32	$18
	(EP)	$20	$12	$20	$12
	(CP)	$23	$14	$23	$14

OLYMPIA HOTEL	(CP)	$18–20	$14–18	$12–14	$ 9–12
Kingston (22 Rms.) **(p)**					
PINE GROVE	(AP)	$26	$14	$26	$14
Kingston (30 Rms.)					
ROSENEATH	(CP)	$13–20	$ 6–12	$ 8–16	$ 5– 8
Kingston (22 Rms.)					
SEYMOUR	(EP)	$15	$ 9	$15	$ 9
Kingston (46 Rms.) **(p)**					
SHERATON KINGSTON	(AP)	$46–48	$29–31	$44–48	$27–31
Kingston	(MAP)	$40–42	$26–28	$38–42	$24–28
(202 Rms.) **(p, g)**	(EP)	$24–26	$18–20	$22–26	$16–20
STONY HILL				$20	$15
Kingston (20 Rms.) **(p)**					
STRAWBERRY HILL	(MAP)	$24–30	$12–15	$20–28	$10–14
Irishtown (6 Rms.) **(p)**					
TERRA NOVA	(EP)	$20	$15	$20	$15
Kingston (13 Rms.) **(p)**					

Montego Bay Area

BAY ROC	(MAP)	$60–70	$45–50	$36–42	$24–30
Montego Bay (92 Rms.) **(b, p, t)**					
BEACH VIEW	(MAP)	$32–37	$16–19	$22	$11
Montego Bay	(EP)	$20–25	$10–13	$12	$ 6
(29 Rms.) **(b)**					
BREEZY POINT EAST	(MAP)	$50–60	$35–45	On Request	
Montego Bay (40 Rms.) **(b, p, g)**					
BLAIRGOWRIE	(MAP)	$20–30	$30–35	$12.50	$15.50
Montego Bay (21 Rms.) **(b, p)**					
CASA BLANCA	(EP)	On Request		$12–15	$ 8–10
Montego Bay (46 Rms.) **(b)**					
CASA MONTEGO	(MAP)	$56–60	$35	$38–40	$22–24
Montego Bay (98 Rms.) **(b, p)**					
CHATHAM	(EP)	$26–31	$12–15	$14–16	$ 7– 8
Montego Bay (67 Rms., 20 Ctgs.) **(b, p)**					
COLONY	(MAP)	$55–65	Not	$37–43	$27–33
Montego Bay (94 Rms.) **(b, p, g)**		Available			
CONTINENTAL	(MAP)	$40		$25	$15
Montego Bay (20 Rms.) **(p)**			(CP)	$15	$10
CORAL CLIFF	(MAP)	$36	$23	$22	$13
Montego Bay	(EP)	$22	$16	$12	$ 8
(20 Rms.) **(b)**					
CORNICHE STUDIO					
APTS.	(EP)	$22–25	On	$13–17	On
Montego Bay (20 Rms.) **(p)**			Request		Request
FAIRFIELD INN					
& MONTEGO	(EP)	$30	$25	$18	$12
BAY COUNTRY CLUB	(MAP)	$48	$34	$34	$20
Montego Bay (30 Rms.) **(p, t, g)**					
GLOUCESTER HOUSE					
HOTEL	(MAP)	$38	$20	No rates available	
Montego Bay (43 Rms.) **(b)**					

GOOD HOPE	(AP)	$56–60	$42–45		Closed
Falmouth (23 Rms.) **(b, p, t)**					
HACTON HOUSE	(CP)	$20–25	$12	–	–
Montego Bay	(EP)	–	–	$12	$ 6
(27 Rms.) **(b)**					
HALF MOON	(MAP)			$36–56	$22–36
Montego Bay	(AP)	$70–85			
(116 Rms.) **(b, g, t)**		(Dec. 16-April 15)		(April 16-Dec. 15)	
HARMONY HOUSE	(MAP)	$26	$13–14	$20	$10–11
Montego Bay	(CP)	$22	$11–12	$14	$ 7– 8
(21 Rms.) **(b)**	(EP)	–	–	$12	$ 6– 7
HOLIDAY HOUSE	(EP)	$30–36	$30–36	$13–20	$10–15
Montego Bay	(CP)	$35–41	$33–39	$18–25	$13–18
(10 Rms.) **(b, p)**					
HOTEL 35	(CP)	$22	$12		On Request
Montego Bay (10 Rms.)					
IRONSHORE LODGE					
Montego Bay (10 Rms.)		On Request			
MIRANDA HILL	(MAP)	$75–95		$38–50	$30
Montego Bay (40 Rms.) **(p)**		(Dec. 16-April 15)		(April 16-Dec. 15)	
MONTEGO BAY					
RACQUET CLUB	(MAP)	$48–56	$38–44	$28–34	$18–24
Montego Bay (25 Rms.) **(p, t)**			(CP) $22–28		$14–20
MONTEGO BEACH	(MAP)	$55–70	$45–50	$36–42	$24–26
Montego Bay (90 Rms.) **(b)**					
MONTEGO INN	(EP)	$22	$17.50	$12	$ 8
Montego Bay (30 Rms.)					
RIDGELY PLAZA	(EP)	$16–22	$10	$ 9–12	$ 6
Montego Bay (18 Rms.)					
ROUND HILL		On Request			CLOSED
Montego Bay (97 Rms.) **(b, p, t)**					
ROYAL CARIBBEAN	(MAP)	$50–75	$34–45	$34–44	$18–22
Montego Bay (116 Rms.) **(b, p, t)**					
SUNSET LODGE	(AP)	$70–100	$50	CLOSED	
Montego Bay (40 Rms.) **(b, t)**					
VERNEY HOUSE	(CP)	$24	$15	$12	$ 7
Nr. Airport, Montego (25 Rms.) **(p)**					
WHITE SANDS INN	(CP)	$32–36	$26–30	$16–20	$12–15
Montego Bay (15 Rms.) **(p)**					

Ocho Rios & North Shore

CARIB-OCHO RIOS	(MAP)	$45–60	$35–50	$35–40	$20–24
Ocho Rios (63 Rms.) **(b, p,. t)**					
CASA MARIA	(MAP)	$35–46	$20–26	$24–30	$14–18
Port Maria (24 Rms.) **(b, p)**					
GOLDEN HEAD	(MAP)	$42–52	$30–38	$28–36	$18–20
BEACH Oracabessa (70 Rms.) **(b, p, t)**					
HIBISCUS LODGE	(MAP)	$28–30	$14	$24	$12
Ocho Rios	(CP)	$20–25	$10	$16	$ 8
(14 Rms.) **(b)**					
ISLAND INN	(MAP)	$40–54	$25–37	$32–38	$20–25
Ocho Rios (50 Rms.) **(b, p)**			(EP) $18–24		$13–18
			(CP) $22–28		$15–20

Hotel	Plan				
JAMAICA HILTON Ocho Rios (176 Rms.) (b, p, t)	(MAP)	$48–65	$40–57	$36–42	$26–32
JAMAICA INN Ocho Rios (35 Rms.) Boscobel (b, p, t)	(MAP) (AP)	$60–70		$38–42	$24–26
JAMAICA PLAYBOY CLUB (162 Rms.) (b, p, t)	(MAP)	$48–65	$40–57	$36–44	$23–29
PLANTATION INN Ocho Rios (48 Rms.) (b ,t)	(MAP) (AP)	$60–68		$34–36	$22–24
RUNAWAY BAY Runaway Bay (100 Rms.) (b, p, t, g)	(MAP)	$56–70	$46–60	$34–38	$18–22
SANS SOUCI Ocho Rios (22 Rms.) (b, p)	(MAP)	$48–52	$38–42	$32–36	$20–24
SHAW PARK BEACH HOTEL Ocho Rios (78 Rms; 3 Suites) (b)	(MAP)	$50–70	$40	$34–39	$20
SILVER SEAS Ocho Rios (55 Rms.) (b, t)	(MAP) (EP) (CP)	$40–50 $30–40 $32–42	$30–35 $25–30 $26–31		
SILVER SPRAY Runaway Bay (22 Rms.) (p, g)	(EP) (MAP)	$45–55	On Req.	$15	$10
TOWER ISLE Ocho Rios (100 Rms.) (b, p, t)	(MAP)	$44–58	$20–50	$34–40	$15–30
TROPIC WINDS MOTEL Port Maria (16 Rms.) (b, p)	(EP) (CP) (MAP)	$16 $20 $26	$10 $12 $15	$12 $16 $22	$ 8 $10 $13
WINDSOR HOTEL St. Ann's Bay (21 Rms.) (p)	(MAP) (AP) (CP)	$36 $40 $27	$18 $20 $14	$32 $36	$16 $18

Port Antonio Area

Hotel	Plan				
BONNIE VIEW Port Antonio (23 Rms.) (p)	(MAP)	$28–35	$18–25	$22–28	$12–18
DE MONTEVIN LODGE Port Antonio (15 Rms.)	(AP) (MAP)	$16 $14	$14 $12	$14 $12	$12 $10
FRENCHMAN'S COVE Port Antonio (36 Rms.) (b, g, t)	(AP)	$145–215	$100	$55–104	$40–60
JAMAICA REEF Port Antonio (54 Rms.) (b, p)	(MAP)	$45–60	$35–50	$32–40	$20–30

LEGEND FOR HOTEL LISTINGS: (AP) American Plan (room and 3 meals); **MAP)** Modified American Plan (room, breakfast and dinner); **(CP)** Continental Plan (room and breakfast); **(EP)** European Plan (room only). All rates quoted on a per-day basis and subject to change. Confirmed reservations at specific rates desired are always recommended.

HOTEL FACILITIES: (b) beach; **(p)** pool; **(t)** tennis; **(g)** golf.

MARTINIQUE

Sugar cane, bananas and pineapples fill the fields of Martinique, and above them are the green hills, dominated by Mont Pelée. The island is the birthplace of the Empress Josephine (and of the beguine) and home to some of the finest French cooking in the hemisphere.

Where they begin the beguine

I came to Martinique the lucky way—by sailing yacht.

There was no fasten-seat-belts, no baking runway, no crowds and queues and customs. As we coasted north-to-south down the leeward shore of the island, there were only the sparkling sea and castled mountains, transfixed in stillness under the tropic sun.

Northernmost and highest of the mountains is Pelée. And it has not always been still. At 7:52 on the morning of May 8, 1902, it exploded in a volcanic eruption that was one of the major disasters of history. But on this later day, as we sailed past, it was as calm and gentle as the white clouds that fringed its cone.

Then it faded astern, but Eden continued: a long luxuriant coast of hills and valleys, palms and beaches. After some fifteen miles it angled inward, and, following it, we came into a deep, broad bay. On the bay's northern shore was Martinique's capital city, Fort-de-France, but we didn't go there just yet. Crossing to the south shore, we dropped anchor off the sheltered beach of l'Anse Mitan.

It was a Sunday midafternoon and the beach was crowded—not with tourists but with holidaying Martiniquaises. The voices that came to us across the water were all French. The breeze ruffled a *tricouleur* on a hilltop flagpole. If the breeze had been less soft, the skins of the bathers a few shades paler, we could have been at anchorage off a beach on the Côte d'Azur.

Then as the sun declined, the bathers left. Remaining were only a few moored yachts like our own. In the dusk we rode our dinghy ashore to a beach-front inn called Auberge de l'Anse Mitan, and here we felt ourselves even more in the heart of France. We sipped apéritifs. We dined on *langouste* with white wine and *tournedos* with red. We ended with salad and cheese and fruit and liqueurs, and somehow staggered back to the dinghy and found our way to our boat.

Lying on the deck in the darkness, we watched the distant lights of Fort-de-France and the seemingly closer lights of the enormous stars. Across the bay, from somewhere, came the faint, plangent music of a Martiniquaise beguine.

*View of the quay along the River Madame in Fort-de-France
on the island of Martinique*

Yes, this was the way to come to Martinique. Or to any island.

The next morning we cruised over to Fort-de-France, and Eden gave way to the 20th century. The island capital is not just a town but a city of almost 100,000 inhabitants: a jam-packed, active, clangorous minimetropolis that, next to Trinidad's Port-of-Spain, is the biggest in the Lesser Antilles.

It is also, like l'Anse Mitan—like all the island—very French, and not by accident. In contrast to Britain, which has allowed its West Indian domains to slip steadily away toward independence, France has been holding hers with a tenacious hand.

The two largest, Martinique and Guadeloupe, no longer rank as colonies but as integral *départments,* or states, of the Republic. The officialdom is as deep-down French as on Paris' Quai d'Orsay. Le Grand Charles makes periodic visits. On Martinique you can scarcely go a mile *(pardon, un kilometre)* in any direction without being reminded that here was the birthplace of Napoleon's Empress Josephine.

Not that you will mistake Fort-de-France for the homeland's impeccable City of Light. To begin with, it is dark at night. By day it runs to the frowsily decrepit, and while many new buildings are going up—mostly government-built or financed—the majority are still of antique vintage. In the heart of town, the municipal park, called La Savane (featuring a statue of Josephine), is a long shaggy way from the Tuilleries or Bois de Boulogne.

There are oases, however. Also in the midst of downtown are two restaurants, Chez Gérard and Foyal, that are as good, and as expensive as you could find anywhere. The Roger Albert Free Port Shop is a treasure house of French and other European luxury products: perfumes, china, silverware, handbags, watches. As a treasury of a different sort there is the Centre d'Arts, exhibiting and selling the works of local painters and sculptors, who, along with Haiti's, are the best in the Caribbean.

(It is not too widely known, incidentally, that Paul Gauguin tried Martinique as an island of escape before taking off for Tahiti. His several months there, however, seem to have been chiefly devoted to keeping alive, and were not one of his more productive periods.)

To date, Martinique's tourist trade has been strictly limited. The great majority of visitors have been cruise ship passengers, ashore for only a few hours, and those coming for days and weeks have been few and far between. A major deterrent, for Americans, has been the language problem: few Martiniquaises, even in the tourist business, speak English. On the islanders' side it has been largely a matter of simply not wanting outsiders, and therefore doing little to attract them. Their economy was based on agriculture: sugar, bananas, pineapples. The old landowning families were entrenched and content. No nationality can be as xenophobic as the French, when they set their mind to it, and for years the Martiniquaises set theirs very strongly indeed.

Now this is changing, as is everything in the Caribbean. The jets are coming. The tourist tide is coming. And a new generation of islanders has reached the conclusion that they can no longer live in splendid Carib-Gallic isolation. The Tourist Board is becoming ever more active. New projects are being financed, and new hotels built. Ultimate of ultimates, the Martinique Hilton is being built in the outskirts of Fort-de-France.

The current roster of hotels consists of four in the deluxe category and another dozen-odd rating from "almost" to "perish the thought." Three of them, in town, are at the middle of the scale, designed for the traveling businessman rather than the lotus-seeking tourist.

Of the Big Four (though none are really big, ranging from 17 to 45 rooms), the nearest to Fort-de-France is the Lido, perched on a west coast hillside not far from where the new Hilton Hotel is rising. Two are across the bay: the aforementioned l'Anse Mitan and the brand-new Bakoua—both best reached by boat. And the fourth, the Cap Est, is, as its name indicates, well off by itself on the Atlantic shore. All have beaches. (Not the best in the Indies, but no hardship posts either.) All but l'Anse Mitan have swimming pools. And all, most emphatically, have cuisines to be cherished. Indeed, one of a guest's major problems is that of eating so well, and so much, that he has no energy left for anything else.

And there is plenty else. Historically and scenically, in its land and its people, Martinique has attractions to match any in the Caribbean.

First, as to people—almost 330,000 of them in all. As on every West Indian island, they are racially mixed, but here even more so than elsewhere, for the French are no segregationists either in theory or fact. One of the delights of Fort-de-France is to watch the women—well, the young women— go by: white, black, and all shades of in-between.

At occasional parties and festivals they wear the traditional island costume, topped by a multicolored, multipointed headdress called a *madras*. But here in the streets they are dressed like their cousins in Paris, or better. Their ensembles may have cost them twelve francs fifty at a bargain counter; but with straight backs and swaying hips, they wear them as if they were straight out of a *salon de haute couture*.

As one leaves the city, to be sure, *couture* fades behind. We are in agricultural country. Sugar cane, bananas and pineapples fill the fields, and above them the hills are green, the streams lively, for Martinique gets ample rainfall.

The roads are good. But they twist and turn, and traffic is heavy. Though it costs more, I suggest you do your driving behind a chauffeur; otherwise you'll spend the whole time coping with what's coming at you front and rear. Indeed, one of the major surprises to me was the number of cars on the island. And if it was annoying in one way, it was pleasing in another, for it bespoke a prosperity I had not expected to find.

Also pleasing were the schools: a new and handsome one in almost every village. And apparently this is not just a matter of concrete and glass. I have been told by several people who should know that the level of education in the French islands is by far the highest in the Caribbean.

Out of Fort-de-France, there are in general three routes you can take through the countryside. One, leading to the east coast and then southward along the Atlantic, has no particular "sights," but provides a continuously lovely panorama of land and sea. And for a midday break of beach and lunch there is, just when you need it, the Cap Est Hotel.

A second tour leads first either across or around the Bay of Fort-de-France to *l'Anse Mitan* (Middle Bay) with its two side-by-side hostelries, the Auberge and the Bakoua. Here also is the village of Trois Ilets, and close by it, a bit inland, the childhood home of Marie Rose Josephine Tascher de la Pagerie—later Beauharnais—still later Bonaparte.

The actual house in which the future empress was born was destroyed by a hurricane in 1766, when she was only three years old. But much of the surrounding estate, called La Pagerie, remains as it was in the days of her sugar-planter father; and at its center has been built a small museum containing memorabilia of both Josephine and Napoleon.

Interestingly, the establishment is not owned by the government but by an individual Martiniquais named, no less interestingly, Dr. Robert Rose-Rosette. All details of construction, restoration and collection have been handled by Dr. Rose-Rosette as a labor of love. The result is a happy one. Even more appealing than the museum, to my taste, are the surrounding lawns and groves, carefully tended and stocked with horses and cattle. Compounded of stillness and tropic sunlight, the scene is idyllic. Two centuries vanish. One would scarcely be surprised if the young Josephine herself came tripping across the lawns on the way to her date with history.

A few miles on from La Pagerie is more history, of a different sort. Here, on Martinique's south shore, is Diamant Beach and, offshore, the *Rocher du Diamant* (Diamond Rock), a 600-foot-high natural fortress on which, during the colonial wars, a small British garrison held out for almost 18 months against the whole of French-occupied Martinique. Diamant Beach itself is perhaps the best bit of strand on the island. Today there are several away-from-it-all villas in the area, and in time there is sure to be a resort hotel.

The third and longest of Martinique tours is also the most memorable. This is the one to the north, to Mont Pelée and Saint-Pierre—the destroyer and the destroyed. The approach is arduous but beautiful, winding up the headlands and valleys of the west coast, until one comes to the last valley before the volcano and the small town that lies there beside the sea.

Small now. But once Saint-Pierre was a city of 40,000, one of the great commercial centers of the West Indies—until that May morning in 1902 when it ceased to exist. For some time previously, during that spring, Pelée had been muttering and rumbling, but so had other volcanoes on neighboring islands, and few worried greatly about it. The governor of Martinique came up from Fort-de-France to show by his presence that there was no cause for concern. On the night of May 7th the city went to bed as usual, on the next morning woke up as usual, was having breakfast, was setting to work—when Pelée blew its top.

It was not lava that came down from the heights. Far swifter and more lethal, it was a *nuée ardente*, a blazing avalanche of gas and flame that engulfed Saint-Pierre in a matter of minutes and literally burned it to a crisp. Of all the ships in its busy harbor, only one was not destroyed. More incredibly and terribly, there was also exactly one survivor among all its inhabitants. This was a prisoner in a jail, a Negro laborer called Cyparis, who, though badly burned, lived on to become a prize exhibit in circus side shows.

Following the holocaust, there was talk of abandoning Martinique, of evacuating its whole population. But this of course did not happen. On the contrary, people eventually began resettling on the very site of the disaster, until there was a new Saint-Pierre, though with only one-tenth the population of the old. Some of the old still remains: notably the ruins of a theater that was once the city's proudest edifice. And among them stands the Museum of Mont Pelée, built, largely by American enterprise, as a memorial to the great cataclysm. Some of its exhibits are scientific, showing the why and how of the eruption. Others are pathetically human: remnants of homes, clothing, implements: a burnt-out pot, a stopped watch, a cornet twisted by heat into a blackened pretzel.

Above the town sits the volcano, calm and still. When I was there—as on the morning when I had seen it from the sea—its summit was ringed with innocent white clouds. Beyond Saint-Pierre a road curves up around Pelée's flanks. Where poisonous gas and flaming mud once raged, there is now only greenness—first of broad pineapple fields, then, higher, of lush forests of fern. Circling, we came to villages on the mountain's eastern and northern slopes, and here, too, in human terms, the world of the living replaced the world of the dead. In one village we were emphatically reminded that the next Sunday was Mother's Day. A banner streaming across the main street proclaimed HONNEUR AUX MAMANS.

Finally we came to the town of Grande Rivière on the northernmost point of the island. And it is quite a point. Behind it, of course, stands the mass of Pelée. Ahead, beyond road's end, are tall cliffs and foaming breakers. Off in the distance, across shining water, rises the craggy purple shape of the island of Dominica.

This is as "far-out" as you can get on Martinique. There are no hotels here, deluxe or otherwise. "Is there any place to have lunch?" I asked Félix, our driver, dubiously. And Félix's cheerful and unexpected answer was, "*Mais oui.*"

Presently we found ourselves in a tumbledown sort of place which a small sign announced was Restaurant Chez Louisin. A few tables were set up in a courtyard, and as companions we had three dogs, two cats, assorted poultry and a tethered goat. On the human side there was, as cook, not a mere honored *maman* but a *grandmaman*, an elderly mulatto with gnarled hands and stooped back. As waitress, there was her somewhat bedraggled daughter, and as spectators, along with the livestock, two of *her* small children, ragged and barefoot.

The prospect was not encouraging. In a comparable place—if such were possible—back home, the fare would have been a greasy hamburger or frankfurter, with perhaps a slab of sodden pie. But this was not back home. This was Chez Louisin in the hell-and-gone village of Grande Rivière, Martinique. And presently the miracles began.

First came a checkered tablecloth, clean and crisp, and equally clean-crisp, carefully folded napkins. Then followed glinting silverware and, as first course, *écrevisses au sauce verte*—small crayfish as delicate and succulent as I have ever tasted. On the side was white wine: *ordinaire*, but as cool and crisp as the napery. When the crayfish were gone, there appeared a dream of an omelette, and more wine. Then a camembert cheese that could have won a prize at an exposition. Then coffee, liqueurs.

Was there a place to eat in Grande Rivière? *Mais oui!*

Among the fascinations of the Caribbean are its never-ending contrasts, and that very night we encountered one for the book. "Have you been to La Bananeraie?" a Martiniquais friend asked us. No, we had not been to La Bananeraie. So from Fort-de-France we headed off into the country for the island's best-known roadhouse.

What we had expected, I'm not sure. But it was not what we found—beginning with the parking lot. Outside Chez Louisin ours had been the only car, indeed almost the only car in Grande Rivière. Here it was one of hundreds, fender to fender, bumper to bumper, as in a lot in Los Angeles or suburban Chicago. One almost expected a sign on the roadhouse saying TONIGHT SINATRA PLUS STREISAND.

Inside there was neither Frankie nor Barbra. But there *was* what seemed to be half the population of the island under thirty years old. The big orchestra was playing, *comme il faut*, beguines and merengues. But there was little of the deep-down Caribbean in the scene. Except that they were almost all Negro and spoke French, the customers, like their cars, could have fitted anywhere into an American landscape. They were dressed in conventional sports clothes. They were drinking beer, Cokes and Pepsies. On the dance floor they were swinging, but it was the swing of the Age of Jukebox, not of Africa of faraway and long-ago.

Like all of the West Indies, Martinique is in transition. It has its Chez Louisin and its Bananeraie. It has its goats and its traffic jams, its *madras* and its bikinis, its ruins of Saint-Pierre and its *Honneur aux Mamans*. Inwardly, I would say, it is still torn between an attachment to old provincial ways and a drive toward new ones; between Martinique backwater and Martinique Hilton.

Map of Martinique showing Grande Rivière, Mont Pelée, Saint-Pierre, Atlantic Ocean, FORT-DE-FRANCE, Caribbean Sea, Trois Ilets, J'Anse Mitan, Diamant. Scale 0–5 Miles.

Among all the changes, however, there are two constants. No one has yet succeeded in spoiling either Martinique's beauty or its food. If you do nothing else, simply looking and eating will repay a visit—and if you can say "bonjour" and "vive la France," so much the bettter.

—*J. R. Ullman*

Instant facts

Location: Midway between St. Lucia and Dominica, 60 miles south of her sister island, Guadeloupe.

Population: About 330,000.

Capital: Fort-de-France.

Nationality: Overseas department of France.

Language: French, very little English.

Currency: New franc, 20¢ U.S.

Documentation: International certificate of vaccination. Passport required by all except French nationals (holding National Identity Cards) and U.S. and Canadian citizens with alternate proof of identity, and entering as bona fide tourists for a maximum of 10 days.

Climate & Clothes: The temperature averages 79° throughout the year, with cooling trade winds and abundant rainfall (as much as 192 inches in the mountainous northern region). There are two "seasons," the first cooler and dryer (December-May), with a period of drought beginning in February. The second season is warmer (June–November), with a rainy season called "hivernage." Light summer clothes.

Food: Accent is on French cuisine, supplemented by spicy local seafood specialties. Soups are even more of a staple than in France, and tropical fruits and vegetables a standard fare on local menus.

Geography: While the island is 50 miles long, 22 miles at its most extreme points, its coastline is so indented that no part of it is more than seven miles from the sea. A total of 385 sq. miles in area, Martinique is ringed with low mountains which form steep cliffs along the coasts. In the mountainous northern region is Mont Pelée, its highest peak (4,428 feet).

History: Although Christopher Columbus landed on the island in 1502, it was a Frenchman who established the first settlement, the town of Saint-Pierre, in 1635. Martinique remained French from that time on, with the exception of two brief periods during the Seven Years' War and the French Revolution. The late 19th century saw the little island battered twice by destructive hurricanes but the worst blow came in 1902, when Mont Pelée erupted, destroying the town of Saint-Pierre and its more than 30,000 inhabitants. In 1946 Martinique became a French Overseas Department, at the request of the islanders.

Who flies here

There are flights to the Lamentin Airport, some seven minutes from Fort-de-France, from the following cities:

New York: Pan Am, Air France. Round trip: $272–$363; 17-day excursion $175–$241.

Miami: BWIA, Pan Am. Round Trip: $221–$291; 17-day excursion $149–$210.

Paris (via Guadeloupe): Air France. Round trip: $690–$950 (3409–4693 francs).

San Juan: Air France, BWIA, Pan Am. Round trip: $107–$147; 17-day excursion $75–$100.

Island transportation

Martinique traffic functions under a law unto itself: brilliantly unorganized, alluringly individualistic, and ultimately fascinating. Observing the *modus operandi* is instructive. Participation is dangerous.

First of all, there are the gutters. Lining both sides of the steep, winding, narrow roads, they are deep-veed in shape and tank traps in nature. They explain in large part the preference of Martinique drivers for small French cars. When you go off into the gutter, it isn't too difficult to pick up the car and set it back on the road.

The **buses** in Martinique are called *bombes* because of their usual rate of speed. They are open-sided, and when it rains canvas canopies are lowered making it impossible for anyone to see out and, on long trips, providing a communal steam bath.

Package racks are located on the open roof and run the full length of the bus. They usually are overloaded with fruits, vegetables, building materials and assorted boxes which are in jeopardy everytime the *bombe* rounds a curve.

Those who don't own cars or ride in them drive motor scooters and ride bicycles. The pushcarts vie for space in the middle of it all, often colliding with pedestrians.

Though the traffic is exotic and the French road signs are interesting, a stranger to Martinique will find one familiar constant. Everywhere the driver is advised to *"Mettez un tigre dans votre moteur."* For those who dare, cars can be rented at most hotels through Hertz agents (Martinicars S.A.R.L.), central office at rue Ernest-Deproge (Tel: 20-84). Rates are high—$9–$12 a day ($8–$10 if rented by the week), 7¢–8¢ per kilometer depending on the type car (Fiat, Peugeot, Citroen, etc.)—and getting lost is not difficult in Martinique. Rentals are also handled by Ets Louis Crocquet, Kerlys (Tel: 60-76) and S.H.O.T.T.A. (Service Hôtelier de Transport Touristique Automobile), at Hotel Bristol (Tel: 21-79). American licenses are valid here.

S.H.O.T.T.A. also handles tours around the island, as do the following touring and taxi agencies:

Guy de la Houssaye
1 rue de la Liberté
Tel: 21-72, 31-85

Roger Albert
7 rue Victor Hugo
Tel: 44-44

Places of interest

Mont Pelée and **Saint-Pierre:** The morning of May 8, 1902, dawned clear and bright after a night of torrential rains. It was to be a day of parading in the streets, carnival masks, dancing and music. But shortly after 8 A.M., as the first crowds began to gather, two violent explosions ripped apart Mont Pelée, the 4,428 foot mountain that brooded over the city.

Unable to burst through the solid lava at the top of the volcanic cone, Mont Pelée split its side and poured out a hell of gas, glowing rock and ashes at a temperature of 3,600° F. Within 45 seconds Saint-Pierre ceased to exist, and 30,000 people were dead. It was one of the worst natural disasters in the history of the world. Today, Saint-Pierre consists of crumbling walls and other ruins standing in the shadow of the great volcano. A small museum contains remnants dug up from the debris and records of the eruption.

Trois Ilets (La Pagerie): Small village, across the bay from Fort-de-France, where Marie Rose Josephine Tascher de la Pagerie, later the Empress Josephine, wife of Napoleon I, was baptized. The little church still stands after two centuries and nearby is the estate where she was born in 1763. The remains of her childhood home, destroyed by hurricane, have been restored by the present owners. They have also furnished a small museum where souvenirs of the empress and her family are exhibited.

La Savane: Fort-de-France's municipal park, with its statue of the Empress Josephine, unveiled in 1859. This was the site of heavy fighting against the Dutch and the English in the 1700's.

Rocher du Diamant (Diamond Rock): Off the south shore. Last outpost of a group of British soldiers who, starting in 1804, managed to hold out for 18 months until they were cut down by the French.

The sporting life

Martinique has few good **beaches.** The finest beach by far is at Diamant, though the surf can be rough. It is located several miles outside of Fort-de-France on the south shore of the island. Most of the white sand beaches are on the south coast, while black sand beaches can be found along the west coast on the Caribbean Sea.

Best **fishing** spots are at l'Anse Mitan, Diamant, Sante-Luce, Sainte-Anne, Vauclin, Francois, Robert and Tartane. If you do not bring your own fishing equipment, it is available from:

Société Commercial et Industrielle Martiniquaise
M. Carreau-Gaschereau
7 rue Francois Arago, Tel: 43-91

Prisunic
rue Lamartine, Tel: 42-80

Tanon
rue Victor Hugo

Charter boats can be rented from the following agents:

l'Anse Mitan
M. Hamel

Hotel Gallia
M. Berty Chalono
La Savane, Tel: 52-23

S.H.O.T.T.A.
rue de la Liberté, Tel: 21-79

Centers for nautical sports are Centre Nautique, in Fort-de-France (with a sailing school), and the Nautique du Francois. Martinique also has an **olympic swimming pool** and the Louis Achille sports stadium. Cock fights are a local favorite.

Best shopping buys

In addition to fine French goods such as perfume and Limoges china, there are also Swiss watches, Baccarat crystal, Christofle silver and locally made souvenirs such as dolls in native costume, straw hats, baskets, hand-painted pottery, carvings, embroidery, ceramics and earthenware, paintings, and wall hangings of particular color and charm.

Duty-free shops are:

Beaufrand
23 rue Victor Hugo
Lamentin Airport
Tel: 69-00, 24-01

Printemps
10 rue Schoelcher
Tel: 38-66

Roger Albert
7 rue Victor Hugo
Tel: 44-44 and 55-55

Le Centre des Metiers d'Art, a famous art center, has a permanent exhibit of locally hand-crafted wood carvings, tapestries, jewelry, shell work, dolls and other surprisingly sophisticated souvenirs. All items here are for sale.

Dine and dance

The following restaurants are recommended and prepare both Creole and French specialties.

Auberge de L'Anse Mitan: L'Anse Mitan, Trois Ilets. Tel: 12.

Auberge du Vauclin: Vauclin. Tel. 20.

Auberge du Vieux Chalet: Morne Rouge. Tel: 44.

Au Mahogany: Sainte-Anne. Tel: 27.

Aux Fruits Défendus: Francois. Tel: 43.

Bakoua: Trois Ilets. Dinner, dancing Tuesday, Thursday, Saturday. Tel: 55-95.

Bristol: Route de Schoelcher, Fort-de-France. Tel: 31-80.

Cap-Est: Francois. Tel: 87.

La Caridad: L'Anse Mitan, Trois Ilets. Tel: 19.

Chez Gerard: 96 Rue Victor Sévère, Fort-de-France. Tel: 52-70.

Chez Louisin. Grande Rivière. Tel: 5.

Delices de la Mer: Sainte-Luce, Tel. 12.

La Dunette: Sainte-Anne. Tel: 9.

Europe: Place de la Savane, Fort-de-France. Tel: 52-46.

Foyal: Fort-de-France. Tel: 67-13.

Hong Kong: 39 rue Garnier Pagès, Fort-de-France. Tel: 42-63.

Lido: Schoelcher, Anse Colas. Closed Monday. Tel: 45-50.

Louisiane: Route de Didier, Fort-de-France. Tel: 62-82.

Martinique: Route de Schoelcher. Tel: 25-37.

Miami Plage: L'Anse Mitan, Trois Ilets.

Piment Vert: Sainte-Luce. Tel: 7.

Reflets des Isles: Route du Lamentin, Fort-de-France. Tel: 54-15.

Le Relais: Schoelcher, Fond Lahaye. Tel: 45-46.

La Vague: Saint-Pierre. Tel: 40.

Vieux Moulin: Didier, Fort-de-France. Tel: 33-82.

For dancing and night life there is **El Moroco** (closed Sunday), Route de Redoute (Tel: 35-01); **La Bananeraie** (closed Monday), Route de Robert; and **Luna Rock** (closed Saturday), Pont de Chaines, Fort-de-France.

Devils' and saints' days

Carnival: Celebrations held throughout February. Mardi Gras parade in red costume.

Jour des Diables: "Devils' Day," when paraders march in black and white costume. Funeral of King Carnival on Ash Wednesday. February 28.

Bastille Day: Parades, fireworks. July 14.

All Saints Day: Illumination of cemeteries with candles. November 1.

Victory Celebrations: Parades, fireworks. November 11.

Real estate and retirement

There is an extreme shortage of housing, due to the rapid increase in population. Complicating this is the fact that most of the present housing is in need of modernization, or even demolition. However, the following agents in Fort-de-France can help you find some sort of domicile:

Camille Becrite
39 rue Galliéni

Cité Appolinaire
105 rue E. Renan

Sometimes the Tourist Board can help visitors who want to rent a villa for vacations.

Commerce and industry

Martinique's economy is still primarily agricultural, despite a boost in the field of tourism. Sugar cane, followed by bananas and pineapples, make up 97% of her exports. At one time vanilla, cotton, coffee and pepper were also important cash crops but hurricanes and the eruption of Mont Pelée in the early part of the century wiped them out.

The government of Martinique offers investment incentives to industries but, as yet, there are mostly small-scale plants on the island. The main response has been from the hotel industry, and construction has begun on the new Martinique Hilton, to be operated jointly by Martinique's Hotel and Tourist Assn. and Hilton International. There are, at present, over a dozen other hotels.

In addition to the industries centered about Martinique's agricultural produce (sugar refineries, rum distilleries, pineapple canneries), the island has a small but thriving fishing fleet and raises some of its own livestock. It is hardly wealthy, however, and gets a major financial boost from the French government.

Meet the people

Organization	Official	Phone
Rotary Club	Georges Xavier	31-04
Ciné-Club	Roland Suvelor	20-52
French Red Cross	Jacques Tarrin	23-19
Alliance Francaise	Mme Dormoy	33-57
Chamber of Commerce	Robert de Jaham	38-08
Jeune Chambre Economique	Bernard Hayot	38-08
Tourist Bureau (SETMA)	M. Garsonnin	31-19
Town Hall	Aimé Cesaire	33-96
Dispensary	Pierre Clement	35-53, 58-22
Police	Edmond Barraud	68-40
Historical Society	Jacques Petitjean-Roget	41-44
Horse Racing Assn.	Yves Hayot	38-08
Yachting Club	Henri-Robert Hélénon	69-09
Tourism Information	Mme. Roult	5961

WHERE TO STAY — In Martinique

	Plan	Dec. 15–April 14		April 15–Dec. 14	
		U. S. Currency			
		Double	Single	Double	Single
AUBERGE de L'ANSE MITAN Trois-Ilets (22 Rms.) **(b)**	(AP)	$22–30	$14–17	$20–25	$13–16
BAKOUA BEACH Fort-de-France (56 Rms.) **(b, p)**	(MAP)	$50–70	$35–50	$34–50	$25–35
CAP EST Pointe de la Prairie (46 Rms.) **(b, p)**	(MAP)	$42–48	$26–32	$24–28	$12–16
LA MALMAISON Fort-de-France (20 Rms.)	(CP)	$14–21	$11–16	$12–18	$ 9–14
L'EUROPE Fort-de-France (20 Rms.)	(CP)	$12–16	$ 8–12	$ 9–13	$ 6– 9
L'IMPERATRICE **Fort-de-France** (20 Rms.)	(AP)	$22–25	$13–16	$22–25	$13–16
	(MAP)	$18–22	$11–14	$18–22	$11–14
	(EP)	$12–16	$ 8–11	$12–16	$ 8–11
LIDO BEACH **Schoelcher** (26 Rms.) **(b, p)**	(AP)	$41–57	$23–29	$33–41	$21–29
	(MAP)	$32–48	$18–34	$24–32	$16–24

MARTINIQUE	(AP)	$34	$22	$24	$16
Fort-de-France	(MAP)	$30	$20	$20	$14
(14 Rms.) (p)					
NAUTI VILLAGE	(CP)	$ 6	—	$ 6	—
Anse a l'Ane		(Tents, huts for camping)			
VIEUX MOULIN	(AP)	$28	$18	$25	$16
Fort-de-France	(MAP)	$20	$14	$18	$12
(19 Rms.) (p, t)					

LEGEND FOR HOTEL LISTINGS: **(AP)** American Plan (room and 3 meals); **MAP)** Modified American Plan (room, breakfast and dinner); **(CP)** Continental Plan (room and breakfast); **(EP)** European Plan (room only). All rates quoted on a per-day basis and subject to change. Confirmed reservations at specific rates desired are always recommended.

HOTEL FACILITIES: **(b)** beach; **(p)** pool; **(t)** tennis; **(g)** golf.

French bread is delivered right to your door at
Fort-de-France on the island of Martinique

MONTSERRAT

The traveler in the West Indies will often hear from a resident islander, "Yes, it is lovely, but you should have been here ten years ago when it was really beautiful and unspoiled." The beautiful and the unspoiled islands are still there for the finding. One of these is the green island of Montserrat which rises steeply from the Caribbean Sea just 27 miles southwest of Antigua.

Emerald isle

Any description of Montserrat, written or verbal, almost invariably includes the word "lush." The entire island is clothed in green forests and shrubs, clear streams wind down the mountain slopes in the interior, and a waterfall of breath-taking beauty tumbles over a rock cliff to splash into a hidden forest pool. Ferns grow everywhere, and the soil and climate are so mutually agreeable that the vegetable produce of the island is famous in the Caribbean.

Montserrat is called the Emerald Isle of the West, both because of its green beauty and, more specifically, because the island's most numerous early settlers were Irishmen sent over by Oliver Cromwell in the 17th century. Even today, a brogue is occasionally heard, and a shamrock adorns the center gable of Government House.

Flashing neon and nightclub noises are un-Montserratian, but this is not to say that the island has not made its peace with the 20th century. Modern and comfortable hotels and guest houses are available to meet the needs of almost any budget and many American and Canadian citizens have bought land on the island to build vacation or retirement homes. There are two theater groups: the Summer Festival Theater, which has sent touring companies to other islands, and a local troupe, the Shamrock Players.

Plymouth, the capital, is a busy little town on the southwest coast. GOVERNMENT HOUSE, with shamrock, may be visited, and at the southern end of town the Old Fort St. restoration well repays a visit. Here is the Quarter Deck, a delightful restaurant with a patio bar on the beach and a profusion of shade trees to make it a comfortable spot for viewing life on land and at sea.

For the theater-minded the SHAMROCK PLAYERS periodically present light comedies, often with an assist from tourists with professional theater experience who contribute suggestions and advice. Several of the hotels have midweek barbecues with steel bands, and parties, Calypso dances, beach picnics and snorkeling, sailing and fishing expeditions are easily arranged.

On a list of sightseeing things to do, possibly the first stop out of Plymouth could be the OLD FORT on St. George's Hill. This is a 20-minute

Parasols and palms beneath the Caribbean sun

drive from town along the main road, and then up a side road that leads to the fort 1,184 feet above sea level. The fort has an old magazine in a good state of preservation, and a number of cannon placed there by the English in the 18th century, but it is the view that you have come to see—the panorama of Montserrat and her surrounding seas.

ST. ANTHONY'S CHURCH, just outside Plymouth, was built between 1632 and 1666, and rebuilt in 1730. An ancient, gnarled tamarind tree, some two centuries old, stands next to the church, and it is said the site was chosen because the tree provided a ready-made hitching post for horses. The church contains two magnificent silver chalices, gifts of freed slaves after emancipation was proclaimed.

Along the northwest coast is one of Montserrat's most interesting restaurants boasting the island's most intriguing menu. This is the HIDE-AWAY at Rocklands, near St. Peter's Village, where you dine on an open terrace with a fine view of mountain and sea. The setting is informal and the people who come there gregarious. Specialties of the house are mountain chicken (a species of frog) and stuffed mountain dove. Both delicious.

A natural wonder of Montserrat is GALWAY'S SOUFRIÈRE, south of Plymouth and reached by a mountain road lined with tree ferns and the exotic incense tree. At one moment you are surrounded by all the tropical beauty of Montserrat, and in the next the open, boiling crater of the Soufrière

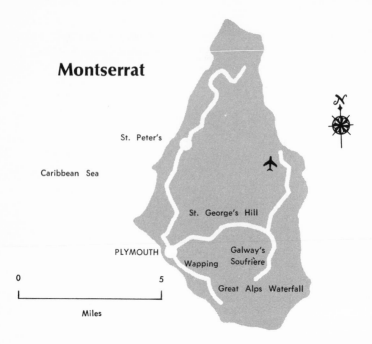

Montserrat

St. Peter's

Caribbean Sea

St. George's Hill

PLYMOUTH

Galway's
Wapping Soufrière

Great Alps Waterfall

0   5

Miles

presents itself, with yellow sulphur spilling over the side in stark contrast to the forest.

But the great wonder of Montserrat and one of the great sights of the Caribbean is GREAT ALPS WATERFALL. It takes a bit of doing to see it in all its beauty, but the effort is amply repaid by the reality.

The first step of the journey is easy—a 15-minute car ride south from Plymouth. Here the trail begins, and ahead lies an hour's walk (if you choose to do it leisurely) over grassy plains and through the lush interior. The route follows along a rippling stream zigzagging its way down the mountainside, tunnels of deep green lead up alongside the moss-covered rock faces, and the thirsty walker can knock down a juicy mango from a tree by the side of the trail.

The final corner is rounded and there is the waterfall, an immense horseshoe-shaped formation with a cascade of crystal water plunging some 70 feet into a mountain pool. The best time to view the falls is around mid-day, when the noontime sun bathes the water and the foliage in a glistening light. (On a practical note, it is decidedly more pleasant to make the trek during the relative coolness of the morning.)

The pool at the base of the falls, fresh and cool as a mountain lake, is perfect for splashing around in, and the forest offers innumerable private places for changing.

Sturdy shoes and a touch of suntan lotion are recommended for the climb, and would-be viewers (40 and over) whose constitutions are on the neglected side should think twice before they start off.

Plans are underway to make the waterfall a prime attraction. Regularly scheduled tours for small groups are now available, a rustic shelter offering cold drinks at the beginning of the trail has been built, and several picnic tables are to be placed near the falls for woodsy lunching.

Great Alps Waterfall may not be one of the Caribbean's most accessible sights, but it is certainly one of the most dramatically beautiful.

Instant facts

Location: 267 miles southeast of San Juan and 27 miles southwest of Antigua, midway between Nevis and Guadeloupe.

Population: 14,000.

Capital: Plymouth.

Nationality: British Crown Colony, with ministerial form of government. An Administrator represents the Queen.

Language: English.

Currency: East Caribbean (same as West Indian) dollar—60¢ U.S., 64¢ Canadian and 4s 2d sterling.

Documentation: International certificate of vaccination. Passport required by all except U.S. citizens with alternate form of identity.

Climate & Clothes: Montserrat is in the direct path of the northeast trade winds, and the mean maximum temperature is 86.5° F. Average annual rainfall is 62 inches. Dress is for sporty and casual living.

Food: Montserrat grows some of the best vegetables in the West Indies and is famous for its tomatoes. A popular native dish is a goat stew known as **goat water,** and many meals include breadfruit (a vegetable served much like a potato), and the root vegetable somewhat mysteriously referred to as tannia-seed.

Geography: Small (7 x 11, or 39 sq. miles) and mountainous. The land is well watered and fertile, and its gray-black beaches reflect the island's volcanic origin.

History: Columbus, the great namer of islands, first saw the peaks of Montserrat in 1493 on his second voyage. Struck by its similarity to "the sawtoothed mountain" of Spain, he named his New World discovery Montserrat after its Old World counterpart.

The island was visited by the Carib Indians, but was not settled until 1632 when a group of Irishmen of "Warner's Company" came from St. Christopher (St. Kitts). The French took possession of Montserrat twice, in 1664 until 1667, and in 1782 to 1783, but except for those two brief periods it has been continuously under British control.

In common with the neighboring Leeward Islands, Montserrat was the scene of intensive missionary activity during the middle and later periods of the last century. The missionaries were also pioneers in mass education, a contributory factor to a literacy rate reckoned in excess of 90% of the present population. Montserrat also has the distinction of being the first island within the area to have passed an act instituting island-wide compulsory education (1921).

Who flies here

LIAT operates twice-daily air-bus service from Antigua, $16 round trip. The trip takes 15 minutes and reservations are not required—just check in 30 minutes prior to flight time. A round-trip flight from St. Kitts via LIAT is $20.90 and Air Antilles has a flight from Guadeloupe, $17 round trip. Charter flights may be arranged from Antigua, San Juan, or the U.S. Virgin Islands.

Island transportation

Self-drive cars are available at moderate prices from the Vue Pointe and Emerald Isle Hotels. Montserrat Car Rentals operates at the Texaco Service Station, Church Rd., Plymouth. There are 60 miles of roads suitable for travel.

Taxis charge 24¢ a mile and fare from the airport to hotels around the island ranges between $3.60 and $5.40. One-way fare to the farthest point of scenic interest is no more than $6. **"Motor omnibuses"** run between Plymouth and almost a dozen areas, charging at the most 30¢.

The sporting life

Golfers will find a nine-hole paradise at the **Belham River Valley Golf Course.** This superb course covers an area of almost 100 acres and is located on the western side of the island by the sea. Fees are $3 a day or $15 a week. Clubs and caddy carts can be rented.

There are no stables but horses and donkeys are available for **riding** along the island's many bridle paths. There are turf courts at the island's club in Plymouth, visitors welcome. **Netball** is one of the island's main sports and **cricket** matches are held weekly.

Water sports

The beaches of Montserrat are a delight (and a surprise) to city folk who have never seen black sand. The volcanic origin of the island has provided a wealth of tiny coves laced with strands of black, shading the beige. A couple of the beaches, to be sure, are a bit more conventionally beach-colored, notably **Carr's Bay,** 35 minutes from Plymouth along the north coast. This is an excellent swimming beach, with clear, clear waters, and a picturesque backdrop of fishermen of the northern coast with their boats and nets.

Little Bay and Rendezvous Bay, on the northwest coast, also are good beaches, but cannot as yet be reached by car. There is no charter service for yachts or boats but the Montserrat Yacht Club has several Sunfish and one Mirror Dinghy. Smaller boats are available for fishing, cruising or water skiing.

Shopping buys

Local handicrafts include straw goods and little ceramic souvenirs. There is a large selection of the well-known sea island cotton fabrics. The island grows some cotton which is sent to England for processing and imported back to Montserrat. These goods are available in Plymouth at the following shops:

The New York Store
Strand St.

Cottage Crafts
George St.

The Island Shop
Parliament St.

The Sugar Mill
Parliament St.

Dining Out

Anchorage: Wapping. Light luncheons and dinners, by reservation. Specialty: Sunday night barbecue. Occasional floor shows.

Hide-Away: At Rockland's, near St. Peter's. Specialties: mountain chicken, stuffed mountain dove.

Merry Kettle: Wapping. Morning drinks, luncheon plates or sandwiches. English afternoon tea. Try their hot pancake sandwich.

Quarterdeck: Wapping. Luncheon, cocktail patio on the beach.

There are also dining rooms and cocktail lounges at the Vue Pointe, Emerald Isle and Wade Inn Hotels.

Special events

Agricultural Show and Livestock Exhibition: Exhibit of agricultural produce, local handicrafts, flower gardens, etc. February.

Whit Monday: Boat racing featured on this bank holiday. June 3.

Christmas Celebrations: Carol singing at the War Memorial, masquerades, float parade, steel and string band competitions, election of beauty queens, folk and calypso competition, buffet dinners and dances at hotels, West Indian Jump-Up on streets of Plymouth. December 24–January 1.

Meet the Montserratians

Organization	Official	Address
M/rat Sports Assn.	F. Edwards	Water Lane
Netball Management Comm.	Mrs. M. Tuitt	George St.
M/rat Yacht Club	W. White	Fort Barrington
Belham Golf Club	F. George	Richmond Hill
Shamrock Players (Drama)	J. Sturgen	The Ridge
Play Reading Group	Mrs. P. Rustin	Old Towne Estate
Angelican Young Peoples Assn.	Miss Annette Allen	Kinsale
YWCA	Mrs. W. H. Bramble	Taylor St.
Young Christian Workers	Melvin Casell	Chapel St.
Social League of Catholic Women	Mrs. J. C. Nanton	Wall St.
Church Lads Brigade	Cpl. L. Thomas	Kinsale
Boys Brigade	Rev. L. Crichton	Wesley Manse
Girl Guides	Miss Betty Browne	Cork Hill
Boy Scouts	S. McCallum	Spanish Point
Youth Council	J. Bass	St. Peters
Red Cross Society	S. Meade	Richmond Hills
St. John's Ambulance Brigade	J. Vanderpool	Police Head/qts
Junior Chamber	C. Osborne	Osborne St.
Chamber of Commerce	H. S. Mercer	Trescellian House
Extra-Mural Dept. (U.W.I.)	H. Williams	Parliament St.
Old Peoples Welfare Assn.	Mrs. E. Herman	Old Towne Estate
Credit Union Council	Mrs. F. Butler	Grovesville
Family Planning Assn.	Mrs. D. R. Gibbs	Vue Pointe
Teachers Union	V. Weekes	Cork Hill
Parent Teachers Assn.	E. R. White	Plymouth
Taxi Drivers Assn.	J. N. Edwards	Salem
Christian Council	Rev. L. Crichton	Wesley Manse
M/rat Mirror (Newspaper)	C. H. Meade	Parliament St.
St. Anthony's Masonic Lodge	W. O. Barzey	Cork Hill

Real estate and retirement

Montserrat's income tax structure is the lowest in any of the islands. The maximum tax payable (either personal or corporate) is 20%. Allowances are generous—$1,000 resident allowance, $750 marriage allowance, and allowances of up to $800 for children, dependent on the age of the child and the place of education.

Double taxation relief agreements are in operation with the United States, the United Kingdom, Canada and many other countries. There are no death or succession duties. As on all the Caribbean islands, food—most of it imported—is more costly than in the States. In Montserrat, however, a large variety of home-grown fruits and vegetables can be bought quite cheaply.

There are furnished homes and cottages for rent but the big real estate activity is in four large developments—Spanish Point, Montserrat Beachettes, Foxes Bay and Isles Bay. Spanish Point, a Canadian project, is almost all sold out and Beachettes (actually somewhat lacking in beach area) is already a bustling community. The other two offer land at $12,000 an acre. Building costs have been estimated at $20 a sq. foot. There is a definite shortage of contractors, considering the present real estate boom. Information on the residential developments is available from:

Burl Johnson & Associates
P.O. Box 290, Plymouth

Montserrat Estates Ltd.
(representing Foxes Bay), Plymouth

Leeward Island Development Co.
Spanish Point

Arthur Lennsen, Jr., Montserrat

Montserrat Beachettes
Dept. YB, Plymouth

Home Services, Box 267, Plymouth, can help newcomers find finished homes and cottages for rent.

Commerce and industry

The stony shells of former windmills still dot many a hilltop in Montserrat, a firm reminder of the days when "sugar was king." The quality of her lime juice and sea island cotton gave the island a world prominence unmatched by her size.

Today, Montserrat produces vegetables and livestock, a fair proportion of which are exported to neighboring islands. Recent increases in land prices have triggered a real estate boom which is expected to contribute significantly to economic growth. The government has passed legislation to encourage outside investment. The Development Incentive Ordinance No. 9 of 1964 enables the developer under the terms of the ordinance to import duty free all materials and equipment for the construction and fitting out of his factory, store, etc. It also confers an income tax holiday of seven years starting from the date of production. This ordinance applies also to the extensions to development enterprises.

To encourage hotel development, the government has enacted the Hotels Aid Ordinance No. 11 of 1954. This permits duty-free importation of all materials and equipment for the hotel and gives general tax concessions during the first 10 years of operation. There is particular need for a small preserving plant, a laundry and dry cleaning service, a printing plant, repair and maintenance services for home appliances and more construction firms. Additional information may be obtained from the Ministry of Finance, Plymouth, Montserrat.

WHERE TO STAY — In Montserrat

| | Plan | Dec. 15-April 14 | | April 15-Dec. 14 | |
		Double	Single	Double	Single
		U. S. Currency			
CANADIANA **Spanish Point** (6 Units) (EP)		$12.50	–	$10	–
COCONUT HILL (AP) **Plymouth** (10 Rms.)		$20	$12	$12	$8
EMERALD ISLE (AP) **Plymouth** (16 Rms.) **(b)**		$30	$20	$18	$12
MACLEOD GUEST (AP) **HOUSE Plymouth**		$25	$15	$15	$9
WADE INN (MAP) **Plymouth** (10 Rms.)		$25	$15	$15	$9
VUE POINTE (MAP) **Old Towne** (54 Rms. **(b, p, g)**		$36	$24	$24	$14

LEGEND FOR HOTEL LISTINGS: (AP) American Plan (room and 3 meals); **MAP)** Modified American Plan (room, breakfast and dinner); **(CP)** Continental Plan (room and breakfast); **(EP)** European Plan (room only). All rates quoted on a per-day basis and subject to change. Confirmed reservations at specific rates desired are always recommended.
HOTEL FACILITIES: (b) beach; **(p)** pool; **(t)** tennis; **(g)** golf.

PUERTO RICO

Fortifications dating back to the Spanish conquistadores still stand grim guard next to luxury resort hotels on the ocean-front of San Juan. In the country there are fields of sugar cane and coffee plantations and in some places teams of oxen till the soil.

Out on the island

Puerto Rico, perhaps more than any other island of the Caribbean, presents a slightly schizophrenic face to visitors. It is hymned by travel agents and advertising agencies as the complete vacationland, the tropical isle *non pareil*. There are beaches and palm trees and warm aquamarine waters. There are luxury hotels and mountain retreats and history and culture in old forts and international music festivals.

Puerto Rico has all of these. It also has hundreds of new factories, oil refineries, petro-chemical complexes, a booming construction industry and a lively economy. It is an island busily going about its work.

The tourists who arrive by the planeful and the boatload can see as much or as little of this working face of Puerto Rico as they wish. They cannot, of course, completely avoid the sights and sounds of progress, the rush and bustle that may appear unseemly in an island of the Indies.

But the old ease is there, too, side by side with the new progress, and the trade winds blow gently over the island just the way they did before anyone ever heard of Operation Bootstrap.

What Puerto Rico has to offer, both from its past and from the present, has made it one of the major tourist islands of the Caribbean.

There is the big and plush—the opulent pleasure palaces that line the shores of the Condado and Isla Verde, complete with gambling casinos, big-name entertainment and the requisite beach plus pool plus acres of lounge chairs. The big hotels of San Juan provide so much largess in the way of poolside and beachside, bars and restaurants and nightclubs that many a visitor feels no need to leave the enclave. At the most, there may be a quick safari into Old San Juan to look into the shops and perhaps gaze at history in the form of an old fort.

There is no denying that the hotels and shops of the metropolitan area are the hub of tourism in Puerto Rico. But "out on the island"—which means any place outside of metropolitan San Juan—the tourist will by no means feel he is isolated from the amenities. There are a number of hotels, ranging from the deluxe to the simple, great stretches of golden sand beaches and a network of good highways and good-to-passable roads that facilitates around-the-island travel. (A cautionary word: Most Puerto Rican drivers operate on a principle of fatalism, or what will be will be. It generally isn't considered necessary to pull off the road if one is going to stop the car. Hand signals, if any, are subject to individual proclivities.)

One of the most popular short trips out of San Juan is to the tropical rain forest of EL YUNQUE, a site any aficionado of the primeval green should not miss. The Luquillo range lies east of San Juan, its peaks rising well over 3,000 feet. Giant fern trees and tropical shrubs and flowers grow in wild profusion, and under the jurisdiction of the U.S. Forest Service. Clear streams and waterfalls course down the mountainsides and, in the La Mina Recreation Area (altitude, 2,100 feet), there is a spring-fed swimming pool and a restaurant serving drinks and Puerto Rican specialties. From this point foot trails lead to three peaks: El Yunque (round trip 2½ hours), Mount Britton (1¼ hours) and El Toro (8 hours).

Near El Yunque (in fact the mountains form a dramatic backdrop for it) is LUQUILLO BEACH, Puerto Rico's most famous strand. The crescent-shaped beach, lined with thousands of coconut palms, has been called one of the world's most beautiful. The Puerto Rican government maintains it and its surroundings in well-kept order and there are facilities for changing, a snack bar and picnic accommodations.

At the northeastern end of the island, near the town of FAJARDO, is the cliff-top El Conquistador Hotel. The hotel stretches along the crest of a 300-foot hill overlooking the Atlantic and the fishing village of LAS CROABAS. A string of small cays breaks the blue expanse in the middle distance, and on a clear day St. Thomas in the Virgin Islands appears on the horizon.

El Conquistador has facilities for nearly every conceivable water sport, as well as bowling greens, tennis courts and an 18-hole golf course. Guests travel from cliff-top to beach and dock area on an aerial tramway. The hotel recently completed an expansion from 82 rooms to 300, including ocean-front lanais.

The little harbor of Las Croabas is crowded with native fishing sloops, many of which can be chartered for a day sail to the offshore cays and reefs. The usual destination is Icacos, an uninhabited islet that offers a dazzling white sand beach, reefs for snorkeling and some of the clearest waters around.

In years past, Icacos was a favorite Sunday goal for a small band of island sailing enthusiasts who had the beach pretty much to themselves and their picnic lunches. It is now so popular that a weekend can see it looking like a parking lot for yachts and, unheard of in the old days, an empty beer can may now and again be seen floating on the pristine water.

A few miles from Las Croabas as the road winds is PUERTO REAL, or Playa de Fajardo (Fajardo Beach), the "seaport" of the east coast town of Fajardo. Here is the pink Customs House for sea voyagers who may have something to declare to the government, and the pier where the ferries to the offshore islands of Vieques and Culebra and the passenger boat to St.

El Morro, for centuries Puerto Rico's chief defense, lies at the northwest tip of Old San Juan

Thomas dock. Facing the harbor activity is the 20-room Hotel Delicias, built around an interior patio.

Until recently (it was saddening for many when it disappeared) there was a sign on the road leading to the Playa advertising "Hielo—Hecho en Puerto Rico" (Ice—Made in Puerto Rico).

ISLETA MARINA, on Cayo Obispo about a mile off Fajardo has four overnight cabins, a restaurant and a marina for 100 boats.

Puerto Rico is sharply divided, from east to west, by a central mountain range whose peaks rise to 3,000 and 4,000 feet. On the southern side of the range roads twist down escarpments that drop to a broad coastal plain bordered by the Caribbean Sea. The southern coast is still a long way from rivaling the north in tourist attractions, but it has many points of interest.

Some of the island's best seafood restaurants are found here, among them Ladi's Place, beside the beach near SALINAS. Ladi's is most definitely on the rustic side, but the fare is excellent and it is a favorite with local people. Another well-known seafood restaurant is the Aquarium at SANTA ISABEL. It is considerably more formal than Ladi's, featuring as it does air-conditioning and tablecloths.

PONCE, Puerto Rico's second largest city, dominates the southern section of the island. No conscientious tourist returns from a visit without having posed for a picture beside the old Parque de Bombas (firehouse), an eye-stopping structure painted in red and black stripes with green and yellow embellishments.

The pace in Ponce is considerably more relaxed than that of San Juan. It is even possible to hire an old horse-drawn carriage for a leisurely ride past the double plaza and through Ponce's quiet streets.

The city boasts a first-rate cultural attraction in the Ponce Museum of Art, designed by architect Edward Durell Stone. The museum is cool, white and tropical, and houses a collection of paintings and sculpture representing all schools of Europe and America of the past five centuries. There are works by Velasquez, El Greco, Reynolds, Van Dyke and Gainsborough, as well as examples of pre-Raphaelite and Italian baroque painting.

The collection and the museum are the gift of the Luis A. Ferre Foundation, headed by Ponce-born industrialist Luis Ferre.

Across the street from the mad firehouse is the Hotel Meliá. There is a cozy bar with evening entertainment, and an American-style cafeteria that is very popular among the *ponceños* for coffee breaks and lunch.

Also in downtown Ponce is the San José Guest House, with 17 air-conditioned rooms, two blocks from the plaza. Another guest house, El Coche, is located in the La Rambla section of town toward the airport. It has 20 rooms and a popular restaurant that specializes in German, Puerto Rican and American food.

The largest hotel in Ponce is the 170-room El Ponce Inter-Continental Hotel, atop El Vigia hill on the northern edge of town. The Ponce Inter-

Continental is a complete resort, and the ample terrace beside its two swimming pools overlooks a burst of bougainvillaea down the hill, and the Caribbean far below.

Just off the modern four-lane highway that runs west from Ponce is EL TUQUE BEACH, recently opened by the Puerto Rican government, which has swimming pools, lockers, a restaurant, and picnic tables scattered among the palms that line its strand.

Thirty miles west of Ponce is YAUCO, a curious little town thrown as a tablecloth over a small hill on the plain. If you happen to be stopping there, the Casa Roig, at 10 Betances Street, has 16 comfortable rooms in a Spanish colonial setting.

The town of GUÁNICA, a few minutes' drive south from Yauco, is the site of the landing of U.S. troops in 1898 during the Spanish-American War. Just outside Guánica is the Copamarina Hotel, a quiet, charming hotel strung out along a most inviting beach. The Copamarina has 24 rooms, a pool, and a modern restaurant that features seafood.

Further west is the fishing village of LA PARGUERA, long a favorite vacation spot for both visitors from abroad and island residents. On the waterfront at La Parguera is the Villa Parguera, a very relaxed little 40-room hotel that serves excellent seafood in its open-air dining room. Villa Parguera has a swimming pool—with poolside dining a regular fair-weather treat—and a dock from which you may rent boats to go fishing, snorkeling and swimming among the many mangrove cays along that section of Puerto Rico's shore.

La Parguera is also famous for its phosphorescent bay, where the water, when agitated, glows at night with the bright luminescence of marine microorganisms. Illuminated fish can be seen darting below the water's surface.

BOQUERÓN, a small resort village on Puerto Rico's southwest shore, was first a pirate haunt, later a popular place for the wealthier Puerto Ricans of that sector to keep a summer home. You may still see a number of these small wooden gingerbread houses in the town. The Villa del Mar is an unpretentious 20-room inn on the water, where you can eat good seafood and rent an outboard motorboat for a spin around the bay. Boquerón's beach is long, wide and excellent. Further inland is the beautiful little town of SAN GERMÁN, one of the island's best-preserved examples of Spanish colonial living. Sites of interest include the Porta Coeli museum of religious art on the plaza, and the campus of Inter American University. Inter American has guest accommodations at Costello Hall, 10 rooms, all meals served.

North of San Germán is Puerto Rico's third largest city, MAYAGUEZ. The 150-room Mayaguez Hilton on a hill at the edge of town has two restaurants, a bar with musical entertainment, and a casino. Recreational facilities there include a swimming pool and tennis court, and the hotel's staff—which is by the way very amiable—can arrange sightseeing and deep-sea fishing excursions.

For those who prefer to stay in town, the La Palma Hotel near the plaza has 105 rooms, some with air-conditioning, and a restaurant-cocktail lounge with a view of the city.

If you seek a comfortable retreat from pressurized living, you might enjoy the Sea Beach Colony near the town of RINCÓN. Sea Beach, 10 miles north of Mayaguez, is a fine colony of cabins in a palm grove along a great beach. A modified American plan is available, but several of the 27 rooms there have kitchenettes. Many technicians from Puerto Rico's first nuclear reactor—also located near Rincón—live here permanently with their families, so reservations should be made well in advance.

At the northwestern corner of the island on a hillside above AGUADILLA is the Montemar Hotel. The Montemar has 40 rooms, a swimming pool, beach bathing and other water sports facilities, and a terrace restaurant with a magnificent view of the surrounding countryside and the sea.

Aguadilla and the nearby town of Aguada have been arguing since the beginning of time as to which one was the site of Columbus' landing in 1493. Both towns celebrate Discovery Day with pomp and certainty, scornful of the fact that another school of scholarly thought puts the landing down around Cabo Rojo in the southwest. All three sites share the same coastline, if not the same opinions.

GUAJATACA BEACH, on the north coast, is a pleasant strip of sand in a notch between two rather precipitous hills, at the mouth of the Guajataca River. The surf here is fairly heavy, and bathers should not venture out too far because of the strong currents. Beside the beach is an old railroad tunnel, cut through a rock cliff, now spruced up (and trainless) as an unusual night spot. On weekends there is music for dancing, and the place is popular with young people from that part of the island. There is also a row of modest cabins near the beach for those who wish lodging.

In ARECIBO, 70 miles west of San Juan, there are comfortable accommodations at the 45-room Mir Hotel on the plaza. The world's largest radar-radio observatory, and two Peace Corps training camps, are located south of the city.

Between Arecibo and Manatí on the road to San Juan are extensive pineapple fields. Numerous roadside stands are filled to overflowing with the sweet, juicy Puerto Rican pineapple and other island produce.

Fifteen crow-flight miles west of San Juan is the DORADO area, with two large complete resorts—the Dorado Hilton and the Dorado Beach hotels. Both are located in seaside palm groves, and both have beautiful golf courses. The Dorado Hilton has 210 rooms with private balconies, as well as a dozen deluxe cabañas near the ocean and pool. There are ample facilities for tennis, boating, fishing, and badminton, as well as ocean swimming, of course.

The Dorado Beach has 308 rooms in elegant units along an extensive ocean frontage. (Room service waiters and bellhops ride bicycles to get from one end to another.) Guests may ride bicycles, too, if they wish, or Spanish carriages, or golf carts. At Dorado Beach you may rent small sailing craft, water skiing equipment, or all the gear needed to explore the underwater reefs.

Any road you take across Puerto Rico's "mountainous middle" is fascinating, both for the countryside and for the friendly people you may meet along the roadways. If you have a camera and like photos of children, you've come to the right island. With very rare exceptions the children of Puerto Rico are born "hams."

There are fruit trees, flowering trees, coffee and tobacco growing in the mountains, if your interests run toward botany.

There are several small resorts scattered across the island's ranges. One is Hacienda Roses, a coffee plantation and guest house on a high ridge off highway 140 near UTUADO.

The Roses family lives on the premises, and they see that guests are well taken care of. The food is marvelous, the view is lovely any time of day, and the Hacienda has horses for guests to ride. Peacocks strut about the lawn.

On a high hillside near the town of BARRANQUITAS is the Barranquitas Hotel, with 42 rooms, none of which is air-conditioned. You will never need it up there. The days are just warm enough to enjoy lounging around the hotel's pool, and at night you may need a blanket. This is an excellent place to spend a honeymoon, or recover from tensions you may have picked up. There are horses and burros to ride, a putting green, tennis courts, and a very comfortable wood-glass-and-stone living-roomish lobby with a huge fireplace in the center. In the town of Barranquitas, below the hotel, is the Luis Muñoz Rivera Museum.

One day, tourists will be able to get a real taste of the island via La Ruta, the scenic mountain route that will run the length of Puerto Rico. Travel will be by foot and on horseback, with occasional stretches accessible by jeep or helicopter. The plan also calls for rustic *posadas*, or hotels, at intervals of every 15 miles or so. La Ruta was proposed in 1962 by former governor Luis Muñoz Marín. He envisaged a lofty trail meandering across the top of Puerto Rico's mountainous divide, where harried urban dwellers could go to rediscover tranquillity and escape the geometric confusion of the cities.

When La Ruta becomes a reality, Puerto Rico will truly have everything to offer the tourist. Opening night with Sammy Davis, or the music of the *coquí*, the Puerto Rican tree frog, outside the *posada* window.

Instant facts

Location: 1,600 miles southeast of New York, 1,000 miles southeast of Miami and 500 miles north of Caracas, Venezuela. Bounded on the north by the Atlantic Ocean, on the south by the Caribbean Sea.

Population: Roughly 2.7 million.
Capital: San Juan.
Nationality: Commonwealth of the U.S.
Language: Spanish, English is widely spoken.
Currency: U.S.
Documentation: Regulations applicable to the U.S.A. apply. International certifi-

cate of vaccination required for re-entry from foreign territories.

Climate & Clothes: Only a slight variation exists between mean temperature in the winter (74.5°) and the summer (80°). The mountains are somewhat cooler, though coastal areas are refreshed by trade winds. While there is no official rainy season, most rainfall occurs between May and November with short, heavy rainstorms around December–January. The hurricane season is from July to November. Despite these seemingly gloomy forecasts, Puerto Rico's days are usually sunny and showers only briefly interrupt eager sunbathers. A summer wardrobe is appropriate throughout the year with a wrap for cooler evenings and air-conditioned night spots. Jacket and tie compulsory after sundown in most hotels and many restaurants. A word of warning: ladies and gentlemen who go shopping and sightseeing in short shorts or bermudas must be prepared for derisive stares and comments.

Food: Puerto Rican cuisine often blends Spanish recipes with new world fruits and spices. Commonly used seasonings are oregano, garlic and pimiento, though the dishes are not "hot" like Mexican food. Unique to the island is **asopao** (a wet rice dish with chunks of lobster, shrimp, chicken or a combination of all three). **Arroz con habichuelas** (rice and beans) is the "national dish" and other local favorites are **arroz con pollo** (chicken with rice), **lechón** (roast pig) and Spanish **paella** (saffron-seasoned rice with seafood and chicken).

Native seafoods include oysters, *jueyes* (land crabs), *mero* and *sierra* (both white fish), *camarones* (shrimp) and *langosta* (Caribbean lobster).

Most popular snacks are **pastelillos** (crisp turnovers stuffed with cheese or ground meat), **alcapurrias** (plantain croquettes stuffed with meat), **papas rellenas** (potato balls stuffed with meat). **Platanutres** (fried plantain chips) are sold in cellophane bags along with peanuts and pretzels. **Tostones** (larger slices of fried plantain) are offered like French fries—as a snack or side dish. For a cool treat,

piraguas (sweetened ices) are sold from pushcarts.

Native fruits include *papaya* (pawpaw), extra-sweet pineapple, vitamin-C *acerola*, *guanábana*, *mamey*, *guava* and *mango*. Many of these fruits, as well as chilled coconuts, can be bought at road-side stands along the highways.

Puerto Rican coffee, long ago exported to European royalty, is strong as **pocillo** (demitasse) and delicious with hot milk as **café con leche.**

Geography: Three fourths of the island's 3,435 sq. miles (100 x 35) is mountainous. Highest peak is Cerro de Punta, some 4,400 ft. above sea level. Fertile coastal plains stretch along both north and south shores, and the central mountain range extends from west to southeast. Very little rain occurs in the "enclosed" southwest corner and the area is dry and desert-like. This is in contrast to the abundant green vegetation throughout most of Puerto Rico, culminating in the moist splendor of El Yunque rain forest.

History: Heeding the word of some friendly Indians, Columbus came across the island of "Boriquén" in November 1493 and, in claiming it for Spain, promptly renamed it San Juan Bautista. The first settlement, called "Puerto Rico," was built by Ponce de Leon at Caparra, and later moved to what is now Old San Juan. Eventually names were exchanged, but for a time Puerto Rico was the capital of San Juan. For the next few centuries, settlers were busy fighting off the fierce Carib Indians, then the French, the English and the Dutch. Puerto Rico was, in effect, a fortress island protecting Spain's sealanes. At the end of the 19th century, Puerto Rico obtained a "Charter of Autonomy" from Spain, particularly through the efforts of Luis Muñoz Rivera. But it was too late. The Spanish-American War broke out and, in 1898, the island was ceded to the U.S. Governors were appointed by the President until 1948, when Muñoz Rivera's son, Luis Muñoz Marín, became the first elected governor. Puerto Rico became a Commonwealth in 1952. Residents do not have voting representation in Congress and do not participate in national elections. The island is represented in the U.S. Congress by a non-voting Resident Commissioner. Island residents do not pay Federal income taxes, except on income derived from outside Puerto Rico. They do pay some Federal taxes, notably excise taxes on certain goods purchased from the continental U.S., and there is Social Security coverage.

Commonwealth status is favored by many for providing what has been described as "all the advantages of being allied with the U.S. and none of the disadvantages." Supporters of statehood, however, claim that as a Commonwealth Puerto Rico is neither fish nor fowl and its residents are "second-class ciitzens." The "independentistas" (supporters of independence from the U.S.), a small but vocal minority, argue that U.S. authority in Puerto Rico merely constitutes colonialism. In a plebiscite held July 23, 1967, Puerto Rican voters supported the present Commonwealth status by giving it 60.5% of the total vote cast. The Statehood formula received 38.9% and the independence formula ran well out of the money, receiving less than 1%.

Who flies here

There are direct flights from the following cities to San Juan's International Airport:

New York: Eastern, Pan Am, Trans-Caribbean. Round trip: $90–$222; 10-day excursion $104, 30-day first-class excursion $179.

Miami: Eastern, Pan Am, BWIA. Round trip: $93–$143.

New Orleans: Delta. Round trip: $181–$258.

Montreal and **Toronto:** Eastern. Round trip: $204–$285 (Canadian $220–$307).

Madrid: Avianca, Iberia. Round trip: $574–$842.

Paris: Air France, Avianca. Round trip: $583–$931.

Lisbon: Air France, Pan Am. Round trip: $543–$804.

Frankfurt: Avianca. Round trip: $621–$965.

Caracas: Iberia, Pan Am. Round trip: $104–$238.

Air France, BWIA, Pan American and Caribair connect San Juan with numerous islands throughout the Caribbean. Other services include Dominican Airlines (Santo Domingo only), Delta (Jamaica), Trade Winds Airways (St. Thomas), Trans Caribbean (Aruba) and V.I. Airways (the U.S. and British Virgin Islands).

Island transportation

By Car: There is no scarcity of car rental dealers in and around San Juan. A casual stroll down Ashford Avenue, where most of the hotels are located, will reveal representatives of the majority of them. The two largest car rental agencies are Hertz and Avis and they have offices at the airports in San Juan, Ponce and Mayaguez. Rates vary, depending on the model of the car, but there is actually not too much variation between agencies. While one may advertise rates of $5 a day, 5¢ a mile (for a Volkswagen), it pays to check into such "extras" as gasoline and minimum mileage which an agency charging $5.75 or $6 a day, 10¢ a mile, may not charge for. Newcomers to the island may drive for 120 days on their stateside driving licenses.

The following companies offer sight-seeing tours in the metropolitan area and around the island. Besides these, there are over 100 independent operators authorized by the Department of Tourism to act as tourist guides. These can be identified by the Tourism shield displayed on the windshield.

National Tours
Gallardo Apt.
1102 Magdalena, Santurce
Tel: 722-0428, 723-9277

Borinquen Tours
Caribe Hilton Lobby
725-0303, Ext. 1110 or 1112

Gray Line
Suite 405, First Federal Bldg.
Stop 23, Santurce
723-0569, 724-3431

Southerland Tours
1052 Ashford, Condado
724-6281
Sheraton Hotel
724-2734

Turismo International
Lobby, San Juan Darlington
724-1297, 723-5192

Uncle Sam's Tours for the Young
("For boys and girls 7 to 70")
725-1890, 724-6234

All authorized **taxicabs** carry red license plates and are metered. Rates are 25¢ for the first 1/5 mile, 5¢ for every additional 1/5 mile. Make sure the driver turns the meter handle completely around to the left. It is not advisable to use meterless taxis although "públicos," the island's unique contribution to transportation, are very popular. Those who don't like being crammed into a car (ranging from standard sedan to small bus) with 8–10 other people or who have back-seat driving tendencies should avoid the public car. It is identifiable by red license plates, a sign on the front windshield announcing the car's destination and, very often, pom poms, stuffed animals and other paraphernalia hanging wherever minimal visibility permits. Públicos collect fixed rates, depending on their route, from each passenger.

Buses run throughout San Juan and the metropolitan area and fares are 10¢. It is convenient to take a bus between Santurce and San Juan as buses run regularly between these two points. Outside of Santurce, however, relying on public transportation is a major frustration, with schedules largely unheeded and more than one bus often necessary. Yellow posts or metal standards reading "parada" mark bus stops, though the term "parada," followed by a number, in addresses refers to the old trolley-car stops—now functionally obsolete but used to mark off sections of town.

For getting around the island, Puerto Rico Motor Coach offers daily scheduled services between San Juan and Mayaguez with stops at Arecibo, Ramey and Aguadilla. Main office starting point: 317 Recinto Sur, near San Juan post office. Tel: 725-2460. One-way fares: Arecibo 75¢, Ramey $1.50, Aguadilla $1.75, Mayaguez $2.

By Plane: There are daily flights to Ponce, $14 round trip, by Caribair, Prinair and Trade Winds Airways. Caribair and Prinair fly to Mayaguez, $16 round trip, while Trade Winds Airways and Prinair have scheduled flights to Vieques.

By Ferry: The ferry to Cataño, across San Juan Bay from San Juan, leaves the Old San Juan terminal every 10 or 15 minutes, 10¢ one way. There are regular trips to Vieques at 9 A.M. and 5:00 P.M. daily, leaving from Playa de Fajardo. A ferry leaves Vieques at 7:30 A.M. and 3:30 P.M. for the hour ride to Fajardo, $2 per person one way.

Walking in and around San Juan

Puerto Rico's Spanish heritage is nowhere more evident than in the complex of narrow streets, pastel-tinted buildings, open courtyards and ancient forts and fortifications that is Old San Juan. The 20th century has, of course, intruded in modern shops and art galleries, in drugstores and cafeterias, and in cars sardining their way through streets originally designed for horses; but the shops and galleries are likely to be housed in an 18th-century town house, the cars drive over blue blocks brought to the New World as ballast on Spanish galleons, and the drugstores may sell freshly squeezed fruit juices in a choice of pineapple, papaya, mango or grapefruit.

The old city is actually an islet that guards the entrance to San Juan Bay. Its small size, coupled with its wealth of historic sites and beautiful vistas, make it ideal for an afternoon of sightseeing. And so the following tour is designed for walkers who don't want to miss a single old brick or commemoratory plaque.

Most of the sites (and shops) are concentrated in the western end of Old San Juan. And at the extreme northwestern tip is the supreme historical site of them all: **El Morro Fortress.**

The way to **El Morro** lies through **Fort Brooke,** a U.S. Army base now deactivated. The walk from the Fort Brooke gate leads down a road lined with Australian pines and coconut palms (and through a nine-hole golf course where the fairways dogleg around old walls, and moats and arches are the hazards. As of now, the golf course is also deactivated.) The massive fortress rises on a headland above the Atlantic, its shell-marked walls still guarding the entrance to the harbor. Begun in 1539 and finished in 1776, its guns repelled an attack by Sir Francis Drake and a siege by the Dutch. Inside the fort there are the huge assembly plaza, soldier's quarters, gunrooms, kitchens, dungeons and a labyrinth of ramps, tunnels and stairways that give access to every part of the fortress.

A walk (more a climb) up the steep cannon ramps to El Morro's topmost level is repaid with a sweeping view out to sea and over the harbor to Isla de Cabras (Goat Island). Down in the depths of the fortress are a stairway and interior ramp that lead to an iron grilled gate where you can get a waterline view of the ships passing through the narrow harbor entrance. The U.S. National Park Service conducts free guided tours.

Plaza San José: Exiting from Fort Brooke, a turn to the right will bring you to this brick-paved square with its statue of Ponce de Leon, Puerto Rico's first governor. The focal point of the plaza is the Church of San José, one of the oldest churches in the hemisphere and one of the most beautiful. The church was begun around 1530 by Dominican friars, and its Gothic ceilings are among the few traces of Gothic architecture in the Americas. The church houses a number of religious and historical relics.

The church stands at the top of **Cristo Street,** which is probably the most visited thoroughfare in Old San Juan. It descends straight and narrow (and paved with the inevitable blue blocks) down a steep slope, and then levels off as it approaches the old city walls. On and just off Cristo Street can be found the interesting shops, art galleries and a goodly number of buildings restored to their original Spanish colonial elegance.

The most impressive of these is **Hotel El Convento,** a luxury hotel facing a small, tree-shaded square. (Note: The square was tree-shaded as of press time. There has been a movement afoot to remove the single large leafy tree and replace it with a statue of an early Puerto Rican bishop.)

The hotel building was formerly a Carmelite convent, built in the 17th century. It was later abandoned and fell into disrepair and eventually was used as a parking area for trucks. This sorry state of affairs was rectified when the building was restored with unstinting attention to detail and taste and unstinting outlays of money.

The dining room, formerly the convent chapel, has a 50-foot vaulted ceiling and leaded glass windows patterned in Spanish coats of arms. It is dramatically gracious for dinner but a little awesome for lunch. If lunchtime finds you in or near El Convento you may repair to the interior patio, shaded by trees and striped awnings over the tables and with a small swimming pool tucked away at one end. Guest rooms and suites are entered from the tiers of cloistered galleries that rise above the patio.

Near El Convento are San Juan's two remaining step streets, **Callejon de las Monjas,** one block west of Cristo St., by the hotel, and **Caleta del Hospital,** one block west of Cristo between Sol and San Sebastian Streets.

The **Cathedral of San Juan Bautista** (St. John the Baptist), on the opposite side of Cristo St. from El Convento, holds the remains of Ponce de Leon. The cathedral's collection of religious treasures may be viewed upon request.

Opposite the Cathedral, Caleta de San Juan (San Juan Lane) leads down from Cristo St. to **San Juan Gate.** Completed about 1635, this was the main entrance from the waterfront to the walled city of San Juan. (Huge wooden doors, studded with brass headed nails, bear the date 1749.) Travelers from Spain climbed the hill to the cathedral to give thanks for a safe voyage.

There is a little park outside the gate and you can walk or drive through the gate and along the sea wall, circling back into the city at the Paseo de la Princesa, once a favored promenade.

If you walk back up Caleta de San Juan to Cristo St. and turn right you will be strolling into the prime shopping area. Here is an abundance of goods and goodies, although do not expect bargain prices. San Juan is not a free port. A compensation, however, is that you will be browsing and buying in beautifully restored buildings with the charm and proportions of Old Spain. One excellent example is **Casa Cavanagh** on Cristo St., which purveys wares from clothes to Spanish-styled furniture in a high-ceilinged, Spanish-styled building with interior courtyard and latticed balconies. Of the art galleries in the old city, one of the most elegant is **La Casa del Arte** (one and a half blocks down on Fortaleza St., which crosses Cristo) housed in a meticulously restored building.

One block to the right on Fortaleza St. is **La Fortaleza** (The Fortress), official home of the Governor of Puerto Rico and the oldest Governor's mansion in continuous use in the Western Hemisphere.

The mansion sits atop the city walls (48 feet high at this point) and commands a magnificent view of San Juan Bay. Begun originally in 1533 as a fortress to protect the bay, it was equipped with ammunition and pieces of artillery but its location was soon found wanting. The Spanish Crown decided to erect another fort at the entrance of the harbor, but until El Morro was completed La Fortaleza served as the main defense structure of San Juan. The building has two 16th-century towers and a sweep of walls that are among the earliest examples of military architecture in the Americas. Tours may be taken through the gardens and certain portions of the mansion.

A pleasant (but longer) way to get back to Cristo St. is to climb the flight of stairs that leads up from Fortaleza St. some 100 yards from the Governor's mansion. At the top is the all-but-hidden little **Parque de las Palomas** with its trees for shade and benches to sit on and watch the ships sailing in and out of the harbor. You may also watch the pigeons, for whom the park is named.

Built along the top of the city wall, the park overlooks La Princesa Jail and the Coast ·Guard installation at La Puntilla. At the far end the park adjoins the southern end of Cristo St. and the **Cristo Chapel,** an 18th-century oratory with an intricately formed silver altarpiece. The chapel was built in memory of a young caballero who plunged over the precipice during a horse race down Cristo St. It also served to close the street and prevent further accidents.

Near the chapel, at 255 Cristo St., is **La Casa del Libro** (The House of the Book). This 18th-century house has been lovingly remodeled to show to best advantage the collection of rare books of early and modern printing and documents dating from the time of Queen Isabella. Nearby is the Institute of Puerto Rican Culture's **Museo de Bellas Artes** (Museum of Fine Arts) with paintings and sculpture by Puerto Rican artists.

One block down Fortaleza St. and a turn to the left will bring you to the **Plaza de Armas,** which was an open-air market in the 16th century. Today it is lined with department stores and shops and government buildings (City Hall, for one), and on one corner of the square is a drugstore that sells the aforementioned freshly squeezed fruit juices. They taste like nothing that ever came out of a can.

As you stroll through the old city you'll find on many corners pushcarts full of fresh fruit and vegetables. The vendors do a brisk trade in peeling oranges in neat spirals. The orange you eat while walking.

At 319 Fortaleza St. is **Casa del Callejon,** an 18th-century building owned and restored by the Institute of Puerto Rican Culture. The building contains two museums: the **Museum of Colonial Architecture,** with scale models of El Morro, La Fortaleza and private homes, together with photographs and original plans and examples of typical woodwork; the **Museum of the Puerto Rican Family** is on the second floor and is furnished to show how a typical San Juan family lived a century ago. The building also houses the Colibrí Gallery and the Fonda del Callejon restaurant.

A block away is the **Plaza de Colón,**

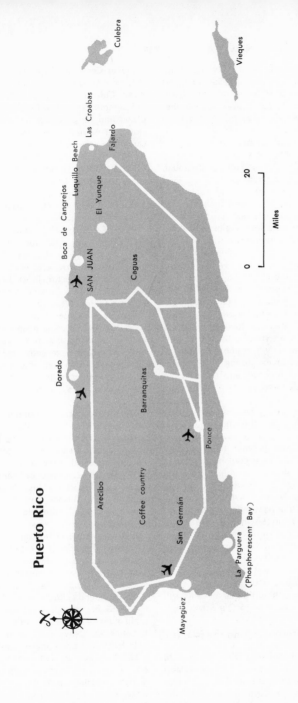

Puerto Rico

at the entrance to the old city. There are trees and benches (and the San Juan bus terminal) and a statue of Puerto Rico's discoverer, Cristobal Colón (Christopher Columbus). A large gray building next to the square houses the Institute of Puerto Rican Culture, which may be visited.

Just up the hillside street, Calle Norzagaray, from the plaza is **Fort San Cristobal**, built by the Spanish to protect the land approach to the city. San Cristobal has a plaza de armas surrounded by gunrooms and barracks. Tunnels lead up to a main gun deck and on a higher elevation there is a massive two-tiered gun platform 150 feet above the ocean, and with a panoramic view. If you peer over the parapet you can see the "haunted" sentry box, "Garita del Diablo." The legend of the sentry box is that a soldier assigned to this lonely post disappeared one night and was presumed kidnaped by the devil.

In recent years the fort's battlements have rung with the immortal lines of Shakespearean drama during local theater productions of *Macbeth* and *Othello*.

All the sights and points of interest in Old San Juan should not be attempted in one day. The sun is hot and the paving blocks hard, and the horns of the crammed-in autos apt to blare.

If at any point in your tour you feel that all you want is a cool breeze and a chance to sit down, you might try a sea voyage on the Cataño Ferry that crosses San Juan Bay. Ferries leave from the terminal behind the post office on 15-minute schedules (10 minutes in rush hours) and for a modest outlay of ten cents you can gaze back upon Old San Juan and its walls and buildings while enjoying the breeze off the bay. At the Cataño terminus do not get off. There is probably nothing for you in Cataño. An additional 10 cents will buy your passage back to Old San Juan.

Places of interest around the island

Arecibo Ionospheric Observatory: On Route 129, south of Arecibo. The largest radar-radio observatory in the world, operated jointly by Cornell University and the U.S. Air Force. Open to the public on Sundays, 2 to 4:30 P.M.

Indian Ceremonial Ball Park: On Route 111, near Utuado. The Institute of Puerto Rican Culture is restoring this 700-year-old ceremonial area with its paved walks, plazas and long parallel lines of standing stones in varying height and colors, some carved in low relief with the figures of gods.

Loíza Aldea Ferry: Along the sandy coast road past Boca de Cangrejos. The raft-like ferry, poled by hand, takes cars and passengers ($1 fare) across the Río Grande de Loíza.

Peace Corps Training Camp: Route 621. The camps are open for tours without prior notice on Sundays only. Week-day tours may be arranged either by letter addressed to Director, Peace Corps Training Center, Camp Crozier, Arecibo, P. R., or by phoning 878-0952.

University of Puerto Rico: On Ponce de Leon Ave. (Rt. 25). The main campus is in Rio Piedras. Spanish architecture and carefully landscaped grounds make a visit worthwhile. Also on the grounds are several museums, a library, art gallery and the theater, site of the annual Casals Festival.

The Agricultural Experimental Station: Off Hwy. 1, Rio Piedras. Part of the University, a veritable oasis in the middle of unscenic city traffic. Acres and acres of unusual tropical vegetation, hills cultivated in "steps," fields of pineapple and many varieties of orchids. Other agricultural stations further out on the island are located in Gurabo and in Mayaguez, adjacent to the University's College of Agriculture and Engineering.

Coffee Plantations: Visitors interested in seeing coffee plantations can tour the Monte Verde farm—contact Herb Abel, Ponce Inter-Continental Hotel (Tel: 842-1140). Hacienda Roses in Utuado (Tel: 894-9946) has accommodations for overnight guests. The best months to visit are October and November, when all available hands are attending the harvest.

Fish Hatchery: Rt. 410, entrance to Maricao. Since Puerto Rico has no indigenous fish, the hatchery produces 25,000 fingerlings yearly to stock lakes and streams. Here, in a park-like setting, are the spawning and rearing pools.

Rum Distilleries: During the week it is possible to tour the Ronrico Rum Distillery, on Rt. 2 in Arecibo, the Bacardi Rum Plant on the way to Dorado (Rt. 165) and Don Q on Rt. 1 near the Ponce Airport.

The Indian's Cave: At Punta Las Tunas, between Barceloneta and Arecibo. Ancient Indian petroglyphs are carved into the walls of the cave—actually one large cave and a number of smaller ones. Located along the ocean, a few of the smaller subdivisions are eroding and may be entered only at your own risk.

The sporting life

Golf: There are many beautiful and unusual golf courses, all private, with privileges limited to beach club members, A favorite course, at El Morro, is closed down presently while the land is being transferred from the U.S. Army to the Commonwealth government. The Dorado Beach Hotel has two 18-hole championship courses and its neighbor, the Dorado Hilton, has a new 18-hole course. Other greens are at El Conquistador in Fajardo and at Berwind Country Club, now located in Rio Grande, both 18 holes. The Ponce Country Club has a nine-hole course which can be used by guests of the Ponce Inter-Continental Hotel.

Horseback Riding: The Barranquitas Hotel (Barranquitas) has horses for riding the mountain trails and donkeys for children to ride. The Dorado Beach and the Dorado Hilton (Dorado) also have horses available. Sportsman's House (Vieques Island) has a stable of both American Saddle Breeds and the smooth-gaited *paso finos*.

Bowling: There are two modern bowling alleys in the metropolitan area, Paradise Bowl-a-Mat on Matadero Rd. in Hato Rey and Star Bowling Center on Muñoz Rivera Ave. in Rio Piedras.

Tennis: In the San Juan area and around the island courts are available to guests of most large hotels. (See "Where to Stay" listing.)

There are free courts at the University of Puerto Rico in Rio Piedras and in Baldrich (Hato Rey), next to Station WIPR.

Spectator Sports — Baseball: The island's favorite U.S. sport. In addition to rooting for such big league teams as "los Yanquis" of New York or "los Cachorros" of Chicago from April to October, local fans can continue in their own winter league from October to March, topped off by a grass-roots "world series." There are six teams (the San Juan Senators, Santurce Crabbers, Caguas Creoles, Arecibo Wolves, Mayaguez Indians and Ponce Lions) and the final victor faces play-offs in other Latin American countries. Among the players are major leaguers from the States, some of them islanders who have "made good."

Cockfights: There are over a hundred *galleras* (cockpits) throughout the island. (Easily accessible is The Canta Gallo on the airport road in Santurce.) This colorful and bloody sport is legal, and popular; here and in December many of the better cockpits have an annual government-sponsored festival featuring new cocks. Cockfights are held between November 2 and August 31, usually on Saturday and Sunday from 9 A.M.–6 P.M.

"Bull Fighting": This is not the sport that Hemingway immortalized. The bulls are half-Brahman, the matadors a bit paunchy and, thanks to animal-loving organizations, there is no kill. It's fun, though, and certainly different. The corrida can be seen at a small bullring near the Americana Hotel in Isla Verde (admission: $5 shady side, $3.50 sunny side, children $2.50) and occasionally at the Sixto Escobar Stadium in San Juan.

Horse Racing: El Comandante is a modern track, with all computing done by electronic tabulators. For proper drainage and texture, the surface of the track contains "bagasse," sugar cane residue mixed with top soil, giving the mile-long track its peculiarly sweet odor. In addition to pari-mutuel and daily-double wagering, El Comandante features the "cinco-seis" (5-6) pool. Over 300 *agencias hípacas* (off-track agencies) handle betting throughout the island.

A special tour leaves leading San Juan hotels at 2 P.M. on racing days. Children under 18 are not permitted and shorts are prohibited. Post time for the first race is

2:30 P.M. For further information, call the track at 769-0040.

Boxing and Wrestling: Championship matches are frequently scheduled at the Hiram Bithorn Stadium on Roosevelt Avenue or in San Juan at the Sixto Escobar Stadium.

Basketball: Indoor and outdoor games are held in late spring and summer by eight professional island teams.

Water Sports — Swimming: Most visitors will find delightful swimming weather in Puerto Rico throughout the year. During the busy "winter season," however, when the plot of sand behind every hotel looks like Jones Beach during a heat wave, you will find beaches outside San Juan almost deserted. Natives of this sunny isle, sensitive to the few degrees drop in temperature, generally avoid the water during the "winter" months. But visitors should keep in mind that tropical sunshine takes some getting used to. Many an unwary sunbather has been burnt on his first day out, deceived by cool trade-wind breezes that seem to subdue the heat of the sun.

A few hotel-affiliated beaches have been blocked off by manmade reefs and the waters are as calm as a lake. For those who like their surf white-capped, and don't mind doing without lounge chairs, mats and rafts, there are public beaches all around the island. In San Juan proper the new **Escambrón olympic pool,** built especially for the Tenth Caribbean Games in 1966, has ultra-modern diving facilities and occasional problems with juvenile and adult delinquents. The pool (admission: 25¢, children 10¢) is complemented by a pleasant, middle-sized beach, lockers, parking space, a cafeteria and massage parlor, located adjacent to the Caribe Hilton Hotel on the way to Old San Juan.

East of San Juan, across from the airport, is the huge new **Isla Verde public beach,** complete with parking facilities, picnic area, restaurant, and facilities for showering and changing. Further along this road is the beautiful and untamed shoreline starting at **Boca de Cangrejos** and continuing past Loíza Aldea. No facilities of any sort here but beaches for all tastes—calm, rough, sunny, shady—and

coconut groves galore. This area is still off the beaten track to visitors, in part because of bad roads (avoid them after a rainy day). It seems destined for future development, however, and will one day probably rival the Condado coastline.

Further east, along Route 3, is the renowned **Luquillo** (Loo-kée-yo) **Beach,** very crowded on summer weekends and holidays. Facilities are similar to those at Isla Verde though added attractions are its striking view of the mountains and the row of thatched huts selling native snacks. Nearby, if you go for ice-cold water, is a woodsy swimming pool at La Mina Recreational Area, high in **El Yunque.**

Continuing along Route 3 past Fajardo is the public beach at **Humacao,** also well-equipped with lockers and restaurant. Ponce, too, got its long-deserved **El Tuque Beach Resort,** located several miles west of the city. In addition to modern facilities it has an olympic-sized swimming pool (admission: 50¢, children 10¢).

On the dusty southwest coast, not far from La Parguera, is the newly developed beach area at **Boquerón,** a veritable oasis. Complete facilities are available for daytime visitors and, for those wishing a weekend or week's change of pace, there are family-sized cottages renting for $7 a day. These cottages are very popular with year-round residents—so popular, in fact, that reservations must usually be made several weeks or even months in advance.

To most visitors, the name **Dorado** is synonymous with the Dorado Beach Hotel or the nearby Hilton hostelry, both a good hour's crawl from metropolitan San Juan. There is also a small public beach, **La Sardinera,** on Rt. 693, Km. 6.8. Facilities for changing and a picnic area are supplied but bring your own food. West of Dorado is the grotto-like **Mar Chiquita Beach.** There is a restaurant and facilities for changing.

Admission to government-developed public beaches is nominal (parking 25¢, lockers 10¢). A word of advice in general: don't underestimate the ocean's undertow, particularly strong in the rougher winter season. Also, to avoid the gnatlike "mimis" and mosquitoes, do your swimming early and prepare to leave around 3 P.M.

Skindiving and Water Skiing: In San Juan.

At the Americana and El San Juan Hotels, Bob D'Ascuito and Gene McHugh are in charge of water skiing, snorkeling, skeeter boating.

At the Caribe Hilton and San Jerónimo Hilton, Charlie McCarthy and Jerry Crossman offer skindiving, snorkeling and water-skiing lessons. All equipment provided.

At the Condado Beach and La Concha, Greg Korwek is the certified instructor in charge of water sports. Skindiving instruction and also skindiving boat trips to submarine gardens when water permits. Certified scuba lessons in swimming pools. Water-skiing instruction and tows. Surfing lessons in groups or surfboard rentals.

At Holiday Inn, Chuck Bangert offers skindiving, scuba and water-skiing classes, also boat tours. All equipment provided.

At the Puerto Rico Sheraton, Joe Baker is the certified instructor in charge of water sports, which includes snorkeling, scuba, water skiing, surfboarding and swimming. Also tows, trips by boat. All equipment provided.

Bill Brown conducts all-day snorkeling and sailing trips in the clear waters of the Icacos Island group. He furnishes equipment, complete instruction for beginners, identification of fish and corals, and transportation to and from your hotel. Groups of six people daily, $15 per person. (791-0726, 724-3013, ext. 300). Also available, arrangements for underwater photos of yourself.

Skindiving & Water Skiing: Around the Island.

Aguadilla: The Hotel Montemar offers skindiving and snorkeling for anyone interested.

Dorado: The Dorado Beach Hotel offers water skiing, snorkeling, scuba-diving, surfboarding. Equipment provided. The hotel makes arrangements for surfcasting for anglers.

At the Dorado Hilton, Jaime Garcia is sports manager, in charge of snorkeling, skindiving, scuba, water bicycling. Equipment provided.

Fajardo: At El Conquistador Hotel, Walt Hendrick is the certified instructor for all water sports. Equipment provided. Call Fajardo 560 for further information and reservations.

La Parguera: Villa Parguera makes arrangements for anyone who wants skindiving, snorkeling or water skiing. Equipment provided.

Ponce: Canadian athlete Jim Wilson offers skindiving instruction and trips and provides full equipment as well as transportation from the Ponce Inter-Continental Hotel. For information call Ponce, 942-5780.

Fishing: Deep-sea fishing is excellent in Puerto Rico throughout the year, due to the very deep waters that surround the island. Off the north coast, blue marlin has been a record-breaker and other top catches include white marlin, dolphin, sailfish and tuna (yellowfin, bluefin, Allison's). Best reef fishing is off Arecibo, Fajardo, around Ponce and La Parguera, and near Mayaguez. Billfishing is good off the south coast during the spring months, particularly around La Parguera and Guánica. There is also excellent deep-sea fishing on the west coast, for those who find the island's northern waters too rough.

Calmest weather is during the summer months, particularly August–October, and some of the best fishing, not coincidentally, is between April and October. While the waters off the northern coast of the island are rougher than those of the south or west, winds usually die down after noon. Best months for blue marlin are April–November, white marlin April–August, sailfish October–June, Allison's tuna April–August, yellowfin tuna May–July, dolphin in February and wahoo December–January.

It is not always necessary to charter a boat for fishing. Fishing in Puerto Rico is done from bridges, through grating bars, off reefs, on the beach and in rivers. Lakes and streams are stocked by the fish hatchery in Maricao and some of the best fresh-water fishing is in Guajataca,

Utuado, Guayama, Yauco and Cidra. However, heed this warning: it is not wise to swim or even wade in Puerto Rico's lakes or rivers. A parasite that breeds in freshwater snails can enter the human body through the skin causing schistosomiasis, a seriously debilitating disease.

Boating: In San Juan, modern boats are available with crew for cruising and, fully equipped, for fishing. Arrangements may be made with Capt. Mike Benítez at the Tourism Fishing Pier, Fernandez Juncos, Stop 9 (Tel: 725-0139). Short cruises around the harbor are offered as well as overnight trips aboard a yacht to neighboring islands. The Club Náutico, at the Dos Hermanos Bridge in Santurce, accommodates sailboats and cruisers.

For a 1½ hour cruise around San Juan Bay, the Borinquen Ferry leaves the San Juan–Cataño terminal at Old San Juan Sunday and holidays only, 2:30 and 4:30 P.M. 75¢ adults, 35¢ children.

Cruisers only at the Boca de Cangrejos club, east of San Juan. A low bridge between the club harbor and the sea prevents masted vessels from passing through.

In Fajardo, El Conquistador Hotel offers daily trips on a 35-foot catamaran, *Barefoot*, which holds 15 people. Half-day trips are $7 per person with box lunches available for $2.50. (Tel: Fajardo 560 for reservations). Crude but sturdy fishing sloops can be rented at the nearby village of Las Croabas for about $25 for an enjoyable day of cruising, swimming and picnicking at the nearby islets of Icacos and Palominitos. No reservations are necessary. From four to six people per boat and bargaining is done on the spot with the village's enterprising fishermen. Kiko Toro, Inc., has a sailboat for charter accommodating four but it is usually booked up months ahead on weekends.

Playa de Fajardo is the departure point for Isleta Marina, on an islet about a mile offshore with covered docking facilities for 35 boats and slips for 70. There are boat lifts with up to 200-ton capacity, a repair yard and maintenance shop, and full service including fresh water, electricity, telephone, ice, gas, fuel, marine supplies, guest house, playgrounds, restaurant and bar. Call 724-4147 in San Juan

or Fajardo 1013 for more information.

Other yacht clubs are located in Cataño, near the Ferry Slip, and in Ponce, on an island near the commercial docks. Sailfish are available at the Dorado Beach Hotel. In Aguadilla, fishing trips are organized by the Montemar Hotel on boats belonging to local fishermen. The $5 per person fee includes equipment (Tel: 891-0885).

At La Parguera, home of the Phosphorescent Bay, Wiko's Marine Service has boats available for cruising and fishing. In addition to an early evening tour of the famous bay ($1.50), a boat can be chartered for an hour's cruise ($7) or for a day of picnicking and swimming on nearby secluded beaches ($30). A 5 P.M. sunset cruise ($1.25 per person) meanders through the mangroves and a half-day cruise, with time for swimming (lunch is extra), is $20. Most tours accommodate no more than six persons. Deep sea and small outboard boats are available for fishing, with crew and equipment, at rates by the hour, half-day or day. Sunfish and day sailers can also be rented (with or without instruction or guide) and motorboats can be chartered, with captain, for cruising or water skiing. For reservations, write to Wiko's, c/o Villa Parguera Hotel, Lajas, P. R. 00667 or call (892-9588). There are no extra privileges, pricewise, for guests of the hotel.

Best shopping buys

Most visitors prefer to do their shopping in Old San Juan as the narrow streets and old buildings provide interesting sightseeing as well as good buys. The main streets in Old San Juan run in parallel formation from the bus stop at Plaza de Colón to the San Juan Gate, making it hard to get lost. Most stores are, one after another, on Cristo, San Francisco and Fortaleza Streets, though some of the newest and most interesting ones are somewhat off the beaten track.

Merchandise available in San Juan ranges from the shoes, jewelry, fashions, materials and other goods that can be bought anywhere in the States to Caribbean souvenirs, locally designed resort wear and merchandise imported from Thailand, India, Hong Kong and the Philippines. Prices on imports are about the same as in the States, sometimes lower, often higher. San Juan is not a free port but, as it is U.S. territory, there is take-home duty only on rum.

Some of the more interesting locally made buys are paintings and sculptures by Puerto Rican artists; handwoven fiber mats, lampshades and window blinds; primitive musical instruments and bowls shaped from gourds; tortoise-shell jewelry; "antiqued" maps of Puerto Rico and the Caribbean; packages of shells for lazy beachcombers; records by Puerto Rican composers; and silk-screen posters. For yuletime visitors, Pava Prints has a wide selection of seasonal and note cards printed locally and featuring, in a lighter vein, a tropical Santa Claus and sunbathing reindeer.

Outside of San Juan are many new and modern shopping centers which sell anything and everything but are hardly geared to tourist tastes. Most visitors, in fact, will probably be disappointed as a second-glance at these huge, well-stocked stores reveals a great deal of low-cost, often shoddy merchandise. With a few exceptions, visitors looking for quality buys and interesting gifts are better off in smaller specialty stores.

Dining, dancing and night life

The following listing includes restaurants both elegant and humble and night spots for all tastes. Most hotel restaurants demand jacket and tie in the evening and, particularly on weekends and during the peak winter season, prior reservations.

On the whole, night spots are geared to the young-at-heart but several cater almost exclusively to the young-in-age. Corky's and the Latin Q in Santurce and Gatsby's and The Scene au Go-Go are current teenage favorites, complete with go-go dancers and psychedelic lighting.

The most varied menus are found in San Juan, of course, but more reasonable prices, and often delicious seafood cooked to order, can be found in restaurants scattered around the island. At seaside villages baby barracuda, squid or octopi may be presented freshly caught to the diner for his approval. The major problem to date has been finding the "island" restaurants, which scorn advertisements but serve superbly. Included in the listing are a few for visitors who venture out of San Juan.

OLD SAN JUAN

Barrachina: 104 Fortaleza. Spanish restaurant in open courtyard. Features paella. 11 A.M.–1 A.M. daily except Wednesday. Spanish dancers evenings. Tel: 725-7912.

El Cofre: 149 San Justo, corner Luna. Native food, moderate prices. 8 A.M. till late. Entertainment nightly. 723-1991.

El Convento Hotel: Cristo St. Converted convent, Spanish Renaissance decor. Luncheon in poolside patio, with fashion shows Thursday, Friday. Dining, dancing, entertainment nightly (Monday dinner only) in **Ponce de León Room.** Reservations recommended. Satirical reviews by the Lamplighters Monday–Thursday 10:30 P.M. Friday and Saturday 10:30 P.M., 12:30 A.M. at **Le Club.** 723-9020.

Corral de Marcelo: 203 Tanca. Spanish flamenco shows nightly 11 P.M., 1 and 3 A.M. Dancing till late. Jacket and tie, reservations necessary. 725-0089.

Las Cuevas de Altimira: 353 San Francisco. Flamenco nightspot with singing waiters, dancing, shows at 11 P.M., 12:45 A.M., 2:30 A.M. Hors d'oeuvres served, open 9:30 P.M.–3 A.M. nightly. 725-2415.

La Danza: Corner Cristo and Fortaleza. Typical native cuisine. Dining noon–midnight daily. Bar features 50¢ rum punch 4–7 P.M. Songfests, guitar, piano music 10 P.M.–wee hours nightly except Monday. Jacket and tie after 10 P.M. 723-1642.

Focolare: 150 Cristo. International cuisine, Mexican and Spanish specialties. Ultra-modern cocktail lounge serves Mexican snacks. Dining upstairs, mariachi music 6 P.M.–2 A.M. Reservations recommended. 725-0093, 725-0041.

La Fonda del Callejon: 319 Fortaleza. Native cuisine, cocktails noon–11 P.M. daily in quaint, recently restored building. Also, gallery and museums. 725-8529.

La Gallega: 309 Fortaleza. Spanish specialties 11:30 A.M.–11:30 P.M. daily except Monday. 724-9128, 725-8018.

Gatsby's: 209 Cristo. Go-Go dancers. Recorded music. $3 minimum, drinks from $1.50 (including Coke and beer). 10 P.M.–4 A.M. nightly.

La Gitana: 257 Cruz. Native and Castillian cuisine in Spanish setting. Luncheon, dinner. 725-9862.

La Gondola: 305 Recinto Sur. Italian food and wine in attractive European atmosphere. Air-conditioned. Noon–midnight. 723-1029.

Ko-Bai: 207 Tanca, corner Fortaleza. Cocktails, dining in fancy Chinese decor noon–midnight. Mandarin specialties. Nightly entertainment. 725-0232.

Mago's Saxony: 257 Tanca. A favorite among locals for prime charcoal-broiled steak. Lunch, dinner. 724-9398.

La Mallorquina: 207 San Justo. San Juan's oldest restaurant. A landmark. Native and Spanish cuisine in gracious Spanish setting. Lunch, dinner. 724-9165.

El Mediterráneo: 254 San Justo. Spanish and local cuisine, superb paella. Noon–midnight. Entertainment. 725-1280.

Mesón Vasco: 47 Cristo, corner San Sebastián. Basque specialties 11 A.M.–1 A.M. daily. Continuous piano entertainment. 725-7819.

Ocho Puertas: Corner Cristo and Fortaleza. Lounge in elegant Victorian trappings. Piano, guitar and offbeat vocal entertainment. Nightly from 9 P.M. except Monday. 723-4253.

Ruben's: Across from Customs House. American cooking, 4 P.M.–4 A.M., with musical accompaniment. 725-9712.

Scene Au Go-Go: 253 San Jose. Live entertainment Saturday and Sunday 1–6 P.M. for the teen set. $1.50 minimum, free Cokes. Open other nights until the last dancer drops.

Spot in the Sun: 206 O'Donnell, Plaza de Colón. Casual entertainment by jazz pianist Danny Apolinar till sunup. Closed Tuesday. 725-9773.

The Staircase (formerly The Owl): 151 Tetuán. Entertainment nightly except Sunday, geared to both local and tourist audiences. Shows at 11:30 P.M., 2 A.M. during week, 11 P.M., 12:30 A.M., 2 A.M. weekends. 723-5943.

La Tasca: 257 Cruz. Dining, drinks with a musical backdrop in this Spanish-style "taverna." Open nightly from 11:30 P.M. except Sunday. 724-4980.

La Zambra: 107 Fortaleza. Latin and American cuisine for lunch and dinner. Musical entertainment evenings except Sunday. 724-9748.

La Zaragozana: 356 San Francisco. Spanish, Cuban and American cuisine for lunch, dinner. Excellent black bean soup, paella. Air-conditioned elegant dining. Reservations recommended. 724-9540.

METROPOLITAN AREA

Cathay: 609 Fernández Juncos (opp. U.S. Naval Base). Cocktails, Cantonese luncheon and dinner. 723-5738.

Caribe Hilton: Lighter fare overlooking the pool or at recently opened coffee shop, off the lobby. Cocktails can be sipped poolside, but indoors, under new bar's huge copper hemispheres. Luncheon (except Saturday and Sunday), dinner and cocktails at the **Rotisserie Castillo.** French cuisine, with some entrees prepared tableside. Reservations a must. Dining, dancing, floor show nightly except Monday at the **Club Caribe,** buffet supper Sunday 6:30–9 P.M. Shows start 11 P.M. Tuesday–Friday, midnight Saturday, 10:30 P.M. Sunday. Reservations necessary. Dancing nightly at **Caribar Lounge.** 725-0303.

L'Elegante: 2029 Loíza, second floor. Italian and native cooking, open for lunch and dinner except Tuesday. 722-4176.

Mirabelle's: Puntas Las Marias. Sophisticated night spot. Recorded music.

El Nilo: Ponce de León, Stop 22. Restaurant and cafeteria serving native, American food. 724-9670.

Red Rooster: Across from Caribe Hilton. American cooking with an accent on bagles'n'lox-type fare. 722-0872.

San Juan Darlington: Scenic dining in the new **Cloud Room,** atop San Juan's tallest building. American, German cuisine—excellent roast beef. Cocktails from 5 P.M., dinner 7 P.M.–midnight. Dancing. 725-1212.

Swiss Chalet: Swiss specialties. Popular luncheon spot for local businessmen.

Pleasant dining, piano entertainment nightly. **Café Pierre** open 7 A.M.–midnight; specialty: cheese fondue. 724-1200.

Top-of-the-First: Penthouse, First Federal Bldg., Ponce de León, Stop 23. Elegant spot. Continental cuisine complemented by view of entire metropolitan area. Cocktails from 5 P.M., dinner and dancing 7 P.M.–midnight except Sunday. 723-9210.

CONDADO

Armando's Hideaway: 51 Barranquitas St., opp. Condado Beach Hotel. Live music, dancing till 6 A.M. No cover or minimum. 725-2285.

Atlantic Beach Hotel: Vendig St., off Ashford Ave. Italian dishes at **Mama's Little Italy,** rooftop, open 5 P.M.–midnight. 723-0453.

Bonanza Steak House: 1014 Ashford Ave. near Condado Beach Hotel. Charcoal specialties, roast beef Tuesday. Open daily to 5 A.M.

La Concha Hotel: On Ashford Ave. Informal light luncheon noon–3 P.M., dinner from 7 P.M. at breezy **Sala del Sol,** overlooking the ocean. More formal dining, floor show at shell-shaped **Club La Concha.** Buffet dinner Thursday 7:30–11 P.M.; show begins 10:30 P.M. Monday–Thursday, 11 P.M. Friday and Saturday. Reservations recommended. Dancing, continuous entertainment from 9 P.M. at rooftop **El Mirador.** Dancing also at **Solimar** cocktail lounge from 9 P.M. 723-6090.

Condado Beach Hotel: On Ashford Ave. Elegantly remodeled **Coffee House** open from 6:30 A.M. for breakfast, buffet luncheon, also dinners. French cuisine, eight-course meals at sophisticated **Salón Real,** with guitar entertainment. Dining and floor show at the **Fiesta Room** except Monday. Show starts 11:30 P.M. Saturday, 10:30 P.M. other nights. Celebrated buffet dinner Wednesday 7:30–10 P.M. Reservations recommended. 723-0010.

Condado Lagoon Hotel: 6 Clemenceau, off Ashford Ave. American food with a New England accent at the **Captain's Table,** 7 A.M.–midnight. For the teeny-boppers: **Corky's.** Live organ music by Corky with drum accompaniment, go-go dancers in cage. 723-0150.

Hotel Da Vinci: Ashford Ave. Wide variety of Italian dishes, from fettucini al Alfredo to pastas and pizza, at **La Locanda,** open 7:30 A.M. till late. Dinner, music (except Sunday) at the **Frascati,** formal grill room and cocktail lounge. 725-2323.

Dobbs House: 1357 and 1050 Ashford Ave. Open 24 hours. American cooking. 724-8140, 724-7622.

Flamboyan Hotel: Ashford Ave. Scandinavian smorgasbord, luncheon and dinner, at the **Scandia Room.** Dinner, dancing, floor shows nightly except Sunday at **Club de Oro.** Shows start 10:45 P.M., 1 A.M. Dancing nightly at **Cocolobo Lounge.** 725-7700.

Howard Johnson's Nabori Lodge: Ashford Ave. Native and American food, 7 A.M.–11 P.M. daily. 725-7300.

Latin Q: Ashford Ave. above Red Rooster. Discotheque with live music, go-go dancers.

Las Nereidas: Ashford and Magdalena Aves., across from La Concha. Native, American and Kosher cuisine, served indoors or at sidewalk café. Open daily, around the clock. 725-7446.

La Rada Hotel: 1020 Ashford Ave. **Nino's Steak House,** open noon–11 P.M. daily. Music nightly, bar open 11 A.M.–2 A.M. Dinners a-la-carte from $3.95. 725-2970.

Red Rooster: 1058 Ashford Ave. Lox con bagels and other Kosher and American plates. 724-0022.

San Jerónimo Hilton: Ashford Ave. Informal dining 7 A.M.–midnight at **Café del Mar.** Dine in Spanish setting at the **Castillian Room,** with guitar serenades, 7–11 P.M. nightly except Sunday. For dining and floor show, **La Ronda,** also closed Sunday. Show starts 11 P.M., reservations recommended. Dancing, entertainment at **Siboney Lounge** till 4 A.M., except Monday. 724-4000.

Santa Lucia: 64 Condado. Specializing in Italian food. Moderate prices. 11:30 A.M.–midnight. 725-0425.

Sheraton Hotel: Elegant dining at rooftop **La Alhambra Room,** luncheon and dinner. Guitar music nightly, beautiful view. Cocktail lounge. Dinner, dancing and floor show at **Salón Carnaval** except

Sunday. Floor show Monday–Thursday 10:30 P.M., Friday 11 P.M., Saturday 10 and 12 P.M. Reservations recommended. Dancing to combos nightly at **Zanzibar.** 724-6161.

MIRAMAR

Capitol Hotel: Ponce de León, Stop 12. Native and American food, moderate prices. Open 7 A.M.–midnight. 724-1884.

Hotel Excelsior: 801 Ponce de León. Delicatessen specialties at **Del Continent,** restaurant and cocktail lounge. Open for dining 8 A.M.–11 P.M. weeknights, 8 A.M.– 1 A.M. Friday and Saturday.

Miramar Hotel: Rooftop **Rib Room** has nightly entertainment, smorgasbord buffet at lunchtime. 723-8040.

Olimpo Court Hotel: Varied menu at **La Linterna,** including local and Cuban dishes. Open 7 A.M.–midnight, musical entertainment. 725-5145.

ISLA VERDE

Alberto's: Marginal St., Isla Verde Rd., Villa Mar Shopping Center. Native and Lebanese dishes—specialty: shish kebab. Open daily 11 A.M.–2 A.M., "scotch party" Friday 5–6 P.M. on the house. 791-2837.

Americana Hotel: Prime charcoal-broiled steaks, dinner only, at **El Gaucho Steak House.** Dinner, dancing, floor show at **La Copa** except Sunday. Show starts 10:30 P.M. Reservations recommended. **Port O'Call** features dancing, three shows nightly (10:30 P.M., 12:30 A.M., 2:15 A.M.). Dancing nightly at the smaller **Carioca Lounge.** 791-2020.

Bonanza Steak House: Isla Verde Rd. Informal dining, barbecued specialties. Roast beef Tuesday. Open till 5 A.M. daily. 791-0397.

Cecilia's Place: Rosas St., between El San Juan and Holiday Inn. Seafood, prime steaks, native dishes. Moderate prices, nightly entertainment. 791-9171.

Holiday Inn: Native, American cuisine at **Candlelight Room.** 6–10 P.M. nightly. Entertainment weekends. 791-2300.

Mago's Saxony: Km 2.1, Isla Verde Rd. Prime charcoal-broiled steak. 791-0209.

Mario's: Isla Verde Rd. Favorite family restaurant. Charcoal steaks, seafood specialties for lunch and dinner. Occasional piano, guitar music. 791-0289.

Racquet Club: Continental cuisine nightly in the Tudor Room 7-11 P.M. Musical entertainment except Monday. For cocktails, the **Trophy Room** open 6 P.M.–1 A.M. nightly. Dancing to small combo except Monday. 791-3535.

Salón Ruiseñor: At International Airport. Native and American dishes for lunch and dinner. 791-0300.

El San Juan Hotel: For luncheon and dinner, **Four Winds and Seven Seas** offers American and continental cuisine. Seatings at 7 and 9 P.M., musical background. Dining with a French flair at **Le Pavillon,** evenings only. Dinner, dancing and floor shows nightly at **Tropicoro.** Shows start 9 P.M. and 11 P.M. Saturday, 10:30 P.M. other nights. Reservations recommended. Dancing nightly at **El Chico Bar, Hunca Munca Room** and **Cofresí Lounge.** 791-1100.

Stage Delicatessen: Across from Americana Hotel. Kosher and American dishes, sandwiches. Open 24 hours, takeout and delivery service. 791-1853, 791-2056.

El Taquito: Boca de Cangrejos Rd. Tacos, tamales and other Mexican specialties. Open till 4 A.M. daily. 791-2825.

Tropimar: Isla Verde Rd. at public beach. Native seafood specialties for lunch and dinner. 791-0174.

HATO REY

Bird's: 452 Ponce de León. Popular with businessmen, open weekdays only 7 A.M.– 8 P.M. American, native cuisine. 767-3400.

La Fontana: 843 Hostos Ave., across from Sears. Int'l meals served from noon-midnight except Monday. Specialty: passion fruit drinks.

Malambo: 224 F. D. Roosevelt Ave. Argentine cooking and entertainment. Open lunch and dinner, specialty: steak. 765-3262.

Rovic's: 253 F. D. Roosevelt Ave. Spanish, int'l cuisine. Open 11 A.M.–2:30 P.M., 6:30 P.M.–midnight daily except Sunday. Nightly musical entertainment. 767-5017.

Zipperle's Bavarian Tavern: 352 F. D. Roosevelt. Specialty: German cuisine in typically teutonic setting. Air-conditioned, open for lunch and dinner daily except Saturday. 766-9631.

RIO PIEDRAS

Café Valencia: 944 Muñoz Rivera Ave., Hyde Park. Spanish food served in pleasant air-conditioned setting. Open 8 A.M. till the wee hours. 766-2825, 766-9687.

Phil's Shrimp House: 1273 Jesus T. Piñeiro, Caparra Terrace. Seafood specialties. Open Saturday 6 P.M.–midnight, Monday 11 A.M.–3 P.M. other days 10 A.M.–midnight. 783-3329.

PUERTO NUEVO

Beaumont Café: Open daily 7:30 A.M.–11 P.M., buffet Sunday noon–6 P.M. Free pony ride. 782-2954.

Dobbs House: Borinquen Towers, Roosevelt Ave. American cooking, open 24 hours. 782-7854.

Ko-Bai: 322 De Diego at F. D. Roosevelt Ave. Chinese food, 11 A.M.–midnight. 782-5125.

AROUND THE ISLAND:

ADJUNTAS: Hotel Monte Rio—Air-conditioned restaurant, bar. Native, American food.

AGUADILLA: Hotel Montemar—Restaurant, bar. Native, American food. Native entertainment. Sunday afternoon and evening buffets.

ARECIBO: Half-Way Inn—On Hwy. 2. Air-conditioned restaurant, coffee shop. Native, American food.

El Gran Café—On Hwy. 2. Air-conditioned. Native, American food.

Ricky's—Next to Mir Hotel, main plaza. American, native food. Open 7 A.M.–9 P.M. daily, except 2:30–5:30 Sunday.

BARRANQUITAS: El Barranquitas Hotel—Breakfast, lunch, dinner in the **Torrecilla** dining room. Native, American food. Sunday buffet.

La Unión de Todos—Off Hwy. #156 (Comerio Rd.). Rural family establishment, native food. Great reputation.

CAGUAS: Caguas Highway Inn—Hwy. #1, Km 34.3. Air-conditioned restaurant,

coffee shop, bar. Nightly piano entertainment; buffets, fashion shows Tuesday eves. Native, American food. 731-8668.

Roosevelt Inn—On main square. Restaurant, pastry shop. Light meals.

CANOVANAS: La Fortaleza—Hwy. #185, Km 7.2. Native, American food. Open 8 A.M.–midnight daily.

CAYEY: Jajóme Cocktail Terrace (La Taberna)—Cayey-Guayama Rd. (#15), Km 18.6. Cocktails, snacks served on scenic terrace overlooking mountains, valleys, Caribbean Sea. Open 10 A.M.–9 P.M., closed Monday until 6 P.M.

CIDRA: Treasure Island Hotel—Native cuisine in country atmosphere at *Salón Pomarrosa.*

DORADO: Dorado Beach Hotel—Air-conditioned dining room. *Ocean Terrace Grill* for lunching, dining, dancing. "Su Casa" featuring Spanish specialties. Outdoor, candlelight dining. Reservations necessary for dinner only. Dinner 7–9 P.M. 796-1600.

Dorado Hilton: Air-conditioned dining room, native and int'l cuisine. Nightly entertainment. Also, open-air restaurant for informal dining, cocktail lounge. 796-1515.

FAJARDO: El Conquistador Hotel—Air-conditioned dining room open for lunch and dinner. Beautiful view of ocean. Cocktail lounge, open till midnight. Pool terrace restaurant.

Hotel Delicias—Facing wharf at Puerto Real, Fajardo. Native, seafood specialties. Open 6 A.M.–9 P.M. daily.

Isleta Marina—Cayo Obispo, 3/4 mile off Fajardo Port. Native, American food served 10 A.M.–7 P.M. daily except Monday. Ferryboat service every 1/2 hour. Tel: Fajardo 1013.

Ponce de León—Playa Barceló, center of town. Native, American food—seafood specialties.

Puerto Chico—At Playa Sardinera, on route to Las Croabas (Hwy. #987, Km 2.3). Seafood specialties 11 A.M.–10 P.M. daily. Attractive fenced-in grounds make it a good place to bring children.

GUAJATACA: El Tunel—Just off Hwy. #2 beyond Guajataca Resort. Seafood specialties.

GUANICA: Copamarina Hotel — Hwy. #333 off Guánica, beyond Caña Gorda

Beach. Seafood specialties at *El Galeón*.
LOIZA ALDEA: Rodríguez—Hwy. #188, Km 5.8. Seafood. Open 10 A.M.–10 P.M. daily, till midnight on weekends.
MAYAGUEZ: Bolo's Place—At Playa Guanajibo. Seafood dinners. Air-conditioned.
Mayaguez Hilton—Air-conditioned restaurant serving lunch and dinner. Cocktail lounge, coffee shop. 832-7575.
MAGUABO PLAYA: Corsino's—Follow Hwy. #3 past Roosevelt Rds. Native seafood, by the sea, in fishing village.
PARGUERA: Villa Parguera Hotel—Near Lajas. Native, American food—seafood specialties. Indoor dining terrace overlooks Caribbean and outlying cays. 892-9588.
PONCE: El Castillo—16 Ave. de Hostos. American, native food. Open-air dining. 842-9378.
El Coche—La Rambla section. Open for breakfast, lunch, dinner. German specialties, also native, American food. 842-9338.
Hotel Meliá—on the plaza. Air-conditioned restaurant, bar. American, native food.
Nain's Restaurant—La Rambla section. Air-conditioned. Charcoal broiled steaks and seafood. 842-1132.
Ponce Inter-Continental Hotel—Elegant dining room serving continental and native dishes. Coffee shop for light meals.
SALINAS: Ladi's—Near Ponce. Specialty: fish and tostones (fried plantains). Rustic shore-front pavilion.
SAN GERMAN: Don Mon—Dr. Veve, corner of Javilla, near Porta Coeli. Native specialties 8 A.M.–11 P.M. daily. Piano entertainment Saturday night.
SANTA ISABEL: El Aquarium—Hwy. #538. Modern air-conditioned restaurant, bar. Fresh lobster, seafood specialties. Open 11 A.M.–10 P.M. daily. 845-9997.
EL YUNQUE: La Mina Restaurant—High in the mountains of this National Forest. Spanish and native food in rustic setting.

Casinos

Gambling casinos in Puerto Rico, operated under the watchful eye of the government, are located in the following hotels: Caribe Hilton, San Jerónimo Hilton, Flamboyán, La Concha, Condado Beach, Puerto Rico Sheraton, Americana, El San Juan, El Convento, Dorado Hilton, Dorado Beach and Ponce Inter-Continental.

Special events, festivals, celebrations

Three Kings Day (Epiphany): Traditionally celebrated with gift giving, parades, public and private parties, open house at the City Hall. Exhibitions of elaborate replicas of the Nativity, art works, Santos (hand-carved religious figurines). Strolling street musicians sing carols. Gradually assuming second place to Christmas though still a favorite in the mountain towns. Marks end of the holiday season. January 6.
Dr. Eugenio M. de Hostos Birthday Anniversary: January 11.
Dorado Hilton Agents Golf Tournament: January.
Annual Pro-Amateur Invitational Golf Tournament: At Dorado Beach Hotel. Professionals and amateurs from the U.S., Canada, Central and South America and the Caribbean participate. Teams consist of one professional and three amateurs. The tournament is a 54-hole Medal Play. January.
La Virgen de la Candelaria: At night huge bonfires light up the countryside to celebrate the beginning of the "zafra" (sugar harvest). From this day through June, the countryside is filled with spectacle of cane cut by hand by thousands of workers. February 2.
San Juan Carnival: Parades with floats, public and private parties, masquerade balls, coronation of queens, regattas and general celebrations. Celebrations also in the cities of Arecibo and Ponce and on Vieques Island. Preceding Lent.
Caribbean Mid-Winter Regatta: Open to sailors from all nations. Participating classes: Finn, Snipe, Flying Dutchman, Sunfish, Sailfish, Jet 14, Multihulls, Rhodes 19, etc., and open races from all other types of small sailboats with less than three in class. Beginning of February.
Theater Festival in Ponce: February–April.
Holy Week: Pageants and processions,

particularly elaborate in some of the smaller towns. Majestic floral monuments. On Good Friday evening the fourteen scenes of the Via-Crucis are re-enacted in front of the Capitol Building in San Juan. Week before Easter.

Inter-American Skeet Tournament: At Club Metropolitano de Tiro in Rio Piedras. March.

Annual Open Easter Surfing Championship: End of March.

Semiannual State Game Fish Tournament Opens: Fishermen are invited to register their catches with the Department of Tourism, GPO Box 2350, San Juan, for trophies to be awarded later. April 1–September 30.

Orchid and Garden Show: In Patio del Fauno, Condado Beach Hotel. More than 100 species of orchids and other exotic tropical flora. Also stateside exhibits. April.

International Invitational Tennis Tournament: At Caribe Hilton Hotel. World's top tennis stars compete for "Governor's Bowl." April.

Theater Festival: At Tapia Theater in Old San Juan. April–May.

"Santa Cruz" Patron Saint Festival: In Bayamon and Trujillo towns. A week-long festival featuring masquerades, parties and parades. May 3.

Festival Casals: At the University of Puerto Rico in Rio Piedras. Music festival under the direction of Pablo Casals. Famous featured soloists. May or June.

"San Juan Bautista" Patron Saint Festival: In San Juan. Public parties, bonfires on beaches, street dances, concerts throughout the celebrations, which start a few days before. On the eve of St. John's Day, tradition decrees a dip in the ocean after midnight for good luck. June 24.

U.S. Independence Anniversary: Parade in San Juan. Sports car races at Ramey Air Field, Aguadilla. Road races and drag races. Open entry. July 4.

Patron Saint Festival of the "Virgen del Carmen": In Cataño, Ponce and Cabo Rojo. Various water sport activities and sailing regattas are held in honor of the benefactress of fishermen. July 16.

Patron Saint Festival of Santiago Apostol: In the small north coast town of Loiza Aldea. Colorful festivities, three days prior and three days after July 25th, with traditional costumes, music and street dancing, celebrated in the same manner for more than three centuries.

Constitution Day: In San Juan: parades, fireworks, boat races mark the anniversary of the creation of the Commonwealth Status. Sailing regattas in Santa Isabel, Cabo Rojo and other cities and towns. July 25.

Annual Inter-Club Fishing Tournament: At Cangrejos Yacht Club, San Juan. End of July or beginning of August.

Dorado Beach Hotel Annual Regatta: Mid-August.

Annual Deep Sea Fishing Tournament: Sponsored by the Hunting and Fishing Club in Arecibo. Mid-August.

"Paso Fino" Horse Races: At Salinas. Open entry. Late August or September.

Patron Saint Festival of Our Lady of Monserrate: In Salinas: dancing, fireworks, fairs, sailing regattas, fishing and nautical competitions. In Hormigueros: a pilgrimage of the faithful, which ends with their climbing on their knees up the long flights of steps to the church. September 8.

Annual Flower Show: At Dorado Beach Hotel, sponsored by the Orchid Society of Puerto Rico. September.

Invitational Int'l Game Fishing Tournament: At San Juan's Club Nautico. Top anglers (25–35 teams) from all parts of the United States and hemisphere fish for huge marlin and other game fish. Late September.

Semiannual Commonwealth Game Fish Tournament: Fishermen are invited to register their catches with the Department of Tourism for trophies to be awarded later. October 1–March 31.

Puerto Rican Composers Festival: October.

Puerto Rico Kennel Show (AKC): At Dorado Beach Hotel. Fall.

Cyclist International Race: October.

Puerto Rico Symphony Orchestra Season: 20 free outdoor and indoor performances in San Juan and throughout the island. October–November.

Baseball season: At Hiram Bithorn Stadium in San Juan. Partisanship and rivalry is high, crowd participation as lively and interesting as the play. October–January.

Cockfighting season: Trainers and breeders bring their best fighting cocks to more than a hundred cockpits around the island. Season opens November 2.

Discovery Day: Celebrations honoring discovery of Puerto Rico in 1493. November 19.

Culinary Art Exposition: At a hotel in metropolitan area. Sponsored by the Department of Tourism and the Puerto Rico Hotel Association. Trophies awarded. Generally a November event.

Puerto Rico Open Golf Championship: At the Dorado Hilton Hotel. Professional golfers compete for trophies and prizes. November.

International Theatre Festival: Under the auspices of the Institute of Puerto Rican Culture. At Tapia Theatre in Old San Juan. November–December.

Annual Winter Surfing Contest: December.

Celebrity and Professional Golf Tournament: El Conquistador Hotel and Club. December.

Meet the people

Organization	Official	Phone
Altrusa Club of San Juan	Mrs. Rose Ann Reynolds	766-1129
British Commonwealth Society	D. E. Hastwell	791-0539
Civil Air Patrol	Col. Clara E. Livingston	725-0012
Daughters of the American Revolution	Mrs. Frances Mendin	765-4565
Elks Lodge No. 972, B.P.O.E.	Hector Ledesma	724-5029
Garden Club of P. R.	Mrs. Victor Bernal	789-2202
Hadassah, P. R. Chapter	Mrs. Sylvia Kosson	725-2197
The Little Theater of P. R.	Charles Arndt	767-3490
League of Women Voters	Mrs. David Chang	782-3169
Rotary Club of San Juan	Herbert E. Warfel	766-0872
Women's College Club	Mrs. Ralph S. Miller	723-1995
Yale Club	Herbert E. Warfel	766-0872
P. R. Natural History Society	Eugene Dávila	766-1162 (3)
Sales and Marketing Executives Club	Mrs. Rose Ann Reynolds	766-1129
P. R. Bridge Assn.	Karl J. Kristiansen	765-2958
Scottish Rite of Freemasonry Ancient & Accepted	C. W. Parkhurst	722-4519
Shrine Club of P. R.	Angel Martínez	724-5621
USO	Leo D. Ellingson	722-5752
Kiwanis	John Fucile	725-4980
Lions Club–San Juan	Ricardo Betancourt	767-3349
Credit Granters Assn. of P. R.	Mrs. Rose Ann Reynolds	766-1129
University of Pennsylvania Alumni Club	Angel M. Martín	725-4860
Cornell–Pennsylvania Alumni Club	Dr. Luis R. Garcia Margarida	722-5851
Puerto Rico Kennel Club	Mrs. Harley Miller	767-4504
Welcome Wagon	Mrs. Jane Ward	722-3013, Ext. 225
Newcomers' Club	Mrs. Irene Sheehan	725-5589
Jaycees–San Juan branch	Troy Fields	782-3030
Ex-Stewardess Club	Mrs. Norma Daniel	791-3285
Boy Scouts of America	Manuel López	767-0320, 767-0323
Girl Scouts of America	Miss Rosario Chico	724-5771
Hospital Volunteer Service	Mrs. Margaret Moura	782-4857

Music, drama and galleries

Puerto Rico is rapidly assuming, as it should, a satisfactory place in the world of fine arts. The Festival Casals draws renowned musicians to the island annually;

local theater productions are offered in both English and Spanish. There are many small galleries in Old San Jan and Ponce is now the site of the modern, multimillion dollar Museum of Art, already the recipient of design awards.

In addition to the Festival Casals, which is usually held in May or June, the Puerto Rico Symphony Orchestra holds 8–10 week-long concert tours in San Juan and throughout the island. Other concerts and recitals are sponsored by the University of Puerto Rico, the Conservatory of Music and the Institute of Culture.

The Institute of Culture was established as part of "Operation Serenity," a cultural version of Operation Bootstrap aimed at preserving, as well as furthering, Puerto Rican culture. The Institute maintains a center for folk art in Old San Juan, serving as an outlet and an encouragement to island artisans. Most important, perhaps, is the Institute's restoration program, covering both historic monuments and centuries-old homes. Through institute-sponsored tax exemptions and loans, old homes in San Juan that once were rapidly depreciating into slums are now being acquired by talented tenants who restore them to their former Spanish-style elegance.

Another Institute project is the Spanish-language drama festival, held annually at the Tapia Theatre. The University of Puerto Rico also has a fairly active drama department, complemented by its touring "Teatro Rodante," and English-language plays are put on by several groups, including the Little Theatre of Puerto Rico. English plays, however, are relatively few and far-between and local critics deride their selection, which they claim is not sufficiently intellectual. It is questionable how much support more "intellectual" performances would receive from the paying public, whose present attendance is hardly overwhelming. And despite Operation Serenity, support is also noticeably lacking from the government. The Tapia Theatre in Old San Juan is charming but ill-equipped, and long overdue for some backstage updating.

Also in the old city are the following art galleries and museums. Art exhibits range from the old *santos,* miniature wood carvings of the saints, to psychedelic spatterings.

José E. Alegría: 152-4 Cristo. Paintings, sculptures, antiques. Daily exc. Sunday and holidays 9 A.M. to 6 P.M.

Galerie Roi Christophe: 202 Cristo. 2nd floor, Casa Cavanagh. Haitian art. Daily except Sunday 9 A.M.–6 P.M.

Don Roberto: 205 Cristo. Watercolors, oils and graphics by Puerto Rican artists. Also handicrafts. Daily except Sunday 9 A.M.–6 P.M.

Galería Santiago: 207 Cristo. Contemporary Puerto Rican art and antique santos. Daily exc. Sunday 9:30 A.M.–5:30 P.M.

Galería Botello: 208 Cristo (also in the "new" wing of the Caribe Hilton). Paintings and sculptures by Angel Botello Barros and collection of antique *santos.* Daily exc. Sunday and holidays 9:30 A.M.–5:30 P.M.

Museo de Arte de Puerto Rico: 253 Cristo. Collection of Puerto Rican art from Indian times to present. Daily 8:30 A.M.–5 P.M.

La Casa del Libro: 255 Cristo. Museum and library devoted to the art of the book. Continuous exhibitions. Daily exc. Sunday 11 A.M.–5 P.M.

Galería Colibrí: Callejón de la Capilla. Prints by European, North American and Puerto Rican artists. 11 A.M.–5 P.M. Closed Sunday and Monday.

Galería John St. John: 65 Fortaleza. Paintings by John St. John. 10 A.M.–5:30 P.M. Closed Sunday.

La Casa del Arte: 152 Fortaleza. Large gallery of Puerto Rican art. Daily exc. Sunday 10 A.M.–6 P.M.

Casa Fortaleza: 308 Fortaleza. Specializing in paintings of Puerto Rican landscapes.

Museum of Colonial Architecture: 319 Fortaleza. Small museum illustrating four centuries of Spanish colonial architecture in Puerto Rico. Daily 9 A.M.–5 P.M.

Museum of the Puerto Rican Family: 319 Fortaleza, 2nd floor. Furnished to show how typical urban families lived 100 years ago. Daily 9 A.M.–noon, 1–5 P.M. Admission adults 25¢, children free.

Galería San Cristóbal: 406 Luna. Local

paintings, prints, sculptures and stained glass.

Guillermo Cruz, Inc.: 367 Tetuan. Scheduled exhibits.

Institute of Puerto Rican Culture: Plaza de Colón, Old San Juan. Permanent exhibition of *santos*, monthly art exhibitions. Monday through Friday 9 A.M.–noon, 2–5 P.M. Closed weekends and holidays.

Other galleries around the island are:

Museum of Military History: In Fort San Jerónimo, beside Caribe Hilton. Military history of Puerto Rico from 1493 to 1898. Daily 9 A.M.–5 P.M. Admission: adults 25¢, children free. Free Saturday.

UPR Extension Division: University of Puerto Rico, Rio Piedras. Small gallery for monthly art exhibits. Monday through Friday 9 A.M.–noon, 1:30–5 P.M. Saturday 9 A.M.–noon. Closed Sunday.

University Museum: Campus, University of Puerto Rico, Rio Piedras. Permanent archeological and historical exhibitions, monthly art exhibitions. Monday through Friday 9 A.M.–noon, 1:30–10 P.M.; Saturday 9 A.M.–noon, 1:30–5 P.M. Closed Sunday and holidays.

Ponce Museum of Art: Las Américas Ave., Ponce. Five centuries of European painting and sculpture in a handsome new building designed by U.S. architect Edward D. Stone. Adjacent to the building are concert facilities and a Spanish garden around a fountain and sculpture. Tuesday through Saturday 10 P.M.–noon, 2–5 P.M.; Sunday 1–5 P.M. Closed Monday.

Porta Coeli Museum of Religious Art: San Germán. Collection of antique religious objects in old restored chapel. Monday through Friday 9 A.M.–5 P.M.; Saturday, Sunday 9 A.M.–4 P.M.

Galeria El Cemi: Across from Porta Coeli Museum, #61 Dr. Veve, San Germán. Native historical items, ceramics, books, recordings, woodwork and paintings. Open 9 A.M.–6 P.M.

Real estate and retirement

While residents of Puerto Rico save on such cold-weather expenses as heating and winter clothes, settling here is still a costly proposition. To begin with, transporting goods from the States is expensive and there is an excise tax on certain household goods, especially rugs and electrical appliances. There is also an excise tax on cars, but it is generally less expensive to ship one here than to buy it on the island (at nearly double stateside costs). Taxes favor wage-earners in lower income brackets and bachelors; married couples cannot split their income.

Puerto Rico is in the midst of a building boom and housing is readily available, but usually not at bargain prices. In Santurce, adjacent to the capital, condominiums now dominate the skyline and can be purchased for no less than $18,000 or rented for $250–$500. The higher up the apartment, the higher the cost. There are only a limited number of private homes for sale but modest apartments can be found, furnished or unfurnished, in the Condado, Miramar and Punta Las Marias sections and further east in Isla Verde. Old San Juan is an ideal locale for the slightly more adventurous with a bent for interior decorating. Many old apartments have been bought and restored under the watchful eye of the Instituto de Cultura.

Whereas a little over a decade ago Rio Piedras, some 20 minutes by car (without traffic) from San Juan, was cow-grazing countryside, it is now—along with other areas such as Hato Rey and Puerto Nuevo —a built-up part of Metropolitan San Juan. Highways linking these areas with each other and San Juan are somewhat overburdened, but new expressways are presently under construction. In the meantime, air-condition your car!

Mass housing facilities have been made available to people of all income brackets, not only in San Juan but in Caguas, Mayaguez, Ponce and throughout the island, via the *"urbanización."* This term connotes a huge cluster of concrete, box-like homes built on the smallest parcel of land legally permissible with little or no regard to architecture or eye-appeal. The homes are usually ranch-style and equipped with stove and refrigerator. Prices begin at about $16,000, though "better" homes are usually over $20,000. More spacious and luxurious homes are available at usually no less than $45,000. Some of the most expensive and luxurious can be found in such "older" areas as Santa María, Beverly Hills, San Francisco, Garden Hills and Tintillo. There are newer "luxury" areas but, like the lower-cost urbanization, they are also dominated by look-alike, landless houses.

One alternative has been private home building, slowed up in the last year or two due to tight money conditions on the island which are now easing up. Privately built homes and old Spanish-style villas, when available, are quite costly. The high-rise trend has not been limited to Santurce and there are many apartment buildings throughout the metropolitan area, ranging from the humble two-story type to large complexes of buildings. Rents start at about $150, pretty much the same as rents on urbanization homes.

Shopping centers are plentiful and well located. Supermarkets carry all foods available in the States at slightly higher prices. A major problem for those resettling in Puerto Rico, however, is the schooling. Public school curriculums are, at best, poor and almost anyone who can will send his children to private or parochial schools. The few really good schools have waiting lists sometimes several years long and tuition is higher every year. New schools are constantly being opened but there are still not enough good high school facilities to meet the present demand.

Commerce and industry

Like most of the more flourishing Caribbean islands, Puerto Rico found itself well into the 20th century and entirely reliant on sugar. With wealthy plantation owners monopolizing great tracts of land, islanders were divided into the very rich or abjectly poor. Furthermore, the coffee industry had been almost wiped out by a hurricane and changes in the world market.

By the 1940's, when Luis Muñoz Marín came into power, changes had to be made—and they were. A law was passed limiting land holdings and "Operation Bootstrap" was launched—a program of self-help. The conversion from an agri-

cultural to industrial-oriented society has not been easy. Workers had to be trained and skilled technicians are still in short supply to this day.

Today, investors are offered the following incentives for manufacturing on the island: from 10–17 years of complete tax exemption; freedom from Federal taxes or income from sources within P.R.; financial incentive grants to help cover the cost of personnel training, rent payments, freight and so on; loans through the Government Development Bank, the P. R. Industrial Development Co. and some federal agencies; vocational education and training; assistance in the selection of industrial sites and the construction of buildings. The Economic Development Administration, known on the island as "Fomento," reports over 1,500 manufacturing firms now on the island. For further information, potential investors may write them at GPO Box 2350, San Juan, P.R. 00936.

In addition to industry, tourism has also been a major success on the island. Hotels monopolize the beaches from San Juan to the airport and large hotels have been built in more out-of-the-way locales such as Ponce, Mayaguez and Fajardo. Despite the abundance of places to stay, vacancies are a rare commodity during the winter season and various "package deals" and other offers keep tourists coming most of the year. Many islanders, however, question the island's future as a resort. While volume has kept air fare down, hotel rates continue to soar and it has been estimated in one government report that it will soon be less expensive to vacation in some European cities than to visit this sunny isle.

Vieques

The island of Vieques, a municipality of Puerto Rico, lies some ten miles off Puerto Rico's east coast. Although there is little tourism activity there as yet, it has great potential as a resort area.

Vieques has beautiful white sand beaches ringed with coconut palms and sea grapes, green, gently rolling hills stretched between the coastlines and an excellent climate. The bar to development has been the fact that the U.S. Navy controls 26,000 of the island's 33,000 acres, and twice a year Vieques and the surrounding waters are the scene of large-scale amphibious training exercises.

Until recently, the island had only a rudimentary airstrip which could take only small aircraft, and the Navy had refused permission for larger commercial planes to use the military runway. Last summer a new 2,500-foot airstrip was completed, and the future for tourism looks brighter. There are flights to Vieques from San Juan, St. Thomas and St. Croix.

Vieques (pronounced Vee-YAY-kes) has a few small guest houses and cottage accommodations, and the chief town of Isabel Segunda is generously endowed with bars and grilles which do a brisk business during maneuvers.

The most luxurious accommodations on the island are at Sportsmen's House which sits on a hill overlooking the south shore near three perfect crescent-shaped white sand beaches. Formerly called Frenchman's House, it was built in the early part of this century by a sugar planter from the French West Indies. The rooms are high-ceilinged, all opening on to an interior courtyard, and there are tall trees, gardens, a swimming pool and paso fino horses for riding along Vieques' beaches.

Mona

The most ruggedly interesting of Puerto Rico's offshore "domains" is the small island of Mona, which rises up in splendid isolation midway between Puerto Rico and the Dominican Republic.

The Arawak Indians settled on Mona 1,000 years ago, using the island's caves for shelter and the fertile coastal plain to grow root crops and wild cotton. Unfortunately for the Arawaks, the Spanish began stopping off to replenish their water supplies and demand food, and later French corsairs used the island as a resting place between raids on the south and west coasts of Puerto Rico. Pirates, in fact, used Mona as a sort of rest camp for more than two centuries, and there is the legend that several chests of gold, hijacked from an English ship, are buried near El Uvero beach.

Mona emerged some 500 million years ago when lateral pressures on the ocean bottom squeezed a portion of sea floor upward more than 1,000 feet. On three sides sheer 200-foot cliffs rise from the water. On the lee side of the island there are three white sand beaches bordered by groves of Australian pines, where the water is so clear that objects are clearly visible 40 feet down. There is a small landing strip on the northwestern end of the coastal plain, although most visitors arrive by boat. The island lies 40 miles off the west coast of Puerto Rico.

Mona offers none of the comforts, but it is popular with hunters and fishermen and intrepid visitors who want to explore the unusual. The major portion of the six-by-five mile island is a broad, flat plateau covered by cactus and scrub trees. Wild goats and pigs live on the plateau, and the prehistoric survives in the native iguana, which may grow to a length of five feet.

Man's hand is seen only in the remains of an old CCC camp and the relics of a phosphate mining operation, and the lighthouse that flashes its beacon over the turbulent waters of the Mona Passage.

WHERE TO STAY — In Puerto Rico

Beginning Dec. 15, 1967, most hotels are increasing their room rates approximately $2, according to the Puerto Rico Hotel Assn.

San Juan Hotels		Dec. 15-April 14		April 15-Dec. 14	
		U. S. Currency			
	Plan	Double	Single	Double	Single
AMERICANA OF	(EP)	$33–48	$29–44	$23–33	$19–30
SAN JUAN		(Dec. 16-Apr. 30)		(May 1-Dec. 15)	
Isla Verde (450 Rms.) (b, p. t)					

ATLANTIC BEACH	(EP)	$18–25	$15–22	$14–18	$10–16
Condado (40 Rms.) **(b)**		(Dec. 15-Apr. 30)		(May 1-Dec. 14)	
CAPITOL	(EP)	$12–16	$ 8–10	$10–12	$ 7–8
Santurce (135 Rms.)					
CARIBE HILTON	(MAP)	$58–70	$42–54	$45–54	$30–40
San Juan	(EP)	$33–45	$29–41	$23–32	$19–29
(474 Rms.) **(b, p, t)**					
CONDADO BEACH	(MAP)	$50–67	$35–52	$37–47	$24–35
Condado	(EP)	$28–45	$24–41	$19–29	$15–26
(350 Rms.) **(b, p, t)**		(Dec. 16-Apr. 30)		(May 1-Dec. 15)	
CONDADO LAGOON	(MAP)	$37–39	$26–28	$29–33	$19–23
Condado	(EP)	$24–26	$19–21	$16–20	$12–16
(50 Rms.) **(p)**		(Dec. 16-Apr. 30)		(May 1-Dec. 15)	
DARLINGTON	(MAP)	$35–46	$22–32	On Request	
Santurce	(EP)	$17–28	$13–23		
(550 Rms.) **(p)**		(Dec. 15-Apr. 30)		(May 1-Dec. 14)	
DA VINCI	(MAP)	$52–62	$38–52	$39–60	$26–40
Condado	(EP)	$32–42	$28–42	$19–40	$16–30
(150 Rms.) **(b, p)**					
EL CONVENTO	(MAP)	$49–59	$33–43	$32–36	$20–26
Old San Juan	(EP)	$27–37	$22–30	$16–20	$12–18
(92 Rms.) **(p)**					
EL MIRAMAR	(MAP)	$40–48	$25–33	$32–36	$20–24
Condado Lagoon	(EP)	$24–32	$17–25	$16–20	$12–16
(216 Rms.) **(p)**					
EL PORTAL	(EP)	$15–19	$12–16	$12–16	$10–14
Condado (48 Rms.)					
EL SAN JUAN	(AP)	$57–67	$41–50	On Request	
Isla Verde	(MAP)	$33–43	$29–38		
(394 Rms.) **(b, p, t)**					
EXCELSIOR	(EP)	$16–24	$14–22	$12–20	$ 9–18
Santurce (140 Rms.) **(p)**					
FLAMBOYAN	(MAP)	$53–63	$38–47		
Condado	(EP)	$29–39	$26–35	$20–28	$14–15
(160 Rms.) **(p)**	(Dec. 15-Apr. 30)		(May 1-Dec. 14)		
HOLIDAY INN OF	(MAP)	$42–53	$29–35	$34–40	$24–30
SAN JUAN	(EP)	$27–38	$21–27	$19–25	$16–22
(270) Rms.) **(b, p)**		(Dec. 16-Apr. 30)		(May 1-Dec. 15)	
HOWARD JOHNSON'S	(EP)	$22–40	$20–40	$20–36	$16–36
NABORI LODGE					
Condado (147 Rms.) **(p)**		(Dec. 16-Apr. 30)		(May 1-Dec. 15)	
INTERNATIONAL	(EP)	$21	$17	$16	$12
AIRPORT HOTEL					
Airport, Isla Verde (55 Rms.)	(Dec. 16-Apr. 30)		(May 1-Dec. 15)		
LA CONCHA	(MAP)	$57–69	$40–52	$42–52	$28–38
Condado	(EP)	$33–45	$28–40	$24–34	$19–29
(235 Rms.) **(b, p, t)**					
LA POSADA	(EP)	$19–24	$14–18	$14–16	$ 9–14
Isla Verde (52 Rms.) **(b, p)**					
LEANDER'S	(EP)	$20–30	$15–18	$16–25	$12–14
Miramar (100 Rms.)		(Dec. 16-Apr. 15)		(April 16-Dec. 15)	
NORMANDIE	(EP)	$18–24	$15–17	$16–20	$12–14
San Juan (160 Rms.) **(p)**					
OLIMPO COURT	(EP)	$15–17	$10–13	$ 9–16	$ 7–13
Miramar (116 Rms.)					

PIERRE (MAP)	$48	$32	$38	$25
Santurce (154 Rms.) (p)				

PUERTO RICO SANDS (MAP)	$46–62	$30–46	On Request	
Condado (EP)	$26–42	$20–36		
(46 Rms.) (b, p)				

PUERTO RICO (AP)	$43–61	$37–65		
SHERATON (MAP)	$40–58	$34–52	On Request	
Condado (EP)	$27–45	$21–39	$23–32	$19–28
(450 Rms.) (b, p, t)		(Dec. 15-Apr. 30)	(May 1-Dec. 14)	

RACQUET CLUB (MAP)	$48–61	$34–47	$36–44	$24–32
HOTEL (EP)	$29–42	$24–37	$19–27	$15–23
Isla Verde (185 Rms.) (b, p, t)	(Dec. 15-Apr. 30)		(May 1-Dec. 14)	

REGAL HOUSE (EP)	$12–20	$ 9–16	$ 9–16	$ 6–12
HOTEL & APTS.				
Miramar (14 Units)		(Dec. 15-Apr. 30)	(May 1-Dec. 14)	

SAN ANTONIO GUEST (EP)	$16	$10	$ 8–10	$ 7
HOUSE Ocean Park (7 Rms.)				

SAN CRISTOBAL				
Old San Juan (90 Eff. Apts.)	$10	$ 5– 6	$10	$ 5– 6

SAN JERONIMO (MAP)	$55–70	$39–54	$41–52	$27–39
HILTON (EP)	$30–45	$26–41	$21–32	$17–29
Condado (338 Rms.) (b, p)				

TANAMA (EP)	$20–23	$16–18	$13–17	$10–12
Condado (95 Rms.)				

Around the Island Hotels

BARRANQUITAS (EP)	$18–22	$14–18	$14–18	$10–12
Barranquitas (42 Rms.) (p, t)	(Dec. 16-Apr. 30)		(May 1-Dec. 15)	

DORADO BEACH (MAP)	$60–85	$50–75	$40–55	$30–45
Dorado (307 Rms.) (b, p, t, g)				

DORADO HILTON (MAP)	$60–124	$50–116	$32–60	$22–50
Dorado		(Dec. 21-Mar. 31)	(May 1-Oct. 20)	
(222 Rms.) (b, p, t, g)			$40–80	$30–70
		(Apr. 1-Apr. 30 Oct. 21-Dec. 20)		

EL CONQUISTADOR (MAP)	$62–66	$52–56	$38–44	$25–31
Las Croabas (300 Rms.) (b, p, t, g)				

EL PONCE INTER- (AP)	$43–53	$28–38	$40–50	$25–34
CONTINENTAL (MAP)	$37–47	$25–35	$34–44	$22–31
Ponce (170 Rms.) (p, t) (EP)	$20–30	$16–26	$17–27	$13–22

MAYAGUEZ HILTON (MAP)	$33–39	$22–28	$30–34	$19–24
Mayagüez (EP)	$19–25	$15–21	$16–21	$12–17
(150 Rms.) (p)				

MELIA (EP)	$14–20	$ 9–15	$14–20	$ 9–15
Ponce (70 Rms.)				

MONTEMAR (EP)	$18–22	$14–18	$13–17	$10–13
Aguadilla (40 Rms.) (p)				

SEA BEACH COLONY (EP)	$16–33	−	$13–28	$ 9–11
Rincón (29 Units) (b)				

| VILLA DEL MAR | (EP) | $ 9 | $ 6 | $ 9 | $ 6 |
| Boquerón (20 Rms.) (b) | | | | | |

LEGEND FOR HOTEL LISTINGS: (AP) American Plan (room and 3 meals); **MAP)** Modified American Plan (room, breakfast and dinner); **(CP)** Continental Plan (room and breakfast); **(EP)** European Plan (room only). All rates quoted on a per-day basis and subject to change. Confirmed reservations at specific rates desired are always recommended.
HOTEL FACILITIES: (b) beach; **(p)** pool; **(t)** tennis; **(g)** golf.

Bright lights bedeck the plaza at Arecibe on the island of Puerto Rico as a pre-Lenten festival begins

*A quiet lane in the village of Windwardside, on
the island of Saba, one of the Dutch Windwards*

SABA

A scattering of neat Dutch-style villages clinging to a mountaintop form the unique and isolated community of Saba. Because of its geography, getting to Saba is as interesting as being there.

Top of the world

The tiny island of Saba is the Bali Ha'i of the Caribbean. It rises majestically from the sea to a height of 3,000 feet and its summit is generally wreathed in rain clouds. Cliffs plunge straight to the ocean's depths, and no soft stretch of beach breaks the coastline. Saba, at first glance, appears both beautiful and inaccessible.

The entire island is a five-square-mile volcanic outcropping smothered in lush green foliage and brimming with flowers. It also has one of the Caribbean's most interesting populations, and certainly the most interesting distribution of towns.

Saba's principal village is called The Bottom, which, despite its name, sits some 800 feet above sea level and is reached by a steep, winding concrete road. Actually, the name is an English corruption of the Dutch word "botte," meaning bowl, for the little town is built in the bowl of the extinct volcano. Derivation aside, few visitors can resist saying "We're going up to The Bottom."

The Bottom has immaculate white houses with bright red roofs and chimneys, and burgeoning gardens. Because of the protecting warmth of "the bowl," vegetation runs riot.

Even more spectacularly placed than The Bottom are the tiny villages of Hell's Gate and Windwardside, clinging to the crest of the volcano. At 1,400 feet, Windwardside is neat and cozy. There are white picket fences, tidy little houses with red shingled roofs and green shutters, and the curtains in the windows are neatly starched. Vegetable gardens flourish here, tended by the Saban women.

Some of the women do exquisite embroidery—locally called Spanish Work—which you can buy.

Saba is sometimes called "the island of women." There is no industry, and consequently many of the men work in the oil refineries of Curacao and Aruba, or join the world's merchant marines.

The inhabitants (about 60% of the population is white) are descended from a long line of Caribbean seafarers. There is little intermarriage between the races, although there has been a good deal of inbreeding among the white population, especially among those in the topmost reaches.

The seamanship of the Saban is immediately evident if you arrive at the island by boat. Saba has no beaches, no wharf, and only two points, at Fort Bay and Ladder Bay, where ships can anchor several hundred yards offshore. Passengers, and cargo, are transferred to small, wooden surf boats and guided through the surf and reefs by experienced Sabans.

Brightly colored jeeps carry passengers up the corkscrew road to The Bottom, and on to the airier villages.

The alternative to arriving on Saba by sea is to arrive by air, and it is equally interesting. The airstrip, on the island's only relatively flat piece of land, is about the size of an aircraft carrier's deck. The only planes authorized to land are STOL (Short Take Off and Landing) aircraft.

Although Saba is one of the Netherlands Antilles, English is the official language.

Saba has several guest houses, including a government guest house in The Bottom, and one super-elegant hostelry called the Captain's Quarters. The Captain's Quarters features spacious rooms furnished with Dutch antiques, gourmet quality meals accompanied by fine china and crystal, a swimming pool, tennis court and skeet and trap shooting. Naturally there is mountain climbing.

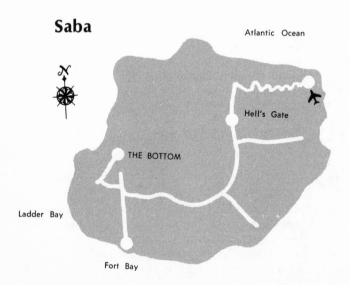

Saba

Atlantic Ocean

Hell's Gate

THE BOTTOM

Ladder Bay

Fort Bay

Instant facts

Location: Between Sint Maarten and St. Eustatius, 28 miles south of Sint Maarten and 17 miles northeast of St. Eustatius.

Population: Slightly over 1,000.

Capital: The Bottom.

Nationality: With Sint Maarten and St. Eustatius, one of the Netherlands Antilles windward islands, an autonomous part of the Kingdom of the Netherlands.

Language: English.

Currency: The Netherlands Antilles guilder (53¢ U.S.), though the U.S. dollar is generally used.

Documentation: International certificate of vaccination and passport or birth certificate required by all.

Climate & Clothes: The Bottom, Saba's principal village, sits in the bowl of an extinct volcano and is tropically warm. The villages near the top of the mountain are cooler and windswept. Casual clothes and sturdy shoes if you plan to do any hiking.

Food: Home-grown vegetables and well-prepared food. One guest house enjoys a gourmet reputation.

Geography: Saba is the five-square mile conical top of an extinct volcano. Its mountains rise directly from the sea so that there are no beaches, only cliffs. Highest peak, known as The Mountain, is the 3,000-foot high Mount Scenery.

History: On a busy September day in 1493, Columbus, in the midst of discovering Caribbean islands, sighted the island of Saba. The tiny island was passed back and forth among the Dutch, English, French and Spanish 12 times. This is less than the number of nationality changes suffered by St. Eustatius and Sint Maarten as the Sabans, taking advantage of their unusual mountainous topography, pelted aggressors from above with rocks and boulders. Saba has always been an English-speaking island, apparently due to the influence of English missionaries and English seamen who settled there.

How to get there

A small airstrip on the only flat stretch of land connects Saba with its two Dutch neighbors, St. Eustatius ($16 round trip) and Sint Maarten ($21 round trip), as well as with St. Kitts ($28 round trip) via Windward Island Airways. Only a specially designed STOL (Short Take Off and Landing) aircraft can maneuver onto the 1,200 feet of runway.

Regularly scheduled transportation by sea is via the *Antillean*, a small freighter linking Sint Maarten, Saba and Sint Eustatius with the rest of the Netherlands Antilles. Island schooners make the run from Sint Maarten on a more casual basis.

The cost of "chartering" a jeep for the trip from the airport to any of the island's guest houses is $10, with a tour and return trip to the airport included.

WHERE TO STAY — In Saba

	Plan	Dec. 15-April 14 U. S. Currency		April 15-Dec. 14	
		Double	Single	Double	Single
CAPTAIN'S QUARTERS (AP) (10 Rms.) **(p, t)**		$35	$25	$35	$25
CARIBE GUEST HOUSE (AP) (5 Rms.)		$16	$ 8	$16	$ 8
THE BOTTOM (AP) **GUEST HOUSE** (4 Rms.)		$16	$ 8	$16	$ 8
WINDWARDSIDE (AP) **GUEST HOUSE** (6 Rms.)		$16	$ 8	$16	$ 8

LEGEND FOR HOTEL LISTINGS: (AP) American Plan (room and 3 meals); **MAP)** Modified American Plan (room, breakfast and dinner); **(CP)** Continental Plan (room and breakfast); **(EP)** European Plan (room only). All rates quoted on a per-day basis and subject to change. Confirmed reservations at specific rates desired are always recommended.
HOTEL FACILITIES: (b) beach; **(p)** pool; **(t)** tennis; **(g)** golf.

ST. BARTHELEMY

According to Indian legend, all Caribbean islands were originally
angels' workshops except one, which was reserved for the chief gods.
The Carib Indians wanted this place, the Swedes once ruled it and now
it is French soil. Tiny and off the tourist route, St. Barts retains an
Old World culture refreshingly removed from the carnivals and general
exuberance of its Caribbean neighbors.

About St. Barts

The first thing that strikes you about St. Barts is that it has a mood and manner unto itself. A distinct personality has emerged from a way of life clutched tightly against a swelling wave of tourism that's washing a certain ultra-modern, man-maneuvered sameness across much of what it touches.

The island has no nightclubs, neon signs, jukeboxes, television sets or local radio stations. The *Sans Pareil* (without equal) restaurant is also the town's pastry shop and movie house.

St. Barts (short for St. Barthelemy, pronounced San Bar-te-le-MEE), is 15 miles southeast of St. Martin and 140 miles north of Guadeloupe in the area of the French West Indies often referred to as the Uppermost Corner— the farthest extremity of the graceful arc of islands between Florida and South America.

The single Caribbean island with a strain of Sweden in its personality, St. Barts appears, at first impression, like something out of a misty bucolic film by Ingmar Bergman set in the 18th century. The wind sweeps constantly around the huge volcanic boulders that dwarf the tiny homes spotted about the hilly landscape of its eight square miles. Bone-dry branches clutter the shores below the craggy cliffs. Billowy clouds block the sun so that in a matter of seconds a cheery Swiss-like hillside is transformed into a moody, gray-green shadowed landscape. Then around the very next turn of the narrow concrete roadway, you are apt to find a garden of jumbo cacti replete with strange-looking blossoms of red, yellow and white.

The men of the countryside wear white, long-sleeved shirts and dark bell-bottom trousers that flap in the breeze. The women tend toward colorless farm outfits and a single style of straw hat as round and flat as a frying pan cover. Older women still wear Breton-style bonnets that hide their faces in a semi-cylinder of starched fabric.

St. Bartians are a lean people with a gaunt look one associates with seafarers. They are remarkably friendly, unsuspicious of strangers and fiercely proud of their homes, their children and their sense of parental responsibility.

Sailfish sailing is a popular tourist sport throughout the Caribbean

Illegitimacy is almost unheard of among the island's population of 2,200. In Guadeloupe, for contrast, they will tell you, "at least half the births are out of holy wedlock."

Inbreeding over a very long period, in St. Barts, has resulted in isolated cases of loss of vigor in youngsters, albinism and even feeble-mindedness. The natural acceptance of these conditions, though, is a phenomenal thing to observe.

The people are adept in the tradition of utilizing the island's flora for medicinal concoctions. The pulp of the calabash is used to remedy diarrhea, coughs and fevers, and the white frangipani provides a milky sap that heals flesh wounds. Wine is mixed with verbena leaves and serves as a throat gargle.

Noticeably poor teeth appear to be a common characteristic. Some years ago the island had a "real" dentist, but he packed his forceps and departed for lack of business. "All he did," relates one elderly man, "was yank out teeth—by the hundreds. Hell, we could do that ourselves. So people just stopped going."

The island's single town and seaport, Gustavia, is named for a Swedish king. Originally colonized by France, St. Barts was a Swedish possession from 1784 to 1877. Its inhabitants (descendants of Norman and Breton fishermen) are mostly blue-eyed and fair complexioned. They speak English and French.

The French West Indies are Departments of France. The French government passed a law (1949) which designated these islands in the New World "a part of French soil." The government had two things in mind: it wished (1) to do away with the negative connotation of "colonies," and (2) circumvent the hands-off-our-hemisphere implications of the Monroe Doctrine. St. Barts, in turn, is officially a dependency of Guadeloupe, the capital and legislative seat of the French West Indies.

The island is probably *the* best free-port shopping center in the Caribbean. Handmade embroideries, perfumes, and Baccarat crystal sell for less than in France. Liquors such as Dewar's, Grant's, Johnnie Walker and Old Smuggler retail at $1.75 a fifth. Chivas Regal goes for $3 a bottle, and French table wines sell for 50¢ to $1.50 a bottle.

One popular Caribbean guidebook notes that "sinister forces" are at work to prevent the general public from discovering the island of St. Barts. It further implies that several extremely wealthy families are prepared to spend untold amounts to "keep it undeveloped."

The fact of the matter is, according to long-time residents, that it is extremely difficult to get accurate information about land available for sale, or for homesite development projects, because more than half the people who own portions of the island's meager eight square miles are not here. They are away mostly for economic reasons.

"You see," you are told, "a man here will not marry unless he has a house in which to put his new wife. A young man might have inherited a nice piece of land. But you can't find this landowner because he's away— maybe in the Virgin Islands, maybe on a boat—holding down a job to earn money to build a house so he can start married life in our traditional way."

David Rockefeller maintains a magnificent hideaway on the island's northwest shore (a half-million dollar project). Edmond Rothschild owns some 25 acres on St. Barts, so does the Moore family, of Moore-McCormack Lines. But these are architectural exceptions. For the most part St. Barts houses are box-shaped affairs with a distinct look of do-it-yourself-with-tenderness about them.

The personal orderliness of the people is surpassed only by their ingrained frugality. Some years ago when the French government changed the currency (and thereupon called in all its old francs) some of the poorest hillfolk trekked down the hillsides carrying heavy padlocked boxes.

Weaving straw around bottles of any size or shape continues to be one of the chief "kitchen table" industries. And able-bodied yachtsmen are one of St. Barts' major exports.

While statistics are unavailable, the lobster trade brings a sizable income. The island is surrounded by reefs and shallows that make the waters highly

St. Barthelemy

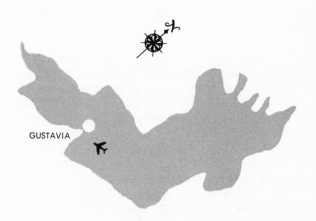

GUSTAVIA

suitable for lobster fishing. Some 80 sq. miles of bank, about 15 to 25 fathoms (a fathom is six feet), surround St. Barts.

Four guidebooks we boned up on before our trip to St. Barts tell of a fabulous "three-mile" or "four-mile beach." Well, strange as it may seem, there is no such length of sand at the surf. Local residents bristle when you mention it. One school teacher suggests (not without bitterness) that some present-day travel writers by-pass St. Barts and apparently copy erroneous information from the published works of others. "And all they are doing is repeating misinformation about a so-called four-mile beach that doesn't exist," she noted.

What the visitor finds, though, are some small but extravagantly beautiful silver-sand beaches on the concave north shore.

The island's chief resorts include Eden Roc Guest House, an idyllic colony of bungalow-cabins set upon a boulder that juts into the sea. It is located in the center of St. John's Bay on the island's north coast. Autour du Rocher (Around the Rock), another guest house with half a dozen cabins, is enlarging its accommodations. It is a handsome, modern stone and wood building, built originally as a private home. There's a small businessman's hotel in Gustavia, called La Presqu'ile, and the St. Barts Yacht Club opened a charming little hotel (eight rooms) tastefully restored in a centuries-old building.

The creator of Eden Roc is Remy de Haenen who holds the unofficial (but undisputed) title of Mr. St. Barts. He is the island's mayor and elected representative to the General Council of the F.W.I. He flies the mail to and from St. Barts, with an occasional mail pouch to and from St. Martin. He conducts a lively lobster export business, and heads the "airline" (one twin-engined Cessna) that brings visitors from Puerto Rico and St. Martin. He designed and built Eden Roc almost with his own hands and tends the small resort's landscaping on weekends. He is married and the father of four lovely daughters.

Remy is a vital man, slowed down only by the flypaper characteristic of interisland red tape, but smiling through as only a Hollander can because of an ingrained respect for international law that was acquired in grade school.

Born in London of Dutch parents, Remy first came to the Caribbean in 1938 as a seaman. He returned many times on lobster boats. His knowledge of West Indies waters was put to use during World War II when he served in the French Navy.

A dozen years ago Remy purchased for $100 the "bare rock" on which the resort now stands. The rock's owner, an old woman, laughed when he offered to pay for a rock. She tried to dissuade him. But his mind's eye could see the possibilities of a cozy seaside resort jutting out into the bay and flanked by two magnificent beaches. (He didn't have to purchase the beach-front property because by law all beaches on French islands are "forever and always" the property of the people.)

Wine is served at lunch and dinner and meals can contain an element of surprise. Your response to the food will depend on where on the cuisine scale, between the extremities of international chow hound and squeamish soul, you place yourself. The cold lobster we had—in vinaigrette sauce—was superb. So was the goat fricassee (succulent beyond compare), and the round roast served with fresh tarragon leaves. But the special variety of jellied madrilene spiked with anchovies, and topped off with a poached egg, was a little much, to say the least.

—*Al Dinhofer*

Instant facts

Location: 15 miles southeast of St. Martin, 140 miles north of Guadeloupe, in the French West Indies.

Population: 2,200.

Capital: Gustavia.

Nationality: French dependency of Guadeloupe.

Language: French, but English widely spoken.

Currency: New Franc (20¢ U.S.).

Documentation: International certificate of vaccination. Passport required by all except French nationals who hold alternate proof of identity.

Climate & Clothes: Dry with temperatures ranging from 60°–90°. Coolest months are November and December, and hurricane season is July–October. Prevailing trade winds come from east and northeast. Casual summer dress is suitable before six. Evening wear should include jacket and tie for men, late afternoon dress for ladies.

Food: French cooking, cheese and wines. Lobster is a specialty. Also recommended: goat, **chatron** (an octopus stew), **matete** (fricassee of land crab), **Madame Jackass** (a red fish dish with hot peppers). Unusual fruits include the sugar apple, which has the taste of rose water, and the St. Barts pineapple, which is sweet-sour.

Geography: Eight square miles of hills, the tallest forming two ridges running northeast from coast to coast.

History: First occupied by French adventurers who sold rights to Knights of Malta in 1651. Carib Indians pushed the Knights out in 1656. France gained control in 1674, then ceded her rights to Sweden from 1784–1877. French and Dutch pirates buried treasure onshore during this time, and Carenage, now Gustavia, became a free port, good roads were built, and the economy prospered. For a short time in the 19th century Britain held the island, but in 1878, through a plebiscite, France regained permanent control.

Who flies here

One of the most interesting aspects of a flight to St. Barts takes place upon arrival. The novel approach to the airstrip is between two hills and the runway is downhill.

Windward Islands Airways, Antilles Air Service and De Haenen Aviation offer regular flights from St. Martin, $16 round trip. The round-trip fare from Pointe-à-Pitre, Guadeloupe is $32.40 and this route also is serviced by Air Caraibes. Charter flights from these airlines can be arranged.

If you wish only a brief look around, Windward Islands Airways offers a one-day trip from St. Martin. In addition to a tour of the island, there is also plenty of leisure time for shopping, swimming and lunch at Around the Rock Guest House. The visit can be arranged any day for $23 per person, round trip—a minimum of four people to a plane.

Activities and facilities

Cars may be rented at reasonable prices. A valid state license secures a local permit. Taxis with guides are available through your guest house or the St. Barthelemy Yacht Club.

Excellent **fishing** is one attraction here. Bring your own spear gun or rod and reel as local fishermen prefer the handline. Best months for catching major species: lobster, year round; March–July, dolphin; September, wahoo, small tuna, marlin, Atlantic bonito. There are also albacore, amberjack and barracuda. Sailfish are occasionally caught. **Sailing** trips to nearby islands can be combined with fishing. Boats and guides are available through the Eden Roc Guest House or St. Barthelemy Yacht Club. Prices are arranged on the spot. (Eden Roc advertises at $15 per day.)

Swimming and **snorkeling** are popular in the very clear waters. Gustavia Harbor has the calmest surface for **water skiing.** Bring your own water sports gear as equipment available for rent is limited. One diversion from lounging is a walk about town. If you are lucky you may see some of the women embroidering and weaving the headgear for which they are famous. Some Swedish visitors have enjoyed perusing legislative records and town plans—all in Swedish—written 200 years ago and kept in **City Hall.**

Shopping buys

Goods are duty and tax free, prices are among the lowest in the Caribbean. Bargains: hi-fi, stereo equipment, microscopes, tape recorders, film projectors, cameras, outboard motors, yacht parts, Dutch pewter, porcelains, perfumes, liquors, embroidered sweaters. There are seven stores in Gustavia, and two of the best are Alma and the Little Switzerland.

Dining

Around The Rock Guest House (Autour du Rocher): Lorient. Dining in open patio. Specialties: lobster and steak cooked by Parisien chef. Good wine cellar. Tel: 73.

Charlie's Bar: The Point. Bar with island atmosphere and packaged liquors to take home.

Eden Roc Guest House: St. Jean. French cuisine, seafood, goat. Overlooking sea. Well-stocked bar. Tel: 1.

La Presqu'ile (The Peninsula): Gustavia, center of town with harbor view. French kitchen, cool dining room, bar. Specialties: pork curry, turtle. Tel: 19.

Philippe Berry Hotel: Gustavia. French cuisine—a favorite place to relax. Tel: 14.

St. Barthelemy Yacht Club: Gustavia harbor. One of oldest Swedish buildings, with bar and restaurant. Barbecue served on Delft tiles, in patio or aboard visiting yachts. Famous bar is bow of Newfoundland schooner. Stereo music accompanies drinks and dining.

Sans Pareil: Gustavia. Restaurant, pastry shop and movie house.

WHERE TO STAY — In St. Barts

| | Plan | Dec. 15-April 14 | | April 15-Dec. 14 | |
| | | U. S. Currency | | | |
		Double	Single	Double	Single
AUTOUR DU ROCHER (MAP) Lorient (10 Rms.) **(b)**		$24	$12	$24	$12
EDEN ROC (MAP) St. Jean (12 Rms.) **(b)**		$35	$25	$35	$25
PHILIPPE BERRY HOTEL Gustavia		On Request			
LA PRESQU'ILE (MAP) Gustavia (12 Rms.)		$20	$12	$20	$12
ST. BARTHELEMY YACHT CLUB Gustavia Harbor (8 Rms.)		On Request			

LEGEND FOR HOTEL LISTINGS: (AP) American Plan (room and 3 meals); **MAP)** Modified American Plan (room, breakfast and dinner); **(CP)** Continental Plan (room and breakfast); **(EP)** European Plan (room only). All rates quoted on a per-day basis and subject to change. Confirmed reservations at specific rates desired are always recommended.

HOTEL FACILITIES: (b) beach; **(p)** pool; **(t)** tennis; **(g)** golf.

SINT EUSTATIUS

One of the true backwaters of the West Indies is the small island of St. Eustatius. One of the Dutch windwards, "Statia" has yet to feel the first ripple of a tourist tide, but it has its attractions. Peace and quiet, for one, and available land at reasonable prices.

The statia salute

If you trip over the name of this tiny island, don't worry about it; everyone calls Sint Eustatius "Statia" (*stay*-shah).

During the American Revolution, Statia offered the new nation called the United States of America her first official recognition.

Fort Oranje saluted the new flag flown by an American privateer but the gesture had tragic consequences. Admiral Rodney used this as an excuse several years later to attack and capture the town of Oranjestad, which was at the time the richest trading port in the Caribbean.

Along with Fort Oranje and Oranjestad, Rodney captured 150 ships and $15,000,000 in merchandise. He sailed away, leaving smoking ruins behind him, and the island has never regained its economic eminence.

Statia is Dutch and uses Dutch currency, but English is widely spoken along with the national language.

There are many interesting sights to see in and around Oranjestad, principally the old warehouse from which Rodney took his plunder, and ruins of the Jewish synagogue which served the community of Jewish traders that contributed so much to the island's brief period of prosperity.

It is interesting to speculate what Statia might have become had she not angered Rodney and the British by firing a salute to the 13-star flag of the United States. Ruins of the little fortress which played a tragic role in this moment of history still stand, and there is a plaque presented by President Franklin D. Roosevelt in 1939 commemorating the event.

Statia differs from many other Caribbean islands in that it is underpopulated and has land available at reasonable prices. There are no hotels yet (there are a few guest houses) but plans are being made for a retirement project called Fair Play.

Although only 7½ square miles in area, Statia boasts a volcanic cone, The Quill, rising to 1,960 feet on the southern edge of the island. The slopes of The Quill have fertile volcanic soil and there is a crater inside the cone.

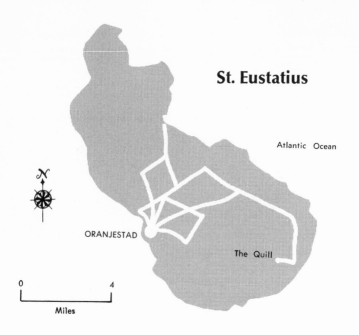

St. Eustatius

Atlantic Ocean

ORANJESTAD

The Quill

0   4

Miles

Instant facts

Location: 20 miles southeast of Saba.

Population: About 1,000.

Capital: Oranjestad.

Nationality: With Sint Maarten and Saba, one of the Netherlands Antilles windward islands, an autonomous part of the Kingdom of the Netherlands.

Language: Dutch, though English is widely spoken.

Currency: The Netherlands Antilles guilder, 53¢ U.S.

Documentation: International certificate of vaccination and passport or birth certificate required by all.

Climate & Clothes: Tropically warm with cooler evenings. Very casual attire.

Food: Dutch-Creole, not gourmet but quite palatable.

Geography: This tiny island is dominated by two high peaks, actually extinct volcanic cones, on either end. The largest, known as The Quill, is 1,960 feet high. Total area of the island is 7½ sq. miles.

History: Statia has little more than his-tory to cling to as its glories are in the past. Once a wealthy center of sugar export and slave trade, the island was known as the "Golden Rock." As many as 200 vessels might be anchored there at one time and the population was many times its present size. However, in 1776, the *Andrew Doria,* an American privateer flying the new thirteen-star flag, entered Oranjestad harbor and was accorded a salute by the cannon of Fort Oranje. Four years later the British fleet, under Admiral Rodney, attacked and looted the island so extensively that it never recovered its former prosperity.

Who flies here

Flights are available from the following nearby islands:

Antigua: LIAT. $29.30 round trip.

St. Kitts: LIAT. $8.40, Windward Islands Airways. $12 round trip.

St. Martin: Windward Islands Airways. $21 round trip.

Exploring the ruins of the old Dutch Reform church on the island of St. Eustatius

WHERE TO STAY — In Sint Eustatius

	Plan	Dec. 15-April 14 U. S. Currency Double	Single	April 15-Dec. 14 Double	Single
CANWORD'S GUEST HOUSE (4 Rms.)	(AP)	$16	$ 8	$16	$ 8
GOVERNMENT GUEST HOUSE (2 Rms.)	(CP)	$13.50	$ 6.75	$13.50	$ 6.75

LEGEND FOR HOTEL LISTINGS: (AP) American Plan (room and 3 meals); **MAP)** Modified American Plan (room, breakfast and dinner); **(CP)** Continental Plan (room and breakfast); **(EP)** European Plan (room only). All rates quoted on a per-day basis and subject to change. Confirmed reservations at specific rates desired are always recommended.
HOTEL FACILITIES: (b) beach; **(p)** pool; **(t)** tennis; **(g)** golf.

*Golden Lemon Guest House on the island of St. Kitts
was once a colonial plantation house*

ST. KITTS / NEVIS / ANGUILLA

For dedicated escapees there are three islands in the Leeward group that offer imposing credentials. St. Kitts, Nevis and Anguilla are, at this date at least, not to be classified as swingers. No big nightclubs, no hotel strips, no organized fun and games. But lots of beautiful scenery, miles of uncrowded beaches, and pleasant accommodations ranging from the modest to the luxurious.

ST. KITTS

Largest of the three islands, St. Kitts is—as the Carib Indians called it— "the fertile land." Mile upon mile of sugar cane stretches away to a central mountain range dominated by cloud-wreathed MOUNT MISERY. On the lower slopes of the mountains cotton and market produce grow along with the cane, and above the 1,100-foot level the mountains are heavily wooded, perennially lush and green.

The volcanic origin of the island, which acounts for its rich soil, also provided a dramatic formation of black rocks that thrust up from the ocean floor near the village of DIEPPE BAY on the northeast coast. Black Rocks, with the sea foaming around them, are worth a visit. Dieppe Bay also has a charming guest house faithfully converted from an airy colonial plantation house.

One of the most impressive sights of St. Kitts is BRIMSTONE HILL, an 18th-century fortress that rivals the Pyramids of Egypt in size. The British erected a battery on top of Brimstone Hill in 1689 and built extensive fortifications during the years of the wars of empire. There were three redoubts, Commanding Officer's quarters, quarters for officers and men, hospital, ordnance stores, kitchen and an amazing system of drainage. Brimstone Hill was greatly damaged by a hurricane in 1834, but it has been partly reconstructed and its guns remounted. A car can be driven up a winding road nearly to the top of the 750-foot fort, and a short climb up the stairs to the main fortifications affords a spectacular view—Montserrat and Nevis to the southeast, Saba and Statia to the north, St. Barts and St. Martin to the west.

The remains of the CHATEAU OF M. DE POINCY may be visited after obtaining permission from Fountain Estate House. The scarlet poinciana tree is named after Phillipe de Longvilliers de Poincy who ruled French possessions in the Caribbean for 21 years from this chateau. The present-day estate house is built on the cellars and foundations of the old house (1640) and the original small red French bricks used in the construction of the chateau show plainly.

At Wingfield Estate and West Farm there are large stones with Carib inscriptions, and the public library in Basseterre has a collection of Carib stones and artifacts. (The library also houses some rare first editions of early books on the West Indies.)

An expedition to Mount Misery is recommended both for scenery and for exercise, but a full day should be allowed for the excursion. A truck will get you part way there, and then it's a steady climb to the lip of the crater at 2,600 feet. (The peak is at 3,792 feet.) It is possible to descend into the crater, holding on to vines and roots. If all this sounds a little too strenuous, there is the trip to Bos D'Ane Pond, a lake in another extinct volcano, which is easier to reach.

The best swimming is from Conaree Beach, Frigate Bay, Friar's Bay and the beaches of the Salt Ponds on the southern peninsula. A modern hotel on Cockleshell Bay on the peninsula collects guests from Basseterre by boat. St. Kitts, like many other islands of volcanic origin, has black-sand beaches.

Basseterre, the capital, is a small town of white-painted colonial houses with a high green Victorian clock tower standing squarely in the center of the Circus, the town's round "square." Basseterre is also a port busy with schooners from Nevis, Antigua, St. Martin, Montserrat and St. Barts, and freighters from the United States, Canada and England call here regularly. The waterfront is also the marketplace, where women who walked in from the country, their straw baskets brimming with yams, breadfruit, carrots and pumpkins, make the morning produce market one of the colorful sights of the island.

At one corner of the Circus a staircase leads up to a cool veranda, the entrance to a waterfront hotel where the bar is the social center of the island. It's a pleasant place to enjoy a good island drink while watching the life of St. Kitts unfold around you.

At the southern tip of St. Kitts is Great Salt Pond where evaporation flats yield two to three crops a year. The Pond is also a resting place for migratory fowl, but, since it is somewhat difficult to reach, visitors are advised to travel in by jeep.

Unfortunately, for this picture of tranquility, political unrest has been simmering since last May when Anguilla declared its independence from the three-island state. The St. Kitts government has jailed many of its political opponents both in St. Kitts and in Nevis.

Instant facts

Location: In the northerly leeward group of the Lesser Antilles. 50 miles west of Antigua.

Population: 40,000.

Capital: Basseterre.

Nationality: St. Kitts, Nevis and Anguilla comprise an Associated State within the British Commonwealth.

Language: English.

Currency: East Caribbean (same as West Indian) dollar—60¢ U.S., 64¢ Canadian and 4s 2d sterling.

Documentation: International certificate of vaccination required. Passport required

Spectacular view from the ancient fort on Brimstone Hill on the island of St. Kitts

by all except U.S., Canadian and U.K. citizens with alternate proof of identity.

Climate & Clothes: Cooling trade winds are steady throughout most of the year and humidity is low. Highest recorded temperature this century was 92° and the lowest 62°. Although there is ample precipitation, there is no rainy season as such. Casual dress and sports clothes.

Food: West Indian dishes, plus here and there continental cooking. Some favorite local foods are **roast suckling pig, turtle steaks, chicken pilaf, crab back, curried lobster, pepper pot** and **peas with rice.** Meat and fish are often served with hot pepper sauce. European vegetables are grown and served alongside West Indian vegetables such as paw-paw, christophine, breadfruit, plantain and occasionally hearts of palm. There are also many native tropical fruits.

Geography: A mountainous island, 33 miles by 5 miles, dominated by 3,792 foot Mount Misery. The long southeastern peninsula of the island has low hills and salt ponds.

History: The official name of St. Kitts is St. Christopher, but no one has called it that for several centuries. Columbus discovered the island in 1493 and named it after his patron saint, but the British anglicized St. Christopher to St. Kitts shortly after they arrived in 1623.

St. Kitts, the oldest British settlement in the West Indies, sent out colonizing parties to other islands, and so became known as the "Mother Colony of the West Indies." The French established a settlement in 1627 and co-existed more or less peacefully with the British (in an alliance against their common enemies, the Spanish and the Carib Indians) until the end of the 17th century. The English drove the French from St. Kitts in 1713, and received full title to the island by the Treaty of Versailles in 1783. Echoes of the French settlement still linger in the name of the capital, Basseterre, and in the village of Half-Way-Tree, where a large tamarind tree marked the halfway point in English territory on the south side.

Numerous forts, ruined and often buried under tropical vegetation, their cannon thrown down, remain as a memorial to those times. The most impressive and best preserved is the fort on Brimstone Hill, once known as the "Gibraltar of the West Indies."

The Caribs called St. Kitts *Liamuiga,* "the fertile land." Its rich soil sloping down gradually from a central spine of mountains has sugar cane growing on virtually every inch of it.

Who flies here

There are no direct flights from main U.S. cities. St. Kitts' Golden Rock Airport, with its new and modern terminal, does connect with the following Caribbean locales:

San Juan: LIAT, Caribair. Round trip: $58–$90; 17-day excursion $45.

St. Thomas: LIAT, Caribair. Round trip: $46–$67; 17-day excursion $45.

Antigua: Caribair and LIAT. Round trip: $16–$22.

St. Martin: ALM, LIAT, Caribair, Windward Islands Airways. Round trip: $16–$21.

Nevis: LIAT. Round trip: $5.

Anguilla: LIAT. Round trip: $21.

Island transportation

A valid hometown driver's license or, preferably, an international license is all you need for a permit to drive in St. Kitts, available from police headquarters. Cars can be rented for about $6 and up and there is a good road around the island. The southeast end of St. Kitts can be reached by car but a jeep is recommended for the trip to Friar's Bay.

Taxis are readily available for guided tours and transportation.

The sporting life

There is good **swimming** at Conaree Beach, Frigate Bay, Friar's Bay, Cockleshell Bay and other beaches in the Salt Ponds area. This is also the best area for **skin-diving** but, unless special arrangements can be made with your hotel, it is best to bring your own equipment. There is

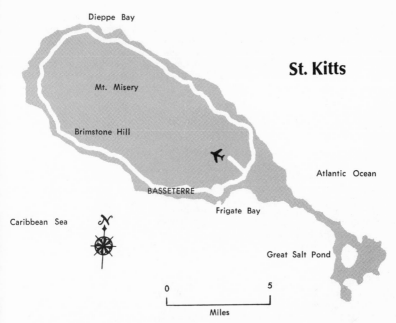

Dieppe Bay

St. Kitts

Mt. Misery

Brimstone Hill

Atlantic Ocean

BASSETERRE

Caribbean Sea

Frigate Bay

Great Salt Pond

0   5

Miles

no **water skiing** equipment available.

Arrangements for **boating** and **fishing** can be made through hotels or with the local fishermen. There are some schooner and charter boats to Saba, St. Eustatius, St. Barts, St. Martin and other islands. A government boat makes regular trips, except Thursday and Sunday, between Nevis and St. Kitts. There is a new pier at Sandy Point.

Visitors interested in **mountain climbing** can make arrangements through hotels. There is also the seasonal **shooting** of mountain dove, migratory duck, plover, ramier and pigeon. There are special **riding** paths up into the mountains. Arrangements should be made through hotels. There are two **tennis** clubs with temporary membership available to visitors—the St. Kitts Tennis Club and the Olympic Club. There is a 9-hole golf course, greens fees $1. Contact the secretary, Golden Rock Golf Club.

Shopping buys

Main shopping area runs through Liverpool Row, the Circus and Bank St. While Basseterre is no St. Thomas, there are some pretty good buys here and there. Liquor prices are low and the small amount of imports includes such miscellaneous items as Indian brassware, ivory, silks, linen, toiletries and camera supplies. Some local handicrafts also are sold.

Restaurants

Blakeney: Basseterre. Tel: 2222.
Four Seasons: Basseterre.
The Palm: Basseterre. Tel: 2424.
Seaside: Basseterre. Tel: 2077.
Wings: Golden Rock Airport. Tel: 2271.

Restaurants serve both Creole and continental food. There are no nightclubs or cocktail lounges on the island.

Special events, festivals

New Year's celebrations: Competitions for musical bands, masquerades, etc. January 1.

Queen's Birthday: Ceremonial parade at Warner Park. June 8.

Arts Festival: Drama, music, art exhibits. August.

Prince Charles' Birthday: November 14.

Boxing Day: December 26. Traditional Christmas festivities usually begin around the middle of December with an island-wide motorcade. Other events are a kiddy costume party, Queen Show (on Boxing night), parade of bands (skin drum, string and steel bands) and street dancing (on the 26th and 27th). Celebrations continue through New Year's.

Meet the people

Organization	Official
Cricket Assn.	S. B. Daniel
Football Assn.	A. Knight
Lawn Tennis Assn.	R. Manning
Netball Assn.	Miss B. Weston
Table Tennis Assn.	D. Ward
Basketball Assn.	F. C. Bryant
Extra Mural Dept.–U.W.I.	V. Joss
Guild of Graduates	G. Bradley
St. John's Ambulance Brigade	W. V. Samuels
British Red Cross Society	Dr. D. Boyd
YWCA	Mrs. C. Sealy
Chamber of Commerce	C. Malone
Junior Chamber of Commerce	M. Redhead
Child Welfare Assn.	Mrs. G. Jones
Mental Health Assn.	C. S. Elmes
Girls Guide Assn.	Mrs. Rhoda Osborne
Boy Scouts Assn.	W. F. Dore
Boys Brigade Council	M. L. Woods
Nurses Assn.	Miss B. Welsh
British Medical Assn.	Dr. A. W. Lake
Civil Service Assn.	Eustace John
Primary School Teachers Union	Mrs. E. Quinlan
Secondary School Teachers Union	Mrs. V. Jacobs
Sugar Assn.	R. S. Vanier
Sugar Producers' Assn.	R. S. Vanier
Employers Consultative Confederation	R. S. Vanier
Labour Party (Workers League)	J. N. France
Trades and Labour Union	J. N. France
Taxi Assn.	Earle Clarke
Waterfront, Airport and Manual Workers Union	Warren Thomas
Central Union of National Employees	C. W. Christmas
Grand United Order of Odd Fellows	Stanley Procope
Freemason's Lodge	J. A. Springer
Heart and Hand Society	Icen Wharton
Unity Friendly Society	Vernon Wilkes
Sandy Point Women's Institute	Miss W. Armantrading
Anglican Mothers Union	Mrs. L. John
Anglican Young Peoples Assn.	I. Beach
Peoples Action Movement	R. Caines
4-H Club Councils	B. H. Henderson
Mutual Improvement Society	H. C. Byron
Christian Council	Archdeacon C. P. J. Walker
Golden Rock Gulf Club	Keith Laurie

Official

Olympic Club
Men's Club
Lawn Tennis Club
Amateur Group
Christmas Festivities Committee
Police Welfare Assn.
Bar Assn.
Ballroom Dance Club
Girls Industrial Union
Service League
Society for the Restoration of
  Brimstone Hill Fortress
Cotton Growers' Assn.

Real estate and retirement

Under the Alien Land Holding Regulation, persons of alien status must obtain a license before they can purchase or lease property in the state. Any alien who wants to stay for an indefinite period, in fact, should make formal application to the Ministry of Home Affairs. There is only one real estate agent in the territory: Mr. J. A. Claxton, Basseterre, St. Kitts. However, there are a number of attorneys who handle real estate. Located in Basseterre, they are:

Adams, Walwyn & Brookes
Central St.

Sir Geoffrey Boon
Bank St.

Kelsick & Kelsick
South Square St.

Mrs. Arlene Fraites-Gomez
Adlam St.

Kawaja, Wigley & Crawford
Liverpool Row

C. F. Henville
Liverpool Row

M. H. Davis
Cayon St.

Organization

J. Humphrey
R. Bollers
K. A. Pencheon
Eustace John
Miss B. Weston
Corporal F. Marshall
R. M. Crawford
Eustace Warner
Mrs. Doris Sheppard
H. M. Dinzey

Sir Geoffrey Boon
C. M. Birkett

Dr. W. V. Herbert
Church St.

The estimated cost of building a house (hollow concrete blocks, concrete floors and galvanized iron roof) is approximately $15 per sq. foot. Personal income tax is not high and property tax 5% of the assessed annual rental value. Necessities, particularly food, are quite a bit steeper than in the U.S., due of course to the importation cost.

Commerce and industry

There has been some noticeable improvement in the field of commerce over the past decade but industrial development has been slow. The St. Kitts Breweries Ltd. is the only major industry which has been established in recent years. A new company, known as Cane Commodities (St. Kitts) Ltd. has recently been granted pioneer status to manufacture sugar cane by-products (cane wax, epidermis, rind, pith, fiber and protein). Production is due to begin in mid-1968. Sugar today still accounts for 90% of the island's foreign income. Over a third of St. Kitts' fertile land area has been set aside for sugar and molasses. Tourism is still a fledgling.

WHERE TO STAY — In St. Kitts

	Plan	Double	Single	Double	Single
		Dec. 15-April 14		April 15-Dec. 14	
			U. S. Currency		
BLAKENEY HOTEL (AP)		$22–32	$13–18	$22–32	$13–18
Basseterre (11 Rms.) (MAP)		$17–28	$11–15	$17–28	$11–15
CHARDON VILLA (AP)		$40	$12	$22	$12
GUEST HOUSE Basseterre (3 Rms.)					
COCKLESHELL (AP)		$40	$32	$30	$20
Cockleshell Bay (10 Rms.) (b)					
GOLDEN LEMON (AP)		$425	$225	On Request	
Dieppe Bay (6 Rms.) (b)		weekly	weekly		
PALMS (AP)		$22	$11	$22	$11
Basseterre (6 Rms.)					
SEA SIDE (AP)		$25	$15	$25	$15
Basseterre (18 Rms.)					
SELF CATERING BEACH					
BUNGALOWS (2 Units)		$15 per unit		$10 per unit	

LEGEND FOR HOTEL LISTINGS: (AP) American Plan (room and 3 meals); **MAP)** Modified American Plan (room, breakfast and dinner); **(CP)** Continental Plan (room and breakfast); **(EP)** European Plan (room only). All rates quoted on a per-day basis and subject to change. Confirmed reservations at specific rates desired are always recommended.
HOTEL FACILITIES: (b) beach; **(p)** pool; **(t)** tennis; **(g)** golf.

Tourists can have skindiving lessons on most islands in the Caribbean

NEVIS

Two miles south of St. Kitts, across The Narrows, lies Nevis, known in the 18th century as the "Queen of the Caribbee Islands." It is still quite unspoiled, with graceful white weather-board houses, fretted verandas and neat gardens.

Nevis is well ahead of many small islands in facilities for visitors. There are a good number of small resort hotels, many of them new and all of them extremely comfortable and even luxurious.

There are tennis courts, and sport fishing boats are available for charter at some of the hotels. And, for the escapee from the clamor and crowds of modern life, there are miles of golden sand beaches where an escapee can walk without meeting a soul.

Nevis also has a wealth of interesting places to visit. There is BATH HOUSE (now partially restored) where the hot mineral springs made Nevis the leading spa of the West Indies in the 18th century.

The island was the site of the wedding of England's most famous naval hero, Admiral Horatio Nelson, to Mrs. Frances Nisbet, a widow. In ST. JOHN'S CHURCH, FIG TREE VILLAGE, the register records the marriage in 1787. The wedding actually took place in a plantation house close to the new Montpelier Hotel, and the story holds that the ceremony was held under a tree in the gardens.

ALEXANDER HAMILTON was born in Nevis, and the ruins of his childhood home can be seen on the beach near Charlestown, the capital.

A drive around the island is well worthwhile. To the north lies St. Kitts, to the south Antigua, Montserrat and Redonda. There are good trails and pleasant roads for walking or horseback riding. Mount Nevis itself can be climbed from either the ZETLAND or DUNBAR ESTATES, but it is usually capped with cloud and is more than 3,500 feet high. This expedition should be started early to escape the heat of the day.

The JETTY in Charlestown is a lively place, with the passenger boats from St. Kitts and inter-island sloops putting in and out. Many of the sloops were built at yards south of the town, where the boat builders are always busy.

Instant facts

Location: Two miles south of St. Kitts.
Population: 14,000.
Capital: Charlestown.
Nationality: St. Kitts, Nevis and Anguilla comprise an Associated State within the British Commonwealth.
Language: English.
Currency: East Caribbean (same as West Indian) dollar—60¢ U.S., 64¢ Canadian and 4s 2d sterling.

Documentation: International certificate of vaccination required. Passport required by all except U.S., Canadian and U.K. citizens with alternate proof of identity.

Climate & Clothes: Cooling trade winds are steady throughout most of the year and humidity is low. Highest recorded temperature this century was 92° and the lowest 62°. Although there is ample precipitation, there is no rainy season as such. Casual dress and sports clothes.

Food: West Indian dishes, plus here and there continental cooking. Some native recipes feature the avocado pear, served either as a salad or soup but also baked, braised, mashed and stuffed. Eggplant too can appear in soup or entrée form. More extravagant dishes are **suckling pig** and **pixilated pork,** both roasted with many spices. Seafood favorites include sea urchin (served much like scrambled eggs!), turtle steak, turtle stew, or turtle pie, and crabmeat, in the shell or in soup.

Geography: Nevis is a round, 36 sq. mile volcanic island with forested slopes rising from the sea to 3,596 foot Nevis Peak. Miles of palm-lined beaches, protected by coral reefs, ring the island.

History: Nevis today is a dramatically beautiful but quiet island. Its social heyday was back in the 18th century when it was the most fashionable spa in the West Indies. Gouty (and wealthy) British planters from other islands came to bathe in the waters at Bath House, and their wives brought along their marriageable daughters for the social season. Admiral Horatio Nelson married the rich young widow, Fanny Nisbet, in a friend's plantation house in 1787, and his best man was the Duke of Clarence, later King William IV of England. Alexander Hamilton was born in Charlestown, the island's present capital, in 1757, and the ruins of the house where he was born may be visited. Nevis' first capital was Jamestown, destroyed by an earthquake in 1680 and claimed by the sea.

Columbus discovered Nevis in 1493 and named it *Las Nieves* (The Snows) after a snow-covered range in the Pyrenees. His "snow" is a wreath of white clouds that usually rings the top of Nevis Peak.

Who flies here

LIAT serves the island with scheduled flights from St. Kitts ($5 round trip) and Antigua ($21 round trip). Air-bus service

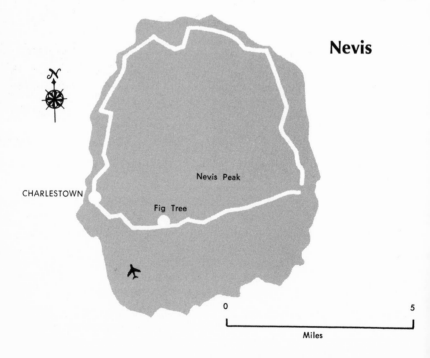

Nevis

CHARLESTOWN

Nevis Peak

Fig Tree

0   5

Miles

Lofty palms beneath the Caribbean sun

between Nevis and St. Kitts, daily except Tuesday and Sunday, makes the trip in 5 minutes.

Real estate and industry

Once a fashionable spa and the site of successful sugar plantations, commercial activity in Nevis today consists of a few farmers on a few small farms who culti-

vate cotton, sugar and coconuts. Housing regulations and taxation are the same as for St. Kitts. Detailed information on homesites or rentals can be obtained from the law firm of Byron & Byron, and attorney Theodore L. Hobson, Charlestown.

Island transportation

A valid driver's license or, preferably, an international license is all you need for a permit to drive in Nevis, available from police headquarters. Cars can be rented for about $6 and up though taxis are also readily available for tours and general transportation.

The sporting life

Best **beaches** here are Pinney's Beach and the strands near Newcastle. Arrange-

Meet the people

ments for all other activities—fishing, boating and riding—must be made through hotels. **Tennis** courts can be found at several of the island's hotels.

Special events, festivals

See "Special Events" for St. Kitts. The Christmas program is also similar to that of St. Kitts.

Organization	Official
YWCA	Miss Maude Crosse
British Red Cross Society	Miss Maude Crosse
Junior Chamber of Commerce	Melford Henville
Nevis Hotel Assn.	Norman Rappard
Nevis Taxi Assn.	Anderson Clarke
Dulcina Island Club	S. Greene
Cricket Assn.	Hugh Claxton
Co-operative Society	Miss Eugenie Huggins
Boy Scouts Assn.	G. L. Bellot
Boys Brigade Assn.	Earle Jeffers
Cotton Growers' Assn.	F. A. Parris

WHERE TO STAY — In Nevis

		Dec. 15-April 14 U. S. Currency		April 15-Dec. 14	
	Plan	Double	Single	Double	Single
GOLDEN ROCK **ESTATE Gingerland** (11 Rms.) **(p)**	(AP)	$44	$25	$26	$14
MONTPELIER **Near Charlestown** (18 Rms.) **(p)**	(AP)	$38	$25	$26	$15
NISBET PLANTATION **Beachlands** (10 Rms.) **(b)**	(AP)	$30	$20	$20	$12
REST HAVEN **Charlestown** (9 Rms.) **(b)**	(AP)	$20	$12	$20	$10
THE CLIFF DWELLERS (15 Rms.) **(b, p, t)**	(AP)	$50–60	$48–50	$28–35	$23–30

LEGEND FOR HOTEL LISTINGS: (AP) American Plan (room and 3 meals); **MAP)** Modified American Plan (room, breakfast and dinner); **(CP)** Continental Plan (room and breakfast); **(EP)** European Plan (room only). All rates quoted on a per-day basis and subject to change. Confirmed reservations at specific rates desired are always recommended.
HOTEL FACILITIES: (b) beach; **(p)** pool; **(t)** tennis; **(g)** golf.

ANGUILLA

North of St. Kitts and Nevis, just 12 miles from St. Martin, is Anguilla, a narrow, 15-mile long island whose size is entirely out of proportion to the political turmoil which erupted last May. After forcibly evicting the 17-member police force (which returned to St. Kitts), Anguilla declared its independence from the St. Kitts–Nevis–Anguilla federation, an unofficial proclamation later supported in a referendum by all but five of its 5,000 citizens.

England refused to step into the fray and other nations (namely the United States) could not commit themselves without some word from the British.

Because of its coral foundation, Anguilla has beaches of unsurpassed beauty, but unproductive soil—the very opposite of St. Kitts and Nevis. With only a small fishing industry, some boat building and the yield of its salt flats, Anguilla would find it virtually impossible to support itself as an independent nation. Parties interested in coming to the "aid" of the small island have included a group of advertising executives and newsmen in San Francisco, which promoted the independence of Anguilla in order to allow an economics professor at the University of Puerto Rico to test his theories on the virtue of smallness; a Greek shipping magnate, and hotel and gambling interests.

Despite its problems, Anguilla has a few striking natural assets. The coastline is a seemingly endless stretch of white coral sand. The water offshore is so remarkably clear that fish can be seen out at sea entering the bays. The swimming is excellent everywhere, and skindivers and snorkelers will find the reefs that almost encircle the island swarming with fish of all kinds. A wide variety of shells washes up on the beaches, especially those at the eastern end of the island.

One of the most picturesque places on Anguilla is Island Harbour, a little town at the east end where schooners are built on the shore and where the fishermen come in with their catches of lobster. Lobstering is the chief industry on the island, and almost all the catch is flown out to larger islands. But there is always one left for your dinner at the small hotel.

Boats and simple fishing equipment can be hired from local fishermen, and indeed the waters of Anguilla are well known for excellent fishing. The small bays off many of the beaches are perfect for water skiing, but the would-be water skier should bring his own equipment. The same also applies for spearfishing and snorkeling.

Instant facts

Location: 70 miles northwest of St. Kitts, and 12 miles from its nearest neighbor, St. Martin.

Population: 6,000.
Capital: The Valley.
Nationality: St. Kitts, Nevis and Anguilla comprise an Associated State within the British Commonwealth. Anguilla, how-

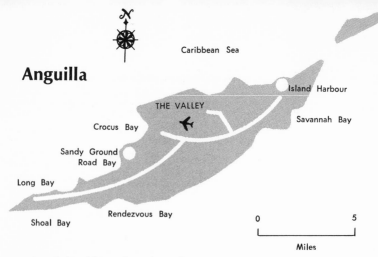

Anguilla

Caribbean Sea

THE VALLEY

Island Harbour

Savannah Bay

Crocus Bay

Sandy Ground
Road Bay

Long Bay

Rendezvous Bay

Shoal Bay

0   5

Miles

ever, has declared her independence from this uneasy trinity.

Language: English.

Currency: East Caribbean (same as West Indian) dollar—60¢ U.S., 64¢ Canadian and 4s 2d sterling.

Documentation: International certificate of vaccination required. Passport required by all except U.S., Canadian and U.K. citizens with alternate proof of identity.

Climate & Clothes: The cooling trade winds are steady throughout most of the year and humidity is low. Casual dress and sports clothes.

Food: West Indian dishes, plus some continental cooking. Fish is particularly abundant in Anguilla.

Geography: 35 sq. miles, a low-lying island encircled by white coral beaches.

History: Anguilla was probably named l'Anguille—the eel—by the French because of its slender, eel-like shape. A French boat called there in 1564, enroute for Florida from Dominica, and the English Captain Harcourt landed in 1609. The island was colonized by the English in 1650, and the settlement was frequently harassed by French and Irish privateers. In 1680 some Anguillans sailed for the Virgin Islands and settled there, while others joined the colony in Antigua in 1689. Life was not easy in Anguilla, and production not abundant. Some sugar and rum were produced, along with tobacco and cotton. The original seed for sea island cotton, which reached Georgia and South Carolina in 1889, is said to have come from Anguilla.

Who flies here

Anguilla is a half-hour from St. Kitts by air. LIAT serves the island with scheduled flights from St. Kitts ($21 round trip), St. Martin ($5 round trip), Antigua ($42 round trip) and Montserrat ($42 round trip). **Windward Islands Airways** also flies from St. Martin, round-trip fare $10.

The sporting life

Beaches are little Anguilla's specialty. Some can be reached by car, others only by boat or on foot. The following is a list of the best beaches:

Sandy Ground: On Road Bay. A semi-circular beach. A small village of fishermen and workers for the salt pond on the strip of land between the salt pond and the sea. Schooners and yachts put in here. There is a small wooden jetty. Excellent **swimming** and **boating** in the Bay, good **fishing** off the promontory to the north. Schooners are built on the beach. A beautiful view of Sandy Ground can be had from the road above the Bay leading to South Hill.

Sandy Isle: An extremely pleasant afternoon's sail from Sandy Ground. A small coral island surrounded by reef—excellent for **skindiving.**

Long Bay: A beautiful stretch of white sand. Good **fishing** in the bay.

Mayd's Bay: A small cove edged by rocky cliffs at the end of Long Bay. Very good **swimming.** A walk over the headland with cliffs descending into Turtle Cove.

The Cove: White sand and beautifully clear water, a broad stretch of sand under clear water before the sea deepens.

Rendezvous Bay: A half-moon bay of white sand.

Blowing Point: A small harbor for sloops and fishing boats. Boats for St. Martin leave from here and from Forest Point, another small harbor.

Sandy Hill Bay: White sand, good bathing, beautiful coloring in the water. A harbor for small sloops and yachts.

Savannah Bay: A broad white beach almost entirely encircled by reef. Very good **swimming** in pools inside the reef. It is possible to wade out about 100 yards over the reef and fish from its edge. Permission from Mr. J. Webster to cross his land to the beach.

Junk's Hole: Very good swimming beach edged by palms and encircled by reef at one end of Savannah Bay. Permission from Mr. Hodge to cross his land to the beach.

Island Harbour: Picturesque small fishing village and harbor. **Boating** from here to Scrub Island, and to beaches along the coast.

Shoal Bay: One of the finest beaches in the Caribbean. Extremely white sand, clear water edged with reef, the shore treelined. It can be reached on foot from the road. Permission from Mr. Harrigan to cross his land.

Crocus Bay: Nearest bay to The Valley. Excellent **swimming.**

Boats and simple **fishing** equipment can be hired from local fishermen, particularly at Sandy Ground and Island Harbour. (Some beaches are especially good for spearfishing but it is necessary to bring your own equipment. There is no snorkeling, skindiving or water skiing equipment available locally.) Best fishing catches here are barracuda, kingfish, cavally, doctorfish, silks, jacks and shellfish. During the winter season, there is good **duck shooting.**

There are daily **boats** (except Sunday) between Anguilla and nearby St. Martin. Charter yachts and schooners also call at Anguilla at regular intervals from the U.S. Virgin Islands.

Meet the people

Organization	Official
Boy Scouts Assn.	Raphael Lake
Girl Guides Assn.	Miss B. Gumbs
British Red Cross Society	Miss B. Gumbs
St. John's Ambulance Brigade	Mrs. D. Richardson
Anguilla Credit Union	Alwyn S. Hodge
Fishing Co-op	Vivienne Vanterpool

WHERE TO STAY — In Anguilla

	Plan	Dec. 15-April 14 U. S. Currency		April 15-Dec. 14	
		Double	Single	Double	Single
LLOYD'S HOTEL The Valley (10 Rms.)	(AP)	$17	$ 9	$17	$ 9
MAUNDY BAY (10 Rms.)		Opening 1968			
RENDEZVOUS Rendezvous Bay (14 Rms.) **(b)**	(AP)	$30	$17	$20	$12

ST. LUCIA

Sheer volcanic peaks rise from the ocean floor, the coastline is ringed
with small harbors and coves that charm yachtsmen, and the beaches
are among the finest in the Caribbean. It is not, at least not yet, an
outpost of the Frantic Set. Night life, in the usual meaning of the term,
is nonexistent. There are compensations. The unrivaled beauty of
the island makes exploring a never-ending pleasure. Roads lead high up
into the central mountain range through deep green forests and along
a pleasantly winding route that almost always keeps the Caribbean Sea
in sight. There is even a drive-in volcano.

A made-to-order paradise

Sightseeing in St. Lucia is *the* thing to do. Artists, photographers (amateur and professional) and just run-of-the-mill nature lovers will rarely find
themselves in a place of more spectacular beauty. Hollywood apparently
agrees the island is pretty enough for a picture and recently made it the
setting of its multimillion dollar production of *Dr. Doolittle*, with Rex
Harrison.

It is also an island rich in history. For 150 years the British and the
French fought over it, and St. Lucia (pronounced *Loo*-shah) changed hands
between the two powers no less than 14 times. The influence of the early
French settlers lingers in colorful forms of dress and a French patois is
spoken by islanders. It is not difficult to imagine in the lushly exotic atmosphere of St. Lucia the sweep of crinoline and lace, sabers and military
uniforms, the tall masts and billowing sails of 18th-century men-of-war,
cannons booming from the forts, the tricolor, the Union Jack.

CASTRIES, the capital, probably was first settled by the French around
1651. It has a magnificent harbor leading inland a mile and a half from a
narrow entrance. At the southern end of the town, the land rises abruptly to
more than 700 feet. This is MORNE FORTUNE (Hill of Good Luck) which
was the principal French fort and where, after it was captured by the British
in 1794, Queen Victoria's father hoisted the colors. There is a monument
to the Inniskilling Fusiliers, ruins of Old Government House and the old
military cemetery.

Across the narrow bay is VIGIE HILL (Watch Hill), a peninsula that
forms the northern arm of the harbor. It was invaded countless times, and in
1778 some 1,300 British soldiers defeated 5,000 Frenchmen at the Battle of
Vigie. Today it is a peaceful, and favored, residential section. There is a

264

*One of St. Lucia's most magnificent sights,
Petit Peton, rising sheer from the sea*

lighthouse atop the hill, and great stone and brick barracks built for the British garrisons still stand.

The harbor of Castries is an idyllic scene today. Yachts and boats of all sizes and types tie up to the dock, and the vegetation on the hills beyond, flowering trees and blooms, is gloriously tropical.

A steep road leads to the top of Morne Fortune, and it is worth a trip. Martinique, and Mont Pelée, rear up in the northern distance, and to the south St. Lucia unfolds in all her mountainous beauty.

Beyond Castries is VIGIE BEACH, a three-mile, palm-fringed strand of pure white sand and crystal clear water. There are dressing rooms available.

A few miles north of Castries is the fishing village of GROS ISLET where boats can be hired to cross the channel to Pigeon Island. PIGEON ISLAND lies a mile offshore near the northern tip of St. Lucia. In 1782, Admiral Rodney had his fleet at Gros Islet Bay and Pigeon Island was his lookout point. It was from there that he observed a French fleet attempting to escape from Martinique, and he ordered his fleet out to give chase. The final battle was fought off Saintes Islands to the north.

The most spectacular sights of St. Lucia—perhaps of the entire Caribbean—are the PITONS (French for pointed peaks). These are Gros Piton (2,619 feet) and Petit Piton (2,461 feet), old volcanic spires which rise sheer out of the sea near the town of Soufrière on the leeward coast.

No one who has seen the Pitons from the sea will ever forget the sight. The twin grandeur of the conical peaks rising fully forested from the sea has been a landmark for mariners for centuries. The Pitons have been scaled, but it is an ascent that should be undertaken only by experienced climbers.

Red-roofed Soufrière, 15 miles down the coast from Castries, is St. Lucia's second city and was an important French colonial center. It maintains much of the charm of its early days. It is from Soufrière that you set out for "the world's only drive-in volcano."

This involves a ride by car up a thousand feet or so, and into the crater of a still lively volcano. The side of the volcano blew out unknown years ago, accounting for its drive-in accessibility. There is a fine inferno atmosphere, with bubbling puddles and pools, and smoke rising from vents and cracks.

Hot mineral springs are all over the area which someday may be developed into a European-type spa. Sulphur baths were opened at Soufrière in 1784 by the French, and the buildings still stand. If you're determined to take a "health bath," facilities are available at nearby Diamond Baths.

The road from Castries to Soufrière passes by MARIGOT BAY, which is considered by yachtsmen the most beautiful small anchorage in the West Indies. The bay, landlocked and with a riot of vegetation growing down to the shore, looks like everyone's dream of an island paradise. There is a hotel and yacht club, snorkeling and swimming in the bay, or you can simply sit at the informal bamboo bar and watch the yachts sail in and out.

The VIEUX FORT drive, south from Soufrière, passes behind the Pitons and then down to the sea in the lush southern part of the island. Beyond the town of Vieux Fort, on the windward side, is one of the finest beaches of St. Lucia, ANSE DE SABLES. Although it faces the Atlantic, the surf is not overly rough because of the protecting reefs. The road continues up the windward coast to the town of DENNERY, then turns inland and crosses the mountains back to Castries. It is as magnificent a drive as can be found anywhere in the Caribbean.

Instant facts

Location: Second largest of the Windward Islands, St. Lucia lies 24 miles south of Martinique and 20 miles north of St. Vincent.

Population: Over 100,000.

Capital: Castries.

Nationality: Independent state in association with Great Britain.

Language: English is the principal language. St. Lucians also speak a French Creole similar to that of Martinique, Guadeloupe and Haiti.

Currency: The East Caribbean (same as West Indian) dollar—4/2 in British sterling, 60¢ U.S., 64¢ Canadian.

Documentation: International certificate of vaccination required. Passport required by all except U.S., Canadian and U.K. citizens with alternate proof of identity and round-trip tickets.

Climate & Clothes: Temperatures vary from 70° to 90°, but, as in her sister islands, the trade winds keep things pleasant year round. The rainy season falls between June and December. Light summer clothes, washable fabrics recommended. Evening wear not essential. Lightweight sweater for the ladies and jackets for men are comfortable on breezy winter evenings.

Food: Cooking with a French accent.

History: St. Lucia was a settlement of the aboriginal Carib Indians long before Columbus arrived in the New World. Columbus probably never landed at the island, and the first Europeans to visit were unknown Spaniards. A party of Englishmen attempted a landing in 1605, but were killed or driven off by the Caribs. Attempts at colonization failed until 1650, when two enterprising Frenchmen purchased the island from the French West India Company. During the next 150 years, St. Lucia changed hands between the French and the British no less than 14 times and much blood was shed around the forts of Castries on Morne Fortune and on Vigie Hill. The Treaty of Paris in 1814 ceded the island to England.

Geography: The oval-shaped island is of volcanic formation, its 238 sq. miles consisting of some mountains covered with tropical rain forest or palms, well-watered alluvial valleys in which is concentrated most of the island's commercial agriculture and numerous attractive beaches which afford ideal sea-bathing.

Who flies here

When booking flights to and from St. Lucia it is prudent to inquire about which airfield your plane will land on or depart from. St. Lucia's Vigie Airport is near Castries, the capital. Beane Field, served by 727 jets, is 45 miles and a $20 taxi ride from the capital though LIAT now flies between Beane Field and Vigie, $7 per seat.

There are direct flights to St. Lucia from the following islands:

Antigua: BWIA, LIAT, Caribair. Round trip: $53–$78.

Barbados: BWIA, LIAT. Round trip: $32–$49; 17-day excursion $20–$30.

San Juan: BWIA. Round trip: $116–$166; 17-day excursion $77–$104.

Martinique: BWIA, LIAT, Caribair. Round trip: $16–$25.

Curaco: ALM. Round trip: $79.

Island transportation

Self-drive cars are available for hire at about $5 a day with a minimum of 20 miles, after which 24¢ per mile is charged. A license to drive is obtained from the Traffic Dept., Police Headquarters, on presentation of an International Driver's License or payment for a local permit costing $3.

Cars can be rented from the following:

Freddy's Garage, Tel: 2177, 2175

Fixit Garage, Tel: 2780

Fletcher's Garage, Tel: 2516

G.B.I. Tours, Tel: 2869

Odlum's Garage, Tel: 2068

St. Lucia Taxi Service, Tel: 2491

Carib Travel Agency, Tel: 2151

St. Lucia also has a number of reliable **taxis** and arrangements can be made with the drivers for sightseeing trips. Rates are set—a short trip around Castries is 30¢ and a detailed listing of longer trips is available through your hotel or the tourist board. The following agencies offer tours and transportation around the island:

Freddy's Garage, Tel: 2177, 2175

Federation Garage, Tel: 2670

St. Lucia Touring Plan Service, Tel: 2266

G.B.I. Tours, Tel: 2869

St. Lucia Motor Garage, Tel: 2715

St. Lucia Taxi Service, Tel: 2491

Carib Travel Agency, Tel: 2151

Peter & Company, Tel: 2771

One motor launch supplies a regular daily service, except on Wednesday and Sunday, between Castries, Anse-La-Raye, Canaries and Soufrière. This launch leaves Castries between 2 and 3 P.M. and returns there the following morning around 11 A.M.

Water sports

Serious sport **fishing** has only recently been introduced in St. Lucia but catches of marlin, bluefin, tuna, dolphin and king-fish have been reported. Motorboats can be rented, for fishing trips or cruising, from the following:

Mr. William Hackshaw
Castries, Tel: 2682

Dr. Nels Johnson
The Reef Marina
Pointe Seraphine
Castries, Tel: 2546

St. Lucia Yacht Charters
P.O. Box 83
Castries

Mr. Richard Egerer
Seven Seas Club
Bridge Street
Castries, Tel: 2168

Mr. S. M. Robinson
P.O. Box 131
Castries

Mr. Robert Elliot
Lunar Park
Vigie, Castries

For the **skindiving** fisherman, the reefs that surround the island also offer an unusual challenge, for they are almost unexplored. With the exception of aqua-lung tanks, most equipment is available locally. Shipwrecks have supposedly been sighted in St. Lucia waters, particularly around Pigeon Island. Boats for skindiving trips may be chartered from Mr. William Hackshaw and from St. Lucia Yacht Charters (see above).

St. Lucia has now become a major **yacht charter** center in the Caribbean. A number of craft make the island their home port and are available for cruises to the nearby French islands of Marti-nique, Guadeloupe, and Saintes; the Grenadines and all of the Leeward and Windward islands; and for skindiving, fishing and day sailing trips around St. Lucia. Information can be obtained from:

Vagabond Cruises
Captain W. C. Boudreau
Yacht Haven Hotel
P.O. Box 194, Marigot Bay

St. Lucia Yacht Charters
P.O. Box 83, Castries

Mr. Richard Egerer
c/o Seven Seas Club
P.O. Box 193, Castries

Dr. Nels Johnson
The Reef Marina
Pointe Seraphine
Castries, Tel. 2546

Mrs. Grace Ganter
Privateer Marine Services
P.O. Box 188
Petit Carenage, Castries

For **swimming,** the beach nearest to Castries is Vigie Beach, a five-minute drive by car. Other nearby beaches are Rat Island, Choc and Reduit.

Best shopping buys

There are no free-port shops in St. Lucia though duty-free liquor may be purchased at some stores. The articles to look for are British imports, on which the duty is low. Native goods include bandana headdresses, straw hats, tortoise-shell goods, pottery, hand-printed fabrics and some primitive art.

The Bagshaws, a studio-workshop "com-plex" overlooking the sea at La Toc, is the place where the knowledgeable vis-itor heads to buy that "something dif-ferent." Designs are silk screened onto linens from Ireland, silks from India and cottons from England and the U.S. These fabrics are then transformed into shifts, beach wear, casual day clothes, cocktail pajamas, unusual hats and linen place mats.

Dine and dance

In and around Castries:
Alleyne's Midway Cocktail Lounge & Restaurant: Tel: 2554
Minvielle & Chastanet's Cafeteria: Tel: 2811
Diamond Slipper: Tel: 2820
The Calabash: Tel. 2864
Seven Seas Club: Tel: 2168
The Flamingo: Tel: 2398
Gaiety Club: Tel: 2696
Blue Danube Club: Tel: 2381
Blue Waters Beach Hotel: Tel: 2427
The Reef: Tel: 2546
St. Lucia Beach Hotel: Tel: 2728

Most of these restaurants also have cocktail lounges, and there is dancing on weekends and holidays at the Havana

Club (Tel: 2135), the Malabar Beach Hotel (Tel: 2533), Diamond Slipper, Gaiety Club, Blue Danube Club, The Reef, Camelot and St. Lucia Beach Hotel.

Days of wine and roses and daisies

New Year's Day: Colorful old French fete, *Le Jour de L'an*, on Columbus Square, Castries. Excursions from neighboring islands. Dances at all clubs. Celebration continues through Jan. 2.

Cricket Season: Begins in February.

Carnival: Dances at all clubs, parades around Castries to steel band accompaniment, crowning of Carnival Queen. February.

Constitution Day: Public holiday. March 1.

Good Friday: Public holiday. April 12.

Labor Day: Public holiday. May 1.

Whitsuntide: Public holiday. June 2.

Queen's Birthday: Public holiday marked by military parades. Second Saturday in June.

Football Season: Begins in July.

Art, Music and Drama Festival: Sponsored by St. Lucia Art Guild. July.

Bastille Day: Celebrations organized by Alliance Francaise. July 14.

Emancipation: Bank holiday. First Monday in August.

Fete La Rose Flower Festival: Feast day of St. Rose de Lima, celebrations in country districts. August 30.

Hunting Season: Begins September 1.

Drum Dances: Begin in country districts on October 1.

Thanksgiving Day: Harvest festivals in the Anglican and Methodist Churches. Public holiday. First Monday in October.

Fete La Marguerete Flower Festival: Celebrations in country districts. October 17.

St. Lucia Day: Public holiday. Aquatic sports. December 13.

Boxing Day: Public holiday. Picnics, dances at all clubs. December 26.

Old Year's Day: Dances at hotels and clubs. December 31.

Meet the St. Lucians

Organization	Official	Phone
Amateur & Athletic Assn.	Charles Augustin	2135
Cricket Assn.	Miss Alicia John	
Basketball Assn.	Miss E. T. Bouty	2841
Yacht Club	Owen King	2327
Netball Assn.	Miss E. T. Bouty	2841
Football Assn.	Burke King	2497
Shamrock Sports Club	John Bristol	2449
Southern Sports Club	L. Auguste	(Vieux Fort)
Ambulance Assn.	David Chase	2607
Chamber of Commerce	C. S. Chase	2785
Jr. Chamber of Commerce	Victor Girard	2230
Red Cross Assn.	Sir Garnet Gordon	2366
Women's Assn.	Mrs. Vincent Floissac	2761
Boy's Brigade	Hiram Isaac	
Nurses Assn.	Miss Jean Isaac	(Vieux Fort)
Police Welfare Assn.	James Nicholls	2284
Press Club	W. St. Clair Daniel	2781, 2599, 2346
Civil Service Assn.	Dr. Graham Louisy	2688
Teachers Union	Irvin Dupres	(Micoud)
Arts Guild	Kenneth Monplaisir	2713, 2182, 2251
Catholic Youth Org.	Benton George	34
National Youth Council	A. Glasgow	2747

Organization	Official	Phone
Anglican Young Peoples Assn.	Miss Patricia James	
Vide Bouteille Cultural Club	Stanley Phillips	
Mental Health Assn.	Julian Hunte	2230
Young Wives Assn.	Mrs. Edward Kent	2473
Anglican Mothers Union	Mrs. H. B. Collymore	2249
V.S.A.D.C.	J. A. Belgrave	2377
Progressive Youth League	Melvin Martial	2650
Boy Scouts Assn.	Winville King	2430
Horticultural Society	S. B. Mullings	2344
Young Farmers Club	Miss Agnes Leonce	(Micoud)
Methodist Youth Fellowship	Miss Cathleen Simmons	2323
Paragons	H. Haynes	
Catholic Boys Club	Timothy James	2854
Wooden Spoon Club	Miss Gail Augustin	(Soufrière)
Anse-La-Raye Social & Cultural Club	Mr. Lamontage	
Girl Guides Assn.	Mrs. Volmar Monplaisir	2101
Employers Federation	M. C. Salle-Miquelle	2709
Alliance Francaise	Madame Le Jeune	
Bar Assn.	Sir Garnet Gordon	2366

Real estate and retirement

Large-scale land development is a relatively new happening under the St. Lucian sun. The island's climate, beauty and accessible beaches are strong arguments for the promotion of vacation and retirement homes, and several companies are now in operation.

One of the most ambitious projects is being developed by the Grand Anse Beach Company, Ltd., which has 2,000 acres on the northeast coast. The company has contracted to deed to Club Santa Lucia, Ltd., a 760-acre tract of land as the site for a 100-suite hotel, golf course, cottage sites and recreational facilities. There is a mile-long sandy beach on the property.

The hotel will be built from sales of shares to 450 club members at $3,950 per share which entitles the buyer to club privileges, dividends from the hotel operation and a share in profits from real estate sales. Each member will have the use of a suite for two persons for a 30-day period at any time during the year at a 50% discount from the regular charge. Friends or relatives of members may spend 30 days between April 15 and December 15 at a 50% discount. Further information may be obtained by writing Caribbean Riviera, Inc., P.O. Box N, Christiansted, St. Croix, U.S. Virgin Islands.

Courbaril Park is part of a private estate close to Castries that is being developed as a residential area. Some 79 house sites have been surveyed, each approximately 3/4 of an acre. The whole property consists of 260 acres, but only 90 acres are being developed. The remainder will be open pasture lands, with an area reserved for a golf course. There is a safe anchorage, and an extensive beach. Further details may be obtained from Trade Winds Land Co., Ltd., P.O. Box 34, Castries.

In the northern part of St. Lucia, Cap Estate spreads over 2,000 acres of pasture land, rolling hills, sandy beaches and mountains. The estate, which is being developed for private homes, includes a working ranch and will have an 18-hole golf course and club house. Each house will stand in its own spacious grounds and will be individually designed by the purchaser or his architect. The cost of land for residences, with sites from one acre upwards, is from $7,000, with ocean-front plots from $15,400. Write: Cap Estate, St. Lucia.

The Morne Development Housing Scheme, a government-sponsored project, is situated approximately 800 feet above sea level and two miles from Castries.

Over 300 lots (5,000 to 20,000 sq. feet) are available for sale at 30¢ per sq. foot. Roads, water and electricity are guaranteed by the government. At least five acres in the center of the project will be set aside for public parks and tennis lawns.

Real estate agents in Castries who can supply up-to-date information on housing are:

Carl G. D. LaCorbiniere
Castries

Louis G. Augier McVane
Bridge St.

Geoffrey Hunt, Manager
St. Lucia Real Estate Agency
P.O. Box 292

Commerce and industry

Agriculture is still the staple industry in St. Lucia but tourism is giving this small windward island its spot in the sun. Although St. Lucia was a relatively late starter in the resort business, several new and fairly large hotels have been added in recent years, more are planned and yachting facilities are being enhanced.

Principal industry is still banana growing, accounting for over 80% of the island's export. Copra and cocoa production are also important agricultural factors on the island though a decline in the price of cocoa has necessitated a major cutback in recent years. The government hopes to make more land available to higher-income crops, such as bananas, and improve local marketing facilities and sources of credit to farmers.

In an effort to attract light industry to the island, the government offers investment incentives such as income tax holidays, tariff concessions, special aid to hotels and carryover of losses. More detailed itemization of these concessions is available from the Ministry of Trade and Industries, Castries. St. Lucia has good roads despite its unusual topography, two airports and an excellent harbor with docking facilities for ships up to 10,000 tons.

WHERE TO STAY — In St. Lucia

	Plan	Dec. 15-April 14 U. S. Currency Double	Single	April 15-Dec. 14 Double	Single
BLUE WATERS BEACH Vigie Beach (27 Rms.) **(b)**	(MAP)	$30	$16	$28	$14
EAST WINDS INN La Brellotte Bay (6 Rms.) **(b)**	(EP)	$20	$17	$10	$ 8.50
MALABAR BEACH (20 Rms.) **(b)**	(EP)	$30	$25	$18	$12
MARIGOT des ROSEAUX Marigot Bay (12 Rms.)	(AP) (MAP)	$34 $30	$24 $22	$24 $20	$16 $14
REEF Castries (10 Rms.)	(MAP)	$42	$24	$28	$16
ST. ANTOINE Castries (16 Rms.)	(MAP)	$24–32	$14–20	$18–24	$10–12
ST. JAMES GUEST HOUSE nr. Castries (11 Rms.)	(AP)	$11–14	$ 6– 8	$11–14	$ 6– 8
ST. LUCIA BEACH Castries (68 Rms.) **(b)**	(MAP)	$52	$40	$30	$16
VILLA Castries (33 Rms.)	(MAP)	$22–32	$12–18	$16–26	$ 9–14

YACHT HAVEN	(AP)	$44	$30	Hotel Closed
Marigot Bay	(MAP)	$40	$27	(May 3-Nov. 14)
(13 Rms.) (b)				

LEGEND FOR HOTEL LISTINGS: (AP) American Plan (room and 3 meals); **MAP)** Modified American Plan (room, breakfast and dinner); **(CP)** Continental Plan (room and breakfast); **(EP)** European Plan (room only). All rates quoted on a per-day basis and subject to change. Confirmed reservations at specific rates desired are always recommended.
HOTEL FACILITIES: (b) beach; **(p)** pool; **(t)** tennis; **(g)** golf.

Marigot Bay, on the island of St. Lucia, is one of the most beautiful anchorages in the Caribbean

SINT MAARTEN / ST. MARTIN

Those on the Dutch side of the island spell it Sint Maarten. On the French side it's St. Martin. This constitutes about the most serious difference of opinion among the inhabitants of this small, pleasant and hospitable island. There is no border as such between the Dutch and the French sectors and everybody wanders back and forth at will.

Designing for the tourist

The half-Dutch, half-French island of St. Martin has long enjoyed a reputation for hospitality. The people are friendly and welcoming to visitors, but unfortunately they have not been able to welcome them in large numbers because there were relatively few places to put them.

This state of affairs is now changing, with the help of Dutch, French, Canadian and U. S. money. At any given time in this small island there are tourism projects in midconstruction, projects about to begin, projects almost completed, projects on the drawing board, projects being "seriously discussed" and "dormant" projects being revitalized.

Most of the island's small hotels are tacking on rooms Habitat-style or adding an upstairs mirador. New construction encompasses hotels, a restaurant, office buildings and seaside homesite developments with all the modern resort accouterments from roulette to Roumanian pastrami. For specific expansions of hotel facilities in and around Philipsburg, on the Dutch side, here's the rundown: The CARAVANSERAI has jumped from 17 to 19 rooms; PASANGGRAHAN GUEST HOUSE has expanded from 12 to 18 rooms; the SEA VIEW HOTEL has added an annex bringing its total to 31 rooms; and MARY'S FANCY has added two rooms for an even dozen.

The GALLERY, a crisp new arcade of shops and offices on Front Street, has allocated space for a mini-restaurant, THE CAPTAIN'S TABLE. Managed by Bud Vass (formerly manager of the Pasanggrahan, and the Captain's Quarters on Saba), the Captain's Table has six tables and offers two sittings per meal. Specialty of the house: Brazilian and East Indian dishes.

The jewelry shop chain of SPRITZER & FUHRMANN now has two elegant free-port shops on Front Street. One's a stone's throw from the other. S & F maintains a small gift shop-boutique at Juliana Airport and another emporium is planned.

Even the *Stad Huis*, the courthouse-city hall on Front Street (dating back to 1783) is undergoing a meticulous restoration. And an ambitious fellow named Valentin Flanders, a resident of the island's French side, has constructed Philipsburg's first cinema for showing new Hollywood 35 mm. products. Before construction was completed M. Flanders decided to make

Philipsburg, the capital of the Dutch island of Sint Maarten, stretches between salt flats and the Caribbean Sea

the tourism scene. He swiftly redesigned his theater building to include four guest rooms.

While most of the undertakings are on the Dutch side (Sint Maarten) a single project on the French side (St. Martin), under the direction of Claude C. Philippe, the renowned restaurateur-maître 'd, overshadows—in scope and imagination—just about anything being done in the Caribbean. It is a striking seaside resort complex in the style of an 18th-century French provincial village. If M. Philippe does pull it off as his blueprints show, it could emerge as one of the resort jewels of the hemisphere.

The building boom here is no surprise to Caribbean tourism pundits. They have been insisting for a decade now that the island is "a natural" and certain to emerge one of the "big winners."

It takes no genius to analyze the island's investment plus factors. St. Martin has been peaceful for centuries; no political-social-economic upsets to impede development. There is the lovely tradition of Dutch cleanliness and orderliness on one side. On the other there's the French flair for cuisine and *joie de vivre*. The beaches can be classified generally as good to superb.

American, British, French and Canadian entrepreneurs are getting involved with gusto, thanks to the absence of linguistic frustrations. The British were among the island's early settlers, which explains why English is

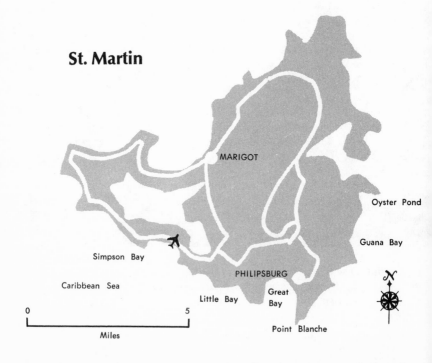

St. Martin

generally spoken. (One meets many St. Martinians with British and Irish names.)

St. Martinians are hard-working and very much aware of the new day that's dawning. One encounters little resentment or anxiety about "outside" money interests. There is some concern, though, that there may emerge a certain incongruity in architectural forms, while attempting to up-date traditional motifs with contemporary Caribbean designs. The effect, some fear, could displace the island's traditional characteristics and centuries-old charm.

French and Dutch citizens of St. Martin have been getting along amicably since 1648 when the momentous Partition Treaty of Mount Concordia was signed. There have been long periods in the past when border demarcations were lost or simply ignored and times when many people were not quite certain to which nationality they owed their allegiance. It was of little significance to the islanders until European mercantile interests bullied them into upholding their inalienable and patriotic rights.

Despite historic compatibility intermarriage between the French and Dutch is surprisingly rare. In Sint Maarten they marry their own and later sigh: "The lass always looks keener on the other side." Married bachelors in St. Martin who maintain *amour clandestine* on Dutch soil will remark: "Better one of theirs."

Meteorologically speaking, the grass *is* greener on the French side. Weather patterns indicate that cloud formations collect on the Dutch side (which is dryer) but the rain falls on the French.

The Dutch are slightly sardonic about this: "God has to be good to them a little more. Our government helps us." The implication is borne out in better roads, schools, and the accelerated economic growth one observes on the Dutch side.

While the British were among the first settlers, the Dutch concentrated their efforts on controlling the key harbor. The Dutch West India Company, instrumental in establishing a colony, was concerned exclusively with trade and shipping.

Incidentally, the French settled the northwest sector of the island for reasons less romantic than legends indicate. It was a case of military necessity. When the French took St. Kitts from the English, they found they had to worry about reprisal from both the north and south. British naval forces defeated at St. Kitts retreated south to their stronghold in Antigua. The French were equally terrified of an attack that might be staged from British-held Anguilla, located directly north of St. Martin. (Armchair admirals, see map.) By occupying the northwest section of St. Martin, the French reasoned they could keep a battle eye on Anguilla and dismiss fears of simultaneous attack from the south—inasmuch as the southern part was Dutch territory.

History lesson over. Back to the constructive present.

Bright as a new Dutch pfennig, SIMPSON BAY VILLAGE HOTEL opened the initial section of a $3 million resort early in 1968. Located on the beach at Simpson Bay (five miles west of Philipsburg), this charmingly modern resort facility was designed by architect William Sigal of Puerto Rico in association with developer Dr. C. B. McDonald and Sint Maarten hotelier Sam Hazel. When completed in mid-1969 it will contain a total of 150 rooms, a marina and gambling casino.

At nearby Oyster Pond, on the island's south-central coast, a yacht-club community called DAWN BEACH CLUB ESTATES is taking form on some 300 acres. A project of the Oyster Bay Development Co., it is headed by Earl Bodin who hopes to provide "a tranquil anchorage for yachts" in the protected harbor of Oyster Bay. Approximately 100 homesite lots (½ to ¾ of an acre) range in price from $7,000 to $14,000. A half mile of protected white sand beach, great for swimming and snorkeling, runs along the project's sea border. Yacht-club facilities are expected to be ready the latter part of 1968, followed by the establishment of a separate tennis club and small hilltop hotel overlooking the coastline.

Just south of Oyster Pond, on the east coast, is the graciously sloping GUANA BAY DEVELOPMENT. This 100-acre project, two miles out of Philipsburg, is offering lots (from one to four acres) selling from $7,500 to $15,000. The project includes a dozen duplex townhouses on the beach fashioned in stucco and shingles. The big news on this slope is that veteran jazzman Benny Goodman and family have built a getaway home in Guana Bay.

CAY BAY HILL ESTATES, the closest real estate development to Philipsburg, is a 180-acre tract that fronts on the east coast beach at Little Bay. The island's first golf course (nine-holes) is to be built alongside Little Bay Pond. Homesites just less than an acre are selling for $10,000–$15,000, according to Rudy Neuss who is directing the Cay Bay Hill project in association with Max Donner and Lew Berkman. Space has been allocated, too, for a 120-room beachside hotel to be constructed sometime in 1969.

Two more rather elaborate projects on the Dutch side are still in blue-print-and-talking stages. The CASTEL SINT MAARTIN's hotel-villa-casino development, a $4-million promotion of Metropolitan Development N.V., is headed by Brigadier Claude H. Dewhurst of Toronto. Situated on the island's southernmost Point Blanche, the plan is to turn the site into a "Mediterranean-like" village with about 100 dwellings, casino and restaurant-lounge on the road that winds down to the deep-water harbor of Point Blanche.

Also in discussion stages is a mammoth New York State-style resort at MAHO BAY (near Juliana Airport). The Dutch government has offered the site to Ray Parker, managing director of the popular 2,000-room Concord Hotel at Kiamesha Lake, New York. As of early 1968 no contracts were signed, no money has exchanged hands. (Background: Ray Parker, a sage Catskill Mountain hotelier, spent a good deal of time in 1965 attempting to link up parcels of land near Luquillo Beach which is on Puerto Rico's north coast. Complications arose, negotiations failed. Mr. Parker took his ideas to Sint Maarten.)

On the beach at the far end of Great Bay, HOTEL BON BINI (meaning "welcome" in Papiamento) was begun in 1965. Financial difficulties put a stop to construction when the hotel was half built. Negotiations to refinance the project were expected to be completed early in 1968, and if so the project should be completed by the end of 1968, with either 130 or 170 rooms, a pool and restaurant-lounge.

On the French side of the island there is news about the restaurant, the old hotel, the new hotel, and the grand project of Claude Philippe.

BEAU SEJOUR is the delightful little restaurant in Marigot. It holds fast to its reputation among gourmets as the best in the island. The hotel on the French side is LE PIRATE, with 12 rooms on the beach. A mile or so out of Marigot, it has an easygoing, windswept mood about it. It also has a reputation for attracting artistic types. To quote a few comments concerning *Le Pirate:* "Its guests are unconventional artistic types" . . . "Those who grow beards and wear sandals" . . . "Brainy ones." We gave the hotel a casual once-over and noted only determined sit-ins at the bar and some loaf-ins at the beach. Guests were as touristy-looking as tourists anywhere.

The new hotel LA PARIS, at Gallows Bay (on the edge of Marigot) opens officially early in 1968. Its architecture is a strange (yet strangely satisfying) composite of modern and traditional. The hotel's 37 rooms are antique-filled and each is dominated by a classic fourposter rigged to the ceiling with frilly fabrics.

Finally there is Claude Philippe's French provincial village. It is so elaborate a resort—at least in blueprint form—that one wonders if three-century-old Marigot, three miles away, is destined to become a ghost town in its shadow.

Hotel de la Pointe des Pierres a Chaux translates loosely as hotel and yacht club at Pebble Point. (It may be named simply La France.) The resort village is to provide deluxe accommodations in the form of 270 rooms and duplex suites, many with patios. The neo-medieval complex is to include a casino, restaurant, cinema theater, tennis courts, and an 18-hole golf course. Alongside the hotel is a 2½-acre natural swimming pool, fashioned (blasted and cemented) from an arc of coral reef at the shore. All of this may take architects Ballard, Todd, Inc. of New York three or four, or maybe five years, if you include plans for a marina in similar stone-covered, 18th-century design. Approximately 100 rooms are expected to be ready early in 1968. Rates? About $65 per person per day—with meals à la Claude Philippe. M. Philippe, one of New York's cuisine kingpins, was associated with the Waldorf-Astoria Hotel for many years and more recently he has been operating the Le Pavilion restaurant in New York City.

Still another touch being considered is a ferry linking this village, on Marigot Bay, with Juliana Airport, across three miles of Simpson Bay Lagoon.

The sight of this stone-faced cluster of 18th-century buildings and archways from the water should be nothing short of breathtaking.

—*Al Dinhofer*

Instant facts

Location: About 150 miles east of Puerto Rico.

Population: About 10,000, more than half of them French.

Capital: Philipsburg (Dutch), Marigot (French).

Nationality: With Saba and Sint Eustatius, Sint Maarten is one of the Netherlands Antilles windward islands, an autonomous part of the Kingdom of the Netherlands. The French side of the island spells it St. Martin and this sector is a dependency of the French department of Guadeloupe. There is complete freedom of movement between the two sections.

Language: Dutch and French, though English is widely spoken.

Currency: The Netherlands Antilles guilder (53¢ U.S.) and the New Franc (20¢ U.S.).

Documentation: International certificate of vaccination, passport or other identification required by all except citizens of the Netherlands and France.

Climate & Clothes: Average temperature is 80°. The coolest month, January, is all of two degrees below that and September "simmers" at an average of 83°. Not much rain falls, though what does falls mostly in November and December. Days are usually sunny and refreshed by trade winds, nights cool. Dress is very casual—sportswear even in town (short shorts not included) and only in a few night spots are jacket and tie necessary.

Food: Thanks to the dual nature of Sint Maarten/St. Martin, the cuisine runs the gamut from superb French dishes to exotic Dutch–West Indian cookery.

Geography: Of the 37 sq. miles, 16 belong to the Dutch and 21 to the French. The island resembles an oddly shaped swiss cheese as its coastline is ringed with bays, some almost entirely landlocked, and a salt pond cuts a hole near the southern shore.

History: Columbus named the island after St. Martin of Tours, whose feast day corresponded with its discovery on November 11, 1493. The island was variously settled by the French, English, Dutch, Spanish and Portuguese but none of them stayed for long. When the Spanish departed, they left behind a party of French and Dutch seamen. The legend of how the island was divided goes this way: a Frenchman and Dutchman were to walk around the island. Where they met, a boundary would be drawn. The stout Dutchman was slower, but he included the better harbor and the most fertile land in his part. Whatever did happen, the settlers signed a compact, the Mont des Accords, on March 24, 1648, and have coexisted amiably ever since.

Who flies here

St. Martin has direct flights from:

New York: Pan Am. Round trip: $208–$282; 17-day excursion $161–$227.

San Juan: Caribair, Air France. Round trip: $48–$71; 17-day excursion $32–$50.

Besides the above airlines, ALM, Air Antilles, LIAT and Windward Island Airways make regular trips to islands throughout the Caribbean.

Island transportation

If you choose to rent a **car** during your stay, rates are about $12 a day (unlimited mileage) for a Volkswagen. There are several agencies in Philipsburg:

Ridson's Car Rentals
Tel: 2378

Reward Rentals
Tel: 2323

St. Maarten Motors
Tel: 2354

Carengie Rent-a-Car
Tel: 2397

Acme Self Drive Cars
Tel: 2204

Simca Drive-U-Self
Barnes & Son, Tel: 2384

In Marigot, Hertz representatives are Martincars S.A.R.L., rue Gourbeyre (Tel: 34). Models include such mini-cars as Renault, Volkswagen, Peugeot and jeeps at $12 a day or $10 when rented by the week. Mileage is unlimited.

Taxis have set rates; for example, $3.25 round trip from Philipsburg to Marigot, $2.70 from the airport to Philipsburg and $2.45 from the airport to Marigot. Tours cost $4 for the first hour and $1 for every additional 15 minutes. A three-hour tour is $10, a four-hour tour $11 and an eight-hour tour $22. Taxi fares are higher in the evening and much higher after midnight.

Water sports

There are many good **beaches** all around the island. **Fishing** is also good here but bring your own gear—only string and fresh bait available. Best catches include dolphin (March–July), wahoo, marlin, tuna and Atlantic bonito (September). Tropical fish are also plentiful for avid spearfishermen.

Center for all water sports is Island Water World, run by Jeff Adams. This enterprising seaside executive can arrange charter boats for island sightseeing, picnics, snorkeling, fishing, water skiing, scuba diving and sailing. Instruction is optional. Island Water World also rents Sunfish and Sailfish for sailing buffs and Hydro-Mite one-man power boats. The boating center is located in Philipsburg on Front St. (next to the town's pier) and at Little Bay Hotel. Of special interest to accomplished divers is an underwater tour of an 18th-century frigate, under 50 feet of water since running aground in 1801.

Best shopping buys

The shopping here is among the best in the Caribbean as both sides of the island are free ports offering great bargains. In Philipsburg, all the stores are on Front St. except for one at Little Bay Hotel. Liquor and cigarette prices are rock-bottom and there are many fine imports from Europe and around the world: Swiss watches, cameras, exotic paraphernalia from the Orient, jewelry and designer apparel.

There are also fine buys on the French side in Marigot, though on a smaller scale. Best selection here, of course, is in French scents.

Dining, dancing and night life

In Sint Maarten—The Caravanserai: On Maho Beach. Continental and West Indian cooking. If you choose to do some fishing before lunch the restaurant will prepare your catch. Dancing to steel band. Tel: 3214.

China Night Restaurant: Back St., Philipsburg. Chinese and local food. Tel: 2375.

Europe Restaurant and Bottle Club: Juliana Airport. French food. Tel: 3215.

Flying Dutchman: Front St., Philipsburg. Lunch (noon–3 P.M.), dinner (7–9 P.M.) and late snacks (9 P.M.–midnight). Specialties include East and West Indian dishes as well as continental cooking. Beer garden setting complete with snackbar, restaurant and nightclub (local combos, steel bands perform several nights a week). Bar open whenever you're thirsty. Buffet featuring West Indian dishes Thursday 7–9 P.M. Reservations recommended for dinner. Tel: 2378.

Little Bay Beach Hotel & Casino: At Little Bay. Music while dining, after-dinner movies. Free drinks while watching the wheel spin at the Las Vegas Casino. Air-conditioned Peter Stuyvesant Bar. Nightly entertainment and dancing. Tel: 2337/8.

Pasanggrahan Hotel: On Great Bay Beach, near the center of Philipsburg. Lounge, cocktail bar, dining room. Tel: 2388.

Seaview Hotel & Bar: Front St., Philipsburg. Dining al fresco, continental cuisine. Tel: 2324.

All the hotels and guest houses have their own restaurants and bars. Reservations should usually be made in advance for dining.

In St. Martin—Hotel Le Pirate: Marigot. French cuisine at their restaurant, drinks in Bar Le Pirate. Tel: 38.

Tackling's Restaurant: Grand Case. French cooking. Bar.

Beau Sejour: Marigot. French cuisine. Great reputation.

Special events, festivals

New Year's Day: Cockfights, French side. Dancing. January 1.

Easter Monday: Cockfights, French side. Dancing. April 15.

Queen Juliana's Birthday: Sports events, parades, fireworks. April 30.

Labour Day: Sports events, parades, dances. May 1.

Sint Maarten's Day: Celebrated jointly by both sides. Ceremonies at the border, sports events, dances. November 11.

Kingdom's Day: Sports, dancing. December 15.

Boxing Day: Second day of Christmas. Cockfights, French side. Dancing. December 26.

Meet the people of Sint Maarten

Organization	Official	Phone
Antillean Girl Guides	Miss Elfleday Brown	
Blitz Cricket Club	Sam Hazel	2309
Boys Brigade	Kenneth Richardson	
Boy Scouts	Dave Hodge	2204
Colebay Girls League	Mrs. P. Cannegieter	
Colebay Womens League	Mrs. A. Bell	
Cubs	Miss Joan Bergland	
Girl Guides	Miss Philomena Watkins	
Methodist Girls League	Miss S. B. Cannegieter	
Methodist Womens League	Mrs. O. A. Illidge	
Orange Benevolent Improvement Assn.	Mrs. Mildred James	
Philipsburg Mutual Improvement Assn.	Alexis Arnell	2360
Sea Scouts	Kitchner Rogers	
Eleven Brothers Football Team	Witfield Vlaun	
Panam Jets Baseball Team	J. Williams	3235

Real estate and retirement

There is, happily, no personal property tax and no income tax on income from outside the island in Sint Maarten. Inheritance taxes are low and apply only to property on the island. In St. Martin, Mrs. Janet Mansen in Marigot knows what housing is up for sale or rent. French income taxes prevail—and they are high. These agents in Philipsburg can supply exact information on housing availability and property costs:

Gay Hill Associates
Mr. Rudy Neuss

Oyster Pond Development Corp.
Mr. Earl C. Bodine

Guana Bay Development
Mr. Richard Soskin

Commerce and industry

A few short years ago the island saw a few hundred visitors at the most trickle in. Today it is becoming an important tourist haven. Most of this growth has been restricted to the Dutch side but in the last year or so the French, formerly bogged down in Gallic red tape and commercial indifference, have been scurrying to catch up. Current and projected land reclamations and road paving projects, and a desalinization plant to augment the water supply, have created a hospitable climate for light industry. Lack of duty, favorable tax rates and tax incentives make Sint Maarten an attractive investment area. Further information on investment possibilities is available from the office of the Netherlands Antilles administration, Philipsburg, St. Maarten

WHERE TO STAY —
In St. Martin/Sint Maarten

	Plan	Dec. 15-April 14 U. S. Currency		April 15-Dec. 14	
		Double	Single	Double	Single
LE PIRATE	(AP)	$27–30	$14–16	$27–30	$14–16
St. Martin (Marigot)	(EP)	$12–15	$ 8–10	$12–15	$ 8–10
(12 Rms.) **(b)**					
CAPT. HODGE'S	(AP)	$24–26	$12–15	$24–26	$12–15
GUEST HOUSE Philipsburg (10 Rms.) **(b)**					
THE CARAVANSERAI	(AP)	$48–55	$30–38	$35–40	$24–28
Maho Beach (17 Rms.) **(b, p)**					
HUNTER HOUSE	(AP)	$34	$22	$26	$16
(8 Rms.) **(b)**					
LIDO	(CP)	$15	$ 9	$15	$ 9
Sint Maarten (5 Rms.) **(b)**					
LITTLE BAY	(MAP)	$48–58	$38–48	$29–36	$19–24
Little Bay (105 Rms.) **(b, p, t)**					
MARY'S FANCY	(AP)	$36	$26	$24	$14
Sint Maarten (12 Rms.) **(p)**					
PASANGGRAHAN	(AP)	$26–30	$18–20	$24–28	$16–18
Philipsburg (12 Rms.) **(b)**					
PRINCE'S QUARTER	(AP)	$30	$21	$24	$17
Sint Maarten (13 Rms.)	(CP)	$24	$15	$19	$13
SEA VIEW	(AP)	$38	$20	$28	$17
Sint Maarten (31 Rms.) **(b)**					
SIMSON BAY VILLAGE Partial completion scheduled for Jan. 1968					
Philipsburg (150 Rms.) **(b, p)**					

   LEGEND FOR HOTEL LISTINGS: (AP) American Plan (room
and 3 meals); **MAP)** Modified American Plan (room, breakfast
and dinner); **(CP)** Continental Plan (room and breakfast); **(EP)**
European Plan (room only). All rates quoted on a per-day
basis and subject to change. Confirmed reservations at specific rates desired are always recommended.
   HOTEL FACILITIES: (b) beach; **(p)** pool; **(t)** tennis; **(g)** golf.

*Boats are beached almost on the street at Kingstown
on the island of St. Vincent*

ST. VINCENT

Of all the islands of the Caribbean, St. Vincent is the one said most to resemble Tahiti. There are thickly forested volcanic mountain peaks, rivers and streams and waterfalls and dramatic views of sea and shore. St. Vincent is where boating is better than driving, picking fruit ripe from the trees more appealing than shopping, and lounging in gardens more popular than catching the new show at the latest night spot. You can, if you wish, go whaling.

Breadfruit and arrowroot

St. Vincent and Grenada are in many ways alike: in size, shape and terrain; in population; in their mixed cultural heritage of African, French and British. Confusingly, they are alike even in the location of their capitals and adjoining resort areas on their southwestern coasts.

Both islands are in the process of coming around the corner from the old days of colonial "plantocracy." But St. Vincent is making the turn more slowly and is considerably behind in all-round development. One reason is that it is having trouble with its basic agriculture. If Grenada is The Spice Island, St. Vincent is The Arrowroot Island, far and away the world's largest producer of this starchy plant. But of late, for various reasons, the market has fallen off. Arrowroot has been overproduced, and the resultant pinch has been serious.

Another problem, more directly involved with tourism—and totally unsolvable—is that, because of long volcanic activity, most of St. Vincent's beaches are not white but black. And dazzling sands traditionally rank as the *sine qua non* of tropical resorts.

As on all islands, there is an Old Guard who doesn't much care; they would be happy if the tourists stayed away. But there are others, more numerous and more realistic, who are working hard for a "new" St. Vincent. One is Fred J. Dare, originally of Lebanon, now the island's leading merchant, general entrepreneur, and a member of its Tourist Board. Others are Pat Huggins, the Board's secretary; George King, its omniscient driver-guide; and Gerry Palmer, realtor and hotel man. They may not be able to sell milady in her bikini on the delights of black beaches, but they have other assets aplenty with which to work and succeed.

To begin with, there is Kingstown, a town of authentic, if rickety, charm; and its marketplace on Saturday is one of the liveliest spots in the West Indies. Its Anglican and Catholic churches, cheek-by-jowl a few blocks inland, are edifices to make an architect, or even a casual passerby, gape. And old Fort Charlotte, high on a neighboring headland, surveys a shining sweep of green mountain and blue sea.

Behind the town is St. Vincent's Botanic Garden, oldest in the Western Hemisphere and a wondrous pageant of tropical vegetation. Among its prime exhibits is a lineal descendant of one of the original breadfruit seedlings that Captain Bligh transported to the Caribbean from Tahiti; for it was here that he brought them on his post-*Bounty* voyage in the *Providence*.

Back on the waterfront the scene changes drastically. Here is not past but present and future, embodied in a big deep-water wharf, recently given to St. Vincent by the Canadian Government. Alongside, when I was there, was the *Maple*, one of twin passenger-cargo ships (the other is the *Palm*) that ply through the length of the British West Indies. Besides them, presently, other ships will be coming in greater numbers than ever before; cruise ships, tourist ships, carrying the import St. Vincent needs most of all.

As to where the "import" will stay, once ashore, there is still not great choice. In town there is the Blue Caribbean Hotel, pleasant but primarily commercial. Out on the southwest coast, lush and lovely, are Villa Lodge, Grand View and, notably, Blue Lagoon, all on bold promontories above the sea. Still higher and somewhat inland (with a swimming pool to compensate) is Sugar Mill Inn, oldest and best known of St. Vincent hotels. As run by

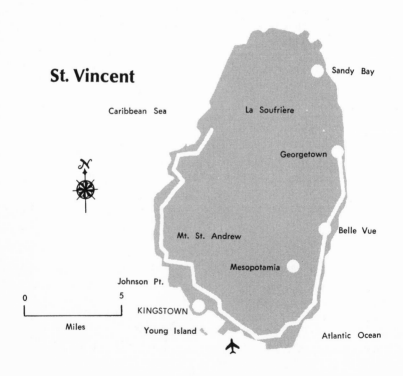

Gerry and Jeanne Palmer, it is very good, plus very English—the only place I encountered in the islands that serves you morning tea in your bedroom. And its landscaped hillside rivals the Botanic Gardens in flowering color.

This leaves Young Island: very new and very special. Situated on an islet of the same name, two hundred yards off the mainland, it is a small but luxurious resort-in-itself, built in the style of a Polynesian village (with improvements) and rimmed by one of the few fine beaches in St. Vincent. To date, it is the only local hotel with amenities, and rates, comparable to those of the top-drawer places on mainline islands.

All St. Vincent's other hoteliers—and many of their guests—are English, Canadian or Anglo-West Indian. But, perhaps not incidentally, Young Island's proprietor is an American. Specifically, he is John Houser, an ex-executive of both American Express and Hilton International, who, weary of package tours and high-rise pleasure domes, decided to build a nonpackaged low-rise retreat to his personal taste. Here is a vote from one visitor that his taste is impeccable.

North and east from Kingstown, hotels and such vanish so completely that for an all-day tour you must bring a picnic lunch. Driving the coastal roads, you pass wide acreages of peanuts, bananas, and, of course, arrowroot, the last sometimes full-grown but left to rot for lack of a market. Then, inland, come the valleys and mountains. They are deeper and higher than Grenada's, wilder and greener. Almost inevitably, as you thread them, rain will fall, but only briefly. There is deluge, then sunburst. The land steams and gleams.

Toward the northern end of the island the roads peter out into tracks. Streams brawl down from the heights, and interspersed with them are black lava flows; for here, 4,000 feet above, is the volcano Soufrière, highest peak on the island. Soufrière last erupted in 1902, a few days after Mt. Pelée's terrible explosion in Martinique, killing some 2,000 persons, as against Pelée's horrendous 30,000. Now, though not extinct, it is dormant. In its summit crater, often shrouded in clouds, is a quiet and gleaming blue lake.

Here, too, in northern St. Vincent, is one of the two places in the Caribbean (Dominica is the other) where there are still pure-blooded Carib Indians. Not many. Of the few who survived the colonial wars, most have long since become absorbed into the predominant Negro population. Now and then, however, you will see a face with almond eyes, high cheekbones and reddish-brown coloring, in which there is obviously no black, or white, at all.

The Caribs called St. Vincent Haroun, Land of the Blessed. But their remnants are not blessed now. They live in poverty and squalor; and it will be a major long-range problem of the island to raise them to a decent modern standard of living.

So it is on all the islands. Side by side, the hotel and the shack, the plane and the donkey, the affluent and the destitute. And paradoxically it is hotel, plane and affluence—the appurtenances of tourism—that, along with the much needed development of light industry, will bring better times, not for a few but all. Especially is this so for an island like St. Vincent, which is just turning the corner from "old" to "new."

—*J. R. Ullman*

Instant facts

Location: 100 miles west of Barbados, 21 miles south of St. Lucia. Lying between St. Vincent and Grenada, 68 miles to the south, is the island chain known as the Grenadines.

Population: 89,000.

Capital: Kingstown.

Nationality: An Associated State within the British Commonwealth.

Language: English.

Currency: East Caribbean (same as West Indian) dollar, about 60¢ U.S., 64¢ Canadian and 4s 2d sterling.

Documentation: Passports, except citizens of the United Kingdom, Canada and the U.S. on visit of no more than six months. Proper identification necessary in place of passport. All visitors must have return tickets. Cruise-ship passengers need no passport while ship is in port.

Climate & Clothes: Temperatures range between 70°–85° with a mean of 78°. Annual rainfall is about 96 inches, slightly heavier in the mountains than on the coast. Dry season is January–April, rainy season May–December. Casual cottons and sport clothes are suitable anywhere. For evenings, some hotels require jackets. Ladies should bring a light wrap for night breezes, rain hat to protect coiffures.

Food: Seafood and Creole cooking with hot spices—such as callaloo soup—are St. Vincent favorites. Fruits are famous for flavor: mangos, cassavas, avocados, and paw-paws. The native passion fruit is eaten for "emotional development." Special drink is **gru-gru swizzle,** a rum punch with exotic ingredients, first made by the Carib Indians.

Geography: 18 miles long and 11 miles wide. Range of volcanic mountains and valleys stretches entire length from Soufrière crater in north to Mount St. Andrew in south. Many small rivers run from hills to beaches on coasts. Vegetation is green, abundant.

History: Discovered by Columbus on St. Vincent's Day in 1498. The Carib Indians, early inhabitants, fought off European settlers for the next 300 years. During this time official possession of the island was fought over by Britain and France. A romantic sidelight to the wars came in 1793 when Captain Bligh of the *Bounty* brought breadfruit trees from Tahiti and planted them—the first in the Caribbean. In 1796 the British defeated the French and Caribs, deported Indian leaders to an island off the coast of Honduras and gained permanent control.

Who flies here

LIAT has regular flights between St. Vincent and the following islands:

Trinidad: Round trip: $57; 17-day excursion $41.

Barbados: Round trip: $32; 17-day excursion $20.

Antigua: Round trip: $72.

Martinique: Round trip: $34.

Guadeloupe: Round trip: $59.

Island transportation

There are buses from Kingstown along the coastal roads. Taxis cost 30¢ a mile or $1.50 per half-hour (whichever is higher!) and car rental services are reasonably priced. Guided tours can be arranged at flat rates. Boat travel is standard in areas where roads are impassable. There are regular launches between Kingstown and Chateaubelair, and boats with guides to other points of interest are easily scheduled.

Information and arrangements for all types of transportation can be made through the tourist bureau, which sends representatives aboard ships and planes upon arrival. Rented cars are easily procured through Hertz or at your hotel, and the Aquatic Club rents boats.

Touring the island

Though a jeep, boat and mountain climbing shoes may come in handy in exploring the countryside, Kingstown itself is a delightful place for lazy sightseeing. Go to **Saturday Market** on the waterfront. Each weekend schooners come in from the Grenadines laden with fruits, goats and infinite varieties of vegetables. Tiny stalls sell local snacks and coffee at the docks. Little boys dive for coins and row any willing passengers around the harbor.

Away from the waterfront, in a peaceful English section, sits an interesting cluster of buildings. **St. George's Cathedral, St. Mary's Cathedral** and **Wesleyan Hall** attract architectural buffs. Built in 1820, St. George's has a regency look and a brass chandelier supposedly presented by George III. A path of scented almond trees leads across a graveyard to St. Mary's. Built by a Belgian priest from his memory of Europe's cathedrals, it combines Gothic, Romanesque and Baroque features. Another fine walk winds through the **Botanic Gardens,** the oldest such park in the Caribbean, and home of the rare tree *Spacthea perforata* which grows only on St. Vincent. Captain Bligh's breadfruit tree is also there. Stop by the **Carnegie Public Library** and see the exhibits of Carib Indian relics. From there it is just a few minutes' drive to **Fort Charlotte** on Johnson Point, commanding an excellent view of the leeward coast and the Grenadines. **Dorsetshire Hill** is also near, with its sweeping view of Kingstown and the harbor.

A drive in the country runs through **Mesopotamia Valley,** a fertile area dotted with small farms and arrowroot plantations. Many tours end at **Belle Vue,** site of the Central Arrowroot Factory, one of the pioneer plants for the manufacture of starch. Also popular is the drive to **Sandy Bay** on the Windward Coast, a village of Carib Indian descendants.

Perhaps the most dramatic sights are reached by **mountain climbing.** An eight-hour excursion for the hardy is scaling **La Soufrière,** the dormant 4,048-foot volcano which last erupted in 1902. Getting to the base of the mountain is half the adventure. You can drive to Georgetown, then strike inland on foot—or take a car or launch to Chateaubelair, then canoe or rowboat to the mouth of the Wallibou River at the base. The actual climb takes about two hours and the lake in the crater and view of St. Vincent and the Caribbean is worth the huffs and puffs. Short-winded travelers may be interested in exploring the **Rabaca Dry River,** where lava once flowed on the lower slopes. A less strenuous climb is **Mount St. Andrew** which has a well-worn trail. From 1,500 feet up a rain forest runs to the peak.

The sporting life

A day on the water can reveal some marvelous sights. At Tyrell Bay, four miles from Kingstown, boats can be hired to explore the ruins of **Fort Duvernette** which rises abruptly from a rock in the sea. There are winding steps from the shingle beach up 260 feet to the top where old cannon and iron rings recall wars, Indians and pirates. The **Falls of Baleine** near La Soufrière are worth a trip. There is no direct road so take a launch from Kingstown or Chateaubelair. The falls tumble dramatically into fresh-water pools by the sea and the journey offers good views of the coast and mountains.

An unusual fishing adventure begins with a visit to the villages of Layou, Barrouallie or Chateaubelair by boat or car. From any of the three you can join one of the **whaling expeditions** that regularly put out to sea. The hunt usually lasts two days and, when the boats return, the village has a fiesta. More leisurely water activity is offered at **Richmond River** near Chateaubelair. A quiet bathing place, the river flows to sea by a black-sand beach, perfect for picnics.

Swimming is exceptionally good at Tyrell Bay and Indian Bay. **Snorkeling** and **water skiing** are popular on the calm seas off the coast. Young Island has excellent **spearfishing.** The Aquatic Club and tourist board can make arrangements for all water sports and are also helpful in arranging the long treks to rivers and fishing grounds.

Tennis players may use the courts of the Kingstown Lawn Tennis Club. **Cricket** can be played or watched in Victoria Park, and there are also facilities for **rifle shooting** and **soccer.**

Shopping buys

St. Vincent is not a free port. British goods are priced lowest. Best buys: Sea Island cotton, English woolens, local handcrafts in straw and mahogany. Liquor is also a bargain.

Dine and dance

Except for the weekly dances at private clubs, and dinner parties and cocktail gatherings at hotels, there is little night life. However, visitors are offered membership in beach and men's clubs and may join in most social activities. Steel bands and Calypso singers are a highlight of many festive evenings.

Aquatic Club: Tyrell Bay, on beach. Favorite place for afternoon snacks, drinks, dancing by the pool. Some guests swim to Young Island Center for water sports and boating.

Blue Caribbean Hotel: Center of Kingstown. Famous for French Creole and native dishes.

Blue Lagoon Hotel: Ratho Mill, on beach. Cozy dining room and bar with gardens for walking. Specialties: fresh fish, Italian and Creole cuisine. Informal dancing evenings, more formal parties some weekends. Party-hopping to Aquatic Club via hotel's skiff.

Coronation Club: Tyrell Bay, on beach. Cocktails and snacks between swimming, snorkeling and lounging.

Grand View Beach Hotel: Villa Point, on beach. Remodeled estate. Excellent views of Young Island and Grenadines from bar and restaurant.

Haddon Hotel: Kingston. Dining room and small nightclub.

Indian Bay Beach Club: Indian Bay. Features bar, informal dancing, swimming and snacks.

Sugar Mill Inn: Ratho Mill on 200-foot cliff. Dining room and cocktail lounge has

one of finest views of Grenadines. International cuisine and barbecues. Informal dancing evenings and more formal parties weekends. Free transportation to Aquatic Club every day.

Several other hotels in town and within a 2½ mile radius also have restaurants: The **Heron, New Haven** and **Olive's Hotels** in Kingstown; **Sea View Hotel** in Edinboro, and **Villa Lodge** in Villa.

Festivities

New Year's Day: Picnics on beaches. January 2 is also a public holiday.

Carnival: Steel band parades, dances, sports events in Victoria Park, competition for queen of the carnival. Late February or early March.

Easter Monday: Dances at clubs and hotels, picnics. April 15.

Labor Day: Public holiday. May 1.

Whit Monday: Picnics, dances. June 3.

Queen's Birthday: Parade by local forces, guides, scouts, etc. In Victoria Park. June.

August 7: Public holiday.

Thanksgiving: Picnics, feasts, parties. November.

Boxing Day: Sharing gifts, greetings with friends. December 26.

Real estate and retirement

British professionals and some titled persons retire here or rent vacation homes. Because St. Vincent is an agricultural economy with few high salaried positions, a guaranteed independent income is advisable for prospective settlers. Immigration requirements provide a special permit enabling a visitor to spend up to one year, so long as he does not work. The permit is available from the Chief Immigration Officer and is convenient for those who wish to stay a season in one of the private houses in the countryside.

The following realtors in Kingstown have information on purchasing and renting properties: Mr. W. J. Abbott, Mr. A. C. Hillocks, Mr. Gerry Palmer.

Homes in particular locations may be rented by writing to the lessor:

Indian Bay:
Mr. O. D. Brisbane, Jr.
Villa Point

Mrs. Vilma Cox
P.O. Box 71, Kingstown

Ratho Mill:
Mr. P. S. Nanton
P.O. Box 117, Kingstown

Villa:
Mr. W. J. Abbott
P.O. Box 124, Kingstown

Mr. Randolph Russell
Russell's Cinema, Kingstown

Commerce and industry

St. Vincent's major exports have seen better times. Besides the declining arrowroot starch market, cotton production has slacked off and sugar cane is no longer even planted. Overproduction of bananas and sweet potatoes have caused drops in prices.

Domestic agriculture has been more successful. Root crops like tannias, yams, and eddoes are locally consumed, as well as peanuts. Tropical fruits are abundant.

Manufacturing is confined to low-return goods like soft drinks, bread and cakes. The Pioneer Industries Ordinance gives fairly generous concessions to new plants, and there is a special need for companies concerned with the canning of fruits and vegetables.

Another incentive to investment is the Hotels Aid Ordinance, which gives a 10-year holiday on income tax and other concessions to new hotels.

Information on business opportunities is available from the Secretary of the Ministry of Trade and Production, Kingstown.

Young Island

Lots of hammocks . . . but only one telephone . . .

Tucked down among the islands of the southern Caribbean there's a little part of the world custom tailored for anyone who has ever said, "Let's get away from it all," and meant it.

This is Young Island, a small, lushly planted private isle 600 feet off the shore of St. Vincent. The island, 20 acres in all, offers accommodations in a tropical village on the beach, with additional facilities on the highest point which offers a magnificent view of the outlying Grenadines.

Young Island was conceived as a small, unpretentious, intimate place where no one has to dress up or follow a schedule. It is a whole island unto itself in a more or less forgotten part of the world where life is casual, unhurried and unorganized.

Although Young Island stresses informality, a good deal of thought and taste has gone into providing comfort and beauty. Guests stay in a cabana village around a tropical lagoon landscaped with exotic flowers and trees. The cabanas are built of native stones with wallabe shingled roofs that gleam in the moonlight.

Each room is furnished for two and offers a private terrace which looks out to sea or to the lagoon. Every room has a private bath and an outdoor garden shower, screened by a bamboo curtain.

There are no television sets, no clocks, and only one telephone is available. But there are hammocks everywhere.

Dining is casual. Meals are served in a beach pavilion surrounded by terraces, pools and flowers. The food is simple and features dishes of the area—fresh fish from the sea or lobster cooked over an open fire, homemade bread and native soups and dishes. If guests get hungry between meals, they are free to pick a banana or a papaya off a tree.

Young Island is probably the only private island that offers another private island for visiting. The second isle, only a few hundred feet away, is Fort Duvernette, once a French fortress. Duvernette is 400 feet high and there are still old cannon at the top.

Young Island itself was once the palace grounds of a Carib chief. He gave the island to a Governor Young in return for a black stallion.

WHERE TO STAY — In St. Vincent

	Plan	Dec. 15-April 14 U. S. Currency		April 15-Dec. 14	
		Double	Single	Double	Single
BLUE CARIBBEAN Kingstown (18 Rms.)	(AP)	$18–26	$10–14	$18–26	$10–14
BLUE LAGOON Calliaqua (12 Rms.) **(b)**	(AP) (MAP)	$28–34 $24–30	$16–18 $14–16	$20–26 $16–22	$12–14 $10–12
GRAND VIEW BEACH Villa Point (12 Rms.) **(b)**	(MAP)	$25–30	$14–18	$15–20	$ 9–12
HADDON Kingstown (15 Rms.)	(AP)	$13–19	$ 7–10	$13–19	$ 7–10
HERON Kingstown (15 Rms.)	(AP)	$12–17	$ 8–10	$12–17	$ 8–10
SUGAR MILL INN Ratho Mill (22 Rms.) **(p)**	(MAP)	$25–35	$18–26	$15–25	$11–19
VILLA LODGE Villa (10 Rms) **(b)**	(AP)	$22–28	$10–15	$18–20	$10–11
YOUNG ISLAND Calliaqua Dock (20 Rms.) **(b)**	(AP)	$52	$31	$32	$21

   LEGEND FOR HOTEL LISTINGS: (AP) American Plan (room and 3 meals); **MAP)** Modified American Plan (room, breakfast and dinner); **(CP)** Continental Plan (room and breakfast); **(EP)** European Plan (room only). All rates quoted on a per-day basis and subject to change. Confirmed reservations at specific rates desired are always recommended.
   HOTEL FACILITIES: (b) beach; **(p)** pool; **(t)** tennis; **(g)** golf.

SURINAM

Surinam has an area of 55,167 sq. miles, about the size of Pennsylvania, and within these relatively small confines can be found luxury hotels, cosmopolitan restaurants, a thriving business and industrial community, broad rivers winding through impenetrable jungles, and tribes of primitive artisans and Amerindians who live today much the way they did in the Stone Age.

Land of contrasts

If you have always yearned to hunt jaguar, track down the exotic sloth, and come face to face with a giant anteater, there is for you a country that allows you to do all this without giving up the rudimentary comforts of civilization.

Or, if you have no desire for the hunt, you can spend a marvelous vacation exploring a land of contrasts, investigating a melting pot of cultures, and in general getting well away from it all.

Surinam, formerly known as Dutch Guiana, lies on the northeast coast of South America between Guyana and French Guiana. The Atlantic Ocean forms the northern boundary. The southern neighbor is Brazil.

Paramaribo, the capital city, lies on the wide Suriname River and the waterfront is lined with buildings of typical Dutch architecture. The name "Paramaribo" is derived from an Amerindian language. Some say it means "place near the water" and others say it means "a place of flowers." Indeed the gardens of the capital are ablaze with flowers of many varieties.

The streets of Paramaribo are a delight in themselves. The passing parade is made up of people of European, Asian and African descent, and various mixtures thereof. One of the most colorful spots in town is the CENTRAL MARKET, where everybody goes at one time or another and where all the sights and sounds and produce of Surinam come together. Here the visitor will hear a goodly part of the world's languages and particularly takkie-takkie (Sranang-tongo), the lingua franca of the country. (Dutch is the official language.)

The market is also a gathering place for the Kotto Missies, the name for Creole women attired in traditional costume. This elaborate garment is high-necked, billowing and floor length. It was designed over a century ago by the cautious wives of plantation owners to cover up the pretty but scantily dressed young slave girls. The Kotto Missie also wears a scarf whose design and arrangement lets onlookers, particularly the male onlooker, know whether or not the lady is eligible and/or interested. Today, these costumes are worn mostly by women of the older generation or by younger women on festive occasions.

*Amerindian mother and her children paddle down
a Surinam river in a corial*

As a melting pot, few countries in the world can hold a candle to Surinam. The first, the original, inhabitants were the Amerindians who have left their traces over the entire country. Rivers and streams, areas, towns and villages are still known by the names given them by the Indian tribes. Amerindians of the Carib and Arawak tribes live today for the most part in remote communities, usually situated along cool, fresh-water creeks and in the neighborhood of the savannas. Deep in the interior but always near a stream are the Bushnegroes, descendants of runaway slaves who found refuge in the jungles. Here they have established their own communities, patterned after the traditions and customs of Africa.

To the south, close to the border with Brazil, are the hunting grounds of two other tribes of Amerindians, the nomad Wajanas and Trios. They seldom come into contact with the people of the coastal area and still use primitive tools and utensils.

The present-day population of Surinam (about 350,000) is not large in relation to the size of the country, roughly that of Pennsylvania. But it is an exotic and multifaceted population. More than 50% consists of Hindustanis, Javanese and Chinese, and the populated areas are dotted with temples and mosques. The largest single group is officially designated as Creole, any mixture of Negro, Dutch, English, Spanish, Portuguese, etc. Also there are Syrians, Lebanese, Europeans chiefly of Dutch descent, and North Americans.

Surinam is an old plantation country. Today the crops are rice, citrus fruits, bananas, sugar cane, coffee, cocoa, plantains, peanuts, corn, tomatoes, green vegetables, sweet potatoes and cassava (the root of the manioc plant). The present economy is based in good part on bauxite, but some oil has been found and a search is going on to find the main source. Tourism is assuming an ever more important role.

Tours in and around Paramaribo are easily arranged, as well as more adventurous treks deep into the interior of the country. A pleasant half-day tour includes a trip across the Suriname River by ferry and a drive through plantations on the north shore to FORT NIEUW AMSTERDAM which formerly guarded the entrance to the Suriname and Commewijne rivers.

At MARIENBURG, a sugar factory and a rum distillery, and a Javanese workers settlement, may be visited.

For visitors with only a limited time to spend in Surinam, a trip up the SARAMACCA RIVER will provide an insight into the jungle life of the Bushnegroes. A short drive through the outskirts of Paramaribo brings visitors to the settlement of Uitkijk, embarkation point for a boat trip upriver to the Bushnegro jungle village of Santigron. The entire trip can be concluded in five hours.

The bauxite mining center of MOENGO, Surinam's second largest city, lies on the Cottica River and can be reached by plane, by boat and by car via the East-West Highway. (Surinam is one of the world's largest suppliers of bauxite, the ore from which aluminum is made.) Further along the East-

West Highway is Albina, on the Marowijne River, and there are many Bush-negro and Amerindian villages nearby. Across the river, in French Guiana, lies St. Laurent, the former French penal colony.

One of the most fascinating trips is to STOELMANS ISLAND on the Maro-wijne River, way up in the vast interior of Surinam. Here, deep in the jungle, is a comfortable guest house where the amenities of civilization co-exist peace-fully with the wild beauty all around. The island can be reached by small aircraft from Paramaribo or by car and boat via Albina.

Exploring the area is an adventure, although a safe adventure. The Marowijne is a beautiful river that runs sometimes broad and tranquil, some-times leaping over rapids and waterfalls. A river safari, in a dugout piloted by skilled native boatmen, is a trip through an unknown world where tropical flora and fauna flourish in abundance.

Jungle river safari

Alcoa operates bauxite mines in Surinam and runs steamers to and from these mining areas via the extensive jungle river systems that crisscross the country. Although passenger accommodations are limited, those who make the trip find a welcome aboard, plus an exciting, yet comfortable experience.

These jungle river safaris start at Trinidad or at Paramaribo. There are

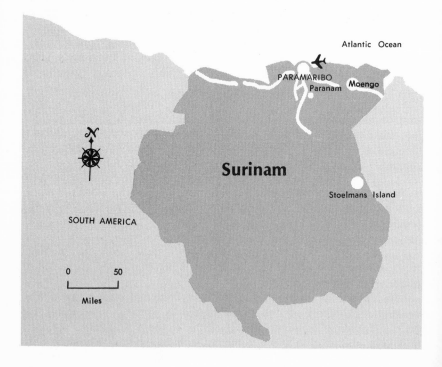

two itineraries, depending on your ship's orders. One cruise takes you to Moengo, about 75 miles from the capital. The other cruise has Paranam as its destination. Both wind through the lush tropical vegetation of the rain forest coming to the water's edge.

Experience is needed to guide the vessels up and down the narrow rivers. Passengers marvel at the maneuvers—until they see the skill of the Bush-negroes in shooting the river rapids in their *corials*, or dugout canoes.

The boat will pass many of these craft. Take the trip to Moengo, for instance, 110 miles inland. The journey begins on the broad Suriname River, at its junction with the lower Commewijne River, at this point fairly broad, too. Twenty-eight miles upstream, however, the steamer moves into the winding and narrow Cottica River, on which Moengo is situated.

Far up the Cottica, early planters made fortunes in coffee, cocoa and sugar by finding cheap labor in slaves and cheap and easy transportation for their produce. Slave labor declined as the slaves, one after the other, bolted off into the jungle to fend for themselves, and joined forces against the Europeans. Their equivalent of our Emancipation Proclamation came by treaty in 1863, recognizing their freedom.

Cheap labor soon became unavailable, and the plantations were abandoned. Plantation names, of curiously mixed linguistic origin (Mon-Desir, Marienburg and Groot Marseille), remain to remind visitors of Surinam's long and polyglot ancestry. Wanhatti is the first large Bushnegro village on the river journey.

Two centuries ago the Bushnegroes' African ancestors, who escaped shortly after their capture and transfer to Surinam, found the dense equatorial jungle very similar to their homeland, and an incentive to resume traditional ways of life. Now they are banded into five tribes, each under a "head man" elected by the tribe and recognized by the government. Empowered under the head man are the "captains" of various villages, whose several assistants are called *bassias*, or bosses.

Some work in the mines. All are skilled woodworkers. Their possessions, including household effects, the wooden doors of their huts, and their *corials* (shaped and hollowed with small hatches from a single tree trunk) as well as the paddles, are intricately carved and often elaborately colored. Their dress is dictated by the jungle—little or nothing, depending on age. Children wear nothing, men are content in just a loincloth. Most girls and women are bare above the waist.

Scenery along the river is mostly dense jungle. But each stretch presents new sights for the traveler. Where the denseness is less intense, towering mangrove bushes line the shores. One also sees thin, woody plants with heart-shaped leaves growing straight out of the water. The view is particularly beautiful at sunrise. Dew-laden cobwebs spread jewel-green fans between tree branches as butterflies seem to dance among them.

Travelers can visit Calbo, the only inhabited Amerindian village on the river. The hollowed-log canoes used by the tribes have a stem and a stern instead of two pointed ends. Clay objects are in considerable demand. Without as much as a potter's wheel the Amerindians fashion jugs and bowls by molding narrow strips of clay together and ornamenting them with designs that are strikingly modern in character.

Along the river, too, are missions of Moravian Brothers and Roman Catholics. Stops are made at some villages to witness ancient rites and rituals —including the Fire Dance in which flames lick at the participants dancing on hot coals and jagged glass.

At Moengo, at the end of the trip, there is a reminder that the past always ends at the present: the settlement's water tower, of gleaming aluminum, shines above the tree tops. Moengo is a company town with many modern houses, supermarkets, and other social refinements of North American and European inspiration.

Passengers may visit the plant where bauxite is crushed, dried and stored according to grades. While it is loaded on their boat, they usually inspect the mine, a low hill rising out of the swamps.

The return journey then gets under way with the steamer traversing the jungles to Paramaribo—the present again waiting at the other end of a journey through the past.

Instant facts

Location: On the northeastern shoulder of South America, bordered on the north by the Atlantic Ocean, on the west by Guyana, on the east by French Guiana and on the south by Brazil.

Population: About 350,000.

Capital: Paramaribo.

Nationality: An autonomous part of the Netherlands Realm, a partner of the Netherlands Kingdom together with Holland and the Netherlands Antilles. A Governor represents the Queen of the Netherlands.

Language: Dutch, and a native dialect called takkie-takkie, or Sranang-tongo, a mixture of English, Dutch and Creole plus a trace of Portuguese, Spanish and French. English is widely spoken.

Currency: The Surinam guilder equals 54¢ U.S. Credit cards are not always honored.

Documentation: Passport and a return ticket required. Smallpox vaccination certicates required.

Climate & Clothes: Temperatures climb highest in September to an average 83°, drop to an average 78° in January; evening temperatures often fall below the 70° mark and may even reach 60°. Summer-weight informal attire in town; on safari, khakis and sports shirts for men, slacks for ladies; raincoats for everyone during the rainy season, May–July.

Food: Continental cuisine in the major Paramaribo hotels; Creole, Chinese, Indonesian and Indian cookery in the native restaurants. Try one of the Indian "Roti Shops" where the tortilla-like roti are served with a variety of fillings.

Some other popular native dishes are **chicken pie,** a much tastier version of our frozen store-bought ones; **rijsttafel,** a multicourse banquet revolving about rice and featuring many exotic side dishes; **peanut soup,** an ordinary chicken or beef broth except for the main ingredient which is peanut butter; and, served as an entrée, **landcrab pie** garnished with garlic, onions and spices.

Geography: Its southern border just 2° above the equator. Surinam (until 1954, Dutch Guiana) covers 55,167 sq. miles. Coastal flatlands stretch inland to merge with dense, almost impenetrable jungle, and, farther south, with mountains—all intersected by many large rivers.

History: Surinam is that rarity among the lands of the Caribbean and South America, a country with very little "history" in the usual bloodstained meaning of the word. In the 17th century both England and Holland claimed the territory for their own, but after a few small skirmishes Holland obtained the country in 1667 through the Treaty of Breda by trading Manhattan island to the British for it.

What is now Surinam was discovered by the Spanish, and in the 1500's bands of adventurers combed the land seeking the legendary "El Dorado." The quest was started by the discovery of clay pots embedded with gold nuggets—actually pyrite crystals, or "fool's gold," which are sprinkled throughout the country's savannas. The "gold" is still mixed with clay to make pots and other utensils.

With the Treaty of Breda, Surinam became Dutch Guiana and remained a Dutch colony until 1954 when it became completely autonomous in domestic affairs and an equal partner, with Holland and the Netherlands Antilles, in the Netherlands Kingdom.

The Dutch spelling of Surinam is Suriname, pronounced Su (as in sun), ri (as in rinse) and nam (as in Vietnam). Scholars believe the name was derived from the Indian tribe of the Surinen, who inhabited the Amazon areas in pre-Columbian times.

Who flies here

Direct flights to Paramaribo are available from the following points:

New York: Pan Am. Round trip: $380–$515; 17-day excursion $270–$390.

Miami: Pan Am, BWIA, KLM. Round trip: $325–$441; 17-day excursion $245–$355.

Amsterdam: KLM. Round trip: $745–$1093.

Frankfurt: KLM. Round trip: $745–$1093.

Lisbon: KLM. Round trip: $716–$950.

San Juan: Pan Am, BWIA. Round trip: $242–$299.

Trinidad: Air France, BWIA, KLM, ALM, Pan Am. Round trip: $109–$151; 17-day excursion $75–$125.

Guyana: Air France, BWIA, KLM, ALM, Pan Am, SLM. Round trip: $61–$88.

Getting around Surinam

Taxis in Surinam are not metered, nor do they have fixed rates. Many of them, however, have standard rates under an unofficial agreement with the tourist board. A list of these drivers, whose fares vary depending on the size (i.e., capacity) of their cars, can be secured at hotels or through the Tourist Information Office, Kerkplein 10 (Tel: 3733). The driver will probably have a Tourist Office sticker on his windshield and should carry the approved rate list.

There are two types of **buses**—the big yellow government-run buses and the smaller private ones. Prices are low for either and all routes are fixed.

For the independent traveler, **self-drive cars** are available from the Hertz representative in Paramaribo, Curacao Trading Co., Dr. Sophie Redmonstraat 2-14 (Tel: 4343). **Tours** can be arranged through:

Succes Tourist Service
Arcade of the Torarica Hotel
P.O. Box 344, Paramaribo (Tel: 6666)

Tonee's Travel & Tour Bureau
Pontewerfstraat 20 (Tel: 6837)

Surinam Travel & Tour Bureau
Tel: 2419

Andre's Tours
P.O.B. 10
Moengo, Tel: 041-207

A Surinam tour can take you on a leisurely three- to four-hour drive through Paramaribo (about $3.25 per person) or on a five-day hunting and fishing safari deep in South American jungle ($65 per person per day). Between these two extremes are a quickie visit to Bushnegro villages ($15 per person) and excursions through Surinam countryside, varying in length from two to six days ($50–$200 per person for the entire trip). Some of the excursions include hiking, canoeing and camping out. Visitors should plan to include at least one tour on their itinerary.

The sporting life

Aficionados, or would-be aficionados, of **hunting and fishing** in South American jungles, will find Surinam an accessible paradise. The jaguar, the puma and the ocelot prowl the land, enormous tarpon may be hooked in the dark waters of the rivers, and duck hunting is superb in the primeval forests. Experienced guides are generally available and arrangements for these inland safaris can be made through touring agencies or the Tourist Information Office (Tel: 3733).

Fishermen will be particularly enthused with Surinam's fishing grounds as they harbor many unusual species. The anjoe-mara is a sort of prehistoric relic who relishes a good fight, and the piranha, also commonly caught here, is well-known for his man-eating tendencies. Other good catches include kwie-kwie, pataca, kubi-fish, walapa, krobia and koemapari, unfamiliar names to most amateur anglers.

Fishing in Surinam is done strictly in rivers, ranging from muddy, overgrown rapids to peaceful, clear-water streams. Heavy tackle is recommended. The fishing trip itself is done safari-style, as most of the good spots are well outside Paramaribo. The boat trip through the jungle is as safe as it is exciting, thanks to the Djukas, the skilled native boatmen.

Back to the tamer things of life, there is excellent **swimming** at Cola Creek near the international airport at Zanderij. The water *is* cola-colored because of leaves that have fallen into it, but it is clean and fresh and always cool. A white-sand beach and picnic facilities make it an enjoyable place to spend an hour or day.

However, except for swimming pools at some hotels and private clubs and public pools at Parima and Moengo, Surinam has no other swimming facilities to speak of. Silt from the Amazon River has ruined most of its beaches and even Cola Creek had to be artificially developed. Someday the government hopes to develop other artificial lakes, both for practical usage (power, irrigation) and as a tourist attraction. One spot being considered is at Torarica, where there is fine white sand and a large luxury hotel.

While there is little sailing and no charter boat facilities here, **boat races** are a feature of most public holidays.

Most popular of the **spectator sports** is soccer, also known here as football. Top teams from Brazil and other championship countries often compete with Surinamers at the 15,000-seat Surinam Stadium, Cultuurtuinlaan. Games are scheduled on most Sunday afternoons and some weekday evenings. Basketball is second only to soccer and games are held Tuesday, Friday and Sunday nights at the Paramaribo Club, Gravenstraat 4. Cricket matches, held on Sundays at the Dr. Snellenpark grounds, Cultuurtuinlaan, enjoy only half-hearted popularity. Fun to watch are bicycle and motorcycle races, usually held in the Surinam Stadium or on public holidays, along public roads.

The only **golf** course in town is at the Paramaribo Golf Club, Pad van Wanica—visitors welcome. Smaller ones are on the grounds of the Surinam Aluminum Co. at Moengo and Paranam. Several of the private clubs have **tennis** courts.

Shopping buys

Shopping in Surinam is exotic in itself. There are the unusual and beautiful Bush-negro and Amerindian articles (wood carvings, pottery); Indian and Chinese jewelry wrought in gold; silks and jade from the Orient; Javanese batiks and wickerwork; stuffed caymans and other jungle fauna. More prosaically, there are ready-made suits of local manufacture, and cameras and photographic materials can be bought at some specialized stores in Paramaribo.

Dining and night life

Bali-Lunapark: Dr. Nassylaan 5, Paramaribo. Indonesian cuisine. Dining in air-conditioned interior or outdoors. Elaborate "rijsttafel" can be ordered on relatively short notice. Tel: 6672.

Garuda Hotel: Jodenbreestraat 41, downstairs. Indonesian cooking, air-conditioned dining room, bar. Tel. 6030.

Het Park: Oranjeplein. Creole cooking. Introduction necessary.

Hong Kong: Keizerstraat 51. Chinese restaurant. Air-conditioned dining room. Tel. 4616.

Hortensia: Dr. Sophie Redmondstraat 125. Creole menu.

Iwan: Grote Hofstraat 6. Chinese cuisine. Tel. 6688.

New Palace Hotel: Oranjeplein. International, native cuisine. Entertainment nightly. Tel: 2815.

Surinam Torarica Hotel: On the waterfront. Continental cooking in the **Plantation Room**, lighter meals throughout the day in the coffeeshop. Casino, entertainment night. Tel: 6666.

Hotel Vervuurt: Dominéstraat 11. Chinese food in **Fa Tai's Golden City** restaurant. Dancing in the **Cactus Club** and floor show every night. Tel: 5045.

Special events, festivals, celebrations

New Year's Celebration: Fireworks, etc. January 1.

Chinese New Year: Chinese shops closed. Parties, fireworks. January 2.

Idul Fitr: End of fast. Muslim holiday. January.

Birthday of H.R.H. Princess Margriet: Military parade. January 19.

Birthday of H.R.H. Princess Beatrix: Military parade. January 31.

Carnival: Costume parties in clubs. Saturday before Lent.

Basant Panchami: Harvest time. Hindu holiday. February 14.

Birthday of H.R.H. Princess Christine: Military parade. February 18.

Good Friday: Shops closed. Special observances in churches. April 12.

Holy Phagwa: Hindu religious holiday. Partygoers are sprinkled with colored and scented waters. March.

Easter Sunday and Easter Monday: Stores are closed. April 14 and 15.

Moharam: Muslim New Year. April 12.

H.M. Queen Juliana's Birthday: Official holiday. Parades. Market women pay homage to Governor. April 30.

Labor Day: Special meetings of unions, dances. May 1.

Ascension Day: Stores closed. May 23.

Whitsunday and Whitmonday: Religious holiday. Stores closed. June 2–3.

Mila Dunnabi: Birth of Prophet Mohamed. Muslim holiday. June.

Birthday of H.R.H. Prince Bernhard: Military parade. June 29.

Freedoms Day: Commemorating abolition of slavery and Surinam's new position as an equal partner with Holland and the Netherlands Antilles in the Kingdom of the Netherlands; also celebration of the Basic Freedoms of Man. Parades. Kotto Missie shows. July 1.

American Independence Day: Celebration by the American Consulate General. July 4.

Birthday of H.R.H. Princess Irene: Military parade. August 5.

Konfriejarie: A Coney Island type of fair held annually around the end of August which attracts troupes and variety artists from abroad.

National Sports Week: Week-long series of games and sports demonstrations. Also at the end of August.

Birthday of H.R.H. Prince Claus: Military parade. September 6.

Commemoration of Peace of Breda: Whereby Surinam was given to the Dutch by the British in exchange for Manhattan in 1667. Weeklong celebrations in September.

Nationalist Chinese Holiday: Chinese community celebrates with fireworks, dragon dances, etc. October 10.

Annual Trade Fair: Entertainment Pavillion of Fair offers nightly shows, beauty contests, etc. Mid-October.

Diwalie: Hindu Festival of Light. November.

St. Nicolaas Day: St. Nick parades through the streets. Day for distribution of gifts to the children. December 5.

Statuutdag or Kingdom Day: Commemorating signing of Charter for Kingdom of the Netherlands, putting Surinam and the Netherlands Antilles on equal political footing with Holland (1954). December 15.

Christmas: Public holidays. December 25–26.

Meet the Surinamers

Sports Organizations	Official	Phone
S.V.B. (Football Assn.)	Dr. F. Essed	2341
Basketball Assn.	Dr. J. Sedney	6841
Paramaribo Golf Club	J. de Vries	4241
Cricket Assn.	C. R. Singh	2527
Lawn Tennis Assn.	R. Fernandes	3445
Badminton Assn.	G. Boymans	5675
Athletic Assn.	W. Axwijk	2625
Volleyball Assn.	Father Mulder	2521
Yachting	W. B. de Haan	2339
Swimming	M. Wijngaarde	5700
Hunting	F. Barend	2141
Surinam Olympic Committee	O. R. G. Vervuut	2672
Table Tennis Assn.	C. Ooft	
Fencing	M. Brugman	6141
Foundation Sports Hall	M. R. Pool	97625
Empire Games	F. L. de Rooy	3733

Clubs

Het Park	Dr. J. Sedney	6841
Officer's Club	Major v.d. Sterren	6141
Oase	M. L. de Kok	99395
Dolfijn	W. B. de Haan	2339
Kwiekwie	E. R. G. Görges	4241
De Witte Lotus	C. Jong Tjien Fa	5753
Kong Ngie Tong Sang	Chiu Hung	2209
Kuo Min Tang	G. Fung	2568
Chung Fa Foei Kon	Tjon Tsoe Jin	2011
N.A.K.S.	E. Drenthe	4639
A.B.O.	Mr. Sof	97235
H.N.S.	E. Abhelak	5438
A.M.O.S. (Muslims)	A. Lall Mohammed	5834

Service Clubs

Rotary	J. van Petten	4557
Lions	M. Abrahams	2685
Jaycees	F. Vanenburg	4717
Toastmasters	A. J. Rondeel	2041
Y.W.C.A.	Mrs. G. Brunings	2089
Boy Scouts	L. Tjon Ajong	4444
Girl Guides	Mrs. M. Oostburg-Cop	97924
Bar Association	G. van der Schoeff	2711
Assn. of Medical Specialists	Dr. P. L. Niemel	5336
Alliance Francaise	H. Speyer	2832
Sociedad Bolivariana	Dr. A. R. Wix	99055
Business Assn.	B. C. de Groot	2287
Red Cross	Dr. E. V. D. Kuyp (B.O.G.)	99494
Green Cross	Dr. J. Lichtveld	3814
White-Yellow-Cross	C. Ooft	99139
National Youth Assembly	R. Cruden	

Service Clubs	Official	Phone
C.C.S. (Cultural Center)	F. Breeveld	3602
Round Table	Dr. S. M. Bellot	4821

Museums, mosques and the finer arts

Also to be visited in Paramaribo are the **Palm Gardens** behind the Governor's Palace, a quiet park shaded by hundreds of palm trees; the **Botanical Garden** with its tropical plants and flowers; the **Hindu temples, Moslem mosques,** Surinam's oldest **synagogue** and the **Roman Catholic Cathedral** which is the largest wooden structure of its kind in the Southern Hemisphere.

The **Surinam Museum,** with its small but interesting collection of historic and prehistoric artifacts, is located on Commewijnestraat 18. Visiting hours are 8 A.M.–noon and 5–7 P.M. during the week, 10 A.M.–noon Sunday. There is also an open air museum, Nieuw Amsterdam, across the Surinam River.

Local theater is a many splendored thing. Most plays are in Dutch or Sranang-tongo and the average visiting theater buff won't even be able to read the reviews. But there is the compensation of the exotic: performances by Indian cultural groups, Indonesians, Creoles and Chinese. On festive occasions, Surinamers of Chinese descent put on dragon parades and scarf dances and shoot off long strings of firecrackers. And if a visitor is lucky, he may find himself at a Hindu wedding ceremony.

Most cultural activities are sponsored by the CCS (Cultural Center of Surinam), located on Gravenstraat 112-114. There is also the Theater Thalia on Dr. Nassylaan 6. Ballet performances and concerts feature moonlighting Surinamers as well as occasional visiting artists. Another cultural group is the N.A.K.S., Thompson Street.

Real estate

The following is a list of real estate agents in Paramaribo who can assist newcomers interested in settling in Surinam:

H. C. Balak Lachman
Herenstraat 13, Tel: 6856

A. N. E. Felter
Calliopsestraat 11, Tel: 99995

J. A. Goedhoop
Weidestraat 60, Tel: 2175

Ch. E. Kruisland
Mr. F. H. R. Lim Apostraat 3, Tel: 6000

H. J. de Vries-Robles
Keizerstraat 81, Tel: 5959

Commerce and industry

With an eye open to Puerto Rico's eminently successful Operation Bootstrap as a prime example, Surinam is working to stimulate its natural potential to create another major economic center for the Caribbean, Central and South America.

A unique combination of vast hydroelectric power, extensive water transportation, a stable democratic government and a high degree of literacy gives Surinam a healthy step up in attracting new investment, and the foreign capital in which it is particularly interested.

New roads have been cut through the jungle to industrial and hydro-electric projects. The great virgin forests of the interior have been further opened up by airstrips. And the government has built an industrial park and new harbor in the capital of Paramaribo to accommodate small and medium-sized industries already under way.

The most sizable stateside investment in Surinam, whose present economy is based in good part on bauxite, has been made by the Aluminum Company of America. Alcoa's confidence in Surinam is marked by its investment of over $150 million in one project alone—the building of a dam at remote Afobaka to convert the flow of a jungle river into electric power, an aluminum smelter to use that power, and a bauxite refining plant which will supply alumina to the smelter.

This mutually profitable working relationship has bound Surinam and Alcoa for nearly half a century.

There is also a rising interest in Surinam in competitive quality food items and U.S. brand names. According to some commerce experts, "another major possibility lies in import agencies." Other open fields of interest to prospective investors are the country's great untapped timber forests. About 92% of the total land area is covered by tropical rain forests with only 19% presently accessible. Oil and gas are also of commercial interest and exploratory work is going forward. The same is true of gold mining and the mining of numerous minor minerals. (During World War II, for example, two-thirds of all bauxite turned into aluminum for U.S. military needs came from Surinam.)

Surinam hopes to stimulate corporate interest from everywhere in this hemisphere by offering industrial incentives to prospective investors. These include a tax holiday of 5–10 years, import duty benefits, investment guarantees, reasonable labor costs and other advantages. Facts and figures may be secured by applying to the Consulate General of The Netherlands, Attention: Mr. E. R. Wessels, Consul, Suite 1123, 10 Rockefeller Plaza, New York, New York. Or you can write directly to the Ministry of Economic Affairs, Economic Information Division, Gebouw 1790, P.O.B. 597, Paramaribo, Surinam, S.A.

While waiting to see what develops, Surinamers are going ahead with the promotion of a tourism industry, and at the same time making extensive inroads into the great bush country to analyze all possibilities for commercial development.

WHERE TO STAY — In Surinam

	Plan	Dec. 15-April 14 U. S. Currency		April 15-Dec. 14	
		Double	Single	Double	Single
KERSTEN HOTEL **Paramaribo** (27 Rms.)	(AP)	$18–21	$10–13	$18–21	$10–13
LASHLEY HOTEL **Paramaribo** (12 Rms.)	(AP)	$12–20	$ 7–11	$12–20	$ 7–11
NEW PALACE HOTEL **Oranje Square, Paramaribo** (32 Rms.)	(EP)	$14	$ 9	$14	$ 9
SURINAM TORARICA HOTEL **Paramaribo** (81 Rms.) (p)	(MAP) (EP)	$35–39 $19–23 (Dec. 16-April 25)	$23–27 $15–19	$31–35 $15–19 (April 26-Dec. 15)	$19–23 $11–15
VERVUURT HOTEL **Paramaribo** (25 Rms.)	(AP) (EP)	$18 $12	$12 $ 9	$18 $12	$12 $ 9

LEGEND FOR HOTEL LISTINGS: (AP) American Plan (room and 3 meals); **MAP)** Modified American Plan (room, breakfast and dinner); **(CP)** Continental Plan (room and breakfast); **(EP)** European Plan (room only). All rates quoted on a per-day basis and subject to change. Confirmed reservations at specific rates desired are always recommended.
HOTEL FACILITIES: (b) beach; **(p)** pool; **(t)** tennis; **(g)** golf.

TRINIDAD & TOBAGO

The two islands of Trinidad and Tobago form a national entity, but they have remained individual in atmosphere and outlook. Trinidad is the polyglot island, busy with commerce and industry but still gaily aware that it is the home of the steel band and the cradle of Calypso. Tobago's ways are quieter. There are unspoiled miles of beaches, birds of paradise nest in sanctuary and the big yearly event is the Eastertide Goat Races.

Trinidad: land of the humming bird

Trinidad is the exotic island of the West Indies, although it has been said that it isn't exotic at all. English is the language, cricket is the sport, and the ghost of Queen Victoria, that most unexotic of ladies, peeps out from much of the architecture. A British passion for neatness and order shows in carefully trimmed lawns and well-kept buildings and the civil service is one of the most efficient in the Caribbean.

Where then is exotica?

Other islands have carnivals. None has one like Trinidad's, where normally staid businessmen join up with the steel band and sometimes are not seen at home for days until Ash Wednesday brings an end to the revels. Booths, bars, fairs and floats are everywhere, and the incredibly colorful costumes give the whole fantastic scene the air of a Technicolor musical gone mad.

But beyond carnival and the neat parks of everyday, are the many faces of Trinidad. An historian once wrote of the island, "Perhaps there is not a local spot in the universe that can boast of such a medley of inhabitants." The population include families of British, French, Spanish, Portuguese, Lebanese, Germans, South Americans, North Americans, Syrians, Muslims, Africans, East Indians and Chinese.

When a visitor thinks he has caught Trinidad in the pulse of the Calypso, he will hear a mussein call from a mosque at sundown. And that procession winding down to the sea, the people dressed in Indian garb. Can this be Trinidad? It is a face of Trindad, the Hindu Ganges festival.

The living faces of Trinidad, especially those of the women, are considered by connoisseurs to be among the most beautiful in the world. Years of intermarriage, the mixing and blending of racial strains, have produced in many cases a poetic beauty and grace. It is here that exotic Trinidad begins to be revealed. A face off an ancient coin prosaically selling woolens in a High Street shop is exotica in paradox.

The mixture of heritages is evident in Trinidad's potpourri of architectural styles. Often the combination of local materials, French grillwork and Victorian gingerbread produces a wedding cake mansion that is uniquely Trinidadian. Splendid examples can be seen surrounding Port-of-Spain's spacious Queen's Park Savannah, the municipal park.

Lying just seven miles off the coast of Venezuela, Trinidad is virtually a channel for wildlife. Living things, flowers and trees and birds, are particularly diverse, and it was this abundance of natural beauty that gave the island its first name. The Indians called it "Iere." The Land of the Hummingbird.

It was from Trinidad that the Calypso went out to the world, and in spite of corruptions in countless cocktail lounges it remains, in Trinidad, a genuine folk art.

Calypso developed out of the folk song and folk music of the Afro-West Indian native in Trinidad, and its structure is strongly African. Moving as the music is, it is the lyrics that matter—always witty, rich in innuendo and frequently satirical. Calypso subjects range from scandal in high places to sporting commentaries, and sometimes a simple love song from a boy to a girl. The writer V. S. Naipaul has called Calypso "the ballad, the broadsheet, the Punch and New Yorker of Trinidad." Calypso is all of those.

It came from Africa, brought to Trinidad by slaves taken from the tribes of West Africa where storytellers called *Tai-Tai* sang in the courts of the African kings and at market fairs.

As slaves, working in the fields of Trinidad, the West Africans sang of the misery they encountered, their hopes and fears, their outrage. When the Negroes were freed, it was an easy matter to wed their songs to existing customs, particularly carnival. That's how Calypso, as we know it today, was born.

Trinidad is also the birthplace of the steel band, the place where more people dance to the music of the oil barrel than to any other instrument. Steel band music has been generously exported to other islands of the West Indies, and it is a rare visitor to the Caribbean who hasn't cha cha'd, merengue'd or even waltzed to the magnetic music of the "pans." But it is in Trinidad that the art of the steel band has reached all but symphonic peaks.

From a rough, and as story has it, accidental beginning, the music of the steel drum has been refined to the point where a Chopin polonaise sounds as much at home as the latest upbeat Calypso. Serious musicians have studied them, and there are those who believe the "pans" will one day be an integral part of the symphony orchestras.

A good introduction to the bands is a walk through John John, a section of narrow streets lined with shacks of tin and wood in Port-of-Spain. The tones of a steel band throb in the air. You follow the sound until you come to a group of men standing in the street pounding out the rhythm on the pans. A few people may be dancing. Somewhere out of sight a man is singing "Ole lady yuh mashin' me toe," a famous Calypso lyric.

Perambulating diner on the island of Trinidad

This is where the steel bands began, and it is here that many of the pans are made. Every pan is carefully designed to fill a particular role in the band in which it is going to be played. Each is a counterpart of, for example, the violin, trumpet or drum of the traditional orchestra, and usually falls into one of three categories: the *ping pongs*, which carry the melody; the *tune booms*, which make up the harmony section; and the *bass booms*, which are rhythm instruments.

There are numerous stories as to how the pans started, but it is generally agreed that they weren't heard until just after World War II. The most widely told story is of the young man who was drumming on a cracker tin when its face was struck by a large rock. Attempting to smooth out the face, he tapped it with a hammer. The tone became mellower. When he tapped it in another place he got a different note.

When he had five notes he found he was able to play "Mary Had A Little Lamb." Off he went to enthrall his friends. Soon everyone was searching for old cracker tins, and then an enterprising soul dragged out an oil barrel. It was discovered that due to the quality of the steel, the barrels had fantastic tone. The steel band was born.

The steel drums probably are the direct descendants of the voodoo drums of Africa. When the authorities banned the drums, brought to the island by slaves in the 18th century, Trinidadians tried everything from rhythmic

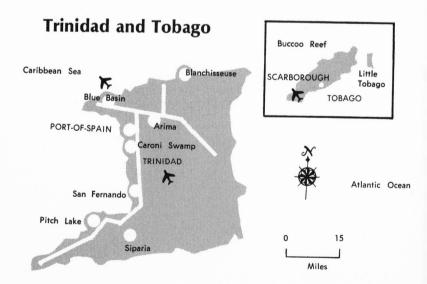

Trinidad and Tobago

Buccoo Reef

SCARBOROUGH   Little Tobago

TOBAGO

Caribbean Sea

Blanchisseuse

Blue Basin

PORT-OF-SPAIN   Arima

Caroni Swamp

TRINIDAD

San Fernando

Atlantic Ocean

Pitch Lake

Siparia

0   15

Miles

handclapping to the ashcan and "bottle bands" of the thirties to satisfy the needs of a musical people. For a time the steel bands were in disfavor, but today they form the basic heartbeat of the island.

Carnival would be unthinkable without their booming rhythms, cafés would be silent deserts and Trinidad would not be Trinidad.

Instant facts

Location: Over 1,900 miles from New York and 1,480 miles from Miami. Trinidad is the most southerly island of the Caribbean, only seven miles from the northeast coast of Venezuela.

Population: Approximately 1,000,000.

Capital: Port-of-Spain.

Nationality: Independent member of the British Commonwealth of Nations.

Language: English.

Currency: Trinidad and Tobago dollar, equal to 60¢ U.S., 64¢ Canadian and 4s 2d sterling.

Documentation: Passport not required by U.S., Canadian and U.K. citizens provided length of stay is not longer than 6 months. Return ticket and identification are required. Smallpox certificate required for re-entry to U.S. and Canada.

Climate & Clothes: Temperatures vary from 72°–82° from December–May, 76°–87° June to November. The rainier season is between June and December, but showers are usually of short duration. Light summer clothing is almost always appropriate; formal attire really not necessary. Short shorts and beachwear are not recommended for the city.

Food: Hotels feature standard British, American and continental fare as well as Creole, Chinese and Indian specialties. **Sancoche** and **callaloo** (crab soup) are typical native soups and the island supplies its own **pastelles** (diced meat and vegetables wrapped in banana leaves), crabmeat and oysters. **Lappe stew** (made from wild hare), **pork souse, wild duck** and **quenk** (wild hog) are favorite Creole dishes. Rum, as on all the islands, is the national intoxicant but Trinidad's real liquid claim-to-fame is her Angostura Bitters.

Geography: Trinidad is roughly rectangular in shape and about the size of the state of Delaware—approximately 1,900 sq. miles. The most mountainous part of Trinidad is the Northern Range which stretches from east to west, actually an extension of the South American Cordilleras. The rest of the island is mainly flat or undulating country except for the central Montserrat Hills and the Trinity Hills in the south.

History: Millions and millions of years ago, when the shape of the world's land was vastly different from present profiles, Trinidad was part of the South American mainland. But in those remote ages volcanic catyclysms crumpled the young crust of the earth. The northeastern corner of the continent was broken away and became the island now known as Trinidad.

Christopher Columbus sighted Trinidad on Wednesday, July 31, 1498. He called it "La Trinidad" (The Trinity) for three low peaks that rose beyond the shore to mark his landfall.

Three groups of Amerindians inhabited the island before the coming of Columbus. The first were the Ciboney, in about 800 B.C., who left their traces in kitchen utensils made of shells. They were followed by the peaceful, agricultural Arawaks. Then the fierce Caribs raided Arawak settlements from the mainland, wiped them out and moved northward up the island chain until they were stopped by the Spanish in Puerto Rico.

Spain annexed the island, but it was not until 1592 that the first permanent settlement of Spaniards was established in the town of St. Joseph on the banks of the Caroni River. The town was sacked by Sir Walter Raleigh who was in search of El Dorado. The Spaniards managed to gain control and made the indigenous Indians their slaves. Despite crops of cocoa and tobacco, the island remained in the depths of poverty until 1780 when, at the invitation of the Spanish King, the French from Haiti and other French islands came by the thousands to settle in the island.

They brought with them sugar cane. And the island prospered. The English captured Trinidad in 1797 and it remained British until Trinidad and Tobago became an independent nation on August 31, 1962.

With the abolition of slavery in 1838, labor became so scarce that from 1845 to 1917 thousands of East Indians were brought in. Chinese and Portuguese came, and many from the other islands of the West Indies in search of employment.

Who flies here

There are direct flights to Port-of-Spain from:

New York: BWIA, Air France, Pan Am. Round trip: $304–$447; 17-day excursion $209–$287.

Miami: BWIA, Pan Am. Round trip: $272–$380; 17-day excursion $170–$240.

Los Angeles: Pan Am. Round Trip: $526–$692.

Montreal and **Toronto:** Air Canada. Round trip: $342–$477 (Canadian $369–$507); 21-day excursion $231–$347 (Canadian $249–$374).

London: BOAC. Round trip: $697–$1093 (£249–£390 sterling).

San Juan: BWIA, Pan Am. Round trip: $170–$246; 17-day excursion $99–$135.

Tobago: BWIA. Round trip: $12.

Island transportation

Car Rentals start at about $10 a day, available from: Hub Travel Ltd., local representatives of Hertz (Tel: 53021), Petter Rentals (Tel: 24959), Henry Pain's (Tel: 52441) and Gordon, Grant & Co. (Tel: 52591) all in Port-of-Spain. Valid driver's licenses issued in the U.S., Canada or United Kingdom are accepted. Parking in Port-of-Spain and driving on the left both require some patience on the part of inexperienced visitors.

For those who wish to avoid such considerations, there is regular **bus** service and no shortage of **taxis.** Taxi rates are fixed by the operator for short trips. Within city limits, charges are about $2.15 an hour for no more than four passengers. Tours can also be arranged. Around the island, about an eight-hour ride, costs $17 per person, including lunch. An unusual night-time tour includes a cocktail, dinner and floor show at $12 per person. Historical sightseeing for 3½ hours is $5 per person. Prices may vary, depending on the number of people in the car. These tours are available through Port-of-Spain hotels or from tour operators. Located in Port-of-Spain, the latter include Hub Taxi Service (Tel: 53011), Battoo Bros. (Tel: 35396/7), Bacchus Taxi Service (Tel: 23023), Chippy's Taxi Service (Tel: 42876) and Mike's Taxi Service (Tel: 41590).

Places of interest

The ridges and rolling hills that surround Port-of-Spain offer matchless opportunities for "skyline" driving. The Saddle is an 18-mile run through graceful arches of bamboo, citrus groves, cocoa and coffee plantations, skirting 600-foot heights overlooking the city. Take the **Skyline Highway** to Maracas Bay and Las Cuevas Bay, good swimming beaches. Wonderful views of the island and sometimes Tobago.

Blue Basin: 2½ hour round trip from Port-of-Spain. A quiet little valley with a pond fed by a very high waterfall. Walden in the tropics, but it's quite a steep climb to reach the falls.

Pitch Lake: 120 mile round trip from Port-of-Spain. One of the wonders of the world, this prehistoric lake covers 100 acres and provides a limitless supply of asphalt to Trinidad and Tobago and many other countries of the world. It was formed millions of years ago by the action of a mud volcano, although legend has a more romantic and simpler explanation of the lake's origin. A tribe of Carib Indians once celebrated the defeat of its enemies by killing and eating the sacred hummingbird. This so angered the Great Spirit that, as punishment, he caused the earth to open and the Indians and their village disappeared and in their place rose a dark and mysterious black lake.

East Coast: Miles of beaches and coves, lush tropical vegetation; drives along beaches at low tide. Ideal for a full day picnic.

Shrine of Our Lady of Laventille: In the hills northeast of Port-of-Spain, illuminated at night and visible from the city. Special services are held on the 13th of every month from May to October.

Shrine of the Black Virgin: At Church of La Divina Pastora at Siparia. Fete with procession in April.

Mount St. Benedict: Hilltop monastery and guest house. A three-hour tour from Port-of-Spain.

Bird Sanctuary: In the Caroni Swamp. The Scarlet Ibis is one of the many rare birds to be spotted here. Visitors allowed between July and September, depending on the behavior of the birds. Permit from Chief Game Warden required.

Gauguin Land: Blanchisseuse is a tiny village on the north coast of Trinidad where a French patois still is spoken. Trinidad once was heavily settled by French planters, and their handsome descendants are straight out of a Gauguin painting. Miles of bamboo-shaded roads, hillsides ablaze with blossoms, thickets humming with jewel-tinted birds—these are the landmarks en route to Blanchisseuse.

The sporting life

If you've always wanted to see a **cricket** match but haven't been able to fit Britain into your schedule, local and international teams play here on the Savannah, the great tree-shaded park of Port-of-Spain. This is also the playing field for other popular "tropical" sports, such as **rugby, soccer** and **hockey.** For **horse racing** enthusiasts, three tracks divide up the racing season between Port-of-Spain, San Fernando and Arima.

There are two 18-hole **golf** courses, one at St. Andrew's in Maraval (Tel: 21415), open both for spectators and visiting players. The course is short (approximately 5,800 yards) but interesting, with a par of 68. Greens fees are $3, caddy service

a little over a dollar and club rental for the 18 holes $1. Club house facilities are included and the only restriction on use of the greens is on some weekends when a competition is in progress. The Pointe-a-Pierre Golf Course, some six miles north of San Fernando, is limited to the staff of Trinidad Leaseholds Ltd. and their guests. Greens fees are 50¢ a day. A nine-hole course at the Brighton Golf Club in La Brea (16 miles from San Fernando) is open to visitors for 60¢ a day greens fees.

There are public **tennis** courts at the Princes Bldg. in Port-of-Spain and in San Fernando. Other courts are in private clubs in Port-of-Spain and St. Augustine.

Hunting (small game type) is there for the hunter. The island is well stocked with deer, possum (manicou), wild hog (quenk), certain birds and other game, and if you've always wanted your own armadillo, you can have a try at getting one in Trinidad. Also the mongoose. And, if you're so inclined, bagging the alligator is thrilling sport.

The hunting season for most game is October 1 to March 31. Animals classified as pests, namely the squirrel and manicou, may be hunted at any time of year by the owner of the land upon which said pest is trespassing. A hunting license, good for a year, costs $3.10 and can be obtained from the game warden at the Inland Revenue Office. To import firearms, application must be made to the Commissioner of Police, Police Headquarters, St. Vincent St., Port-of-Spain. No hunting is allowed in any Sanctuary, such as Caroni Swamp, and the ocelot, monkey and porcupine are strictly off-limits wherever they happen to be.

There is no organized guide service but Sports & Games Ltd., 25 Chacon St., Port-of-Spain, can make arrangements for guides as well as supply equipment.

Water sports

After you have shot and caught your first alligator and have done with it, relax on one of the beautiful **beaches** around the island. Trinidad's swimming shores are not in town, but are accessible via highways that cut over richly forested peaks and down to cliff-sided coves. In fact, the ride is almost more dramatic than the destination. Most popular of the string of beaches reached by the North Coast Road is Maracas, ideal for **surfboards** and water **skis.** For underwater adventurers, **snorkeling** equipment can be purchased in town; air tanks are available only from Sports & Games Ltd. in Port-of-Spain.

Fishing, for tarpon, cavalli, kingfish, mackerel and red snapper, is best from July to September, the experts say. Whether you prefer to troll, cast, fly, spear or harpoon, you'll find your challenge in blue water or in the numerous streams that flow through the island. Bank fishing is usually done in the Gulf of Paria and spearfishing for lobster is best off Maracas Bay. Spearfishing is also good around Gasparee and Monos—contact the Secretary of the Kingfishers Club, c/o Crown Bakery, 101 Charlotte St., Port-of-Spain.

Aquan and Correira in Port-of-Spain rents 28-foot **fishing boats** with outboard motor at $3.60 an hour. All gear must be supplied by the party. This firm also has cabin cruisers for 10–12 persons at $9–$15 an hour. A three-hour sightseeing tour into swamps, with guide, runs to about $9 for 5–6 people. Harpoons, spearfishing equipment and all kinds of tackle are for sale from the following stores in Port-of-Spain:

C. L. Trestrail Ltd.
10 Broadway

Sports & Games Ltd.
25 Chacon St.

Stephens, Todd & Fogarty Ltd.
Frederick St.

Furness, Withy & Co. Ltd.
90 Independence Sq.

Gordon, Grant & Co. Ltd.
10 St. Vincent St.

Sports & Games can also arrange for guides for fishing parties. No equipment can be rented though occasionally a guide will supply the necessary items. The cost of purchasing fishing gear is $7.50 and up for spear guns, $4 and up for casting rods, $20 and up for spinning rods, etc. There is a wide range of rods and reels to choose from and many types of bait.

The **Hummingbird II** is available for individual charter—$80 a day with captain and crew—from Mrs. Q. LaBorde, c/o Mrs. Q. Hosang, Shell Trinidad Ltd., Salvatori Bldg., Port-of-Spain. Groups of 4–10 persons can charter the boat for pleasure sailing at $10 (half day) and $20 (full day) per person, December 15–April 16. Off-season rates are $8 and $12, respectively.

Best shopping buys

There is quite a good selection of imports, including Swiss watches and top brand names in china, crystal and silver, cameras and binoculars, and English and Irish fabrics. From the Orient are silks, Indian saris, carved Oriental furniture and embroidered slippers. Local and imported liquors are available at in-bond prices and island handicrafts run the gamut from straw and sisal goods and wood carvings to hand-embroidered apparel and sea island cotton shirts. There are also duty-free shops at the airport. In town, the stores are mostly on Frederick St., open from 8 A.M. to 4 P.M. Shops close noon on Saturday but stay open late on Friday. Liquor shops are closed a half-day on Thursday. Some stores have branches at the larger hotels.

Dining, dancing and night life

Bel Air Hotel: Piarco Airport. American cuisine, lounge bar. Dancing, floor show Saturday nights.

Belvedere: Lady Chancellor Hill. Local wild game served.

Bergerac Hotel: Dancing at the **Krab Hole** to combo music, Wednesday, Friday and Saturday.

Bretton Hall Hotel: Victoria Ave. European and Chinese cuisine, lounge bar. Dancing Saturday in the **Cyndiana Room.**

Gay Cavalier: Bagshot House. Dining, dancing, entertainment nightly.

Hummingbird: Downtown. Cafeteria.

Inn & Out: 36 Frederick St. Cafeteria.

Kapok: Chinese cuisine, lounge bar.

Kimling: 93 St. Vincent St. Chinese restaurant, lounge bar.

Kowloon: 109 St. Vincent St. Chinese food, lounge bar. Air-conditioned.

Lotus: Henry St. Chinese cuisine, lounge bar.

Mandarin: Western Main Rd. Chinese restaurant built out over the sea.

El Matador: Dancing to combo Friday and Saturday.

Miramar: Dancing, nightly entertainment with a touch of "local color."

Normandie Hotel: 2 Nook Ave., St. Ann's. French and continental cusine, lounge bar. Dancing, floor show Friday nights.

Penthouse Bar & Inn: Salvatori's Bldg., Henry St. and Independence Sq. Lounge bar. Dancing, floor show nightly.

The Pub (Pelican Inn): English-type public house bar. Draught beer, pork pies, Cornish pastry.

Topo Carlo: Downtown. Italian cuisine, lounge bar.

Trinidad Country Club: Dinner-dance Thursday, barbecue and dancing Saturday nights. Limited to members and their guests.

Trinidad Hilton Hotel: Port-of-Spain. International cuisine, dancing nightly. "Tropical fiesta" on pool terrace Monday night, international buffet Thursday night. Floor show, dancing in **La Boucan** nightly except Monday and Tuesday.

Tropical Hotel: Maraval. Dancing in the **Bamboo Room** Wednesday, Friday and Saturday nights.

Upp & Down: Downtown. Cafeteria.

Ying King: Frederick St. Chinese cuisine.

Special events, celebrations (Trinidad and Tobago)

Cricket, Field Hockey Seasons: Begin in January.

Carnival: Competition for Calypso King, king and queen of carnival, "Dimanche Gras" show, street parades of costumed bands, steel bands, dances, etc. Monday and Tuesday before Ash Wednesday (February 26 and 27).

Easter Monday: Public holiday. Eastertide goat races in Tobago. April 15.

May Day: Public holiday. Parade. May 1.

Hosein: Muslim religious festival with processions. April or May.

Whit Monday: Public holiday. Cycle and athletic sports in Port-of-Spain. June 3.

Football Season: Begins in July. Cricket season closes.

Discovery Day: Public holiday. Cycling and athletic sports, Port-of-Spain. First Monday in August.

Independence Day: Public holiday. Military parade, fireworks, etc., in Port-of-Spain. August 31.

Divali: Hindu festival of lights. October or November.

Yachting Season: November-May.

All Saints Day, All Souls Day: Illumination of cemeteries with candles. November 1 and 2.

Remembrance Day: Military parade at War Memorial, Port-of-Spain. Nearest Sunday to November 11.

Boxing Day: Public holiday. Horse racing at Queen's Park Savannah, Port-of-Spain. December 26.

Old Year's Day: Celebrations at local clubs. December 31. Close of football season.

Meet the people

Organization	Official	Phone
Agricultural Society	P. Hosten	42048
Trinidad Art Society	L. E. Beckles	51739
Automobile Assn.	F. Hugh Wilson	38217 or 34445
Mayfair Bridge Club	Mrs. Anne Samuel	637-2894 or 52805
Junior Chamber of Commerce	Dr. Hugh Spicer	24243 or 37067
Lions Club	Olof Johnson	23108 or 36038
Rotary Club	Wilfred D. Best	22252 or 34668
Soroptimist Club	Mrs. Gemma Ramkeesoon	637-4634 or 662-3231

Organization	Official	Phone
Businessmen's Assn.	H. Chan	21645 or 37519
League of Women Voters	Mrs. Nesta Patrick	638-3851 or 41151
Chamber of Commerce	Miss Wendy Gomez	37092
Chess Assn.	K. Phillips	662-3284
Andres Bello Institute	Mrs. D. Millan	54145
Company of Players (drama)	Gabriel Francis	637-3725 or 21151
Dramatic Club	Mrs. Dagmar Butt	268-65
Amateur Fencing Assn.	Mrs. Dorothy Gouveia	41389
Light Aeroplane Club	L. S. Gibson	Piarco 664-4884 or 662-3771
St. Andrew's Golf Club	Major Frisby	21415
Caribbean Kennel Club	Dr. A. R. Acton	637-4631
Philatelic Society	Harold E. Box	42458
Cage Bird Assn.	Richard S. W. Deane	Pointe-a-Pierre 144 or 447
Horticultural Club	Mrs. George Black	24273
Suburb Beautiful Circle	Mrs. Glen Byam	42196
Hunters Assn.	Carl A. Meyer	41021 or 34529
Shooting and Observation of Swamp Birds	C. L. Williams	36523 or 42542
Hunters' Group	Abdool Aziz	652-4415
Trap & Skeet Assn.	Henri de Verteuil	26977 or 32338
Judo Club	C. Woo Ling	24375
La Petite Musicale	Sen. Olive Walke	21454
Nat'l Assn. of Steelbandsmen	George Goddard	53805
S. Trinidad Music Assn.	Miss Grace Abdool	652-2052
Trinidad Music Assn.	Mrs. Robert Johnstone	21547
Field Naturalists' Club	G. E. Laforest	21745
Zoological Society	Ray Shingler	23530
Infocus (camera club)	Wilfred Sharp	23551
Press Club	Dennis Mahabir	637-4566
Assn. of Professional Engineers	K. F. Seheult	662-3502 or 36291
Dental Assn.		38332/37226
Nurses' Assn.	Miss Evelyn Hargraves	23892 or 652-3146
Optical Assn.		22385 or 36639
Society of Architects	B. Broadbridge	42281 or 35135
Teachers' Union		36560
Rifle Assn.	Mrs. Joyce Patience	51294
American Women's Club	Mrs. Robert Bischoff	24544
Canadian Women's Club	Mrs. J. J. O'Flynn	21333
Chinese Assn.	Derry Petit	51401
Himalaya Club	S. M. Hosein	638-2203
Portuguese Assn.	A. M. Querino	41168 or 51171/3
Syrian Lebanese Women's Assn.	Mrs. Souad Sabga	21062
Coterie of Social Workers	Miss Audrey Jeffers	22322
Nat'l Y.W.C.A.	Lady Reece	21798
Fed. of Women's Institutes and Groups	Mrs. Cleopatra Romilly	24130 or 53264
Y.M.C.A.	Solomon Gajadbar	32055
Football Assn.	Eric R. James	22557
Hockey Assn.	Stewart Arrindell	42824
Women's Hockey Assn.	Mrs. Irma de Lima	34280 or 22059
Netball Assn.	Lady Reece	21798
Table Tennis Club	Ronald K. Bates	22417 or 52171

Organization	Official	Phone
Lawn Tennis Club	P. G. Charlett	21554 or 34866
St. Augustine Recreation Club	Dr. Steve Bennett	662-3041 or 21621
Yachting Assn.	Rawle Barrow	637-2062 or 31261
Pegasus (youth group)	Miss Barbara Blenman	37748 or 21476
Girl Guides Assn.		41462
Boy Scouts Assn.	D. Ash	21368

Real estate

There are a number of cottages for rent, either by the day or by the month. Information is available from:

Mr. T. Hosein
32 St. Vincent St.
Port-of-Spain

Mr. R. Lange
29 St. Vincent St.
Port-of-Spain

The following is a list of real estate agents:

John M. Bladon & Co.
31 Frederick St., Port-of-Spain
Tel: 31196, 31274

E. M. Burnett & Co.
70 Queen St., Port-of-Spain
Tel: 31294

Louis E. Kenny
15 Coblentz Ave., St. Ann's
Tel: 42335

L. I. Strasser
Cor. Hololo and Cascade Rds.
Tel: 43628

C. Marquez
46 Richmond St., Port-of-Spain
Tel: 31028

Commerce and industry

Trinidad and Tobago are the islands of sun and fun. The other side of the coin, though, shows a vital nation busy developing in agriculture, industry and commerce.

Trinidad early developed a strong agricultural economy based on sugar, cocoa, coffee and citrus and their by-products. Today, a large cannery encourages the growing of vegetables, and a milk-processing plant stimulates the breeding of high-grade herds. Although the country is industrializing, present trends indicate an effective balance between the agricultural and the industrial.

There is a very active Industry Development Corp. which encourages establishment of industries. To promote a thriving industrial climate, the government by legislation allows incentives to outside investors including an income tax "holiday" and accelerated depreciation allowances.

Trinidad's chief minerals are oil and asphalt. The oil industry has been highly developed for years. Quantities of natural gas provide inexpensive fuel for generating electricity for industry and (in bottled form) for the home. New basic raw materials are now being supplied to a new petro-chemical plant.

WHERE TO STAY— In Trinidad

	Plan	Dec. 15-April 14 U. S. Currency Double	Single	April 15-Dec. 14 Double	Single
BEL AIR Piarco Airport (62 Rms.) **(p)**	(EP)	$13–16	$ 9–10	$13–16	$ 9–10
BERGERAC Maraval (69 Rms.) **(p)**	(AP) (EP)	$24 $14	$15.50 $10.80	$15 $8.50	$10.80 $6
BRETTON HALL Port-of-Spain (100 Rms.) **(p, t)**	(MAP) (CP)	$20–28 $14–22	$12–18 $8–12	$18–28 $12–18	$12–18 $7–12
ERROL J. LAU Port of Spain (18 Rms.)	(MAP) (EP) (CP)	$16–22 $10–16 $12–18	$9–12 $6–9 $ 7–10	$16–22 $10–16 $12–18	$9–12 $6–9 $ 7–10

FARRELL HOUSE (CP)	$16	$12	$16	$12	
Claxton Bay (11 Rms.) (p)					
GULF VIEW APT. (EP)	$19.50	–	$19.50	–	
HOTEL					
Goodwood Park		$300 monthly	$300 monthly		
NORMANDIE (EP)	$14–23	$9–17	$14–19	$8–14	
Port-of-Spain (58 Rms.) (p)					
PAN AM GUEST (EP)	$14	$ 9	$14	$ 9	
HOUSE Piarco Airport (47 Rms.) (p)					
PELICAN INN (AP)	$12–16	$ 7– 9	$12–16	$ 7– 9	
Port-of-Spain (MAP)	$10	$ 6	$10	$ 6	
(26 Rms.) (CP)	$8–10	$5–6	$8–10	$5–6	
QUEEN'S PARK (EP)	$12–15	$7–12	$12–15	$7–12	
Port-of-Spain (130 Rms.)					
SHORELANDS (CP)	$12–13	$ 7– 8	$15–16	$ 9–10	
Point Cumana (18 Rms.) (p)					
TROPICAL (CP)	$12–15	$6–7	$12–15	$6–7	
Maraval (12 Rms.)					
TRINIDAD HILTON (EP)	$22-35	$17–30	$18–26	$13–21	
Port-of-Spain (MAP)	$42–55	$27–40	$34–42	$21–29	
(261 Rms.) (p)		(Dec. 16-Apr. 15)	(Nov. 16-Dec. 15)		

Tobago: Robinson Crusoe's Island

Twenty-one miles northeast of Trinidad lies the tranquil island of Tobago (tuh-bay-go) which, together with Trinidad, forms the independent nation of Trinidad and Tobago.

Travelers have been describing Tobago as an island paradise since 1683. In 1968 one finds no reason to change the billing. There are miles of perfect smooth-sand beaches where you can swim in protected gin-clear waters, sun to your heart's content or relax under the palm trees. Buccoo Reef's beautiful underwater gardens teem with fish (the nondangerous kind) and can be explored simply by wading. And the only birds of paradise in this hemisphere adorn an islet preserve off the northern end of Tobago. These handsome birds were brought here from New Guinea shortly after the turn of the century. They flourished until 1963, when Hurricane Flora blew some of them out to sea. At least seven remain, however, and the bird of paradise is once more one of the island's great natural sights.

Although Tobago has its two or three horse-racing events annually, in an atmosphere of characteristic friendliness and gaiety, it also promotes one of the unusual sporting events of the world—the "Eastertide Goat Races."

Most famous of the descriptions of Tobago is Daniel Defoe's account of Robinson Crusoe's sojourn on a nameless Caribbean island within sight of Trinidad, a tropic retreat "bathed in the currents of the Orinoco River" which flows from Venezuela into the Atlantic.

Defoe's immortal adventure story was published in 1719. Although the author could have landed Crusoe on any number of islands, research led him to believe that Tobago possessed all the ingredients of an idyllic tropical setting. And visitors, ever since, have agreed emphatically.

instant facts

Location: About 20 miles northeast of Trinidad.

Population: Approximately 33,000.

Main Town: Scarborough.

Nationality: With Trinidad, independent member of British Commonwealth of Nations.

Language: English.

Currency: Trinidad and Tobago dollar, equal to 60¢ U.S., 64¢ Canadian and 4s 2d sterling.

Documentation: Customs and entry for Tobago are handled in Trinidad.

Climate & Clothes: Same as Trinidad. Sneakers, usually supplied by hotels, are necessary for exploring the coral reefs. If you plan on doing some intense bird watching in the countryside, long pants and insect repellent are recommended.

Food: Fresh-caught seafood here is particularly good. Crabmeat can be mixed with other ingredients and served in its own shell **(crab backs)** or, boiled with certain seasonings, it makes a soup known as **callaloo.** Another popular fish dish is **accra,** salt fish pounded with seasonings and yeast, fried in small cakes and served with **floats,** a sort of fried dough.

Geography: The island is 27 miles long and 7½ miles wide, a total area of 116 sq. miles. Beautiful sandy beaches ring the island. While the southern end is completely flat, a mountain range of volcanic origin at the northern end culminates in a peak 1,800 feet high.

History: It is generally agreed, though not proven, that Columbus discovered Tobago on his third voyage in 1498. The island then changed hands no fewer than 31 times in less than 200 years. The British were the first to claim Tobago and it was given by Charles I to the Earl of Pembroke in 1628.

For the next hundred years, the island

Early morning on a classic Caribbean beach

was fought over and lost by the Dutch, French, British and Courlanders (from modern-day Latvia).

In 1679, Tobago was formally ceded to the Dutch but the decision was not taken seriously by the other nations and the tug of war continued. By 1704 the European powers mutually declared Tobago a no-man's land. Piracy now flourished and Tobago remained a base for the highwaymen of the Caribbean until 1721, when the British routed them and hanged their leader.

The Swedes were the next to try to settle but were driven off by the Indians and Negroes. For the remainder of the 18th century Tobago was fought over by the British, French and even the American colonists.

Finally, in 1803, British troops recaptured the island and Tobago remained a British colony until it was granted its independence as an entity with Trinidad in 1962.

Who flies here

BWIA has direct flights to Tobago from Trinidad, daily, for $12 round trip.

Island transportation

Car rentals are available through the Hertz representative, Tobago Travel Service (Tel: 2186), Gordon Grant & Co. (Tel: 0304) and Henry Pains (Tel: 2418), starting at approximately $9 a day. Despite the small size of the island, there are over 220 miles of paved road. The Travel Service also offers guided tours around the island. The trip to Buccoo Reef costs $2–$4 depending on the starting point. A five- to six-hour tour of Charlotteville and Man O'War Bay costs $9 per person and the shorter trip to Hillsborough Dam $6 per person.

There is no shortage of **taxis** (Rex, Uptown and Downtown taxi services) and **buses** run regularly from Scarborough to Man O'War Bay.

Places of interest

Scarborough and Environs: Native market on Saturdays is especially colorful. Fort George, approached by way of old Gun Bridge and ruins of old military installations, is on top of a 452-foot hill and affords a wonderful view of harbor.

Government House and **Botanical Garden.**

Plymouth: Tomb of Betty Stivens, famous for its enigmatic inscriptions. Ruins of Fort James, built by French in 1666, first fort in Tobago; overlooking Great Courland Bay.

Roxborough: Beautiful view of Roxborough Bay and Queens Island.

Speyside: Tiny fishing village noted for picturesque scenes and a huge old water wheel in the ruins of a sugar mill. Main starting point for crossing to Bird of Paradise Island.

Craig Hill Falls: Between Scarborough and Moriah; a 100-foot drop of water in a series of three cascading waterfalls.

Little Tobago (Bird of Paradise Island): 1½ miles off northern tip of Tobago and reached by boat from Speyside. Truly a bird watcher's paradise, with its many species of wild birds. This is the only place in the world where the Birds of Paradise have been able to acclimatize in the wild outside of their native New Guinea. A caretaker lives on the island to see that the birds have enough water, artificially supplied to them by "water coolers," and to tend the fruit trees that were planted especially to supply the birds with their accustomed diet.

The sporting life

Hunting regulations are the same for Tobago as for Trinidad. Hunting is not permitted on Little Tobago and those interested in visiting the bird sanctuary must have a permit from the game warden. All arrangements can be made through hotel managers or the Warden's Office, Scarborough. Sports & Games Ltd. sells hunting equipment and has a branch in Scarborough.

Best catches in Tobago waters are wahoo, kingfish, bonito, skipjack, snapper, pargue, barracuda, grouper, tarpon, catfish, porpoise, turtles and ravs. Arrangements for fishing trips with guides can be made through hotels. The guided trip to Buccoo Reef is $3 per person and fishing trips cost about $21–$27. The motor yacht *Fiesta* charters for $12 an hour, maximum 10 persons. Fishing equipment can be purchased at Sports & Games Ltd.

Boats available for charter include a pirogue-type launch accommodating four persons at the most, $6 an hour for a cruise along the coast. A cruise on the motor yacht *Fiesta* is *$10* per person for groups of five to 10 passengers a day (up to eight hours). Sightseeing along the coast is $4 an hour for a maximum of six people and "sail-yourself" Kingfish boats rent for $2 an hour. The trip to Bird of Paradise Island from Speyside takes 15 minutes and, for $4 a person, includes a three-hour guided tour of the island. The boat can accommodate 25 persons.

There are also boat trips to **Buccoo Reef** —$2 from Buccoo Point and $4 from Store Bay and Pigeon Point. From Golden Grove Lagoon, a glass-bottom boat leaves for tours of the reef, $2.50 per person. Best way to see its beautiful coral gardens and colorful marine life, though, is to stick your head underwater. Even non-swimmers can enjoy these sights as bathers can wade over a mile from shore in a "pool" of water only four feet deep. An unexpected submerged plateau halfway between reef and shore explains the mystery. Bring snorkel and mask, and sneakers or old shoes to protect tender feet from the angry fire coral. Near the reef is the "Nylon Pool," a crystal clear body of water carved out of coral by the sea. There's no coral in the pool; just glide down to the white sandy bottom, then look at the boat hanging in "midair" above you.

Tobago specializes in **beaches** and some of the most beautiful are Pigeon Point, Store Bay, Arnos Vale plus a host of secluded coves. Be sure to carry a bathing suit with you wherever you plan to drive. Diving and fishing equipment and instruction is available from Tobago Divers & Fishers at Petit Trou Bay, Bacolet St., P.O. Box 201, Scarborough (Tel: 2484).

Dine and dance

Restaurants are in most hotels, and night-time entertainment is also confined to the hotel beat. There is dancing at the following hotels: Robinson Crusoe (Saturday), Crown Point (Tuesday, Thursday, Saturday) and Bluehaven (Friday). The only nightclub is La Tropicale (run by the Della Mira Guest House).

Meet the people

Organization or Interest	Official	Phone
Agriculture	Claude Job	2570 or 2234
Birds and Shells	Mrs. Kathleen Alford	Plymouth 3
Bridge and Gardening	Lady Dorothy de Verteuil	Plymouth 3
Cultural Affairs	Eileen Guillaume	2178 or 2652, Ext. 36
Football	Alfred Geyette	2480
Rifle Club	Arden Scott	2226
Chamber of Commerce		2669
Music Assn.	Edgar Davidson	2624
Tourist Bureau	Mrs. Josephine Bell	2125

Real estate

Cottages can be rented by the day or month from the following:

Mr. E. G. F. Caston
Heale House
Speyside

Mr. Verner Arnold
Rockley Vale, Scarborough
Tel: 2158

Mrs. Angela Luke
Castle Cove Beach Hotel
Scarborough

For further information on housing or land, the following are authorized real estate agents:

Mrs. J. Bell
Milford Rd., Scarborough
Tel: 217

E. M. Burnett
Scarborough
Tel: 275

Whitaker's
P.O. Box 163, Scarborough
Tel: 2186

Cyril Wildman
Northside Rd.
Scarborough

WHERE TO STAY— In Tobago

ARNOS VALE	**(AP)**	$48–66	$30–35	$28–35	$17–19
Plymouth (21 Rms.) **(b, p)**					
BACOLET INN	**(AP)**	$24–40	$12	$16–20	$8
Scarborough (23 Rms.) **(b)**					
BIRD OF PARADISE	**(AP)**	$25–60	$12–50	$25–60	$12–50
Speyside (16 Rms.) **(b)**					
BLUE HAVEN	**(AP)**	$38–45	$25–30	$26–30	$14–16
Scarborough (40 Rms.) **(b, p)**					
CASTLE COVE	**(AP)**	$30	$17	$18–20	$10
Scarborough	**(MAP)**	$28	$15	$17–18	$9
(18 Rms.) **(b)**	**(EP)**	$22	$12	$11–12	$6
CROWN POINT	**(AP)**	$42–45	$24–27	$29–32	$16–19
Crown Point	**(MAP)**	—	—	$25–28	$14–17
(50 Rms.) **(b, p, t)**					
DELLA MIRA GUEST	**(AP)**	$30	$15	$18	$ 9
HOUSE	**(MAP)**	$26	$13	$15	$8
Scarborough	**(EP)**	$18	$9	$10	$5
(15 Rms.) **(p)**					
ROBINSON CRUSOE	**(AP)**	$38	$22	$24	$13
Scarborough	**(MAP)**	$34	$20	$20	$11
(21 Rms.) **(b)**					
SAM'S GUEST HOUSE	**(AP)**	$16–24	$8–16	$12–14	$7–9
Scarborough	**(MAP)**	$14–18	$10–12	$10–12	$6–8
(26 Rms.)	**(EP)**	$9–12	$7–10	$7	$4–5

LEGEND FOR HOTEL LISTINGS: (AP) American Plan (room and 3 meals); **MAP)** Modified American Plan (room, breakfast and dinner); **(CP)** Continental Plan (room and breakfast); **(EP)** European Plan (room only). All rates quoted on a per-day basis and subject to change. Confirmed reservations at specific rates desired are always recommended.
HOTEL FACILITIES: (b) beach; **(p)** pool; **(t)** tennis; **(g)** golf.